T0124762

STUDIES OF THE BOOK OF MORMON

B. H. ROBERTS

———

STUDIES OF THE BOOK
OF MORMON

———

SECOND EDITION
WITH A NEW AFTERWORD

Edited and with an Introduction by
BRIGHAM D. MADSEN

*With a Biographical Essay by
Sterling M. McMurrin*

SIGNATURE BOOKS
SALT LAKE CITY

Cover design by Brian Bean

All photographs are from the B. H. Roberts Collection,
University of Utah Library, Salt Lake City.

First Edition © 1985
by the University of Utah Research Foundation

Second Edition © 1992
by Signature Books, Inc. All rights reserved.
Signature Books is a registered trademark of
Signature Books, Inc.

Published by arrangement with
the University of Illinois Press

Printed and bound in the United States of America.

Printed on acid-free paper

LIBRARY OF CONGRESS CATALOGING-IN-PUBLICATION DATA

Roberts, B. H. (Brigham Henry), 1857-1933.
Studies of the Book of Mormon / B. H. Roberts:
edited and with an introduction by Brigham D. Madsen;
with a biographical essay by Sterling M. McMurrin.
p.   cm.
Includes bibliographical references and index.
ISBN 1-56085-027-2
1. Book of Mormon — Criticism, interpretation, etc.
I. Madsen, Brigham D.
II. Title.
BX8627.R59 1992
289.3'22—dc20   92-22758
                                                   CIP

Contents

Preface
vii

The Documents
ix

Brigham H. Roberts: A Biographical Essay
xiii

Introduction
1

Correspondence Related to the
Book of Mormon Essays
35

"BOOK OF MORMON DIFFICULTIES: A STUDY"
61

"A BOOK OF MORMON STUDY"
149

"A PARALLEL"
321

Bibliography
345

Afterword
369

Index
371

Preface

The acquisition by the Marriott Library of the University of Utah of major unpublished manuscripts on the Book of Mormon by Brigham H. Roberts, together with related papers, is a matter of considerable importance. Roberts is widely regarded as the foremost historian and theologian of the Mormon Church, although some of his later and more interesting and controversial work is not available to the general public.

Two generous gifts of Roberts's papers were made to the library by separate members of the Roberts family in 1979 and 1981. In the later 1970s Brigham E. Roberts, a grandson of Brigham H. Roberts and a Salt Lake City attorney, indicated his interest in presenting the manuscript "A Book of Mormon Study" to the university, hoping that it would be published with competent editing. Before the gift was consummated, however, Mr. Roberts died. Thereafter, his wife, Virginia D. Roberts, and his sons, William D. and Thom D. Roberts, presented a copy of the manuscript and other Roberts papers to the library. Mrs. Roberts also made a generous cash gift to assist in the preservation and publication of the manuscript material.

In the meantime, Adele W. Parkinson, widow of Wood R. Worsley, a grandson of B. H. Roberts, generously presented the university with portions of the personal library of Roberts, including correspondence and the manuscripts of the three works published in this volume — "Book of Mormon Difficulties"; the larger companion work, "A Book of Mormon Study"; and "A Parallel." Each of the gifts was accompanied by written permission for the university to publish the manuscripts. As requested by the donors, the manuscripts and other materials were placed in the library's Special Collections Department, where they are readily accessible for scholarly study.

The acquisition by the University of Utah Library of the B. H. Roberts manuscripts came during a renewal of interest in the writings and influence of Roberts, who died in 1933. While, as he indicated in a 1932 letter to his former secretary Elizabeth Skolfield, Roberts did not prepare these documents dealing with the Book of Mormon for publication, their presentation in this scholarly edition is intended to allow readers to glimpse yet another dimension of Roberts's work.

Several persons encouraged the publication of these materials. Wallace N. Cooper demonstrated his interest by arranging for his secretary to make a careful transcript of the Roberts Book of Mormon manuscripts. And no one was more enthusiastic in his determination to see Roberts's studies published than George D. Smith of San Francisco, who has special competence as a student of Roberts and his writings. Mr. Smith was persistent in his encouragement of the publication and presented his own analytical synopsis of the manuscripts to the community of Mormon scholars. Certainly the publication of this volume at the present time is in no small measure a result of his efforts.

The project has been under the jurisdiction of the former director of the library's Special Collections Department who, supported by Roger K. Hanson, director of the University of Utah Libraries, and other university officials, negotiated for publication with the University of Illinois Press. Brigham D. Madsen, professor emeritus of history at the University of Utah and widely recognized for his competence as a research scholar in American history, annotated the manuscripts and prepared the requisite introductions and bibliographies. Sterling M. McMurrin, E. E. Ericksen Distinguished Professor at the University of Utah and a student of philosophy and the history of ideas, wrote the essay on Roberts as historian and theologian.

Everett L. Cooley
University of Utah

The Documents

History

The origins and chronology of the three B. H. Roberts's essays now being published are briefly discussed here; further explanation is provided in the biographical essay and the introduction.

The first essay presented, "Book of Mormon Difficulties. A Study," was originally 141 typed pages. It was presented to the General Authorities of the Church of Jesus Christ of Latter-day Saints on January 4, 5, and 26, 1922, and three private meetings were held with Apostles Anthony W. Ivins, James E. Talmage, and John A. Widtsoe over a period from February 2 to May 25, 1922, to discuss the subject further. The Special Collections Division of Marriott Library at the University of Utah, Salt Lake City, acquired copies of the document from the Wood R. Worsley family on December 27, 1979, and from the Brigham E. Roberts family on January 19, 1981.

"A Book of Mormon Study" is divided into two parts. Part I was originally 170 typed pages; Part II was 114 typed pages. It is included in the Papers of Brigham Henry Roberts (1857-1933) in the Marriott Library, and it is the same document referred to by Wesley P. Lloyd in his journal. The decision by Roberts not to present this additional material to the General Authorities of the Church is acknowledged in his October 24, 1927, letter to Richard R. Lyman; according to the Lloyd journal he later sent it to President Heber J. Grant. The Special Collections Department of the Marriott Library obtained copies of the document from the Wood R. Worsley family on December 27, 1979, and from the Brigham E. Roberts family on January 19, 1981.

The final document presented here is "A Parallel," which was originally eighteen typed pages. It presents similarities between the *View of the Hebrews* and the Book of Mormons and is arranged in parallel columns. It was presented to Richard R. Lyman as recorded in the Lyman letter of October 24, 1927. "A Parallel" circulated in the Mormon underground during the late 1920s and through the early 1940s. Ben E. Roberts, the son of B. H. Roberts, acknowledged to Ariel L. Crowley in a letter of July 22, 1939, the existence of this document, and a public distribution of mimeographed copies of this analysis was made at the Timpanogos Club of Salt Lake City on October 10, 1946. It was subsequently published in the *Rocky Mountain Mason* by Mervin B. Hogan in January 1956.

Editorial Method

The correspondence written by B. H. Roberts includes unsigned carbon copies or draft letters sent to individuals. The other letters are either addressed to Roberts or are copies of letters to other individuals sent to him for his information. They are reproduced with all handwritten corrections or additions.

"Book of Mormon Difficulties. A Study" and Part I of "A Book of Mormon Study" are published from the original typewriter ribbon copies. Part II of "A Book of Mormon Study" and "A Parallel" are taken from carbon copies. The text presented here follows the copies on file in the Special Collections Department, Marriott Library, University of Utah, Salt Lake City. In some instances they contain minor, non-substantive differences from copies of portions of these manuscripts that have been circulated over the years.

All of B. H. Roberts's manuscripts contain numerous handwritten changes, corrections, or insertions, and this handwritten material has been included in the text. A number of individuals familiar with Roberts's handwriting consider this material to be his.

In preparing these manuscripts for publication, obvious typographical errors, but not misspelled words, have been corrected. Punctuation has occasionally been added or deleted, for example, "Washington D.C." is given as "Washington, D.C.," and commas are deleted when they appear before dashes. Titles of books and magazines are printed in italics; titles of magazine articles are in quotation marks. Roberts's dots or asterisks to indicate omissions of material have been rendered as a series of three or four ellipsis dots. All brackets and parentheses in the text were placed there by Roberts himself, who used both conventions to insert his comments within the text. Where questions arose as to the meaning of quotations and it was found that incorrect word(s) had been used, the correct word(s) were substituted. Roberts sometimes neglected to provide either opening or closing quotation marks around extracted material; these marks have been supplied where it is clearly evident that they should appear.

Roberts used both numbers and asterisks for his footnotes. When he used numbers, he placed them within parentheses at the end of a sentence, a practice that has been retained; in addition all of his footnotes appear at the foot of the page where cited. In "A Book of Mormon

Difficulties: A Study" Roberts occasionally used fractions to designate footnote numbers (e.g., 25½, 63½, 63⅓); these have been changed to sequential whole numbers. The editor's note numbers appear as superscripts; editorial notes appear at the end of each document, except in the correspondence section, where they follow each letter.

Brigham H. Roberts: A Biographical Essay
by Sterling McMurrin

In one of the earliest scholarly studies of Mormonism, the Mormon philosopher E. E. Ericksen, influenced by the pragmatic principle that "institutions are made and ideals are formed in the process of adjustment," treated the development of Mormon society, religion, and morals in terms of three successive eras.[1] The first, to the death of Joseph Smith and the beginning of the westward movement, was a period defined especially by the conflict of the Mormons with their neighbors.[2] The second, the era of the migration and colonization, was marked by the Mormons' struggle against nature and their troubles with the federal government. The third, following the decline of the Mormon cooperative movement, Ericksen regarded as a time of internal institutional and social conflict and intellectual adjustment. It was in a sense a "scholastic" period, a time for defending the actions of the past, justifying the moral ideals, clarifying the religious doctrines, and constructing a rational philosophy in the light of modern scientific thought and democratic practice.

When allowance is made for the distortion in the description of the historical process that inevitably results from adherence to formulae of this type, Ericksen's thesis is a valuable index to an understanding of Mormon thought and behavior. Today a fourth period might be added, extending from the close of World War II to the present, which has been and is being marked by the worldwide extension of Mormonism, a promised dissolution of its extreme parochialism, and the apparent beginnings of a genuine universalism. But it is Ericksen's third era—the predominance of internal intellectual conflict and a "scholastic" interest and effort—that is of concern here, for the intellectual efforts of that era were dominated by Brigham H. Roberts.[3] Indeed, the era itself effectively came to at least a temporary end with Roberts's death in 1933.

From their beginning as a religious community, the Mormons have had a characteristically pragmatic American temperament, and the history of their institutions and practices exhibits clearly their responses to the political, economic, and natural forces that have affected them. From the financial crisis of 1837 that disrupted their first congregation in Ohio to the economic and social impact of the large-scale federal military installations established in Mormon country during and since World War II, the Mormons as a group have exhibited the social effects of external pressures and internal tensions.

But somewhat less obvious, though evident to any careful observer, are the forces that have contributed to the molding of the Mormon mind, the beliefs and doctrine of the Mormons and the character of their intellectual life generally. Those influences range across a broad spectrum, from the hopes and expectations of Bible-believing Protestant dissidents, who looked daily for a restoration of the primitive gospel, and the enthusiasm of millenarian revivalists to the reverberations of the American enlightenment that joined with the natural optimism of the frontier to strengthen, if not actually induce, the Mormons' life-affirming theology and irrepressible faith in the future. Other factors included the communitarian ideal and experimental attitude of nineteenth-century America, a revisionist Baptist theology that contributed to Mormon doctrine, and the symbolism and ritual of Freemasonry that are found even today in the temple cultus.

The mainstream of the religion, of course, was the watered-down Puritanism that informed the character of the foundation elements in American culture. Although Mormonism revolted against the traditional Christian absolutism, and even more strenuously against the Calvinist doctrines of original sin, divine election, predestination, and salvation by grace only, it was well within the Puritan moral tradition that was grounded in the belief that the proper vocation of man is to create the Kingdom of God. Despite their bout with polygamy, their love of the theater, music, and dance, and their eudaemonistic moral philosophy, the Mormons have been from their beginning essentially Puritan in their morals, committed to the virtues that were built by the English colonists into the basic moral structure of American life.

To recognize the multiple influences on the religious, moral, and intellectual character of Mormonism, or, indeed, to see the Mormon religion as a syncretic product of the cultural amalgam of nineteenth-century America, is not to disparage the creative endowments of the Mormon leaders. Joseph Smith, the charismatic founder of the movement, was remarkably independent in his thinking and possessed uncommon imaginative and intuitive powers. He broke with many facets of the established theological traditions and at least partially freed his followers from intellectual bondage to the past. His successor, Brigham Young, justly celebrated for his administrative talents, which saved the Mormon movement from dissolution and transformed an eschatological sect into a successful church, colonizing much of the American West in the process, had a far greater impact on the intellectual life of Mormonism than is commonly realized. It was especially under the leadership of Young that the basically Puritan character of Mormonism was shaped and the distinctive doctrines made articulate.

Despite the practicality of the Mormon people, whose energies have been devoted primarily to utilitarian pursuits in cultivating the life of their religious community, from the beginning strong intellectual currents have animated and at times strengthened their culture. Mormonism has suffered and continues to experience incursions of anti-intellectualism, but the achievement of knowledge has always been a prominent Mormon ideal; and at least for the past century most Mormons have had a healthy respect for the virtues of reason. For the most part, they are firm in their insistence that religion should be reasonable and conscientious in their conviction that an honest pursuit of knowledge and a genuine respect for reasonableness not only will not discredit or refute the tenets of the faith, but also will clearly establish their truth and justify the claims of the Church. It was here in the domain of knowledge and reason that Roberts was the preeminent leader of the Mormons, committed to the vindication of Mormonism for the defense and edification of the Saints and a warning to the world.

The defense of the faith was an exacting task because the Mormon beliefs were always set forth with the dogmatic assurance of divine authorization. Not only the doctrinal views of the people but also their moral and spiritual ideals and often their social practices were grounded in a sincere belief in the revelation of the word and will of God as their source and sanction. Although believing Mormons, for the most part, have held that their religion requires no defense, in practice they have commonly made serious efforts to construct effective arguments in response to the critics of their religion and, incidentally, to strengthen the foundations of their faith. In a unique way the Mormons even today have tied their faith to their historical roots. They insist that the truth of their religion, the authority of their priesthood, and the divine foundations of their Church depend entirely on the factual truth of certain of their historical claims. The truth of two of those claims is held to be absolutely crucial. If Joseph Smith's vision of the Father and the Son was not in fact an objective, veridical experience, and if the Book of Mormon was not brought forth, as Joseph Smith insisted, by the hand of God, in very fact an account of God's involvement with ancient Americans descended from the people of ancient Judah, then the Church and its priesthood and Mormonism as a religion are abject frauds. This is the position in which the Church has, by its own official pronouncements, voluntarily placed itself. It has tied its faith to its own history and to the authenticity of its distinctive scripture, the Book of Mormon. It is a position that Roberts held and reaffirmed on many occasions.

There is something private, subjective, and inevitably elusive about theophanies. They cannot be repeated and cannot become public experience and knowledge and are therefore in a sense unarguable. But a book is something else—it is a public object. It can be printed and reprinted, translated and sold, placed on a shelf and read, read by whoever cares to invest the time and energy. Here in the Book of Mormon, a truly remarkable production for which strange claims were made, was something that demanded a reasonable and believable explanation. Did it or did it not have the origin claimed for it—gold plates, an angel, a miraculous translation, and all else?

As Mormonism's most competent historian and leading theologian, as well as the most aggressive exponent and capable disputant in its leadership, Roberts quite naturally, and certainly very effectively, filled the role of chief defender of the faith. This, of course, entailed the defense of the Book of Mormon, the claims of its origin, the historical reliability of its narrative, its sometimes strange theology, and the necessity of its coming forth in the "last dispensation." To this task he devoted much of his energy in his earlier years, producing numerous articles and eventually two substantial and, for the Mormons, landmark volumes in its support.[4] He attacked its attackers and responded in detail to its critics, defended its literary style, argued endlessly on the basis of both external and internal evidence for its authenticity as a collection of historical documents, meticulously examined and defended the claims of those who were associated with its production, and justified its existence as a new witness for God with vigor and subtlety.

Of course, Roberts was not the first to undertake a serious defense of the Book of Mormon. He had the advantage of the arguments of the early Mormon apostle-philosopher Orson Pratt and others. But whatever the lasting value of Roberts's work, it was the most effective defense of the Book of Mormon that had been produced, and certainly nothing more impressive has since been forthcoming, even though numerous writers have tried and today efforts are being made to prove its authenticity through such means as computerized word studies, to say nothing of extensive investments in archeological research. Both by his Church histories and his studies of the Book of Mormon, Roberts, more effectively than any other person, made it possible for the generality of Mormons, at least those who were inclined seriously to raise questions and demand answers, to rest assured that their religious beliefs and distinctive scripture were firmly and securely grounded in historical fact. Certainly the acceptance of this new scripture, added as it was to the

Old and New Testaments and the modern revelations, gave Mormonism both a firm confidence and a measure of increased strength.

In the closing passages of his *New Witnesses for God*, Roberts acknowledged that not all the difficulties and objections to the Book of Mormon had been removed. But, he wrote, "a little more time, a little more research, a little more certain knowledge, which such research will bring forth, will undoubtedly result in the ascertainment of facts that will supply the data necessary for a complete and satisfactory solution of all the difficulties which objectors now emphasize, and on which they claim a verdict against the Book of Mormon."[5] It is of considerable interest, therefore, that he returned to the analysis of the book some years later, in the 1920s, again examining its origin, its substance, its authorship, its literary style, and its historical authenticity. In two heretofore unpublished manuscripts, "Book of Mormon Difficulties: A Study" and "A Book of Mormon Study," he treated the book critically and forthrightly rather than defensively.

Roberts's earlier study closed with the sentence: "Until this [the refutation of the positive evidences set forth for the authenticity of the Book of Mormon] is done, I shall hold that the mass of evidence which it has been the effort of the writer through these pages to set somewhat in order, is sufficient, both in quality and quantity, to fill the mind who pays attention to it with a rational faith in the Book of Mormon—the American volume of scripture."[6] But in "A Book of Mormon Study," he found that much of the substance of the Book of Mormon was quite common in the thought and literature of Joseph Smith's time and place, that a literary analysis does not support the authenticity of the book, and that Smith had the talent and creative imagination to have been its author. Whereas in his earlier work he occasionally found passages in Ethan Smith's *View of the Hebrews* that were useful in his arguments for the Book of Mormon's authenticity, he now found *View of the Hebrews* to be a serious threat to that authenticity, and in "A Book of Mormon Study" he devoted extensive space to his treatment of that threat.[7]

Roberts's "A Book of Mormon Study" must speak for itself. But those interested in the author's conclusions set forth in the manuscript should not neglect the statements affirming his belief in the authenticity of the Book of Mormon that appear in the letters that are a part of the record of the controversy that resulted from a reading of the manuscript by Church officials. The contrast of his manuscript, composed as an attempt to come to grips with a basic problem that he apparently believed would yield to scholarly analysis, with his affirmation, in the heat of controversy, of his faith that the objective foundation of Mormonism is not to be doubted raises the interesting question of what Roberts did in fact believe about the Book of Mormon in his latest years. That he continued to profess his faith in the authenticity of the book seems to be without question, despite the strong arguments and statements in his study that would appear to explicitly express a conviction that it is not authentic.

Roberts's biographer, Truman G. Madsen, has argued in a paper published in 1979 that in "A Book of Mormon Study" Roberts was simply playing the role of the "devil's advocate."[8] "The report," according to Madsen, "was not intended to be balanced. A kind of lawyer's brief of one side of a case written to stimulate discussion in preparation of the defense of a work already accepted as true, the manuscript was anything but a careful presentation of Roberts's thoughts about the Book of Mormon or of his own convictions."[9]

Madsen held that Roberts was employing an essentially pedagogical technique to bring attention to problems that should be faced by the Church and by students of the Book of Mormon. In this he had the support of Roberts's letters, written in the context of controversy over his manuscript, but he did not adduce evidence for his interpretation from the manuscript itself.[10] Although he quoted Roberts's statement of faith in his March 15, 1923, letter to the president of the Church, Madsen did not provide his readers with any of the many crucial statements in Roberts's study that appear to a typical reader to throw serious doubt on the authenticity of the Book of Mormon, or at the least on Roberts's belief in its authenticity.[11] The Roberts study was not available to the general reader who might be interested in it, and, except for listing the issues with which the study was concerned, Madsen made none of its contents known in his paper. Roberts's argument and conclusions were not mentioned.

In his authorized biography published in 1980, Madsen devoted comparatively little attention to Roberts's views on the Book of Mormon, referring only to publications that had appeared prior to 1910.[12] Although Roberts's unpublished manuscript, "The Truth, the Way, the Life," a summary of his religious and theological views, received an entire chapter, "A Book of Mormon Study" was not mentioned, nor was there any indication of the important and interesting controversy that it had generated.[13]

Perhaps the importance of "A Book of Mormon Study" lies not so much in the question of the authenticity of the Book of Mormon as in the interest which many have in the personality and thought of Roberts himself, for he was intellectually the most eminent and influential of all the official leaders of the Church. And while Roberts apparently did not prepare the materials in this volume for publication, it is because he is such a key figure in the intellectual history of the Church that the record would not be complete without them.

Roberts lived during a crucial period for Mormonism. The original prophetic impulse was waning, the major feats of pioneering were accomplished, and the struggles with the federal government and their aftermath were taking a severe toll of human energy and threatening the economic and institutional life of the Church. More than anything else, the Mormon Church needed the defenses that would justify its existence, establish its moral and intellectual respectability, and guarantee its own integrity. But there were additional problems that engrossed Roberts—the coming of statehood for Utah, the creation of a political life for the Mormon people, and the secular threat to religion that was carried largely by the new humanism, which enjoyed considerable support from the sciences. It was especially the debate on evolution that captured the attention of the Mormons after the turn of the century. Roberts seemed born to the task of meeting these challenges, and he engaged them with quite remarkable energy, dedication, and self-assurance.

The fundamentals of Mormon thought were quite firmly established in the Church's first generation, but there was considerable confusion in the doctrines, which grew somewhat erratically from the pronouncements of the prophet, the impact of thoughtful converts, and the general experience of the people. It was a later generation, the generation of Ericksen's scholastic period, which pulled the philosophical and theological strands together and brought some order out of the earlier chaos. It was the intellectual leaders of this period, among whom Roberts was preeminent in both ability and influence, who not only shaped the outlines of a systematic theology, but also developed the perspectives that placed the Church as an institution within the framework of history and provided the Mormon people with the instruments for rationalizing and defending their beliefs and practices. Though perhaps less radical and less creative than the first, this generation was more reflective, more reasonable, and intellectually more responsible. The Church had already become defensive where before it had exhibited a quite admirable independence in both thought and action, and argument and scholastic justification had displaced the facile prophetic pronouncements of the first years. Something very important to Mormonism had been lost with the death of Joseph Smith and the passing of those who had known him and were close to him and had been creators with him of the new faith and its rudimentary institutions. But just as inevitably, something was gained by their successors in the necessity for defining, explaining, and justifying the doctrine and exploring and exploiting its numerous entailments for both thought and action. Above all, a new intellectual vitality was gained by the "defense of the faith and the saints."

In his private as well as public life, Roberts was a controversial figure. His autobiography, published in 1990, though obviously unfinished, is a fascinating, moving story of a lonely child in England, left to shift for himself by irresponsible guardians after his Mormon-convert mother had migrated to Utah; his walking barefoot from the Platte River to Salt Lake City; a rough-and-tumble youth; his admirable struggle for an education; his fight with his Church to get into politics; his role in the struggle for Utah's statehood; his dramatic losing battle with the U.S. Congress, which refused him his seat in the House because of his polygamy. The full story of his life will tell of his double struggle against the inroads of secularism in the Church and the anti-scientific bias of some of his ecclesiastical colleagues; of his battle as historian to publish an uncensored history of the Church; of his fight over doctrine and evolution; of his missionary controversies with the Christian sects; of his fight to get into action in World War I, when he was commissioned a chaplain above the age limit because of his demonstrated physical strength and abilities; of his endless battle with the critics of Mormonism; of his struggle to maintain the prestige and influence of his quorum in the central administration of the Church, the First Council of the Seventy, which since his death has been downgraded in the top councils of the Church; of his determination to make Mormonism intellectually respectable and acceptable; and of his internal struggles with his own faith, the struggles of a man who wanted to believe and yet be honest with himself and others.

Roberts belonged to the era of great Mormon oratory, and for almost half a century he was the Church's great orator, in the days when the Tabernacle in Salt Lake City sounded and resounded with the voices of impassioned advocates and defenders, the days before the microphone and camera robbed the Mormon conferences of much of their character and vitality and inspiration, the days when the Mormon Church both valued and invited argument and debate. There was then a kind of intellectual openness about the Church which encouraged thought and discussion; its faith and confidence were firm and aggressive, and it was ready to take on all comers. Its leadership could justifiably boast a roster of impressive talent, but Roberts was at once its chief intellectual exhibit and its most competent advocate.

The high value that the Mormons in the first decades of this century placed on intellectual strength and achievement in matters pertaining to religion yielded a good return, for the thought and writings which issued from their ecclesiastical leaders, among whom were several persons of historical, scientific, and poetic ability, were a permanent impress upon the character of the religion and the Church. Of these Roberts was the recognized leader. Often in rebellion and conflict, he nevertheless commanded both the confidence and admiration of his colleagues and of the rank and file of the Church. His native intellectual powers, his wide and intelligent reading, his forensic skills, the forcefulness of his pen, his enthusiastic and even impetuous speech, and the sheer impact of his uncommon personality and physical bearing made him the intellectual leader of the Mormon people in an era when they both encouraged and prized serious inquiry in religious matters.

Since Roberts's death half a century ago, the Church has suffered a steady decline in matters pertaining to religious thought, a decline accompanied by a growth of irrationalism and anti-intellectualism from which there is no clear indication of recovery in the foreseeable future. Some important sociological studies of Mormonism have been made, and an entire generation of competent historians have produced careful and reliable studies of the Church's history. But comparatively little has been done in leadership circles in matters pertaining to morals, religion, and philosophy, except, of course, to enjoin Church members to accept the established doctrine and live lives of virtue. Notwithstanding a brief respite in the 1960s and 1970s, the Church has discouraged its best historians, and it has consistently resisted serious and competent thought in religion and philosophy. Perhaps a resurgence of interest in Roberts's work will point toward a more productive future.

In general, Roberts's prose style is rhetorical and dramatic. He was at all times the orator. He was lacking in certain capabilities possessed by some others among his colleagues in Church officialdom, whose writings also left important impressions on the Mormon mind. He did not have the precise diction, for instance, of his contemporary James E. Talmage, and there is little indication that he possessed the poetic talents of Orson F. Whitney. But both his oral and written words drew strength from his directness and enthusiasm. He wrote as he spoke, and his written pages often read not as finely composed and polished sentences, but as though they were edited reports of extemporaneous statements—direct, often repetitive, somewhat personal, as though writer and reader were in conversation, sometimes careless in construction, but always to the point and effective.

Like his public address, Roberts's writing was argumentative and polemical. He enjoyed nothing more than argument; indeed, he was at his best in a good fight. If there were no debate in sight, he would produce a battle by monologue. In the heat of controversy he always rose to the occasion, and it is not surprising that his most commendable theological piece, *The Mormon Doctrine of Deity*, certainly the most competent theological statement to come from a Mormon leader, was in its most important part a published debate, an argument with a Roman

Catholic scholar set within the larger dispute on Mormon doctrine that aroused widespread public interest near the turn of the century.

Roberts's strength as a historian resided especially in his intense historical consciousness, his quite spacious perspectives on history, his capacity for historical research and talent for narrative, his sense of personal involvement with his subject, his passion for it, and his sincere desire to be honest and open with his readers. His histories are not without bias and prejudice. They are clearly pro-Mormon and written with a vengeance. They are intended to justify the Mormon Church and bring credit upon it, but they are written with admirable honesty and sincerity, having the mark of a desire for objectivity even when it is not achieved. Often in his writings the Church comes out second best where a man of lesser character under similar circumstances would have found it easy to bring it out on top. In the preface of volume 1 of *A Comprehensive History*, Roberts wrote:

It is always a difficult task to hold the scales of justice at even balance when weighing the deeds of men. It becomes doubly more so when dealing with men engaged in a movement that one believes had its origin with God, and that its leaders on occasion act under the inspiration of God. Under such conditions to so state events as to be historically exact, and yet, on the other hand, so treat the course of events as not to destroy faith in these men, nor in their work, becomes a task of supreme delicacy; and one that tries the soul and the skill of the historian. The only way such a task can be accomplished, in the judgment of the writer, is to frankly state events as they occurred, in full consideration of all related circumstances, allowing the line of condemnation or of justification to fall where it may; being confident that in the sum of things justice will follow truth; and God will be glorified in his work, no matter what may befall individuals, or groups of individuals.

In *A Comprehensive History of the Church of Jesus Christ of Latter-day Saints* (1930), Roberts composed for the historically minded and history-based Mormons a strong and carefully researched historical statement, laid out many of the fundamental issues and basic problems, and did so with courage and honesty. He had a large capacity for work, a fine sensitivity for the controversial, and a talent for research, comprehension, and synthesis. And while he wrote as he argued and debated, he achieved a measure of understanding admirable in a man who was personally living through the impassioned events that he described and who wrote as both a high official of the Church and as the author of its official history.

Though every historian, if he is to avoid confusion and frustration, must adopt a position from which he selects his materials, it is unfortunate that Roberts was so strongly inclined toward what may be called the "political" theme in his history. Perhaps he would have been untrue to his own political nature if he had done otherwise. But it is still disappointing to find so much of political and institutional conflict and controversy and so little of cultural history in his work. Yet he was himself a man of action, and quite certainly he told the narrative where the action was.

Moreover, Roberts did not fully and properly examine and exploit the origins of Mormonism; and partly because of this, the generality of Mormon people today, who depend so heavily upon him for their historical interpretations, do not understand and appreciate the multiple forces that went into the making of their religion and the historical movement of their Church. The picture is altogether too simple and is too much affected by the strong desire to vindicate and justify the Church. In his *Outlines of Ecclesiastical History*, an early text first published in 1893, he mentioned very briefly such matters as the Jewish and Hellenistic backgrounds of Christianity. But here he was interested in making a case for the apostasy of the early Christian church, and for this he was able to draw on numerous able historians for his material. In his official Mormon Church histories—the seven edited volumes of the *History of the Church, Period 1*, and his six-volume *Comprehensive History*—aside from brief references to the revivalism current in western New York in the 1820s and an account of Joseph Smith's ancestry and family religious interests, he totally ignored the American intellectual and religious milieu from which Mormonism issued. "A Book of Mormon Study" partially atones for this serious defect, one that has had an effect on the thought of the Mormon people, who, for the most part, know little or nothing of the cultural and intellectual background of Mormonism.

Roberts's treatments of Christian history were polemical and propagandistic. He treated altogether too casually the large cultural forces that produced Christianity and its institutions; and while his factual materials are in the main reliable, conforming at least to the opinions of some of the best histories of his time, much that he wrote on this subject is difficult to defend. He failed to grasp fully the character of early Hellenistic Christianity, to see its very beginnings in Paul as a departure from the Palestinian religion, and failed therefore, as did most Christian historians, to judge fairly the subsequent course of Christian thought and institutions. Nevertheless, he wrote intelligently, and though he depended excessively on secondary sources, the church historians, he set forth the main historical foundations upon which the Mormons have rested their case, the apostasy of the Christian church as the necessity for a restoration and the necessity of revelation as the basis of that restoration.

Roberts's perspectives on history and his competence to treat some of the large problems in Christian history were due in part to his wide-ranging and intelligent reading. There was much that he neglected in intellectual history, through no fault of his own, for his formal education was at best very elementary. He seems to have known too little of Greek and Roman philosophy and their bearing upon Christianity, or of medieval philosophy and theology. But he profited much from such writers as Andrew White, John Kitto, John W. Draper, and Edward Gibbon. His works are well furnished with telling references to such greats as Johann Mosheim, Alfred Edersheim, Henry H. Milman, and Eusebius. Roberts read extensively in all of these, and in Ernest Renan, Sir William Blackstone, Thomas Macaulay, and an assortment of major philosophers, ancient and modern, when still a youth employed as a blacksmith—no mean accomplishment for one who first learned the alphabet at the age of eleven. He was acquainted with Ralph Waldo Emerson, John Fiske, and William James, even though he neglected some of the major thinkers of his own generation in favor of second- and third-raters.

Roberts's work indicates a rather broad acquaintance with both the Old and New Testaments and with Bible commentaries. Indeed, he was too dependent on such works as Bible commentaries and Bible dictionaries. In treating the history of religion, he was given to extensive quotations from secondary sources that were edifying to his readers but exhibited deficiencies in his own knowledge. However, he gave some attention to biblical scholarship and recognized the claims of "higher" or historical-literary criticism. In an address, "Higher Criticism and the Book of Mormon," published in the *Improvement Era* for June and July 1911, he said, "The Book of Mormon must submit to every test, literary criticism with the rest. Indeed, it must submit to every analysis and examination. It must submit to historical tests, to the tests of archeological research and also to the higher criticism." The thesis of this address, however, was that the Book of Mormon itself exhibited the errors of the higher criticism in certain of its well-established conclusions relative to the Bible, for example, the multiple authorship of Isaiah, which is contradicted by the Book of Mormon. Here and elsewhere, Roberts insisted, it is evident that the Book of Mormon in a very real way will save the truths of the gospel. Referring to passages describing Christ's appearance in the Western Hemisphere, he concluded, "And that testimony of the gospel, its historicity and reality, contained in the Book of Mormon, shall stand against the results of higher criticism" (p. 786). A few years later, in "A Book of Mormon Study," Roberts employed the principles of the higher criticism in his own analysis and critique of the Book of Mormon.

Nevertheless, partly because of the failure by Roberts to appreciate fully the findings of biblical scholarship, the Mormons even today are in general the victims of traditional patterns of biblical thought that often tie them to an outworn and intellectually frustrating scriptural literalism. Despite Roberts's rather high level of historical and theological sophistication, he failed to distinguish effectively history from myth and legend in the biblical writings, accepting literally such accounts as the Garden of Eden and flood stories of Genesis. There is no indication in his writings that the New Testament scholarship of his time, such as the analysis of the relationships that obtain among the synoptics or the impact of the early church on the character and substance of the Gospels, seriously affected his thought or scholarship.

It was in his studies of Mormon history that Roberts exhibited his research talents. Elsewhere he was very dependent on secondary sources, sometimes quoting so extensively from other writers that it is difficult to determine the limits of his own ideas. But this defect in scholarship was in some respects a boon to the typical Mormon who read Roberts's writings, for here he was introduced to historians and occasionally philosophers, theologians, and sometimes scientists whose work otherwise would have remained unknown to him. It was one of Roberts's great contributions to his people that he was determined to raise the level of their historical knowledge and religious thought, and he was remarkably effective in this effort. Many Mormon libraries today still include the works of Josephus, Eusebius, Draper, or White because of his lesson materials that called for the study of these writers. His special responsibility as an official of the Church was to provide leadership in missionary activities, and he firmly believed that missionaries should be adequately armed with knowledge for their task.[14] He was not always supported in this conviction by his colleagues, who often preferred dependence on faith with a minimal concern for relevant learning.

As a historian, Roberts was not free from the dictates of theology, a serious weakness in any historian, but his work as theologian was strengthened by his sense of history as well as by his historical knowledge. It was in part his historical consciousness that made him preeminent among the "official" Mormon theologians. He had remarkably reliable instincts for distinguishing the crucial elements, both theological and philosophical, in the intellectual foundations of Mormonism and was well endowed to treat those problems within a historical framework of large perspectives and vision. He was committed to the intellectual exploitation of the ideas which he found or thought he found in the pronouncements of the Mormon founder, Joseph Smith, and had a healthy respect for the religious thought that issued from others of the earlier generation of Mormon leaders, especially Brigham Young and Orson Pratt. He was not a creator of doctrine like Smith and Young, or even like the early Church leader Sidney Ridgon, Mormonism's chief tie with the Baptist tradition. And he was somewhat less original in his more technical thought than Pratt. Though he shared Pratt's disposition for speculative metaphysics, he lacked his logical and analytical talent. There is no analytical piece among Roberts's writings, for instance, comparable to Pratt's "The Absurdities of Immaterialism," the most impressive philosophical statement in the early Mormon literature. Roberts's philosophical writings had a flamboyance and looseness about them that exhibit his lack of expertise when compared to the thought of his contemporary, W. H. Chamberlin. But Chamberlin was not a Church official, and he died at a comparatively early age. His work would have brought both credit and strength to Mormonism had he lived long enough to publish the results of his religious and philosophical thought. Chamberlin had studied with Josiah Royce at Harvard and George Holmes Howison at Berkeley and had gained a good foundation in formal biblical studies at Chicago. Though he was in a position to bring to Mormonism the fruits of his labors, supporting its basic philosophy with the arguments of personal idealism, even in some Mormon academic circles he suffered considerable neglect, if not derision.

Like Mormon writers generally, in both his theological and philosophical writings, Roberts seriously neglected discussion of fundamental moral philosophy. This omission of an interest that should be basic to religion has had an effect to this day on Mormon literature. Roberts's younger contemporary and admirer Ephraim E. Ericksen, professor of philosophy at the University of Utah, undertook to compensate for this lacuna in Mormon thought, but, like Chamberlin, despite his influence in academic circles, Ericksen did not enjoy the official status that was necessary to produce a large and lasting impact on Mormon thought.

Roberts's most influential colleague among official Mormon writers was the scientist-apostle James E. Talmage. Roberts's talents in treating doctrinal issues were perhaps less refined than those of Talmage, as were his literary abilities, but he was less legalistic and, on the whole, less literalistic than Talmage and had a more expansive intellect, a more creative style, and a far greater sensitivity to historical and philosophical issues. Although he lacked the equivalent of Talmage's scientific education and knowledge, Roberts was more competent than either Pratt or Talmage in his grasp of the large implications of Mormon doctrine and was in a better position to achieve perspective on the place of Mormonism as a religious movement or social structure.

Roberts was not a theologian of the first order, as he was not a major historian. He was simply the best theologian and historian that Mormonism had in its first century. His main strength as a theologian for Mormonism was not in his capacity for theological dialectic or refinement or in any genuine originality for this discipline. It was, rather, in his instinct for the philosophical relevance of the Mormon theological ideas — this and his sense of history. His combination of temperament, talent, and interest brought breadth and depth to his thought, giving his work a profoundness that was uncommon among Mormon writers.

More than any other Mormon thinker of his time, Roberts sensed the radical heresy in Mormon theology, its complete departure from the traditional Christian doctrines of God and man, its denial of the divine absoluteness, and its rejection of the negativism of the orthodox dogma of the human predicament. In those matters he had a fine sense of what was entailed by the basic ideas already laid down by his predecessors, and he did more than any other person to set forth the full character of the Mormonism that followed inevitably from the theological ideas of Joseph Smith, from the doctrine, for instance, of the uncreated intelligence or ego and the denial of the orthodox dogma on the creation of the world. He reveled in the pluralistic metaphysics inherent in Mormon doctrine and saw its implications for the freedom of the will and its possible strengths in treating the problem of moral and natural evil. In this he felt some kinship with William James, but he often failed to follow through on the path that his best instincts had charted for him, in part, perhaps, because he lacked the technical equipment for doing full justice to his own ideas.

Roberts was not embarrassed by the unorthodox implications of the finitistic conception of God indicated in the teachings of Joseph Smith. He delighted in them, for they made room for a positive doctrine of man, genuine freedom, and an unfinished universe. He kept the discussion of the nature of God on a more defensible level than did most of the Mormon writers in theology, who commonly either failed to recognize the radical nature of the departure from orthodoxy or yielded to the naive extremes of anthropomorphism that compromised the very meaning of divinity.

At the turn of the century and for some years thereafter, the Mormons had difficult practical problems of their own, especially of an economic and political nature, which kept them well occupied, but their intellectual leaders did not escape the main controversy of the time, religion versus evolution. The evolution controversy reached the United States rather late, and it reached the Mormons a little later, but Roberts was in the thick of it, determined to make the case for orthodoxy by discrediting Darwinism. An early essay on the subject, "Man's Relationship to Deity," does him little credit, but it is important to the story of his work. It is interesting that his argument was not anti-scientific in spirit, an attitude that would have betrayed his confidence in the virtues of reason. The errors of Darwinism, he insisted, were not due to the scientists. They were the fault, rather, of the churches, whose nonsense regarding the creation and age of the earth had driven the scientists far from the truth in their efforts to find a ground upon which they could make sense.

Roberts's own efforts to reconcile the findings of science with a liberalized biblical literalism were typical of the times and do not deserve serious attention today, but it should be said in his defense that in later years he appears to have developed a somewhat greater sophistication in such matters. He was interested in the science-religion controversy and read quite widely in the field, but he was better prepared to see the dispute in past centuries than to contribute importantly to it in the present. As in his treatments of Christian history and dogma, he quoted extensively from others but made no serious contributions to the subject.

On the whole, Roberts appears as a writer of uncommon good sense, determined to distinguish fact from fiction, history from legend, and meaningful doctrine from meaninglessness. But he had serious lapses, caused especially by his deficiencies in biblical scholarship and his inability to escape the yoke of a sometimes abject biblical literalism. In his final treatment of the problem of Mormonism and evolution, for instance — a problem that should have posed for him no really great difficulties, since the Mormon Church had not then and has not since taken an official stand against organic evolution — his thought was reduced at one point to the level of proposing that Adam and Eve were transplanted full grown from another planet. This piece of fantasy was part of his effort to come to terms with science by way of arguing for a race of pre-Adamites, humans who had been obliterated by some natural catastrophe.[15] Despite such nonsense, Roberts's instincts were generally good; in his later years especially he was a strong defender of science and scientific knowledge. But he knew too little of science and paid far too little attention to the work of really first-rate thinkers who were occupied with similar problems. His work on religion and evolution is less commendable than that of his colleague Talmage, or his contemporary Frederick J. Pack, a Mormon geologist who enjoyed considerable Church approval without holding high Church office.[16]

But above all, this should be said of Roberts — he was intellectually alive to the very last, a person whose later maturity increased not only his wisdom and the general quality of his thought but also his determination to find the truth about the things that for him mattered most. There is little doubt that if he had enjoyed ten more years and had been given full confidence by his ecclesiastical colleagues, very interesting things would have come from his pen.

After his death in 1933, Brigham H. Roberts was a seriously neglected figure in the Mormon Church until very recently. Where once he was easily the most interesting, exciting, and stimulating person in its leadership, its most prolific writer, its chief theologian and historian, and its

B. H. Roberts, probably taken about the period he produced his "Study of the Book of Mormon."

B. H. Roberts in his mid-twenties, possibly taken by Charles R. Savage, circa 1884.

Captain B. H. Roberts when a chaplain with the 145th Field Artillery, U.S. Expeditionary Force in France, 1918, at Camp De Souge.

B. H. Roberts circa 1930.

Bronze bust of B. H. Roberts sculpted by Mahonri M. Young, circa 1946.
The bust is located in the Joseph Smith Building, Brigham Young University,
Provo, Utah.

most capable defender, he has since been eclipsed by writers of varying but lesser talents, many of whom lack even the grace to acknowledge their indebtedness to him, and some of whom seem never to have heard of him. The resurgence of interest in Roberts's work and the reissue of some of his writings are therefore fortunate. His name should be kept very much alive by those who are interested in the intellectual life of Mormonism, who have any attachment to its robust and romantic past, or who have genuine concern for the ideas and institutions that have been the substance and strength of Mormonism.

Brigham Henry Roberts was born in Warrington, Lancashire, England, March 13, 1857, one of six children of Benjamin and Ann Everington Roberts. Both of his parents converted to the Mormon Church, and in 1862, while he was still a child, his mother left his father and emigrated to Utah, placing him in the custody of somewhat irresponsible guardians in England. In 1866, under the auspices of the Church and accompanied by his sixteen-year-old sister, Mary, he made the journey to Utah to join his mother, who had settled in the village of Centerville, now a suburb of Salt Lake City.

Roberts suffered an unhappy childhood in England, and his early years in Utah were difficult, always in poverty or near-poverty. But from an early age he was adventurous and hardworking—as a miner, a blacksmith, and a ranch-hand. As a youth he read widely, especially the historians, and eventually, despite severe financial difficulties, he studied at the University of Deseret, the predecessor of the University of Utah.

Roberts served as a missionary for the Church of Jesus Christ of Latter-day Saints in the central and southern states from March 1880 to May 1882 and again in the South in 1883 and 1884. He married two women, Sarah Louisa Smith in 1878 and Celia Dibble in 1884, and in 1886 was arrested on a federal charge of unlawful cohabitation. He evaded the law, however, and left for England, again as a missionary, on the day following his arrest. In 1888 he returned to Utah and was ordained a member of the First Council of the Seventy, one of the general governing bodies of the Mormon Church. In April 1889 he surrendered to the federal court on the pending charge of unlawful cohabitation and served a term of several months in the Utah territorial prison. He married a third wife, Margaret Curtis Shipp, in April 1890.

Although much involved in theological, biographical, and historical writing, Roberts entered territorial politics, serving in the Utah constitutional convention in 1895. His involvement in politics resulted in considerable difficulty between him and some of his less liberal ecclesiastical colleagues, but in 1898 he was elected to the U.S. House of

Representatives as the Democratic candidate from Utah. Because of his polygamy, however, he was denied his seat by the Congress.

In 1917 Roberts was appointed chaplain of the First Utah Field Artillery and served in France under the command of General John Pershing. He returned to Utah in 1919 and resumed his duties as a Church leader, becoming the senior member of the First Council of the Seventy in 1924. From 1922 to 1927 he was president of the Eastern States Mission of the Church, with headquarters in New York.

Over a period of several decades Roberts was heavily engaged in writing and preaching and, allowing for a brief respite during his prison term and his period of military service, in ecclesiastical duties. He was not infrequently appointed to represent the Church on special occasions, when an exhibit of its finest forensic talents was considered important, if not crucial. In sheer volume his literary output exceeds anything produced by a Mormon Church leader before or since.

Roberts died in Salt Lake City at the age of seventy-six on September 27, 1933, from complications related to diabetes.

NOTES

1. E. E. Ericksen, *The Psychological and Ethical Aspects of Mormon Group Life* (Chicago: University of Chicago Press, 1922; reprint, Salt Lake City: University of Utah Press, 1975). The reprint edition has an introduction by Sterling M. McMurrin.

2. References to the Mormons, Mormonism, the Mormon Church, and the Church are to the people, beliefs, and institutions of the Church of Jesus Christ of Latter-day Saints, which has its headquarters in Utah. I do not mean to include in these categories other groups and institutions that are a part of the Mormon movement and tradition.

3. In commenting on Roberts in this essay, I have drawn freely on "Brigham H. Roberts: Notes on a Mormon Philosopher-Historian," which I wrote as an introduction to a 1967 reprinting of Roberts's early volume, *Joseph Smith the Prophet-Teacher* (Princeton: Deseret Club of Princeton University), first published in 1908.

4. Volumes 2 and 3 of *New Witnesses for God* (Salt Lake City: Deseret News, 1909).

5. Ibid., 3:559.

6. Ibid., 561.

7. A separate and brief manuscript by Roberts comparing Ethan Smith's *View of the Hebrews* (1825 ed.; orig. publ. Poultney, Vt.: Smith & Shute, 1823) with the Book of Mormon, commonly referred to as "A Parallel," was published in the *Rocky Mountain Mason* (Jan. 1956) by Mervin B. Hogan ("A 'Parallel': A Matter of Chance versus Coincidence"). "A Parallel" is reprinted in this volume.

8. Truman G. Madsen, "B. H. Roberts and the Book of Mormon," *Brigham*

Young University Studies, 19 (1979): 427-45. In this article Madsen's quotations from Roberts's statements on the Book of Mormon are almost exclusively from Roberts's earlier period, prior to his work on "A Book of Mormon Study."

9. Ibid., 441.

10. See the section of this volume on "B. H. Roberts's Correspondence Related to the Book of Mormon Essays."

11. Regarding the date of the "1923 letter," see note 65 in the section of this volume entitled "Introduction." Brigham Madsen is of the opinion that this letter was probably originally dated 1922.

12. Truman G. Madsen, *Defender of the Faith: The B. H. Roberts Story* (Salt Lake City: Bookcraft, 1980).

13. Several months after the present volume, including this essay on Brigham H. Roberts, was sent to the publisher, Madsen published in an official magazine of the Church of Jesus Christ of Latter-day Saints an article entitled "Brigham H. Roberts after Fifty Years: Still Witnessing for the Book of Mormon," *Ensign,* Dec. 1983. In this article Madsen gave attention to the Roberts manuscripts, "Book of Mormon Difficulties," "A Book of Mormon Study," and "A Parallel," which are the substance of this volume. Madsen called attention to the basic problems and questions that Roberts raised in his "A Book of Mormon Study," but he did not provide his readers with any information on Roberts's views and conclusions on the problems that were set forth in the manuscripts.

14. Roberts was a member of the First Council of the Seventy, one of the three governing quorums of the Mormon Church.

15. This aberration appears in Roberts's late unpublished work, "The Truth, the Way, the Life," written in the 1920s.

16. See Frederick J. Pack's *Science and Belief in God* (Salt Lake City: Deseret News, 1924). Pack was professor of geology at the University of Utah, as Talmage had been in earlier years.

Introduction

by Brigham D. Madsen

From the beginning of his missionary labors for the Church of Jesus Christ of Latter-day Saints, Elder Brigham Henry Roberts faced hostile critics whose specific attacks on the authenticity of the Book of Mormon he met with skill and a determined pugnacity that came to mark his career as a defender of what the world called the "Golden Bible" and the faith which it helped to forge. Never content with superficial answers to serious questions about the story of Lehi and the peopling of the Americas and impatient with fellow Church members who were satisfied with perfunctory responses, he spent many years in industrious research and written and oral argument to sustain his early belief in the Book of Mormon. He could never understand those who were willing to settle for less.

The new scripture that absorbed so much of Roberts's attention throughout his career as a religious leader had, in the view of its adherents, been revealed to Joseph Smith, Jr., a Vermont farm boy, in 1823, through the visitation of a heavenly being, the angel Moroni. Moroni, it was said, showed Smith some gold plates that he had deposited in a hill near present Manchester, New York, about 421 A.D., just before his death as the last member of his race, the Nephites. According to the Book of Mormon, which Joseph Smith claimed to have translated from the plates by aid of a Urim and Thummim found with them, the American continents were peopled by migrants from the East over a period of many centuries. Smith later summarized the contents of the Book of Mormon in a letter to John Wentworth of the *Chicago Democrat* in 1842:

> In this important and interesting book, the history of ancient America is unfolded, from its first settlement by a colony that came from the Tower of Babel, at the confusion of languages, to the beginning of the fifth century of the Christian Era. We are informed by these records that America in ancient times has been inhabited by two distinct races of people. The first were called Jaredites, and came directly from the Tower of Babel. The second race came directly from the city of Jerusalem, about six hundred years before Christ. They

were principally Israelites, of the descendants of Joseph. The Jaredites were destroyed about the time that the Israelites came from Jerusalem, who succeeded them in the inheritance of the country. The principal nation of the second race fell in battle towards the close of the fourth century. The remnant are the Indians that now inhabit this country. This book also tells us that our Savior made his appearance upon this continent after his resurrection, that he planted the gospel here in all its fulness, and richness, and power, and blessing; that they had apostles, prophets, pastors, teachers and evangelists; the same order, the same priesthood, the same ordinances, gifts, powers and blessings, as were enjoyed on the eastern continents, that the people were cut off in consequence of their transgressions, that the last of their prophets who existed among them was commanded to write an abridgment of their prophecies, history, etc., and to hide it up in the earth, and that it should come forth and be united with the Bible for the accomplishment of the purposes of God in the last days.[1]

Roberts first began wrestling with the Book of Mormon and its problems as a twenty-three-year-old missionary in Tennessee when a Campbellite minister, a Mr. Alsup, challenged him and his companion to a debate, held over a three-day period, February 5-7, 1881, and "limited to a consideration of the Book of Mormon." The opening speech of Alsup, in which he declared the Mormon scripture to be "of no more worth than last year's Almanac . . . a fraud, a cheat, and worthless," was "for the two inexperienced elders in Book of Mormon matters . . . quite appalling," but, as Roberts later wrote, "gradually things righted themselves." The Campbellite minister first contended that the Book of Mormon was in conflict with the Bible in that it taught the gospel of Christ before the appearance of the Savior. Roberts, as the chosen opponent of Alsup, quoted the Old and New Testaments to prove that the gospel taught to Abraham was the same as revealed later in New Testament times, which led the listening congregation to conclude that Alsup's view "had left Abraham in hell and Elder Roberts had dared him to get him out." The Campbellite then attacked the Mormon story that Christianity was preached on the American continents 700 years before the appearance of Christ, to which Roberts again quoted Bible verses to refute his opponent. Other arguments from Alsup were concerned with the use of a mariner's compass by the Israelite emigrants while crossing the ocean, which he said conflicted with known science; the Spaulding theory of the origin of the Book of Mormon, a claim that Smith had based his account on a story written by the Reverend Solomon Spaulding, which "falsehood" was rebutted by Roberts; and the charge that the Book of Mormon was written by one man, which Roberts acknowledged but explained that one author to be Mormon, the ancient chronicler of the Nephite people. Roberts's defense of the book was so successful that Alsup left the debate early and eventually over sixty new members were baptized into the Mormon Church from the nearby community of Manchester, Tennessee.[2]

A number of years later, in 1896, while Roberts was visiting in Cincinnati, Ohio, he spent some time at the local library and discovered an article in Alexander Campbell's *The Millennial Harbinger* in which Campbell had attacked the Book of Mormon.[3] Alsup had used these exact arguments in debating Roberts, who was therefore really taking on the founder of the Campbellite faith. Later Roberts, in reflecting on this early missionary experience in Tennessee, thought that Campbell's attack was "the most powerful criticism of the Book of Mormon that has been written."[4] The confrontation with Alsup fixed for Roberts a determination to prove the authenticity of the new scripture; he wrote in his missionary journal three years later that evidence in support of the Book of Mormon "is intensely interesting to me. . . . I have observed when speaking on this subject I have enjoyed great liberty of the Spirit perhaps more so than with speaking on any subject."[5]

After four years of missionary work in the South, first as one of the traveling elders and later for two years as Mission President, Roberts returned to Utah to become an editor with the *Salt Lake Herald* until December 1886, when he was advised to leave the territory to escape imprisonment for unlawful cohabitation with his two wives. His Church sent him to Liverpool, England, to become an editor of the *Millennial Star,* the most important European publication of the Mormon Church, and during the next two years, 1887 and 1888, he pursued his studies on the origins of the Book of Mormon. When not writing weekly editorials of up to 2,000 words on various gospel subjects, he engaged in public debates, traveled widely in England, and soon gained a reputation as a fearless and articulate defender of Mormonism. He spent many hours in the nearby famous Picton Library, "making an immense collection of notes from American Archeology that was used in the evidences of American antiquities and Archeological works in the external evidences for the Book of Mormon." The results of his research formed the basis for many of the editorials in the *Star* and became the foundation for his three-volume work, published in 1909, *New Witnesses for God,* which, as will be seen, remained his chief defense of the Book of Mormon until his further investigations in the early 1920s.[6]

Roberts gave a number of public lectures on what many newspapers called "The Book of Mormon Controversy," a typical one being a talk at Swansea, Wales, where, after an hour-and-a-half discourse, he fielded a number of questions from a member of the audience, one Adolphus Bolitho, who later corresponded with his Mormon antagonist in the forum of the *Millennial Star.* Bolitho suggested that since there were only 553 years from the first Zedekiah to the Messiah instead of the

600 years as stated in the Book of Mormon that the "Messiah of the Book of Mormon came too late to be the Messiah of the Bible." Elder Roberts replied that Bolitho admitted discrepancies in the Bible but would not admit that possibility in the Book of Mormon. In another exchange Roberts invited his questioner to prove that Jewish and Nephite months were identical, which Roberts said Bolitho could not do. The questions seem dated now but were evidently fiery issues in the Victorian era of biblical polemics.[7]

Returning from England in late 1888, Roberts took over the editorial work for the *Contributor,* a magazine for the youth of the Church, wrote articles under such names as Horatio, which seemed particularly suited for his muscular prose, and continued his interest in the Book of Mormon by writing a series, *Corianton: A Nephite Story.* It was so successful that a book and play entitled *Corianton: An Aztec Romance* were produced in 1902. They were both financial successes, but the play, written by a young playwright named Orestus U. Bean, was so long that diehard theater-goers and Book of Mormon addicts had to wait until after midnight to see the final scene. To Roberts, who was accustomed to hearing two-hour sermons and to using almost limitless quotations in his writing, the dramatic production was perhaps a normal exercise in histrionics. The book very much reflected his knowledge of and attraction to the Book of Mormon. There were the Zoramites, and a Shiblon and a Zoan, in addition to the hero, Corianton, whose "proud, haughty spirit now humbled to the dust, listened with prayerful attention to the instruction of his father and found the faith of the Gospel the stay and hope of his soul." So ended Roberts's one major plunge into fiction, a Book of Mormon romance.[8]

Four years later, he turned his attention to serious history and produced three books which marked the beginning of his work on the history of the Church of Jesus Christ of Latter-day Saints. The first, *Outlines of Ecclesiastical History,* dealt with the establishment of the Christian Church, the apostasy from the "true" faith, and the reformation and restoration of the gospel through Joseph Smith. The two purposes of the book, according to the preface, were to sustain the position of the latter-day church and to teach the principles of the gospel. Roberts expressed his early professionalism as a historian by suggesting that his readers turn to the notes at the end of each section to obtain additional information and perhaps to become interested enough to pursue the subject further. To emphasize his objectivity, he announced that "no fact has been suppressed that has a tendency to support the opposite view."[9]

A second book, *The Missouri Persecutions,* attempted to build the faith of the youth of the Church by delineating, in some detail, the sacrifices of early members in the Missouri of the 1830s and by correcting the misrepresentations and "calumnious insinuations" of anti-Mormon writers. The author was careful to list many books friendly to the point of view of Missourians, so that his readers would have both sides of the story, and he insisted that he was not presenting "argumentative history" or writing "for the purpose of glozing [sic] over the defects in the character of the early members of The Church." In fact, he had tried to point out their "actual sinfulness in conduct." Roberts succumbed to pride of authorship by proclaiming that his history "told more thoroughly" the account of the Missouri persecutions than had any other work; he then blasted certain unnamed plagiarizers who had stolen quotations from the earlier *Contributor* articles on which his book was based.[10]

The final volume in this early trilogy was *The Rise and Fall of Nauvoo,* a "companion volume" in "historical sequence" to his book on the Missouri persecutions. In his introduction Roberts discussed at some length the cruel banishment of the French Acadians from their homes in Nova Scotia by British officials during the French and Indian War and then excoriated the victors for their "atrocious crimes" in depriving the French peasants of their homes, a stain "upon the escutcheon" of England. He concluded by comparing this "execration" with the enforced evacuation and destruction of Nauvoo permitted by the "United States, the boasted asylum for the oppressed of all nations." The only reason for Roberts's selection of the Acadian story to introduce his volume may have been that Illinois was formerly a French province, but his tactic of attempting to prejudice his readers in advance by the tearful comparison of an Evangeline-type recounting of British cruelty with that of similar brutality on the part of Illinois frontiersmen was a ploy he should have reconsidered. The story, told simply, of the expulsion of the Saints from Nauvoo was dramatic enough in its condemnation of unrelenting persecution.[11]

In 1892 Roberts published his one biography, a narrative of the life of John Taylor, cellmate with Joseph and Hyrum Smith at the time of their murders, third president of the Mormon Church, and a hero to Roberts, who "loved" his subject. Roberts could see few defects in Taylor's character, and his recital of Taylor's great qualities reflects the virtues by which Roberts attempted to guide his own life. The Church president had a "universal benevolence, powerful intellect, splendid courage, physical as well as moral, a noble independence of spirit, coupled with implicit faith and trust in God, a high sense of honor, unimpeachable integrity, indomitable determination, and a passionate love of liberty, justice and truth." Above all was Taylor's love of liberty: "I was not born a slave! I cannot, will not be a slave. I would not be slave to God! . . . I'd rather be extinct than be a slave." It is understandable why Roberts's fierce independence thrilled at such statements from his alter ego. Taylor had other attributes of which his biographer approved: scrupulous honesty, little desire for "money getting," his preference for "a faded coat to a faded reputation," his insistence that a plowed field be well done and not merely skimmed over, and finally his desire to be "a preacher of righteousness."[12]

An opportunity for Roberts to apply some of the above qualities to his discipline of history came when he was asked to revise and publish the journal of Joseph Smith, which he had already compiled in three volumes while serving as a missionary in England. The six-volume *History of the Church of Jesus Christ of Latter-day Saints,* publication of which began in 1902, reflected Roberts's determination to present the facts of early Church history as "related by the persons who witnessed them"; to allow the reader to "form his own conclusions"; and to add notes that would give further explanation of some of the important events related.[13] Recognizing that some of the journal material had been prepared by scribes and not Smith himself, the editor felt free to make numerous changes in spelling and grammar to ensure better clarity and to eliminate such indecorous incidents as that of J. B. Nicholls, who kicked a Presbyterian minister "on his seat of honor," and Smith's argumentative reasoning asking for repeal of a hog ordinance passed by the City of Nauvoo.

A more serious challenge to Roberts's editorial methodology was his deletion of significant passages, ranging from an omission of the definition of the word *Mormon* as being "more good," which the editor thought was "based on inaccurate premises and was offensively pedantic," to the more consequential deletion of such detailed accounts as the description of how the "ruffian" who had attempted to decapitate the murdered Joseph Smith at Carthage jail had been paralyzed by a sudden and powerful light "from the heavens." Roberts commented on the latter incident: "It was inevitable, perhaps, that something miraculous should be alleged as connected with the death of Joseph Smith; that both myth and legend, those parasites of truth, should attach themselves to the Prophet's career." Some critics have rightly charged Roberts with thus "mutilating" history, of failing to report the personally written accounts of Joseph Smith's death and of neglecting to differentiate between materials written by Smith and those recorded by his secretaries. It must be remembered, however, that whatever Roberts did had to meet the approval of the First Presidency of the Church, so that his editorial judgment was, at times, somewhat proscribed.[14]

Throughout his early career as an editor and historian, Roberts was always challenging or being challenged by divines and critics, particularly about the authenticity of the Book of Mormon, and he accepted these opportunities for debate with alacrity and the fire of the warhorse scenting battle. An especially pertinent exchange occurred with Dr. William M. Paden, who, in three discourses delivered in Salt Lake City during early 1904, attacked III Nephi of the Book of Mormon as a "Fifth Gospel" that did not add anything to the picture of Christ.[15] In a very lengthy sermon, dutifully reported by the Church organ, the *Deseret News*, Roberts cited several antiquarian historians to prove his contention that signs of cataclysmic events and darkness following the Messiah's death had occurred in the Americas and that the traditions of the native Americans not only proved the divinity of Jesus but also helped authenticate the Book of Mormon and added the new knowledge that Christ had appeared to the people of this hemisphere. Roberts's use of these early evaluations of the monuments and other archeological evidence found in the Western continents was a foreshadowing of his later extensive investigations of written materials concerning these civilizations.

In a more comprehensive examination of Book of Mormon criticism, an individual known only by the signature "M" had published two lengthy attacks on the Mormon scripture in articles in the *Salt Lake Tribune* of November 22 and December 4, 1903.[16] The "Unknown," as Roberts described him, charged that: (1) Nephi quoted Christ's apostles 600 years before they were active in their roles; (2) Nephi quoted from Shakespeare in a sentence from Hamlet's soliloquy; (3) Nephi quoted from the King James version of the Bible, not published until A.D. 1611; (4) Nephi wrote in the "campmeeting exhortation" style of 1828; (5) there was not one item of moral truth revealed by the Book of Mormon; and (6) finally, although the three witnesses to the book explained that "Joseph Smith had nothing whatever to do except simply to read the English sentences as they appeared in translation," apparently the Mormon prophet must have also quoted not only from the Bible and Shakespeare but also from other English works and perhaps from the peculiar views of Sidney Ridgon as well. After noting "M's" lack of courage in hiding behind anonymity, Roberts attempted to dispose of the charges one by one. (1) At times Joseph Smith "used Bible phraseology in representing ideas akin to those found in Jewish Scriptures." (2) The quotation more closely followed Job than Shakespeare, who may have taken his inspiration from the Old Testament prophet in the passage to which "M" referred. (3) The larger question of how the Book of Mormon was translated, Roberts explained in a manner that upset the then current Mormon conception of a simple reading of the English words as they appeared to the eyes of the youthful prophet:

Because Joseph Smith translated the Book of Mormon by means of the inspiration of God and the aid of Urim and Thummim, it is generally supposed that this translation occasioned the Prophet no mental or spiritual effort, that it was purely mechanical; in fact, that the instrument did all and the Prophet nothing, than which a greater mistake could not be made. All the circumstances connected with the work of translation clearly prove that it caused the Prophet the utmost exertion, mental and spiritual, of which he was capable, and while he obtained the facts and ideas from the Nephite characters, he was left to express those ideas in such language as he was master of. This, it is conceded, was faulty, hence here and there [are] verbal defects in the English translation of the Nephite record. Now when the Prophet perceived from the Nephite records that Isaiah was being quoted; or when the Savior was represented as giving instructions in doctrine and moral precepts of the same general character as those given in Judea, Joseph Smith undoubtedly turned to those parts of the Bible where he found a translation, subsequently correct, of those things which were referred to in the Nephite records, and adopted so much of that translation as expressed the truths common to both records; and since our English version of the Jewish scriptures was the one the Prophet used in such instances, we have the Bible phraseology of which the Unknown complains, and of which this, in the judgment of the writer, is the adequate explanation to all of that class of his objections.[17]

(4) Nephi had received in a vision the knowledge that Christ was to appear, to be baptized of John, and to complete his ministry among the people. (5) The Book of Mormon contained a number of new religious truths such as "Adam fell that men might be; and men are that they might have joy." (6) "M" showed what a "back number" he was by referring to the outmoded and disproven theory of the Spaulding manuscript as the origin of the Book of Mormon.

Roberts's detailed explanation of his "new" theory of the method employed by Smith in translating the characters engraved on the gold plates is quoted here because of the prominence it was given by the Mormon faithful and Gentile critics in the next several years. As Roberts wrote later, "The translator is responsible for the verbal and grammatical errors, in the translating"; "to talk of 'literal translation' is to talk of literal nonsense"; and "the translation of the Book of Mormon is English in idiom, and the idiom of the time and locality where it was produced."[18]

At about the same time as the "M" exchange, Roberts had replied in similar fashion to a question about the translating of the Book of Mormon from an H. Chamberlain, who was so satisfied with the Mormon historian's detailed reply that he rejoined, "I am free to say that your reasons for his [Joseph Smith] so doing are not only probable, but the only solution that can be given."[19] As late as 1925 G. A. Marr wrote Roberts that his explanation of the method of translation was "the greatest creative effort of which the annals of controversy bear record."[20] Roberts himself was so satisfied with his reasoning in the matter that he incorporated it as part of his argument in his New Witnesses for God.[21] To modern scholars the controversy over the translation of the Book of

Mormon and Roberts's explanation may seem quaint, but in the early 1900s it tended to end more of the speculation concerning the book.

Another objection raised by "higher" criticism" was that entire chapters of Isaiah are quoted in the Book of Mormon, although these chapters, 40-66, were not written until the time of the Babylonian captivity, 586-38 B.C., by another author and perhaps 125 years after Isaiah's death and fifty years after the Lehi colony left Jerusalem, supposedly with all of Isaiah intact. Of the 433 verses of Isaiah quoted in the Mormon scripture, 199 were repeated word for word, and the remaining 234 were slightly changed from the wording in the King James Bible.[22] In a series of articles Roberts refuted, to his own satisfaction, the "higher critics" and announced that the Book of Mormon "shoots holes into higher criticism! . . . and established the integrity and unity of authorship for the whole book of Isaiah." If Roberts could not have satisfied himself that all of Isaiah was the work of one writer, then, as he acknowledged, the authorship of chapters 40-66, some fifty years after Lehi led his family into the desert, "throws the whole Book of Mormon under suspicion of being fraudulent."[23] As for the exact wording of Isaiah verses apparently copied from the Bible into the Book of Mormon, Roberts's explanation of Smith's method of translation satisfied him and most Mormon adherents, including the First Presidency of his Church, "who approved of Brother Roberts' views regarding this matter as perhaps the best reasons that could be given in the absence of a knowledge of the facts."[24] By the early 1900s Elder Roberts evidently had become the chief Church spokesman in defending the authenticity of the Book of Mormon.

Roberts's interest in the origins of the book and his prompt and eager acceptance of almost any opportunity to debate its virtues led him into written conflict with Theodore Schroeder, a former lawyer in Utah who had been disbarred by the state supreme court for unprofessional conduct. Schroeder, who later led the fight in Washington, D.C., against Roberts being seated in the House of Representatives, wrote a series of four articles for the *American Historical Magazine*, attacking Book of Mormon claims by resurrecting the "old exploded Spaulding story" of its origins. The anti-Mormon *Salt Lake Tribune* was reproducing the articles, and Roberts wrote the editor, Colonel William Nelson, asking the privilege of answering Schroeder, who was claiming to have found a second Spaulding manuscript. At Nelson's suggestion Roberts corresponded with David I. Nelke, the editor of *American Historical Magazine*, who indicated he would consider publishing a response to Schroeder if it met the literary and professional standards of his journal. The first Roberts reply was so satisfactory that eventually all four of his responses were printed, along with Schroeder's attacks, in this magazine (whose title was soon changed to the *Americana*).[25]

In refuting the relationship of the second Spaulding manuscript to the Book of Mormon, Roberts wrote, "We 'mormons' get considerable amusement out of the conflicting theories advanced to account for the origin of our Book of Mormon." The story of the Spaulding manuscript began with Solomon Spaulding, an obscure minister, who, about 1809 and while living in Conneaut, Ohio, produced a manuscript about the ancient inhabitants of America based on a supposed translation of a Latin document that he claimed to have found in a cave near Conneaut, and so the name "Manuscript Found." In 1834, some years after the death of Spaulding, his relatives transferred the manuscript to a former Mormon, D. Philastus Hurlburt, who wished to expose it as the ancestor of the Book of Mormon. This first manuscript was eventually deposited in the library of Oberlin College, and both Mormons and non-Mormons who examined it declared its 112 pages have nothing in common with the Book of Mormon. But then Schroeder claimed that the Book of Mormon was based upon a second Spaulding manuscript, allegedly a story written in scriptural style and asserting that native Americans were descended from Israelites. It was this second manuscript which Roberts spent 114 large printed pages destroying; he never lacked for words or thoroughness in his polemical writing.[26]

The last of Roberts's four articles on the subject was particularly germane in view of his later questions about the Book of Mormon. He first declared that when the twenty-two-year-old Joseph Smith translated the Book of Mormon he did not need the assistance of a Solomon Spaulding, a Sidney Rigdon, or any other man—that Smith was "superior in talents . . . [and] in literary power of expression" to any of the supposed authors of the book. Second, he wrote, if the book had been produced as explained by Schroeder "it would not have been so full of petty errors in grammar and the faulty use of words as is found in the first edition of the Book of Mormon. . . . They are ingrained in it; they are consti-tutional faults" as expressed by the uneducated but brilliant boy prophet. Roberts concluded his four articles with the somewhat immodest but perhaps accurate claim that they constituted "a successful rejoinder . . . [which] exhibits how inherently weak, and foolish this Spaulding theory is."[27]

Roberts's reference to errors in the first (1830) edition of the Book of Mormon came from a very close reading of his personal copy, which is in the B. H. Roberts Collection at the University of Utah and contains copious marginal notes in his own handwriting. He especially marked mistakes in grammar and the repetitive use of such words as "did," which he called the "did series." Localisms like "much horses" and "good homely cloth" were marked. Similarities with passages of the Bible were underlined—for example, he compared Hebrews 3:15 ("While it is said,

To day if ye will hear his voice, harden not your hearts, as in the provocation") with page 139 of the Book of Mormon ("Yea, today if he will hear his voice, harden not your hearts: for why will ye die?"). Contradictions like the slaying of one leader on page 272 and seven on page 274 were noted. Finally, he made occasional cryptic comments, as on page 275 when "king Lamoni saith, Is it above the earth? and Ammon saith, Yea, and he looketh down upon all the children of men." Roberts noted in the margin, "Heaven located."[28]

All of his early investigations into the Book of Mormon and his debates with skeptics finally led him, as the chairman for nine years of the Manual Committee of the Mutual Improvement Association (MIA), the youth organization of the Church, to write three of the annual manuals which attempted to assemble the evidence for the truthfulness of the Book of Mormon. Under the title *New Witnesses for God,* they were first published in 1903 as a single volume and later appeared in three volumes in 1909. The first volume was devoted to Joseph Smith as a witness for God and the last two volumes considered the external and internal evidences of the authenticity of the Book of Mormon. In his "Life Story," Roberts noted that many regarded this work "as his greatest contribution to the literature of the church."[29]

In the manuals Roberts sought to impress the young people of his Church with the importance of the Book of Mormon but recognized that the teachers in the MIA might "have some difficulty with the boys, because they have not had much experience in the matter of literary criticism." Therefore, he listed seven points that should be emphasized: (1) a diversity of style permeated the book, which was only logical when nine men were the authors of the first 156 pages; (2) there was an originality in the several hundred names in the book; (3) the forms of government described were consistent with the circumstances; (4) the events in the book harmonized with the character of the writers; (5) the 40th chapter included such philosophical statements as "Adam fell that men might be, and and men are that they might have joy," a concept only "dull" readers would not discern as being dramatically new and inspiring; (6) the book gave a unique definition of truth as being "knowledge of that which is, of that which has been, of that which is to be"; and (7) the explanation of the doctrine of "opposite existence."[30]

In his lesson outlines for the manual he was more specific, proposing review questions and instructions about methods of teaching the Book of Mormon. Typical questions included: "In what way would the message of Joseph Smith be affected if the Book of Mormon were proven untrue?" "What is meant by burden of proof?" "In any discussion on the truth of the Book of Mormon on whom does the burden of proof rest?" His suggestions for lesson treatment were also typically forthright—"Talk directly to the subject. . . . Practice stopping at the right time and place. Do not allow endless rambling discussions. . . . Master the lesson as thoroughly as possible. . . . Do not be satisfied with 'skimming.' . . . Get the Spirit of God, and work hard under that influence." The type of questions Roberts proposed reflected his wish to establish in the classes open, frank, and honest discussion of the difficulties he saw in proving the divinity of the Book of Mormon.[31] Nevertheless, his personal belief in its authenticity was apparently unshaken in 1905 when he could write, "It is useless to ascribe the knowledge it imparts . . . to human intelligence or learning at all."[32]

In order to understand the development in Roberts's thinking concerning the origin of the Book of Mormon, it is necessary to describe the arguments he advanced in the early 1900s to support his belief in its authenticity, so that a comparison can be made with his point of view as expressed in the studies he completed in the 1920s. An examination of volumes 2 and 3 of Roberts's *New Witnesses for God* provides this perspective, and his preface in volume 2 explains the purposes for which he wrote the book:

While the coming forth of the Book of Mormon is but an incident in God's great work of the last days, . . . still the incident of its coming forth and the book are facts of such importance that the whole work of God may be said in a manner to stand or fall with them. That is to say, if the origin of the Book of Mormon could be proved to be other than that set forth by Joseph Smith; if the book itself could be proved to be other than it claims to be, . . . then the Church of Jesus Christ of Latter-day Saints, and its message and doctrines, which, in some respects, may be said to have arisen out of the Book of Mormon, must fall; for if that book is other than it claims to be; if its origin is other than that ascribed to it by Joseph Smith, then Joseph Smith says that which is untrue; he is a false prophet of false prophets; and all he taught and all his claims to inspiration and divine authority, are not only vain but wicked; and all that he did as a religious teacher is not only useless, but mischievous beyond human comprehending.

Nor does this statement of the case set forth sufficiently strong the situation. Those who accept the Book of Mormon for what it claims to be, may not so state their case that its security chiefly rests on the inability of its opponents to prove a negative. The affirmative side of the question belongs to us who hold out the Book of Mormon to the world as a revelation of God. The burden of proof rests upon us in every discussion . . . for not only must the Book of Mormon not be proved to have other origin than that which we set forth, or be other than what we say it is, *but we must prove its origin to be what we say it is, and the book itself to be what we proclaim it to be—a revelation from God.* . . . To be known, the truth must be stated and the clearer and more complete the statement is, the better opportunity will the Holy Spirit have for testifying to the souls of men that the work is true. While desiring to make it clear that our chief reliance for evidence to the truth of the Book of Mormon must ever be the witness of the Holy Spirit, . . . I would not have it thought that the evidence and argument presented . . . are unimportant, much less unnecessary. Secondary evidences in support of truth, like secondary causes in natural phenomena, may be of firstrate importance, and mighty factors in the achievement of God's purposes.[33]

There could not be a clearer and more honest statement of the case for the Book of Mormon. B. H. Roberts was caught between history and creed, presenting both the objectives and attitude of a trained historian while acknowledging that his belief in the Nephite record would inevitably color his judgments. Nevertheless, he believed that proving the Mormon scripture true was, after all, the proper job of a Mormon theologian.

So there would be no doubt, Roberts listed his intentions in establishing the authenticity of the Book of Mormon in volume 2 of his *New Witnesses for God*. They were: (1) to show the American Indians what the Lord had done for their ancestors; (2) to teach the natives what covenants the Lord had made with their fathers; (3) to convince Jew and Gentile alike that Jesus was the Messiah; (4) to convert the American Indians to Christianity; (5) to convince the Jews that Jesus was the Christ; (6) to be another witness to the truths taught by the Bible; and (7) to restore truths of the gospel which had been lost from the Jewish scriptures. Then, after describing how Joseph Smith had received the plates and translated them and after giving an analysis of the Book of Mormon, the author launched into a discussion of the impossibility of defining the exact locations of the Nephite and Lamanite peoples, their cities and monuments, because of the cataclysmic changes that the Book of Mormon described as having occurred in the Western Hemisphere during a three-hour period at the time of the crucifixion of the Savior. He argued that significant changes in the earth's crust could happen over a short period and that "nowhere else in the records kept by men" had such terrible events occurred. He further doubted that the Nephites, the civilized portion of the Book of Mormon peoples, had occupied lands any farther north than the southern part of Mexico, a "misapprehension" which he thought was widely held by most Church members at the time.[34]

To make clear his methodology, Roberts next defined what he meant by external evidence—"facts outside the book itself": testimony of witnesses, ancient ruins, and the customs and traditions of American native races. (Internal evidence was, of course, concerned with the structure, internal consistency, and theory of organization of the book.) For six chapters he evaluated the testimonies of the three witnesses who had examined the gold plates and had never refuted what they said they had seen; that of the eight witnesses who had also seen the plates and had never denied their stories, evidence "of such a nature that it could not possibly have been the result of deception wrought by the cunning of Joseph Smith"; and finally, the certainty that the Mormon prophet had been visited by angels—"Such phenomena are mistakenly considered supernatural. They are not so really. They are very matter of fact realities; perfectly natural, and in harmony with the intellectual order of a universe where intelligence and goodness govern." After all, Roberts admonished, if electric energy could be transmitted 460 miles from Niagara Falls to New York City, why should humans question the power of God to maintain instant communication with all parts of his creation?[35]

After disposing of these preliminaries, Roberts began to examine what was really the heart of his argument—that American antiquities and traditions could prove the Book of Mormon. His first thesis was that certain evidence led him to believe that the Nephites did not work in stone but had built their temples and other buildings of wood, which accounted for the lack of material remnants of their civilization in South and Central America. He also was of the opinion that, although it would be difficult to produce "in quantity and clearness" the evidence in antiquities to support the Book of Mormon, he was sure that eventually there would be a "development of the fulness of monumental testimony to its truth" still hidden among the ancient ruins of the Western Hemisphere.[36]

In his preliminary considerations of these ancient proofs of Nephite and Lamanite occupation of the Americas, Roberts acknowledged that there had probably been many other adventurers from Europe, Africa, and Asia who had sailed to the Western continents as well as others who had returned to the East. He considered the mingling of early Spanish buildings with those of ancient ones in America as being troubling also. He then recited the difficulties in investigating the writings of antiquarians and more modern authors whose biases and credibilities had to be carefully weighed as one reads their accounts of the Ten Lost Tribes and of their descriptions of old ruins. In his summary before turning to a specific evaluation of archeological evidence and traditions he maintained that he had established that: (1) civilized races existed in both North and South America; (2) the monuments of these people were being found along the western plateau of South America and in Central America, where the Nephites and Jaredites had lived in Book of Mormon times; (3) there were successive civilizations in the Americas with the latest being the most advanced; and (4) the main center of the ancient civilizations was in Central America, where the oldest Book of Mormon races lived. The author was convinced that nothing had been advanced by scholars that conflicted with the claims of the Book of Mormon and that much of their work supported the story.[37]

Looking first at the traditions and mythology of the native Americans, Roberts cited proof that they knew of the creation, the fall of man, the flood, the tower of Babel, and especially of the prophecies concerning the coming of the Messiah, who, as the "traditionary personage" of Quetzalcoatl, visited the peoples of the Western Hemisphere after his resurrection as related in the Mormon scripture. As for the Hebrew origin of the American Indians, after citing some early writers who had advanced evidence to support the theory, Roberts announced that "so much in the foregoing summary of points of comparison between the American races and the Hebrews as may not be successfully contradicted stands as evidence of no mean order for the truth of our Nephite record." He summed up this section of his books by describing several other "gold plates" discovered in the eastern part of the United States; he called one a "hoax," admitted that another's "genuineness" was in question, but concluded that these accounts constituted "at least important incidental evidence" for the authenticity of the Book of Mormon. As for the requirement that the Nephite story demanded a unity of race for modern American natives, he cited two authorities to substantiate this fact, which was only "one more evidence for the truth of the Book of Mormon."[38]

To round out his discussion of external evidence, Roberts first tackled the problem of whether the Book of Mormon was produced after the publication, in English, of works on ancient American civilizations that would have been available to Smith. As Roberts explained, "Was it possible for Joseph Smith . . . to have possessed such a knowledge of American antiquities and traditions that they [Smith and his associates] could make their book's alleged historical incidents, and the customs of its peoples, conform to the antiquities and traditions of the native Americans?" He answered the question by arguing that to become acquainted with the vast knowledge of American antiquities and traditions and then make them conform to the story in the Book of Mormon was an insurmountable task for a youthful prophet who was "not a student of books." Roberts then listed the only works which "so far as I can ascertain" might have been accessible to Joseph Smith: the publications of the American Antiquarian Society, 1820; Ethan Smith's *View of the Hebrews*, second edition, 1825; *The History of the American Indians*, by James Adair, 1775; and Alexander Humboldt's books on New Spain, 1811. Roberts discusses these works more fully in his "A Book of Mormon Study" presented in this volume, but it is interesting how easily he brushed them aside in 1909. This list also revealed how little he knew of the extensive literature on the subject of American antiquities. He was to spend several years in study to rectify that omission.[39]

After a discussion of the "Isaiah problems" in the Book of Mormon, already examined above, Roberts briefly touched on the Bible passages which mention "other sheep . . . which are not of this fold," concluding, as do nearly all faithful Mormons, that the other flocks mentioned were the peoples of the Americas. At this point he announced that it was the Church of Jesus Christ of Latter-day Saints that bore witness to the Book of Mormon rather than the reverse. Then, admitting that the Book of Mormon was not the first account to mention the possible Israelite origin of the American Indians, he maintained that the native traditions established the existence of Christian ideas in the Western Hemisphere; denied that Joseph Smith or any other individual could have had the intelligence or imagination necessary to compose the Book of Mormon; and then took a healthy swing at the "intellectual pride . . . which so often attends upon the worldly learned man" who does not know the meaning of humility and who cannot accept the Mormon scripture because of its "complex, confusing and clumsy" treatment of historical events and its faulty language. In spite of what the world esteemed to be its "contemptible" character, there was, within its pages, the power to "cheer, comfort and encourage men" through the Spirit of God.[40]

In chapters XLIV through XLVIII of volume 3 of *New Witnesses for God,* Roberts came to an important part of his defense of the Book of Mormon as he considered "Objections to the Book of Mormon." After dispensing with "Counter Theories of Origin," including Campbell's charge that Smith was the author, the "shallow story" of Spaulding, the contention of Rigdon's authorship, and the psychological study of Woodbridge Riley that Joseph Smith's inspired visions were in reality hallucinations caused by epilepsy, Roberts repeated his earlier explanation of how the Nephite record was translated, admitting that errors in grammar, localisms, and verbatim copying from the Bible had been introduced by Smith because of his poor education and the attempt to "ease himself" by using Bible passages already in existence.[41]

In considering a series of criticisms of Nephite pre-Christian era knowledge of the gospel, Roberts first noted that if Old Testament prophets could be told of the coming of the Messiah, certainly the inhabitants of the Americas would not be denied those truths. Also, just because the people of the Eastern Hemisphere had lost their earlier accurate knowledge of astronomy, it did not follow that the Nephites could not have an understanding of the movement of the earth and its planetary system as revealed in the Book of Mormon. After discounting accusations that there was no "definiteness" about Book of Mormon geography by explaining that the record was only an abridgement that did not permit detailed descriptions of land forms, the author discussed comparisons between ancient Egyptian writing and a transcript of characters from the Nephite plates made by Joseph Smith. Roberts declared "a strong family likeness" existed, exploding the charge that there was no resemblance between the two.[42]

Roberts's final chapter dealt with some particular objections to which he devoted much greater emphasis in his 1920s study than he did in this brief examination. To the contention that the Book of Mormon had copied incidents from the Bible—for example, that in Alma's conversion he was struck dumb for two days just as Paul had been stricken with blindness for three days, or that the Jaredite use of eight barges was "an attempt to outdo the Bible account of Noah's 'one ark'"—Roberts argued that the same use of parallelisms could be made in comparing the Old and New Testaments. To the objection that there was an absence of Book of Mormon names in native American languages, he recognized "here a real difficulty" but observed, in a rather far-fetched assertion, that the name "Nahuas" was probably derived from "Nephi"; that the river Amazon no doubt got its name from "Ammon," the son of King Mosiah II; and that "Andes" could have come from the common use of "anti" in the Nephi record, such as "Anti-Nephi-Lehi," the name of a Lamanite king. And to the question of how a small group of 100 adults in Lehi's company could "duplicate Solomon's temple," the answer was obvious: it was a very tiny temple, "only like unto Solomon's temple in its arrangement and uses."[43]

In his later study of the Book of Mormon, Roberts was seriously concerned with the fact that while iron and steel had been extensively used by the Nephites no archeological evidence had been found to substantiate this fact. He proposed that the rapid oxidation of the metal left no specimens to be found and that it was easier for the Nephites to convert their plentiful supply of copper into the implements they needed. A similar and important objection that no evidence of horses, cows, asses, goats, and sheep had been discovered among the ruins of ancient America or in the traditions of the natives while the Book of Mormon insisted that such animals existed in Nephite days led Roberts to admit "that it constitutes one of our most embarrassing difficulties." In response, he insisted that during the thousand years that had elapsed between the final destruction of the Nephite civilization and the coming of the Spaniards, some calamity could have destroyed all such animals and adopted the suggestion of one scientist that a "wide-spread epidemic" had eliminated them. But Roberts finally concluded that the "weight of evidence" lay with those who said that horses and the other domestic animals were not found in the Americas before Columbus.[44]

Of the many other objections Roberts attempted to counter, a final one concludes this discussion of his *New Witnesses for God*. A number of writers had ridiculed Smith's claim that he had carried the gold plates from the Hill Cumorah about two miles to his home and on the journey had successfully fought off three assaults while running at top speed. One critic had estimated that the plates, at 7 x 8 inches and 6 inches thick, would have weighed 200 pounds. Roberts refused to "haggle" about the weight, which he said could have been as low as ninety or even fifty pounds, but explained that Smith was a "strong, athletic young man" who, under the stress and excitement of the moment, could have performed this amazing feat. Roberts would not turn to an "appeal to the supernatural, to the miraculous," but chose instead to compare Smith's achievement to that of Samson's feats of strength.[45]

Roberts concluded his three-volume series in defense of the Book of Mormon by pointing out that the arguments made against the book were similar to those made against the Hebrew scriptures and that, while "Sectarian divines" felt free to use such tactics against the Mormon scripture, they complained bitterly when such strategies were employed against the Bible. He acknowledged that not all of the objections to the Book of Mormon had been answered to the satisfaction of critics or even to Roberts himself, but he thought a little more time and research would vindicate his efforts. As his later study demonstrates, the more he studied the problems of the Book of Mormon, the more difficult they became to solve. But in his last sentence he declared that the evidence he had presented was sufficient, "both in quality and quantity," to convince any rational person of the truthfulness of the Mormon scripture.[46]

Less dated now than his work on the Book of Mormon, B. H. Roberts's six-volume *A Comprehensive History of the Church of Jesus Christ of Latter-day Saints* also has more enduring importance for today's investigators of Mormonism. The history was an outgrowth of the four exchanges with A. Theodore Schroeder published in the *Americana*. David I. Nelke of that magazine had invited Roberts to write a detailed history of the Mormon Church, which was eventually published in monthly editions of the magazine, at about forty-two pages per month, over the period from 1909 to 1915, under the title "History of the Mormon Church." The death of Nelke prevented the publication of the articles in book form at the time, and the estimated cost of $50,000 for publication was more than Church authorities could afford. It was not until 1930 and the centenary anniversary of the founding of the Church that arrangements were made to print the six volumes under its present title, wiping "out the years of disappointment through which the author had suffered over it."[47]

In his preface to the volumes and also in his "Life Story," Roberts expressed his purpose in writing the history to be "pro-church of the Latter-day Saints" but also emphasized his intention to follow the precept of Theodore Roosevelt that history to be of any worth must not only tell of your successes, but also of your failures or semifailures. Roberts thought that to "so treat the course of events as not to destroy faith in these men [leaders engaged in the work of God], becomes a task of supreme delicacy; and one that tries the soul and skill of the historian," especially when "it must be said of those entrusted with this great mission of God that they were not always 100% perfect and right in their administrations, neither were those who fought them always and every time 100% wrong." A historian, he said, must follow the truth "justly, firmly and without hesitation, or he will fail in his absolute duty to the truth of things," a quality he insisted he "religiously held" throughout his writing and that was its "chief characteristic." Not all Church members were comfortable with this approach, as was evident in the case of David McKenzie, a clerk in the office of the Church president, who one day accosted Roberts: "Well I have read your story in this month's *Americana* and Aye Mon the frankness of it: the frankness o' it. How dare you do it Mon." Despite such misgivings on the part of some then and perhaps now, if and when the books are read, Roberts may be forgiven his lofty assertion that "undoubtedly it is the masterpiece of historical writings in the first century of the Church's History." He may still be right.[48]

Others have praised his history for its comprehensive treatment, his willingness to meet such issues as the Danites forthrightly, for what one called his "interpretative balance . . . a church history that is free of fustian and prejudice,"[49] while another considered him to be "the greatest Mormon historian. . . . While never objective, Roberts didn't allow his passionate defense of the faith to overwhelm his respect for truth."[50] He had little patience with Church writers who saw miracles in everything. His response to one who claimed that the use of "ouiza" boards as "spiritist" magic had been foretold by the Book of Mormon was to write in the margin of the magazine, "The article here in is of the kind that makes our Mormon argument contemptible."[51] On the other hand, J. Reuben Clark, a sophisticated counselor to several presidents of the Church, could write of the documentary history, "Brother Roberts' work is the work of advocate and not of a judge, and you cannot always rely on what Brother Roberts says. Frequently, he started out apparently to establish a certain thesis and he took his facts to support his thesis, and if some facts got in the way it was too bad, and they were omitted." Clark's evaluation must, however, be placed in perspective. He and Roberts had personal difficulties dating back to a public altercation on September 3, 1919, when then Major J. Reuben Clark had spoken to a Tabernacle crowd against the League of Nations. After Clark had finished, Roberts rose from his seat on the stand to announce that he would answer Clark's arguments, which he did six days later.[52]

There was no doubt of Roberts's honesty, his moderate approach to history, and his industry and tenacity in digging out the facts. He could be abrasive in his independence, despised the maxim "thus far shalt thou come, but no farther," and denounced the "simple faith" which could lead to belief without understanding or to "ignorant and simpering acquiescence." He knew from personal experience that many looked upon thinkers as being troublesome and once wrote, "But some would protest against investigation lest it threaten the integrity of accepted formulas of truth — which too often they confound with the truth itself, regarding the scaffolding and the building as one and the same thing."[53]

His memorial library of 1,385 books in the LDS Archives reveals his studious nature and his preferences for the various disciplines. Of the eighteen categories under which his books have been cataloged, theology leads the list with 171 items; then history with 134; followed by politics, 76; Christian history and the Bible, 71; science, 69; World War I, 68; philosophy, 62; American antiquities, 62; and anti-Mormon writings, 56. Furthermore, most of the books have marginal notes with many asterisks and underlinings. It is a working scholar's library.[54]

From the completion of his *History of the Mormon Church* in 1915 to his discharge from his position as a chaplain in the U.S. Army in January 1919, Roberts was so caught up in World War I that his historical scholarship was placed in reserve except for his *The Mormon Battalion: Its History and Achievements,* published in 1919. The book was well researched and, à la Roberts, presented a new view that the Mormon leaders had appealed to the government to allow them to enlist a battalion in the Mexican War to help get their people to a home in the Great Basin, a much different conception from the one long held by most Mormons that the enlistment was a sacrifice demanded by President James K. Polk. On May 30, 1927, when Roberts delivered the main address at the unveiling of the Battalion Monument on the State Capitol grounds, it was reported that "literal quotations from diplomatic correspondence . . . with Elder Roberts' comments, startled his audience . . . in a manner that was quite unexpected."[55]

The incident that really motivated Roberts to become involved again in historical study and especially to reexamine the origins of the Book of Mormon was a letter from a young man in Salina, Utah, William E. Riter, who, on August 22, 1921, wrote to the geologist and theologian Apostle James E. Talmage, asking for a response to five questions submitted to him by a Mr. Couch of Washington, D.C., who was investigating the claims of the Book of Mormon.[56] Talmage asked Elder Roberts to prepare answers to the questions, which were concerned with the following items:

1. How could the great diversity in primitive Indian languages have occurred in such a short period after about A.D. 400, when the Nephites, whose Hebrew language was so highly developed, disappeared?

2. The Book of Mormon reports that the followers of Lehi, upon their arrival in the New World, found horses, which were not in existence when the first Spanish explorers arrived.

3. Although the Jews had no knowledge of steel in 600 B.C., Nephi was reported to have had a bow of steel after he left Jerusalem.

4. The Book of Mormon speaks of "swords and scimeters," and yet the word "scimeter" does not appear in early literature before the rise of Mohammedanism, which took place after Lehi departed from Jerusalem.

5. Even though silk was not known in America, the Nephites knew of and used silk.

While Roberts began the investigations that led to his first treatise, "Book of Mormon Difficulties: A Study," apparently another apostle, Richard R. Lyman, decided to ask two of his well-educated friends with interests in the Book of Mormon to respond to the questions. Dr. George W. Middleton, a physician, and Dr. Ralph V. Chamberlin, a biologist, wrote the rather brief analyses included in the correspondence herein. There is also a brief letter from Riter inquiring when he can expect a reply from Roberts, who wrote back asking for more time for his research, which had already occupied "several weeks." Then, because he had "found the difficulties more serious than I had thought," Roberts wrote Heber J. Grant, president of the Church, on December 29, 1921, asking for an appointment to present a 141-page typed report to the First Presidency, the Twelve Apostles, and the Council of Seventy, so that from the "collective wisdom" of all them and from "the inspiration of the Lord" they might find a solution which would satisfy both the youth of the Church and outside investigators.

The request was granted, and Roberts presented his treatise to the assembled General Authorities over a period of two days—January 4 5, 1922—from 10 A.M. to 6 P.M. the first day and from 10 A.M. to 4 P.M. and then after a short recess, again until nearly 8 P.M. on the second day. Apostle George Franklin Richards merely noted the meetings in his diary,[57] but Talmage wrote at some length in his journal, describing the substance of the Roberts presentation:

a lengthy but valuable report . . . what non-believers in the Book of Mormon call discrepancies between that record and the results of archeological and other scientific investigations. As examples of these "difficulties" may be mentioned the views put forth by some living writers to the effect that no vestige of either Hebrew or Egyptian appears in the language of the American Indians, or Amerinds. Another is the positive declaration by certain writers that the horse did not exist upon the Western Continent during historic times prior to the coming of Columbus.

I know the Book of Mormon to be a true record; and many of the "difficulties," or objections as opposing critics would urge, are after all but negative in their nature. The Book of Mormon states that Lehi and his colony found horses upon this continent when they arrived; and therefore horses were here at that time.[58]

Apostle Talmage's journal entry for the following day merely noted that Roberts continued his presentation.

The document reveals a Roberts whose dogmatic assertions of his *New Witnesses for God* had been replaced by pained and troubled doubts about the Book of Mormon, which he challenged his colleagues in the hierarchy to help resolve. Based on the five questions asked by Couch, Roberts quoted ancient and modern writers and investigators to attempt to clarify three problems involved in the Book of Mormon story: linguistics; the presence in America, before the Spanish conquest, of domestic animals, iron and steel, silk, wheat, and wheeled vehicles mentioned by the Nephite record; and the origin of the native American races.

The discussions during the two days of meetings were so unsatisfactory and disquieting to Roberts that he wrote a letter to President Grant just four days later, on January 9, 1922, expressing his disappointment about the irrelevancy of the comments expressed but promised to continue his investigations, fully aware that Couch's questions had been inadequately answered. In response, Grant allowed Roberts some time in the council meeting of January 26, 1922, for a further exposition of his report on "Book of Mormon Difficulties." Furthermore, on three other occasions extending from February 2 to May 25, 1922, Roberts met in some evening sessions in a private home with Grant's councilor, Anthony W. Ivins, and with Apostles Talmage and John A. Widtsoe to "consider external evidences of the genuineness of the Book of Mormon" and to approve a letter of reply to Couch. There is no evidence of Roberts's reaction to these meetings.[59]

But not quite two months before his death, Roberts did discuss the episode of his meeting with the Church authorities as recorded in the Personal Journal of Wesley P. Lloyd, former dean of the Graduate School at Brigham Young University and a missionary under Roberts in the Eastern States Mission. Lloyd wrote on August 7, 1933, that he had spent three and a half hours with his former mission president and that "the conversation then drifted to the Book of Mormon and this surprising story he related to me." Lloyd then recounted Roberts's explanation of the background of Riter's request for answers to the Book of Mormon problems and how Roberts had been assigned the task of answering the questions:

Roberts went to work and investigated it from every angle but could not answer it satisfactorily to himself. At his request Pres. Grant called a meeting of the Twelve Apostles and Bro. Roberts presented the matter, told them frankly that he was stumped and ask for their aide [*sic*] in the explanation. In answer, they merely one by one stood up and bore testimony to the truthfulness of the Book of Mormon. George Albert Smith in tears testified that his faith in the Book had not been shaken by the question. Pres. Ivins, the man most likely to be able to answer a question on that subject was unable to produce the solution. No answer was available. Bro. Roberts could not criticize them for not being able to answer it or to assist him, but said that in a Church which claimed continuous revelation, a crisis had arisen where revelation was necessary. After the meeting he wrote Pres. Grant expressing his disappointment at the failure and especially at the failure of Pres. Ivins to contribute to the problem. It was mentioned at the meeting by Bro. Roberts that there were other Book of Mormon problems that needed special attention. Richard R. Lyman spoke up and asked if they were things that would help our prestige and when Bro. Roberts answered no, he said then why discuss them. This attitude was too much for the historically minded Roberts. There was however a committee appointed to study this problem, consisting of Bros. Talmage, Ballard, Roberts and one other Apostle. They met and looked vacantly at one and other, but none seemed to know what to do about it. Finally, Bro. Roberts mentioned that he had at least attempted an answer and he had it in his drawer. That it was an answer that would satisfy people that didn't think, but a very inadequate answer to a thinking man. They asked him to read it and after hearing it, they adopted it by vote and said that was about the best they could do. After this Bro. Roberts made a special Book of Mormon study. Treated the problem systematically and historically and in a 400 type written page thesis set forth a revolutionary article on the origin of the Book of Mormon and sent it to Pres. Grant. It's an article far too strong for the average Church member but for the intellectual group he considers it a contribution to assist in explaining Mormonism. He swings to a psychological explanation of the Book of Mormon and shows that the plates were not objective but subjective with Joseph Smith, that his exceptional imagination qualified him psychologically for the experience which he had in presenting to the world the Book of Mormon and that the plates with the Urim and Thummim were not objective. He explained certain literary difficulties in the Book such as the miraculous incident of the entire nation of the Jaradites, the dramatic story of one man being left on each side, and one of them finally being slain, also the New England flat hill surroundings of a great civilization of another part of the country. We see none of the cliffs of the Mayas or the high mountain peaks or other geographical environment of early American civilization that the entire story laid in a New England flat hill surrounding. These are some of the things which has made Bro. Roberts shift his base on the Book of Mormon. Instead of regarding it as the strongest evidence we have of Church Divinity, he regards it as the one which needs the most bolstering. His greatest claim for the divinity of the Prophet Joseph lies in the Doctrine and Covenants.[60]

As indicated by Lloyd, in a letter to Riter dated February 6, 1922, Roberts briefly answered Couch's questions, covering "the problems suggested" without delving into any of the difficulties that had been discussed by the General Authorities in three separate council meetings. Riter, an evidently tenacious and inquisitive young man, responded by thanking Elder Roberts and then asked another question, "Why can not the Negro hold the Priesthood?" We have no record of an answer to the query.

As for Roberts, an errant buzz saw whose persistent and disturbing clatter and sharp cutting edges increasingly disturbed the tranquility of the elders who controlled the church in Zion, the First Presidency on May 29, immediately after the Book of Mormon confrontation, told him he "might select any mission within the United States as a field of Labor" as a mission president or he might even consider accepting the editorial direction of the Church newspaper, the *Deseret News*. There was no hesitation on the part of Roberts, who chose to go to New York City as head of the Eastern States Mission covering the northeastern section of the United States. For years he had felt "cribbed, cabined and confined in Utah" and had once written a journalist friend, Isaac Russell in New York City, about being "hampered by the restrictions which our peculiar conditions impose on all such workers and which grows no better so far as I can see with the elapse of time." He expressed his discomfort further and explained his own way of dealing with the problem by quoting from a letter he had received from another young friend who had left Utah for the East: "One of my objects, I might say, my chief object in leaving Salt Lake was that I might avoid if possible, causing pain to my friends and relatives by openly announcing my spiritual and intellectual independence and freedom from what had become bondage I could no longer endure." After the frustration of encountering mostly indifference to his report on Book of Mormon difficulties, New York and New England probably looked very inviting to Roberts.[61]

A further inducement, as reported in his autobiography, was that "it had the attraction of including within it the territory of the early activities of the Church — Vermont — the birthplace of the Prophet; New York — the early scenes of the Prophet's life, the first vision and the coming forth of the Book of Mormon, the Hill Cumorah; . . . which naturally would endear this section of the country to the mind and heart of Elder Roberts." As soon as he was located in New York and as he traveled around the mission, he began researching and gathering materials to satisfy himself about the origins of the Church and especially the

Book of Mormon. His file at the University of Utah contains references to books which he read and copied during these travels. Among them were: (1) Jedediah Morse, *Geography Made Easy*, 5th ed. (Boston, May 1796), with the note, "above book in Municipal Museum of Rochester, copied by B. H. Roberts, June 7, 1922," and a marginal comment that "America was peopled from the North East parts of Asia"; (2) Josiah Priest, *American Antiquities and Discoveries in the West*, 5th ed. (Printed by J. Munsel, 1841), with the note, "Title Page of Josiah Priests Work 1841 Copied by B. H. Roberts, N.Y."; (3) Josiah Priest, *Wonders of Nature and Providence* (Albany: Published by Josiah Priest, E. & E. Hosford Printers, 1836), with the note "Copied from the copy in New York Public Library. The above book bears copyright date of June 2, 1824"; (4) Elias Boudinot, *A Star in the West* (Trenton, N.J.: Published by D. Fenton, S. Hutchinson and J. Dunham, George Sherman, Printer, 1786), with handwritten notes by Roberts; and (5) Ethan Smith, *View of the Hebrews* (Poultney, Vt.: Printed & Published by Smith & Shute, 1823), with the note, "Copied by B. H. Roberts from copy in 1st Edition, New York City Library. The second Edition (1825) is about one third larger than the first." These five were perhaps the most important Roberts acquisitions, although there were many others. We thus have a picture of Roberts publicly trimming and nurturing an eastern branch of the tree of Mormonism while privately digging away at its roots trying to determine from whence they came.[62]

While pursuing his investigations of the origins of the Book of Mormon in his spare time, he nevertheless ran a vigorous missionary campaign during the five years he was president of the mission. He established a mission school to ensure that his missionaries were well prepared to present the gospel message, and he sent them out into rural areas on "summer campaigns," away from their comfortable winter lodgings "in the spirit of adventure to extend our borders. . . . Let there be no retreating, nor growing listless, nor weary in well doing. This is the heroic part of your mission. This is where you display manhood or prove that you have none. . . . Be you brave and persistent, and remember, Emmanuel!" His missionaries also learned that "three hateful words" were idleness, listlessness, and restlessness, and in another proclamation they heard, "I want action . . . *I want it done*." He used the Book of Mormon as a chief means of winning converts, announcing in one letter to his missionaries "that it has survived all the ridicule and mockery of those who have scorned it, . . . and that its voice is testimony of the Christ as Eternal God."[63]

One missionary, Roscoe A. Grover, remembered Roberts's resolute independence and especially an incident when Roberts found it difficult "to get into line with the Brethren" and "packed his books ready to go

home until someone talked him out of it." When Grover was released
to go home, he was "flabbergasted" to hear the president tell him he
did not need to depart at once but perhaps should stay and continue
his education in the fine arts. As Grover knew, the General Authorities
of the Church wanted to get the missionaries back home and married
as soon as possible, but Roberts continued, "You ought to be where the
market is. Back home on the farm you have to have a pair of gloves,
work shoes, overalls, and a straw hat. Beyond that then you try to support
your family well enough so that your sons can go on missions. That's
the first priority." Grover once met Roberts in the American Museum
of Natural History and asked what he was doing there. Roberts replied,
"By all means go and see the Golden Plates. And see the things that
Mahonri Young has done." Young was a Utah sculptor whose work
included many motifs from the Book of Mormon. Grover saw the golden
plates, "which had nothing to do with our golden plates." When President
Roberts wrote a farewell message to his missionaries before he departed
the mission for Utah in the spring of 1927, he left a statement of his
convictions: "Concerning my own testimony of the truth of these things
I can say that time the impressions of my youth deeper makes, as streams
their channels deeper wear."[64]

Before leaving for his mission, Roberts had decided to continue
with the presentation of some additional Book of Mormon problems to
the First Presidency and had written a letter dated March 15, 1923
[1922], indicating that "the truth of the Book of Mormon is absolutely
essential to the integrity of the whole Mormon movement" and that his
further studies had seemed only to increase the problems. But, as a letter
of October 24, 1927, to Apostle Lyman shows, he had reconsidered and
had sent neither the letter nor the additional material. Now, back from
the Eastern States Mission, he indicated to Lyman that he had come
upon an "embarrassing" theory about the Book of Mormon based on
quite remarkable similarities between the Nephite record and Ethan
Smith's *View of the Hebrews*, published in 1823 and 1825 and probably
available to Smith before the production of the Book of Mormon. He
indicated that his latest examination was "not one fourth part" of what
could be written about such a comparison but suggested that if Lyman
thought it wise, he might submit it to other members of the Council of
Twelve Apostles.[65]

In addition to his two longer treatises — "Book of Mormon Difficulties" and "A Book of Mormon Study" already described — Roberts
authored a third document based on his investigations of the Ethan Smith
book. This quite brief analysis of Roberts's conclusions about a possible
relationship between the *View of the Hebrews* and the Book of Mormon
was apparently written during 1922 and given the title "A Parallel."

After the death of Roberts, his oldest son, Ben E. Roberts, and perhaps others, informed friends about the document, and soon it was public knowledge that the parallel of the Book of Mormon with Ethan Smith's work seemed to cast doubt on the authenticity of the Mormon scripture. To correct this misapprehension, Ben E. Roberts in a letter of July 22, 1939, declared that his father had "found nothing in his study which reflected upon the integrity of Joseph Smith's account of the Book of Mormon." On October 10, 1946, Ben E. Roberts discussed his father's work on the Book of Mormon before the Timpanogos Club in Salt Lake City and, after the meeting, distributed mimeographed copies of "A Parallel" to members of the audience. Dr. Mervin B. Hogan, of the faculty of the University of Utah, obtained a copy and had it published in January 1956 in the *Rocky Mountain Mason*. The parallel is composed of eighteen typed pages concerned with eighteen items and with notes and quotations from both the Book of Mormon and the *View of the Hebrews* arranged in parallel columns on each page. This short review, since its publication in 1946, has been the object of many evaluations by both supporters and detractors of the theory. "A Parallel," as originally written by B. H. Roberts, including handwritten additions and corrections, is included in this volume. The much longer and more comprehensive "Study," presented here, will now probably take the place of the 1946 publication for argument and debate.[66]

Ethan Smith, the author of *View of the Hebrews,* was a New England minister who was born in Belchertown, Massachusetts, December 19, 1762, and died in Pompey, New York, on August 29, 1849. During his long life he was prominent enough to have a number of his sermons printed, and he also authored or edited several books, including *A Dissertation on the Prophecies relative to Anti-Christ and the Last Times; Memoirs of Mrs. Abigail Bailey;* and his most famous work, *View of the Hebrews.* At the time he was writing this latter book, he was the minister of the Congregational Church at Poultney, Vermont, where he served from November 21, 1821, to December 1826.[67] Early in 1827 the Reverend Smith apparently visited Palmyra, because by December 31, 1826, the *Wayne Sentinel* posted his name for letters remaining in the Palmyra Post Office (*Wayne Sentinel*, January 5, 1827). As some critics who relate Joseph Smith's Book of Mormon to Ethan Smith's *View of the Hebrews* have pointed out, Oliver Cowdery, Joseph's cousin and his scribe during the writing of the Mormon scripture, had lived in Poultney for twenty-two years until 1825. In fact, Cowdery's stepmother and three of his sisters were members of Ethan Smith's congregation, according to the Poultney Church Records, Book 3 (August 3, 1818).[68] Poultney is just a half-mile from the border separating the states of Vermont and New

York and about seventy miles from Albany, which marked the eastern end of the Erie Canal, completed as far west as Brockfort in 1823, about forty miles beyond the village of Palmyra. Today it is difficult to measure the importance of the Grand Canal as the preeminent thoroughfare to the interior of the northern United States during the 1820s and until the 1850s, when the railroad became the carrier of people and freight. To be situated on the canal meant that the inhabitants of a village could receive freight from New York City, about 335 miles away, on boats that traveled forty miles a day; passengers and mail could move eighty to ninety miles in twenty-four hours. Thus, in about a week's time, news and goods could be delivered to families and businesses in the town from the great metropolitan city at the mouth of the Hudson, and a constant stream of freighters and packet boats made Palmyra a bustling and busy stop on the Erie Canal.

Furthermore, a reading of the town's weekly newspaper, the *Wayne Sentinel*, indicates that there were at least three bookstores which advertised wares to the citizens of Palmyra: The Canandaigua Bookstore, and two local establishments, J. D. Evernghim & Co. and the *Wayne Sentinel*, the latter run by Tucker & Gilbert, the publishers of the newspaper. In at least two issues the Wayne Bookstore listed the titles of books just received for sale, a four-column spread in the December 17, 1823, issue, and a similar listing of new books in the November 24, 1826, issue. But usually Tucker & Gilbert merely noted almost weekly "have this day received, several boxes of Books" or "More New Books" at their bookstore, later renamed the Palmyra Book Store. Occasionally, an entrepreneur would import a stock of books to be auctioned off, as did one who advertised on August 30, 1825, "18 Cases of Books, recently received from New York and Philadelphia, being the largest and most varied collection of Books . . . ever offered at public or private sale in this village. . . . The books are fresh and new." With such opportunities to acquire books, it would be unusual if the Joseph Smith family were not aware of Ethan Smith's work.

In addition, Josiah Priest's *The Wonders of Nature and Providence Displayed* was in the local Manchester Rental Library, just five miles from Joseph Smith's home, and the membership records, now located in the Ontario County Historical Society in Canandaigua, show that it was checked out repeatedly during the years 1826 to 1828. Priest's book included a long selection from Ethan Smith's work and attempted to establish that the Indians were of Hebrew descent. Very early in this century I. Woodbridge Riley in his book, *The Founder of Mormonism,* had noted that Ethan Smith's "work was published in Poultney, Vermont, next to Windsor County, where Joseph's parents once lived, and by 1825 had circulated to westernmost New York." But as Fawn M. Brodie, another of the writers to hypothesize a connection between the two books by the two Smiths, has pointed out, "It may never be proved that Joseph saw *View of the Hebrews* before writing the Book of Mormon." Yet at the same time she insisted that the parallel features could not be "mere coincidence."[69]

In Roberts's consideration of origins in his "A Book of Mormon Study," he divided the work into two parts: Part I, an initial discussion of the "Literature Available to Joseph Smith as a Ground-Plan for the Book of Mormon," followed by the major portion of the treatise, "View of the Hebrews as Structural Material for the Book of Mormon," which included a final chapter on "The Imaginative Mind of the Prophet Joseph Smith"; and Part II, "Internal Evidence that the Book of Mormon Is of Human Origin—Considered." After completing his final study of the Book of Mormon by the time he left New York City and his Eastern States Mission, Brigham H. Roberts returned to Salt Lake City and to the life of a General Authority of the Church. He died there in 1933.

During the last six years of his life is there any evidence that Roberts still retained his faith in the authenticity of the Book of Mormon, despite his critical examination of the origin of the book? The record is mixed. In his public statements he was still the defender of the faith. For example, at the semi-annual conference of the Church in April 1928 he was reported to have "defended the Book of Mormon as the word of God . . . [and] closed his address by bearing an impressive testimony to the divinity of the Church."[70] And a year before his death in 1933 he penned an article for the *Atlantic Monthly* on "What College Did to My Religion," in which he declared that God would complete His work of the "New Dispensation of the fulness of times. It will never be destroyed, nor its work be given to another people."[71] But in a sermon in April 1929 he sounded rather enigmatic as he said, "I rejoice at the prominence given the Book of Mormon in this Conference. It is, however, only one of many means in letting God's work be known to the world." He then "told of an experience where the Doctrine and Covenants was instrumental in converting a friend, after the Book of Mormon had failed."[72] In one of his seven last discourses he counseled the youth of the Church to "carefully and thoroughly examine every principle advanced to them and not only intellectually assent to it as a grand system of truth, but also become imbued with its spirit and feel and enjoy its powers."[73] Finally, in a 1932 article, "Joseph Smith: An Appreciation," the fire and conviction of his youth came through as Roberts confessed his love and respect for Joseph Smith, as an admirer "who believes in him without reservation . . . I was influenced by the boldness of his claims, for the tremendous intellectual daring . . . for the very sway and swagger of him, and for his unschooled eloquence. . . . To me and for me, he is the Prophet of the Most High, enskied and sainted!"[74]

Whether or not Roberts retained his belief in the Book of Mormon may never be determined. In his last conference address of April 1933 he referred to the Book of Mormon as "one of the most valuable books that has ever been preserved, even as holy scripture."[75] But in his "A Book of Mormon Study," Roberts presents an intense and probing evaluation of the possibility that Ethan Smith's *View of the Hebrews* furnished a partial framework for Joseph Smith's written composition, that the Mormon prophet had the intellectual capacity and imagination necessary to conceive and write the Book of Mormon, and that internal contradictions and other defects added further evidence that it might not be of divine origin.

As for Roberts himself, one can appreciate his fierce independence, his forthright honesty, his deeply imbedded integrity, and, above all, his fearless willingness to follow wherever his reason led him. He could be abrasive in his defense of stubbornly held beliefs, but he had the capacity to change his views when confronted with new and persuasive evidence. It is easy to admire Brigham H. Roberts, and, to apply his description of Joseph Smith to himself, to enjoy Roberts's "unschooled eloquence," his "tremendous intellectual daring," and "the very sway and swagger of him."

NOTES

1. Quoted in B. H. Roberts, *A Comprehensive History of the Church of Jesus Christ of Latter-day Saints,* 6 vols. (Salt Lake City: Deseret News Press, 1930), 1:167.

2. *Deseret News,* 24 Feb. 1881; B. H. Roberts, "Life Story of B. H. Roberts" (typescript), 115-18, Marriott Library, University of Utah, Salt Lake City; Truman G. Madsen, *Defender of the Faith: The B. H. Roberts Story* (Salt Lake City: Bookcraft, 1981), 126-29.

3. Alexander Campbell, *The Millennial Harbinger,* 2 (Bethany, Va.: Printed and published by the Editor, 1831), 86-96.

4. Roberts, "Life Story," 119.

5. Madsen, *Defender of the Faith,* 129.

6. Ibid., 160-78; Roberts, "Life Story," 154, 161; B. H. Roberts, *New Witnesses for God,* 3 vols. (Salt Lake City: Deseret News, 1909).

7. *Millennial Star,* 50:113, as quoted in Journal History, 13 Feb. 1888, 5-6, L.D.S. Archives, Salt Lake City; Madsen, *Defender of the Faith,* 170.

8. Madsen, *Defender of the Faith,* 296-97; B. H. Roberts, *Corianton: A Nephite Story* (Salt Lake City: N.p., 1889), 111.

9. B. H. Roberts, *Outlines of Ecclesiastical History* (Salt Lake City: George Q. Cannon & Sons, 1893).

10. B. H. Roberts, *The Missouri Persecutions* (Salt Lake City: George Q. Cannon & Sons, 1900).

11. B. H. Roberts, *The Rise and Fall of Nauvoo* (Salt Lake City: Deseret News, 1900).

12. B. H. Roberts, *The Life of John Taylor* (Salt Lake City: George Q. Cannon & Sons, 1892).

13. B. H. Roberts, ed., *History of the Church of Jesus Christ of Latter-day Saints*, Period I. *History of Joseph Smith, the Prophet. By Himself* (Salt Lake City: Deseret News, 1902).

14. For a more detailed evaluation of Roberts as the editor of this history, see Dean C. Jessee, "The Reliability of Joseph Smith's History," *Journal of Mormon History*, 3 (1976):23-46, and Madsen, *Defender of the Faith*, 289-93.

15. *Deseret News*, 29 May, 11 June 1904.

16. B. H. Roberts, "Attack on Book of Mormon" (1903), L.D.S. Church Archives.

17. Ibid., 6-7.

18. B. H. Roberts, "Translation of the Book of Mormon," *Improvement Era*, 9 (Apr. 1906):430; 9 (May 1906):544, 548.

19. H. Chamberlain, "Letter to B. H. Roberts, from Spencer, Iowa, November 13, 1903," *Improvement Era*, 7 (Jan. 1904):193-96.

20. G. A. Marr, "Letter to B. H. Roberts, March 19, 1925," 19, L.D.S. Archives; for further information, see B. H. Roberts, *Defense of the Faith and the Saints*, 1 (Salt Lake City: Deseret News, 1907), 278ff.; for a modern reiteration of Roberts's stance, see Edward H. Ashment, "The Book of Mormon—A Literal Translation," *Sunstone*, 5 (Mar.-Apr. 1980):10-14.

21. Roberts, "The Manner of Translating the Book of Mormon," *New Witnesses for God*, 2:106-21.

22. Paul R. Cheesman, *The Keystone of Mormonism* (Salt Lake City: Deseret Book Co., 1973), 95-96; for an earlier and more critical evaluation of Book of Mormon changes, see also Lamoni Call, *2000 Changes in the Book of Mormon* (Bountiful, Utah: Lamoni Call, 1898).

23. B. H. Roberts, "Higher Criticism and the Book of Mormon," *Improvement Era*, 14 (July 1911):781; B. H. Roberts, "An Objection to the Book of Mormon Answered," ibid., 12 (July 1909):681-89.

24. *Journal History*, 9 Nov. 1903, 3.

25. Roberts, "Life Story," 214-16.

26. B. H. Roberts, "The Origin of the Book of Mormon," *American Historical Magazine*, 3 (Sept. 1908):451, 441-68; 3 (Nov. 1908):551-80; 4 (Jan. 1909):22-44; 4 (Mar. 1909):168-96. The four articles were later reprinted in Roberts, *Defense of the Faith and the Saints*, 2 (Salt Lake City: Deseret News, 1912), 1-229.

27. Roberts, "The Origin of the Book of Mormon," *American Historical Magazine*, 4 (Mar. 1909):179-81, 196. An effective argument against the Spaulding theory about the origin of the Book of Mormon is Fawn Brodie's *No Man Knows My History*, 2d ed. (New York: Alfred A. Knopf, 1979), 442-56 (Appendix B).

28. Joseph Smith, Jr., *The Book of Mormon* (Palmyra: Printed by E. B. Grandin, for the Author, 1830). For a modern evaluation of the many changes made in the language and format of the various editions of the Book of Mormon, see Cheesman, *Keystone of Mormonism,* 75-76, 84, 93-94. For example, Cheesman notes that there have been about 200 deletions of the phrase "and it came to pass" (93).

29. Roberts, "Life Story," 210.

30. B. H. Roberts, "Review of the New Manual," *Improvement Era,* 8 (Aug. 1905):783-89.

31. B. H. Roberts, "New Witnesses for God. Volume II. The Book of Mormon, Part I," *Young Men's Mutual Improvement Association's Manual, 1903-1904,* no. 7 (Salt Lake City: The Deseret News, 1903):i-lxv.

32. B. H. Roberts, "Originality of the Book of Mormon," *Improvement Era,* 8 (Oct. 1905):902.

33. Roberts, *New Witnesses for God,* 2 (1909):iii-viii.

34. Ibid., 45, 169-85, 199-200.

35. Ibid., 237-310, 311, 323, 326.

36. Ibid., 347-55.

37. Ibid., 356-70, 415-16.

38. Ibid., 417-41; 3 (1909):3-66, 82-87. Because Roberts discusses these antiquarian authorities and other more modern writers in much greater detail in his later Book of Mormon Studies included in this work, descriptions and citations of the materials involved have been deferred to the footnotes for those sections.

39. Roberts, *New Witnesses for God,* 3:87-90.

40. Ibid., 115-12, 170-78, 229-30, 329-31.

41. Ibid., 347-460.

42. Ibid., 461-510.

43. Ibid., 511-23.

44. Ibid., 524-33.

45. Ibid., 552-56.

46. Ibid., 557-61.

47. Roberts, *Comprehensive History;* Roberts, "Life Story," 214-15.

48. Roberts, "Life Story," 216-17; Roberts *Comprehensive History,* vii-ix.

49. J.O., "Mormons: Their Social and Economic Development," in the Preface, found in Anthony W. Ivins Collection, Box 17, fd. 1:10, Utah State Historical Society, Salt Lake City; the editor has been unable to identify who "J.O." was and whether or not a book by this title was published.

50. Samuel W. Taylor, *Nightfall at Nauvoo* (New York: Macmillan, 1971), 382.

51. J. M. Sjodahl, "Book of Mormon Facts," *Juvenile Instructor,* 6 (June 1922):305-9; Roberts's marginal note is at the bottom of the first page of a copy of the above article found in "Book of Mormon, Articles," Ms. 106, box 5, fd. 3, Roberts Papers, Marriott Library.

52. J. Reuben Clark statement, 8 Apr. 1943, in "Budget Beginnings," 11-12, Box 188, J. Reuben Clark Papers, Harold B. Lee Library, Brigham Young

University, Provo, Utah, as quoted by D. Michael Quinn in *On Being a Mormon Historian* (Salt Lake City: Modern Microfilm Co., 1982), 8; Madsen, *Defender of the Faith*, 313-14; *Deseret News*, 12 Sept. 1919.

53. B. H. Roberts, "B. H. Roberts on the Intellectual and Spiritual Quest," *Dialogue*, 13 (Summer 1980):123-28.

54. B. H. Roberts's Memorial Library of 1,385 Books, L.D.S. Archives.

55. B. H. Roberts, *The Mormon Battalion: Its History and Achievements* (Salt Lake City: Deseret News, 1919); Junius F. Wells, "The Mormon Battalion," *Utah Genealogical and Historical Magazine*, July 1927, 98-99.

56. In giving a brief descriptive overview of the events and correspondence that led to Roberts's study of Book of Mormon problems, it seems wise to defer exact citations and explanations of the people involved in the story to their appearance in the correspondence and in the meetings that took place.

57. George Franklin Richards, Diaries, L.D.S. Archives.

58. James E. Talmage, Journals, Jan. 1922–July 1933, Harold B. Lee Library.

59. Ibid., 26 Jan., 2 Feb., 28 Apr., 25 May 1922.

60. Wesley P. Lloyd, Personal Journal (in private possession), Monday, Aug. 7/33. Permission to quote the Lloyd Journal has been given by the family.

61. Roberts, "Life Story," 217; "Letter of B. H. Roberts to Isaac Russell, 25 October 1909," and "Letter of B. H. Roberts to Isaac Russell, 9 September 1910," Scott Kenney Papers, Special Collections, Marriott Library.

62. Roberts, "Life Story," 217; B. H. Roberts Collection, Box 5, fd. 5 Special Collections, Marriott Library.

63. Massachusetts Conference of Eastern States Mission, President's Records, June 1923, Jan., 22 Mar., 20 Sept. 1924, 1 July 1926, L.D.S. Archives.

64. Interview of Roscoe A. Grover, by Gordon Irving, Salt Lake City, Utah, Feb.-Mar. 1979, Oral History Program, L.D.S. Archives; Massachusetts Conference of Eastern States Mission, President's Records, 15 May 1927.

65. From a reference in the Lyman letter of Oct. 24, 1927, it is evident that Roberts's letter of Mar. 15 should carry the date of 1922, not 1923. Additional support for this change of date comes from the fact that the original letter in the Roberts file is typed and has the printed letterhead, Salt Lake City, Utah, while the date has obviously been written later in ink and in Roberts's handwriting. By 1923 Roberts was living in New York City as president of the Eastern States Mission and would have found it difficult to meet regularly with the committee composed of James E. Talmage, John A. Widtsoe, and the others who were residing in Salt Lake City.

66. Ariel L. Crowley, *About the Book of Mormon* (Salt Lake City: Deseret News Press, 1961), 131-32; Mervin B. Hogan, "'A Parallel': A Matter of Chance versus Coincidence," *Rocky Mountain Mason*, 4 (Jan. 1956):17-18.

67. James Grant Wilson and John Fiske, eds., *Appleton's Cyclopedia of American Biography* (New York: D. Appleton and Co., 1888), 562-63; Joseph Sabin, *A Dictionary of Books Relating to America* (New York: Biographical Society of America, 1892-1928), 176-78; Zadock Thompson, *History of Vermont* (Burlington, Vt.: Chauncey Goodrich, 1842), 143. Daphne Bartholomew, librarian of the Poultney Public Library, in a letter to the editors of Aug. 20, 1982,

indicates that, according to a *History of Poultney*, published in 1875, Smith was dismissed from his Poultney ministry because of a misunderstanding with one of the deacons of the church. See also Wesley P. Walters, "The Use of the Old Testament in the Book of Mormon" (M.A. thesis, Covenant Theological Seminary, St. Louis, 1981), 98.

68. Hal Hougey, *"A Parallel"—The Basis of the Book of Mormon* (Concord, Calif.: Pacific Publishing, 1963), 5-6; Larry W. Jonas, *Mormon Claims Examined* (Grand Rapids, Mich.: Baker Book House, 1961), 41-42; Robert N. Hullinger, "The Lost Tribes of Israel and the Book of Mormon," *Lutheran Quarterly*, 22 (Aug. 1970): 327-29; Walters, "Use of the Old Testament in the Book of Mormon," 97-98.

69. George E. Condon, *Stars in the Water: The Story of the Erie Canal* (New York: Doubleday, 1974), 4-5, 115; *Wayne Sentinel* (Palmyra, N.Y.), 1 Oct. 1823–13 June 1828; I. Woodbridge Riley, *The Founder of Mormonism* (New York: Dodd, Mead, 1903), 124-25; Brodie, *No Man Knows My History*, 46-47; Walters, "Use of the Old Testament in the Book of Mormon," 99.

70. *Deseret News*, 9 Apr. 1928. As already indicated in the Lloyd Journal, this assertion was in line with Roberts's belief that the Doctrine and Covenants offered the strongest proof of the divinity of Joseph Smith.

71. B. H. Roberts, "What College Did to My Religion," as quoted in the *Improvement Era*, 36 (Mar. 1933):259-61, from an article in the *Atlantic Monthly*, June 1932, by Philip E. Wentworth.

72. *Deseret News*, 8 Apr. 1929.

73. B. H. Roberts, *Discourses of B. H. Roberts* (Salt Lake City: Deseret Book Co., 1948), foreword.

74. B. H. Roberts, "Joseph Smith: An Appreciation," *Improvement Era*, 36 (Dec. 1932):81.

75. B. H. Roberts, Conference Reports, Apr. 1933, 117, L.D.S. Archives.

Correspondence Related to the
Book of Mormon Essays

A letter from a young Mormon, William E. Riter, asking five specific questions about problems with the Book of Mormon inaugurated a series of events that led to a critical examination of the book by Brigham H. Roberts, member of the Council of Seventy of the Church of Jesus Christ of Latter-day Saints and leading historian of the Church. The following correspondence, concerned with the affair and arranged chronologically, is almost self-explanatory, and the notes are provided to help identify the individuals involved in the exchange as well as to give information about the various sources cited by the writers of the letters.

Although only the first nine letters are concerned with Roberts's initial Book of Mormon analysis, "Book of Mormon Difficulties: A Study," we have included the unsent letter of March 15, 1922, addressed to Heber J. Grant and the Quorum of the Apostles and the October 24, 1927, letter to Richard R. Lyman, as they help explain how Roberts eventually came to prepare his more comprehensive "A Book of Mormon Study" and the shorter "A Parallel," both of which are a part of this publication.

W. E. Riter[1] to James E. Talmage[2]

U.S. Expt. Station, Salina, Utah   Aug. 22, 1921

Dear Dr. Talmage:

During the past few years I have associated and had some religious discussions with some non-"Mormons." Mr. Couch[3] of Washington, D. C., has been studying the Book of Mormon and submits the enclosed questions concerning his studies. Would you kindly answer them and send them to me.

Sincerely,
W. E. Riter

ENCLOSURE

1. The "Mormon" tradition states that the American Indians were the descendants of the Lamanites.[4] The time allowed from the first landing of Lehi and his followers in America to the present is about 2,700 years. Philologic studies have divided the Indian languages into five distinct linguistic stocks which show very little relationship. It does not appear that this diversity in the nature and grammatical constructions of Indian tongues could obtain if the Indians were the descendants of a people who possessed as highly developed a language as the ancient Hebrew, but indicates that the division of the Indians into separate stocks occurred long before their language was developed beyond the most primitive kind of articulations. Again the time allowed from the landing of Lehi is much too short to account for the observed diversity.

2. The Book of Mormon states that when the followers of Lehi reached North America they found, among other animals, the horse here. Historical and paeleontological data shows that the horse was not in America at that time, nor did it arrive for 20 centuries afterward.

3. Nephi is stated to have had a bow of steel which he broke shortly after he had left Jerusalem, some 600 years B.C. There is no record that I know of which allows the Jews the knowledge of steel at such a period.

4. Reference is frequently made in the Book of Mormon to "swords and cimiters." The use of the word "scimeter" does not occur in other literature before the rise of the Mohammedan power and apparently that peculiar weapon was not developed until long after the Christian era. It does not, therefore appear likely that the Nephites or the Lamanites possessed either the weapon or the term.

5. Reference is also made to the possession by the Nephites of an abundance of silk. As silk was not known in America at that time the question arises, where did they obtain the silk?

1. William Emerson Riter, born April 26, 1901, in Logan, Utah, was a graduate of Utah State Agricultural College and served a mission for the Mormon Church from 1922-24 in Germany and Switzerland. His career was spent in the employ of the federal government and at the time of his death in Portland, Oregon, on June 3, 1953, he was regional supervisor in the Interior Department's fish and wildlife service. *Deseret News and Telegram*, 4 June 1953.

2. James E. Talmage was born September 21, 1862, in Hungerford, Berkshire, England, and emigrated with his family to Utah in 1876. He studied geology at the University of Pennsylvania and Johns Hopkins University. For three years, 1894-97, he served as president of the University of Utah. He was ordained an apostle in the Church of Jesus Christ of Latter-day Saints on December 7, 1911, and was one of the chief exponents of Mormon theology until his death on July 27, 1933. Among his most important writings are: *The Articles of Faith, The Great Apostasy, The Philosophical Basis of Mormonism, Jesus the Christ,* and *The Vitality of Mormonism.* Andrew Jenson, *Latter-day Saint Biographical Encyclopedia,* 3 (Salt Lake City: Andrew Jenson History Co., 1920), 787-89; Virginia Budd Jacobsen, "James Edward Talmage: A Portrait of the Second President of

the University of Utah," *Utah Alumnus* (Dec. 1926):9, 16; see also John R. Talmage, *The Talmage Story* (Salt Lake City: Bookcraft, 1972).

3. Mr. Couch is not identified any further, but only five men with that surname are listed in the District of Columbia directory for 1921: Arthur O. Couch, an auditor in the U.S. Treasury Department; Frank B. Couch, a district inspector; James F. Couch, a chemist in the Department of Agriculture; John J. Couch, a laboratory technician; and Ralph F. Couch, a correspondent with the United Press Association. *Boyd's Directory of the District of Columbia* (Washington, D.C.: R. L. Polk & Co., 1921), 446.

4. In the Book of Mormon the Lamanites were the nomadic portion of the descendants of the Hebrew emigrants who traveled from Jerusalem to the American continent in 600 B.C.

George W. Middleton[1] to Richard R. Lyman[2]

Salt Lake City   Nov 11, [19]21

My Dear Friend and Brother:

I have given considerable time and study to the questions you forwarded to me concerning the Book of Mormon. The man who framed them was certainly some student, but if he had been a real critical reader of the Book of Mormon text, he could have raised questions much more difficult to answer.

Question 1 regarding languages: Hubert Howe Bancroft in his *Native Races,* Vol. 3 page 553 Says: "First that a relationship exists among all the tongues of the northern and southern continents; and that while certain characteristics are found in common throughout all the languages of America, these languages are as a whole sufficiently peculiar to be distinguished from all the other languages of the world. . . . Nowhere on the globe are uniformities of speech carried over vast areas and through innumerable and diversified races with such persistency as in America; nowhere are tongues so dissimilar, and yet so alike as here."[3]

As to the rapidity with which languages will change among people. I was astounded some years ago to learn that the modern Italian, and the modern Greek tongues bear no resemblance to the Latin and Greek of classic days. These latter are dead languages in every sense of the word.

Bancroft in another volume gives a great array of evidence of the Hebrew origin of the American Indians. Whitney characterises these American languages "The most changeful forms of human speech," basing his opinion on the changes observed since the advent of Europeans.[4]

As evidence of Hebrew origin, Bancroft quoting other authors points out the flood myth, circumcision, the ark of the covenant which the tribes of Honduras had, the conception of trinity, certain distinctions of animals clean and unclean, the doctrine of resurrection, anointing with oil, etc, etc. Lord Kingsborough spent his life and his fortune to prove that the American Indians were the ten lost tribes of Israel. *Native Races* Vol. 5 page 84.[5]

2nd   With regard to the horse recent geological research shows that the original home of the horse was in America. The new *Encyclopedia Americana* Vol 14, page 397 we read: "In the early part of the age of man or quarternary period, wild species of horse were to be found on every continent, except Australia. Remains of these true native horses have been found buried in strata of this age in all parts of the United States, in Alaska, in Mexico, in Ecuador, in Brazil, and Argentina."[6]

Apparently the horse was abundantly represented in American fauna in quarternary times, and I can see no good reason for his extinction, although the spaniards have so far as I know said nothing about the matter. It may easily be that they took it for granted, and thought comment unnecessary!

3rd, The term steel seems to be an entirely modern term. I find no mention of it in the bible nor any ancient history. We must remember though that the translation of the Book of Mormon was in this modern time, and that steel is only a modified form of iron, and any modification of that metal could find only this modern word in our vocabulary to express it. That Iron of a superior quality was in use at a very early date is proven by the fact that an iron crosscut saw made in either Babylonia or Egypt a thousand years before Christ is preserved in the British Museum. Julius Cesar was said to have a sword made from iron procured from a fallen meteor.

4th   The scimeter, although a weapon used much by the Mohamedan peoples, was also a weapon common to all eastern peoples. The highest types of the scimeter were made at Damascus, a city not far from Jerusalem.

That the word does not occur anywhere in the bible may be due to the fact that it is a type of sword, and the term sword may be the generic name which includes all varieties of that weapon. As to the date of the genesis of the scimeter among the Arabs and other eastern tribes I can find nothing definite.

5th   The facts about silk culture seem to be: Hawae-Nan-tze in his Silk Classic states that Se-ling-shi queen of Hwang-te, a province of China in the year 2460 B.C. was the first to rear silk worms, and the emperor Hwang-te was induced to make robes and garments from that circumstance.[7]

The Chinese seem to have kept the matter of the silk worm a profound secret for centuries, but to furnish western peoples with manufactured silk which sold at fabulous prices, sometimes for its weight in gold. The bible frequently speaks of silk at a very early date, but in no way to indicate that the Israelites knew anything about the secret of its production.

The secret of the silk worm was kept absolute with the Chinese until the sixth century A.D. when two Nestorian monks, who had been engaged in missionary work in China solved the mystery by bringing to Constantinople a small quantity of silk worm eggs concealed in their palmer staves. The missionaries had observed in China the various processes connected with the rearing of silk worms, the leaves on which they fed and the process of reeling off the silk fibre. Justinian gave every encouragement to the silk industry and it soon spread to the peoples of the western parts of Europe.

There are a number of different species of moth which produce silk cocoons. Several north and south American species yield silk which has not become commercially important because of the superiority of the (Bombyx textor), the particular specie that seems to yield the finest quality of silk. It would be quite in the possibilities that the peoples of America would learn independently to reel silk from their native cocoons, and manufact[u]re silk. I give the suggestion for what it is worth.

My dear friend I have given your letter considerable study, both because I would like to accommodate my friend, and because I have a peculiar liking for prying into such things and weighing them up in cold blooded logic. With kindest personal regards to you I am

Your friend and Bro.
Geo W. Middleton

1. Dr. George W. Middleton was born in the small village of Hamilton Fort, Utah, December 10, 1866, and received his medical training at the University of Louisville, becoming nationally recognized as a physician and surgeon. His avocations were geology and Utah history, and he was also active in civic affairs, serving as mayor of Cedar City, Utah, and as a member of the Board of Regents of the University of Utah. He died December 8, 1938. *Deseret News*, 8 Dec. 1938.

2. Richard R. Lyman, born in Fillmore, Utah, November 23, 1870, was trained as a civil engineer at the University of Michigan and Cornell University, from which latter institution he received a Ph.D. in 1905. In 1896 he founded and for twenty-six years headed the department of engineering at the University of Utah. The son of long-time Church leader Francis M. Lyman and a descendant of Brigham Young's counselor, George A. Smith, on his mother's side, he was active for many years in his Church and was ordained an apostle on April 7, 1918. He also wrote extensively on Mormon subjects, his most prominent publications being *Pres. H. J. Grant and His Family*, *Pres. Joseph F. Smith*, and *A Century of Mormonism*. He died in Salt Lake City on December 31, 1963. *Salt Lake Tribune*, 1 Jan. 1964; Jenson, *Latter-day Saint Biographical Encyclopedia*, 756-60.

3. The five-volume series by Hubert Howe Bancroft, *The Native Races* (San Francisco: A. L. Bancroft & Co., 1883), was considered to be a basic work in 1921 for investigators interested in the origin and culture of North and South American native peoples. The first volume dealt with *Wild Tribes;* the second was titled *Civilized Nations;* the third was concerned with *Myths and Languages;* the fourth described *Antiquities;* and the fifth examined the *Primitive History* of the native Americans. As will be seen,

Roberts was expecially interested in the materials found in volumes 3, 4, and 5. In the first chapter of volume 5, *Primitive History,* 77-102, Bancroft examined the theory that the American Indians were of Hebrew descent or remnants of the Ten Lost Tribes and included a discussion of the Book of Mormon story.

4. Middleton is referring to William Dwight Whitney, whose ninth lecture from a series of twelve on *Language and the Study of Language* deals with the "changeableness of the different tongues" (346), the unity of American languages "all descended from a single parent language" (348), and the absurdity of the theory that the American Indians should be identified "with the ten Israelitish tribes deported from their own country" to the Americas (352). William Dwight Whitney, *Language and the Study of Language: Twelve Lectures on the Principles of Linguistic Science* (New York: Charles Scribner's Sons, 1888), 346-53.

5. Lord Viscount Kingsborough, over eighteen years (1831-48), published nine volumes of argument based on a number of ancient Spanish, French, and Mexican manuscripts, never in print before, to attempt to prove that the native races of America were of Jewish origin. The effort cost him a fortune of £32,000 and his life, for he died in a debtors' prison. Kingsborough used scriptural analogies, the Mexican tradition of a deluge, and other speculations to prove his theory. Those conjectures which were not entirely spurious may have been "improved" by the imaginations of some Spanish priests. Edward King Kingsborough, *Antiquities of Mexico: comprising facsimiles of ancient Mexican paintings and heiroglyphics, preserved in the royal libraries of Paris, Berlin and Dresden, in the Imperial library of Vienna, in the Vatican library; in the Borgian museum at Rome; in the library at the Institute at Bologna; and in the Bodleian library at Oxford. Together with the Monuments of New Spain, by M. Dupaix,* 9 vols. (London: R. Havell, etc., 1831-48).

6. *The Encyclopedia Americana: a Library of Universal Knowledge* (New York: The Encyclopedia Americana Corp., 1918-20).

7. Huang-ti, the Yellow Sovereign, supposedly the progenitor of the Chinese people and the first of the Five Sovereigns, reigned in China about 2640 B.C. and, in addition to his prowess as a strong ruler, also was noted for his invention of the compass, a calendar system, and bamboo musical instruments, among other novelties. His wife "taught the people how to rear silkworms and to weave silk, and has been regarded as the goddess of the silk industry." Li Ung Bing, *Outlines of Chinese History,* ed. Joseph Whiteside (Shanghai: The Commercial Press, 1914).

Ralph V. Chamberlin[1] *to Richard R. Lyman*

Cambridge, Dec. 3, 1921

Dear Richard:

It was good to hear from you under date of Oct. 28. I would have replied at once were it not that you indicated you were to be out of the State for some time and would probably write to me again before I should write. As you are probably again in Utah by now, I am writing without waiting to hear from you.

With reference to the questions bearing upon the Book of Mormon which you sent, I am enclosing a few comments. I have not felt it necessary, unless the author of the questions may amplify his grounds, to go into the matters any more extensively. In some points I think you will see that he is obviously inaccurate and has made statements without much effort to get at the facts. There are many questions concerning the native races of America that cannot now be answered scientifically; and it may be even generations before the data shall furnish grounds for the answer. In the meantime the opinions of particular men, even where they merit the title of scientists, must not be given as the conclusions of Science. If I have not supplied what you wish, I shall be glad to do anything further that I can in case you will let me know.

Things are going nicely with me here. I am very busy and am trying to be happy and contented for the time being.

I am to be the speaker at our church here tomorrow.

Shall be looking to the letter you promised soon,

Cordially yours,
R. V. Chamberlin

ENCLOSURE

1. The statement that philologic studies on the American Indian languages "indicates that the division of the Indians into separate stocks occurred long before their language was developed beyond the most primitive kind of articulations" is not in accord with the findings of the profounder students of the subject and cannot be substantiated. The conclusions reached by Duponceau,[2] Humboldt[3] and Steinthal,[4] and supported by such recent students as Brinton,[5] have not been successfully brought into question. These conclusions are that there are certain general and distinctive grammatical principles underlying all American languages proving their unity at a date far more recent than the quoted statement intimates. No Indian language when thoroughly understood can be placed in the status regarded as most primitive. Max Müller[6] once declared that the language of the savage Iroquois in its extent and complexity of grammatic forms was comparable to the Sanscrit and that the native intellectual capacity required to maintain this linguistic machinery must be of high order. We are, furthermore, in no position at this time to speak confidently or positively as to the length of time required to account for the diversity in the American Indian languages. We have very little knowledge as to the rate, manner, or causes of change in these languages. The statement of Sagard,[7] author of a dictionary of the Huron language published at Paris in 1632 that the Huron language was constantly changing so that in a generation or two it would be like a new language may be extravagant; but there can be no doubt that languages, particularly those of small groups with no written forms, at times change very rapidly. Dr. Beauchamp[8] once wrote: "The Onandagas have not moved over twenty miles in two hundred and fifty years, yet how much their tongue has changed in half that time! A migration to new and distant homes

would have produced many new words, and then the language would have remained much the same for a time, waiting for other disturbing causes." Certainly if any conditions could favor linguistic change it would be the complete isolation of an initially small band of people in an extensive and entirely new environment. Much of an old vocabulary would become useless almost at once and so quickly abandoned, and a new vocabulary would of necessity be produced. In the absence of all the ordinary conservative influences initially slight changes in structure might quickly become pronounced. We are not in position to speak on scientific grounds as to the rapidity with which changes regressive on the one hand and progressive on the other might occur under such conditions before a harmony might be reached between the requirements of a radically new physical and intellectual life and the language. Scarcely a beginning has been made toward the accumulation of data that must be had before final conclusions can be drawn in this field. In the meantime dogmatism is not in place.

2. It is true that the evidence seems to show that the horse was not in America at the time of the discovery by Columbus. The true modern horse, however, was in existence in America after the ice age; and its remains are found contemporaneously with those of men. It is not known precisely when it became extinct on this continent or what mysterious cause may have brought on its apparent obliteration. Geological estimates of time are not reliable within limits at all narrow; and it would be hazardous now to say just how late bands of horses may have lingered. The evidence is far from all in under any conditions.

3. There is no room for doubt that the Jews may have had a knowledge of steel 600 years B.C., in fact it is practically certain that steel implements were known among them and all neighboring peoples. The remains of iron implements manufactured in prehistoric times are so numerous as to leave no question as to the extreme antiquity of the use of that metal. In the time of the Assyrians iron was in extensive use, "saws, knives and other analogous tools having been found by Layard in Nineveh, many of which are very similar to those in use at the present day. Both Homer and Hesiod refer to the forging of iron, whilst the hardening and tempering of steel also appear to have been operations in common use among the early Greeks." (Encyc. Brittanica, 9th ed., XIII, p. 289, etc.)[9] Certainly, then, if the manufacture of steel was commonly understood and practiced among the early Greeks and other early Mediterreanean peoples the possession of a steel bow by a Jew in 600 B.C. would be easily possible and wholly natural.

4. As to the statement "The use of the word 'scimeter' does not occur in other literature before the rise of the Mohammedan power and apparently that peculiar weapon was not developed until long after the

Christian era," it may be said that any question about the particular word 'scimeter' is irrelevant. The question is wholly one as to the early existence of the curved type of sword to which the Mohammedans applied a word which we have adopted. Contrary to the statement made, there is no distinct evidence as to the origin in either time or place of the crescent-shaped Asiatic sword or sabre now commonly indicated under the general term scimeter. It is sufficient, in showing its antiquity, to refer to the fact that in Egypt in the nineteenth dynasty (1350-1205 B.C.) the Pharaoh is represented as fighting: "He even takes place in the hand-to-hand fight and his dagger and sickle-shaped sword are close at hand." (Cf. Erman, *Ancient Egypt,* p. 527).[10] Other similar cases of the picturing of the curved sabre or scimeter in very early times might be given. The implement was known in pre-Christian centuries even as far west as Italy. It was used by the ancient Etruscans. (Cf. Dennis, *The Cities and Cemeteries of Etruria,* I, p. 201, etc.)[11] There is thus no force or foundation for the statement that the curved sword or scimeter was not developed or known "until long after the Christian Era."

5. It is not clear what is meant by the statement: "As silk was not known in America at that time the question arises, where did they obtain the silk?" If the author of the statement means that the Chinese silkworm was not native to America, he is quite right; if he means to infer that there were not in America related forms he is wrong. Several different species of moths have caterpillars which produce silk that has been put to commercial use; but the superiority of the Chinese species has long since led to neglect of the others. However, a civilized people in America might well have found a way to use another form. Furthermore, silk of very fine quality is produced by some spiders and has been made into cloth, notably in the case of spiders of the genus Nephila, several species of which are common from the southern United States southward into South America. While cloth from this source has not been produced among us on a commercial scale, a method of doing so would doubtless be found if we did not have a better source. So far as natural sources are concerned, the Nephites might have had a true silk in any amount. Aside from this there is the possibility that the word may be used in a translation simply as the nearest equivalent of the name of a fabric not used and not known by us. We ourselves have applied it to an artificial product made from wood, etc.

1. Ralph V. Chamberlin, a biologist, was born in Salt Lake City on January 3, 1879. He received a bachelor's degree from the University of Utah in 1898 and a Ph.D. from Cornell in 1904. He taught at the University of Utah, where he was the first dean of the two-year school of medicine; he later joined the faculty of the University of Pennsylvania, leaving there to serve at Harvard University for fifteen years until 1925, when he returned to the University of Utah as the head of the departments of zoology and

botany. He spent a sabbatical year in Mexico and South America studying biology and Indian archaeological records. He died on October 31, 1967. *Salt Lake Tribune,* 1 Nov. 1967.

2. Peter S. Duponceau was the translator from the German of David Zeisberger's, *A Grammar of the Language of the Lenni Lenape, or Delaware Indians,* presented to the American Philosophical Society at Philadelphia on December 2, 1816, vol. 3 (Philadelphia: Printed by James Kay, Jun. & Co., 1830). In his preface to the book Duponceau held that God has given men a natural logic and that, by instinct, they formulate language. More to the point of Chamberlin's reference, Zeisberger wrote that "the astonishing variety of forms of human speech which exists in the eastern hemisphere is not to be found in the western . . . a uniform system . . . seems to pervade them all [American Indian languages]"(76).

3. Alexander von Humboldt's famous essay on New Spain offers the reader some "precise data on a very great variety of important subjects," according to the translator. There is a long "Geographical Introduction," and then the four volumes are divided into six sections: "First Book," a general consideration of the extent and physical aspects of New Spain; "Second Book," the general population and the division of castes; "Third Book," a statistical view of the intendancies, their population and area; "Fourth Book," the state of agriculture and metallic mines; "Fifth Book," the progress of manufactures and commerce; and "Sixth Book," the revenues of the state and the military defense of the country. Alexander von Humboldt, *Political Essay on the Kingdom of New Spain,* trans. J. Black, 4 vols., 2d ed. (London: Longman, Hurst, Rees, Orme, and Brown, and H. Colburn, 1814).

4. Chamberlin could have been referring to the ninety-one-page pamphlet by Heymann Steinthal, *Die Classification der Spracken* (Berlin: Ferd. Dummler's Buchhandlung, 1850), but he probably meant Heymann Steinthal's "On the Origin of Language," *North American Review,* 225 (Apr. 1872):272-308, which was reviewed by W. D. Whitney. The essay is a refined elaboration and summary of Steinthal's work in linguistics and his philosophy of language. It "treats of the ethnological peculiarities of the different families of language," especially that of English, according to Whitney.

5. Daniel G. Brinton was professor of American archaeology at the University of Pennsylvania. In his book, *The American Race,* Brinton wrote that it was the first "attempt at a systematic classification of the whole American race on the basis of language." He emphasized grammar and lexicography and not physical data, culture, or history and was convinced that "the morphology of any language . . . is its most permanent and characteristic feature." The author divided the North American tribes into the North Atlantic group, the North Pacific group, and the Central group. The South American tribes were divided into the South Pacific and South Atlantic groups. The language stocks followed the same classification. Brinton noted that the U.S. Bureau of Ethnology recognized fifty-nine stocks in that portion of the continent north of Mexico. Daniel G. Brinton, *The American Race: A Linguistic and Ethnographic Description of the Native Tribes of North and South America* (Philadelphia: D. McKay, 1901).

Roberts owned a copy of the book, now in the L.D.S. Archives, which is liberally marked with such marginal notes as: p. 51—"No domestic animals"; p. 156—"Carving without iron or even copper"; p. 156—Brinton wrote, "Cotton was woven into fabrics of such delicacy that the Spaniards at first thought the stuffs *were of silk,*" and Roberts underlined the last three words; and among two pages of notes on the back end sheets, Roberts noted: "The Toltecs important gents 129," and "The *Stone Age.* Had *not* reached age of metals—p. 51."

6. F. Max Müller, *Chips from a German Workshop,* 5 vols. (New York: Charles Scribner's Sons, 1887). In volume 4, Müller uses the Iroquois language as reference to examine the science of language in this series of eight lectures, of which Lecture 2 deals with "On the Stratification of Language" and Lecture 4 discusses "Results of the Science of Language." See also F. Max Müller, *Lectures on the Science of Language,* delivered at the Royal Institution of Great Britain in 1861 and 1863, 2 vols. (New York: C. Scribner, 1866).

7. Gabriel Sagard-Théodat, *Le grand voyage des pays des Hurons, situé en l'Amerique*

vers la mer douce, e's derniers confins de la Nouvelle France, dite Canada (Paris: Chez Denys Moreau, 1632). Sagard was a lay brother in an ascetic order and, in the twenty-two chapters of his book, covers almost every aspect of Huron life, with exceptional powers of description. The appendix includes the account of the Huron language, which is more a phrase book rather than a dictionary. With the exception of Jacques Cartier's brief vocabulary, Sagard's book contains the first published account of the Huron language. For a more recent edition of the work, see Father Gabriel Sagard, *The Long Journey to the Country of the Hurons,* ed. George M. Wrong and trans. H. H. Langton (Toronto: Champlain Society, 1939).

8. At least two of Beauchamp's books would have been available to Chamberlin: William Martin Beauchamp, *The Iroquois trail, or Foot-prints of the Six nations, in customs, traditions, and history* (Fayetteville, N.Y.: Printed by H. C. Beauchamp, 1892); and William Martin Beauchamp, *A History of the New York Iroquois, now commonly called the Six Nations* (Albany, N.Y.: New York State Education Department, 1905). A third book appeared in 1922: William Martin Beauchamp, *Iroquois Folk Lore Gathered from the Six Nations of New York.* Selected and arranged by the Rev. Wm. M. Beauchamp . . . for the Onondaga Historical Association (Syracuse, N.Y.: Dehler Press, 1922).

9. *The Encyclopaedia Britannica,* New Werner ed. (Akron, Ohio, 1904).

10. Adolf Erman, *Life in Ancient Egypt,* trans. Helen Mary Tirard (New York: Macmillan, 1894). The book was a popular work on the manners and customs of ancient Egypt designed for the English public. Page 527 is concerned with a discussion of war as "the highest good for the country."

11. George Dennis, *The Cities and Cemeteries of Etruria,* 2d ed., 2 vols. (London: John Murray, 1883). The purpose of the book was to describe the antiquities of Etruria and to serve as a guide to those who wanted to visit the remains of Etrurian civilization. On p. 201, the author described a "short curved sword" and indicated that similar curved swords were represented on several Etrurian monuments.

William E. Riter to B. H. Roberts

Logan Utah   Dec. 20-1921

Dear Elder Roberts:

Last September I left a set of questions concerning the book of Mormon with Dr. Talmage. These questions were submitted to me by Mr. Couch of Washington D.C. who is very desirous of hearing from them. Doc. Talmage wrote me some time ago and explained that he had turned them over to you for consideration. I appreciate the fact that you are very busy indeed, but if in due time you can give this set of questions consideration I will be very glad.

Respectfully
Wm. E. Riter

B. H. Roberts to William E. Riter

Salt Lake City, Utah, Dec 28/1921

My Dear Brother —

Answering card of inquiry about the Couch Book of Mormon questions will say that I have been engaged upon an investigation of the

problems involved during the past several weeks, but have not yet reached
conclusions that serve as a basis upon which to formulate my answer.

I expect to continue to give attention to the subject and as soon
as may be will make answer to the matter submitted to me.

Very truly yours,

B. H. Roberts to Heber J. Grant[1] and Counsellors, the Quorum of the Twelve Apostles, and the First Council of the Seventy

Salt Lake City, Utah, Dec. 29, 1921

Dear Brethren —

Early in the month of November, Elder James E. Talmage referred
to me for consideration and answer, the letters that here follow and that
will be self-explanatory:

I very gladly undertook the task of considering the question here
propounded, and hope to find answers that would be satisfactory. With
some branches of the field of inquiry I was more or less familiar, having
devoted some attention to them while writing my Book of Mormon
treatise under the title *New Witnesses for God;*[2] and while knowing that
some parts of my treatment of Book of Mormon problems in that work
had not been altogether as convincing as I would like to have seen them,
I still believed that reasonable explanations could be made that would
keep us in advantageous possession of the field. As I proceeded with my
recent investigations, however, and more especially in the, to me, new
field of language problems, I found the difficulties more serious than I
had thought for; and the more I investigated the more difficult I found
the formulation of an answer to Mr. Couch's inquiries to be. I therefore
concluded not to undertake an answer to his questions on my own
account, but decided to make a study of all the problems he submitted —
somewhat enlarging upon them as I proceeded — and then submit the
result of my investigations to all of you who are addressed at the head
of this communication, that from the greater learning of the individual
members of the Quorum of the Twelve, or from the collective widsom
of all the brethren addressed, or from the inspiration of the Lord as it
may be received through the appointed channels of the priesthood of
his Church, we might find such a solution of the problems presented in
the accompanying correspondence, as will maintain the reasonableness
for the faith of all in the Nephite scriptures, as well the faith of those

who with us accept it now, and are assured of its essential truth, as those who are investigating its truth and its message.

I trust I am not manifesting an over anxiety in presenting to you so extensive an inquiry as this paper proposes — 141 type written pages — but I assure you that I am most thoroughly convinced of the necessity of all the brethren herein addressed becoming familiar with these Book of Mormon problems, and finding the answer for them, as it is a matter that will concern the faith of the Youth of the Church now as also in the future, as well as such casual inquirers as may come to us from the outside world.

All which is respectfully submitted,[3]

1. Heber J. Grant, seventh president of the Church of Jesus Christ of Latter-day Saints, was born in Salt Lake City, November 22, 1856, the son of Jedediah M. Grant, early Church leader and a companion of Joseph Smith. The father died when the boy was only nine days old. Heber became a prominent businessman in the western United States and was named an apostle of the Church at twenty-five.

2. Brigham H. Roberts, *New Witnesses for God*, 3 vols. (Salt Lake City: The Deseret News, 1909).

3. In his cover letter of December 29, 1921, to President Heber J. Grant, Elder Roberts added to his typed copy a handwritten note referring to a "Discourse by President Brigham Young," delivered at a special conference held at Farmington, Utah, June 17, 1877, in *Journal of Discourses, reported by D. W. Evans, George F. Gibbs, and others,* 19 (Liverpool: Printed and Published by William Budge, 1878), 36-39. In this sermon Brigham Young recounted an experience of Oliver Cowdery, who had accompanied Joseph Smith to return the Book of Mormon gold plates to the hill Cumorah: "When Joseph got the plates, the angel instructed him to carry them back to the hill Cumorah, which he did. Oliver says that when Joseph and Oliver went there, the hill opened, and they walked into a cave, in which there was a large and spacious room. . . . They laid the plates on a table; it was a large table that stood in the room. Under this table there was a pile of plates as much as two feet high, and there were altogether in this room more plates than probably many wagon loads; they were piled up in the corners and along the walls. . . . I tell you this as coming not only from Oliver Cowdery, but others who were familiar with it. . . . Now, you may think I am unwise in publicly telling these things, thinking perhaps I should preserve them in my own breast; but such is not my mind. I would like the people called Latter-day Saints to understand some little things with regard to the workings and dealings of the Lord with his people here upon the earth."

B. H. Roberts to Heber J. Grant

Jan. 9, 1922

Dear Brother: —

At the close of your remarks following the long day's conference had on the Book of Mormon problems, I arose to make some remarks in relation to what I had listened to throughout the day. But realizing that the hour was late and that everybody was tired, I desisted and concluded to let matters go. Thinking of it since, however, and of the probability of a record being made of the hearing I concluded that I would not like that record to be made without having included in it my impressions of what was said and the suggestions that were made — hence this note which I limit to the very briefest space that will express my view in relation to the results of our consultation.

Permit me to say, then, but in the utmost good will and profound respect for everybody else's opinion, that I was very greatly disappointed over the net results of the discussion. There was so much said that was utterly irrelevant, and so little said, if anything at all, that was helpful in the matters at issue that I came away from the conference quite disappointed. All the facts and arguments that were proposed, outside of the matter of linguistics, I had already made the utmost use of in the third volume of my *New Witness for God,* as may be determined by reference to the part dealing with "Objections to the Book of Mormon."[1] While on the difficulties of linguistics nothing was said that could result to our advantage at all or stand the analysis of enlightened criticism. You perhaps may think differently because of what was said by President Ivins.[2] Referring to that I shall make bold to say, though I trust without giving offense, for that is farthest from my purpose, that what he said, so far as it had any bearing upon the problems before us was most disappointing of all, because I had come to believe from what I had heard of him, that he has so specialized in the Book of Mormon and literature bearing upon it, that one could confidently expect something like substantial help from his contribution of comment. It was this perhaps that made his contribution so disappointing.

You will perhaps remember that what Bro. Ivins chiefly relied upon to satisfy his mind so completely, with reference to our linguistic difficulties was Dr. Le Plongeon's "Maya Alphabet," published in his *Sacred Mysteries Among the Mayas and Quiches,"*[3] and reproduced, photographically, by me in the third volume of *New Witness* (p. 507). If I were now writing my *New Witness* with the larger knowledge of Dr. Le Plongeon's standing as an investigator of and writer upon American Antiquities I would not quote his work even in the very incidental way in which I then used it; much less to use it as Bro. Ivins does to satisfy himself completely in relation to Book of Mormon linguistic difficulties. I am glad he limited the application of Le Plongeon's Alphabet to the complete satisfying of himself, also that even that statement was made where it would not be open to the comment of unfriendly critics who would so easily turn it to ridicule. The facts are that even while Le Plongeon's investigations were in progress and reported from time to time they were discredited by authorities who are certainly accepted as reliable in this field of research. John T. Short, author of *North Americans of Antiquity,* Harper Bros. N.Y., 1880,[4] writes of him — and this before some of his wildest notions were known: — "We cannot refrain from expressing regret that Dr. Le Plongeon's enthusiasm is so apparent in his reports. A judicial frame of mind as well as calmness which accompanies it are requisites both for scientific work and the inspiration of confidence in the reader." (Above work, p. 396-7).

Commenting on Le Plongeon's statements respecting languages, Short says: "He does not hesitate to say that the Maya, containing words from almost every language ancient and modern is well worth the attention of philologists," etc. Referring to its antiquity he (Le Plongeon) says: "I must speak of that language which has survived unaltered through the vicissitudes of the nations that spoke it thousands of years ago, and is yet the general tongue in Yucatan, the Maya. . . . It was used by a people that lived at least 6,000 years ago." "With Mr. Bancroft," says Mr. Short, "we agree that no value can be attached to these speculations, until impartial comparisons are made by scholars who have no theory to substantiate." (Ibid., p. 276).

Mr. E. A. Allen, author of *Pre-historic Races*[5] criticises much to the same effect, and more in his computation of time, and supplies the evidence that throws doubt upon the speculations of Le Plongeon (see above work, p. 658-666). Mr. Allen's standing in this field of knowledge may be judged in part by the list of highly learned men to who various parts of his work was submitted; which list is published on the title page of his book.

Desire Charnay, writing in the *North American Review* for October, 1880, is perhaps the most pronounced in the condemnation of Le Plongeon.[6] He quotes two native Mexican (or Spanish) writers in refutation as to his interpretation of statues which afford Le Plongeon his chief characters of Queen Moo — saying in conclusion — "We hold ourselves to be justified in rejecting as absolutely erroneous and baseless, the name Chac-Mool given by Le Plongeon to the Yucatan Statue." And with the rightfulness of Le Plongeon's interpretation of that statue gone, falls all the fabric of his speculations. Charnay himself commenting on both the Abbe Bourbourg[7] and Le Plongeon, in this same article, says: "Some of these writers comment with deserved severity upon the mad theories of the Abbe Bourbourg, who finds in one of the codices (native books) evidence that the current geological theory was originated by the Mayas 100,000 years ago. Others hardly deign to notice the childish fancies of Le Plongeon who finds that the electric telegraph was in use among the Mayas."

When I visited "Dr." Le Plongeon in Brooklyn, many years ago, I think in 1896, I found him living in very unhappy circumstances of wretchedness. His sole companion then in his forbidding lodgings was a half witted woman — what their relations were I do not know, but she was evidently the scrub woman — for such was her work on my arrival — and was, as he informed me, his medium in receiving spirit communications under direction. He proposed for me a sceance, which, of course, I declined. My visit to the "Dr." and learning then and through him how impossible it was for him to get any recognition for his views from any source of scientific standing, led me to doubt of the value of his investigations.

I think Bro. Ivins, too, will find it necessary to change his views respecting the extent of Nephite literature. While of course no one assumes that the Nephites had a literature in the modern sense of that term, and since the printing press, but they had a literature equal to that of the Jews, previous to the Babylonian capativity, in comparison with their numbers; or the Egyptians, or the Babylonians under the same limits, i.e. according to their number. I think Bro. Ivins must have omitted from consideration in presenting his views on the limitations of Nephite literature, Helaman 3:13-16; and Alma 13:20; 14:1 and 8.[8] If the conditions existed as to scriptures in Ammoniah as there represented, there is no reason why they would not so exist in other cities.

This letter is becoming much longer than I intended. I just wanted the brethren to know that I was quite disappointed in the results of our conference, but not withstanding I shall be most earnestly alert upon the subject of Book of Mormon difficulties, hoping for the development of new knowledge, and for new light to fall upon what has already been learned, to the vindication of what God has revealed in the Book of Mormon; but I cannot be other than painfully conscious of the fact that our means of defense, should we be vigorously attacked along the lines of Mr. Couch's questions, are very inadequate.

Very truly your brother,

1. Roberts, *New Witnesses for God*, 3:407-561.

2. Anthony W. Ivins was born September 16, 1852, at Toms River, Ocean County, New Jersey, and came to Utah with his parents in 1853. He moved with his parents to St. George, Utah, where he became one of the prominent civic and Church leaders. In 1875-76 he served an L.D.S. mission to New Mexico, Arizona, and Mexico; he later worked as a missionary among the Navajo and Pueblo Indians; and in 1895 he was placed in charge of the Mormon Church interests in Mexico as president of the Juarez Stake. He was appointed a member of the Council of the Twelve Apostles on October 6, 1907, became a Second Counsellor to President Grant, and was appointed First Counsellor on May 28, 1925. He died September 23, 1934. *Deseret News*, 23 Sept. 1934; Jenson, *Latter-day Saint Biographical Encyclopedia*, 3:750-52.

3. Augustus Le Plongeon, *Sacred Mysteries Among the Mayas and the Quiches* (New York: Robert Macoy, 1886). Le Plongeon's purpose in writing this book was to present "some of the historical facts that have been brought to light by deciphering the bas-reliefs and mural inscriptions, by means of the ancient hieratic Maya alphabet discovered by me." In his *New Witnesses for God*, 3:507, Roberts reproduced a table included on p. xii of Le Plongeon's work, comparing characters of the Maya hieratic alphabet with those of the Egyptian hieratic alphabet; there were some similarities. Ten years after the

publication of the *Sacred Mysteries*, Le Plongeon published *Queen Moo and the Egyptian Sphinx* (New York: Published by the Author, 1896). This was a study of the ancient Maya relics, which supposedly revealed striking similarities between Mayan culture and that of the ancient civilizations of Asia, Africa, and Europe. The author believed that these similarities were the result of "intimate communications" between the Maya and the Eastern civilizations. According to his book, Queen Moo, the widow of Osiris, the murdered king of Egypt, fled to the Maya colonies "that for many years had been established on the banks of the Nile." Moo became queen of these colonies. Maya archives explain the inscriptions on the Sphinx, which can be read with the aid of a Maya dictionary. It is little wonder that Le Plongeon had to publish the book himself.

4. John T. Short, *The North Americans of Antiquity: Their Origin, Migrations, and Type of Civilization Considered*, 3rd ed. (New York: Harper & Brothers, 1882). The book compares evidence from the mound-builders and the Pueblo cliff dwellings with the traditional history and civilization of the ancient races of Mexico and Central America to determine how they influenced each other. In twelve chapters the author offers a manual of information concerning the earliest period of North American antiquity, an introduction to ancient American history.

5. E. A. Allen, *The Prehistoric World: or, Vanished Races* (Cincinnati: Central Publishing House, 1885).

6. Désiré Charnay, "The Ruins of Central America," *North American Review*, 287 (Oct. 1880):301-21. Charnay describes three Yucatan statues, which he says are identical, and writes, "The Indian Bacchus, Tezcatzoncatl or Izquitecatl, called by Le Plongeon Chacmaal" (303). Later Charnay published *The Ancient Cities of the New World: Being Voyages and Explorations in Mexico and Central America from 1857-1882*, trans. J. Gonino and Helen S. Conant (New York: Harper & Brothers, 1887). The author's expedition to the area involved a "careful reproduction of Central American monuments and a systematic investigation of the so-called 'ruined cities' and other remains of ancient civilization in Central America and Mexico." He hoped that his book demonstrated that the ancient American civilizations had a single origin — "that they were Toltec and comparatively modern."

7. Charles E'tienne Brasseur de Bourbourg, *Histoire des nations civilisées du Mexique et de l'Amérique-Centrale*, 4 vols. (Paris: Arthur Bertrand, 1857). The work is concerned with the history of the Ten Lost Tribes and attempts to prove similarities between the cultures of Egypt and Mexico, citing the Atlantis theory that the continent of North America once extended across the Atlantic Ocean as far as the Canary Islands. Other scholars besides Charnay ridiculed his ideas, Hubert H. Bancroft calling his theories "long, rambling digressions."

8. Of the typed and marginal handwritten notes by Roberts concerned with the extent of Nephite literature, his best reference is the first cited, Helaman 3:13-16, which comments on the records kept by the people "which are particular and very large" and are only "a hundreth part of proceedings of this people."

B. H. Roberts to William E. Riter

Feb. 6, 1922

Dear Sir:

Your letter of Aug. 22nd to Dr. Talmage with accompanying inclosure from Mr. Couch, was referred to me for consideration owing to the necessary absence of Dr. Talmage from the state, shortly after your letter was received. I regret that it has not been possible until now for me to send you the following reply to the questions submitted by Mr. Couch.

It must be admitted that the questions of Mr. Couch respecting American languages and the Book of Mormon present a problem, but not one that may be unsolvable. The solution seems to hinge upon the time element necessary for the production of the differentiation in the language stocks of the American race as now known. Mr. Couch holds that the time period allowed by the Book of Mormon, which he states to be 2,700 years, is not sufficient to produce this variation from some common source. This becomes then a question of the rapidity or slowness with which languages may change.

It should be held in mind that the Book of Mormon notes the changes that had taken place in the language of Book of Mormon peoples even while there were those among them capable of reducing it to written form, a thousand years previous to the discovery of America. This, however, respecting the written languages (see the Book of Mormon—within the Book of Mormon—ch. 9:32).[1] Changes in oral language, unaccompanied by written language—which, so far as known, was the case with American peoples in the thousand years following the closing up of the Nephite period to the coming of Columbus—would take place more rapidly, and would be more pronounced. An illustration of this is given in the Book of Mormon. It tells of a colony leaving Jerusalem about eleven years after the Lehi colony left that city, and who for two hundred or for two hundred and fifty years were settled in the New World before coming into contact with Lehi's people. This colony, known as the colony of Mulek, had brought no records with them, from Jerusalem, no books, had no written language, and when discovered by their race kindred, the Nephites, their language had been so changed in that two hundred or two hundred and fifty years, that they could not understand each other (See Book of Omni in the Book of Mormon—1:14-19).

Authorities are not agreed upon the time element required for producing diversity in languages. The Marquise de Nadaillac in his *Pre-Historic America*,[2] in discussing the character of American language says: "Their diversity may be accounted for by the constant crossing of races, migrations, and by the new customs and ideas which gradually become introduced even amongst the most degraded peoples; still more by the well recognized instability and mobility of many aboriginal languages." Then he adds that which seems almost improbable: "Some missionaries say they have found the language of tribes revisited after an absence of ten years completely changed in the interim." (*Pre-Historic America*, pp. 6, 7.)

John Fiske,[3] on the same subject, says: "The speech of uncivilized tribes when not subject to the powerful conservative force of widespread custom or permanent tradition, changes with astonishing rapidity. Referring to the case of a group small enough to use but one language, and then breaking up—under such circumstances he notes that "the dialects," resulting from such a breaking up, "would change so rapidly as to loose their identity; within a couple of centuries it would be impossible to detect any resemblance to the language of the primitive tribe." He remarks further that "the facility with which savage tongues abandon old expression for new has no parallel in civilized languages, unless it be in the more ephemeral kinds of slang. It is sufficiently clear, I think, under such circumstances that a language will seldom or never acquire sufficient stability to give rise to mutually resembling dialects. If the habits of primitive men were in general similar to those of modern savages, we need not wonder that philologists are unable to trace all existing languages back to a common origin." In evidence of this tendency among savage tribes to changes in language quickly, he first cites the fact that in civilized speech "no words stick like the simple numerals; we use the same words today, in counting from one to ten that our ancestors used in central Asia ages before the winged bulls of Nineveh were sculptured; and the change in pronunciation has been barely sufficient to disguise the identity. But in the language of Tahiti, four of the ten simple numerals used in Captain Cooke's time have already become extinct: —

> Two was rua; it is now piti.
> Four was ha; it is now maha.
> Five was rima; it is now pao.
> Six was ono; it is now feno.
> (*Excursion of an Evolutionist,* pp. 155-6).[4]

In addition to this evidence for the rapidity with which language may change, there is a thousand years from the close of what may be called the Book of Mormon period to the coming of Columbus, in which period there may have been immigrations to the American continents of other peoples from Europe or Africa, or from Asia or the Polynesian Island; and it will not be necessary to remind Mr. Couch that the literature of American race origins abounds with the urgency of such infusions; and I may assure him that there is nothing in the Book of Mormon that pronounces against the possibility of infusions of such peoples, and the consequent modifications of native American languages, or even the creation of language stocks and dialects in the New World, by reason of such immigrations.

Moreover, there is also the possibility that other peoples may have inhabited parts of the great continents of America, contemporaneously with the peoples spoken of by the Book of Mormon, though candor compels me to say that nothing to that effect appears in the Book of

Mormon. A number of our Book of Mormon students, however, are inclined to believe that Book of Mormon peoples were restricted to much narrower limits in their habitat on the American continents, than have generally been allowed; and that they were not in South America at all.

If this be true, it might allow of other great stretches of the continents to be inhabited by other peoples, with other cultures and languages, which would still further tend to solve the difficulties of the Book of Mormon in regard to the existence of the great diversity of language stocks among the American race.

In relation to iron and steel among Book of Mormon peoples and the existence of the horse in America, matters referred to by Mr. Couch, I refer to my consideration of these subjects in New Witnesses for God (Vol. III pp. 524-542), a copy of which I am sending under separate cover, as part of this communication, and which I ask you to forward to Mr. Couch with the report you make to him of this letter.

Relative to the word "cimeter" in the Book of Mormon, no great difficulty attaches to that at all for the reason that it is a word used in the translation by Joseph Smith in the early decades of the 19th century, and may have been used by him as a descriptive term for a peculiar shaped sword among the Nephites, which may or may not have been after the shape of the Mohammedan weapon of post Christian times.

Mr. Couch's remarks in relation to "silk" among Book of Mormon peoples, also presents no serious difficulty. The manufacture of silk is of great antiquity. It was an industry in China before the empress So-ling-she encouraged the cultivation of the mulberry tree in aid of it—2,640 B.C.—; about which time also she invented the silk weaving loom. If this Chinese chronology be allowed then silk was known even before the Jaredites—the earliest Book of Mormon people—left the Old World for the New, and they may have brought knowledge of the fabric and its manufacture with them. Silk was also known to the Hebrews a thousand years before Christ. Of the good wife, the writer of Proverbs says, "Her clothing is silk and purple" (Proverbs 31:22). This according to Usher in 1015 B.C..

It will be said, however, that silk is unknown among the Americans, and it must be conceded that generally that seems to be taken for granted, and chiefly for the reason, I would say, of the absence of the fabric from among the natives when discovered by Europeans, and for lack of evidences of its existence among their discovered antiquities. The absence of silk among the natives when discovered by the Europeans could be accounted for by the debacle which overtook the Nephite civilization at the close of the fourth century, A.D. when the art of producing silk, together with many other arts, may have been lost. And the lack of its existence in native American antiquities, could be accounted for by the perishable nature of the fabric, as I am assured, by those competent to speak on the matter, that the chemical elements of silk are such that when compared with cotton, for instance the former might perish while the latter would persist. Of this however, I am not competent to speak from my own knowledge.

There seems to be no room for doubt but that the native races had the necessary skill to weave silk. Of the weaving art in South America Mr. Wissler, author of *The American Indian*[5] says that "Taxes, fines and tributes were levied in fine cloth. As to the qualities, we have not only the testimony of early observers, but in the desert burial grounds of Peru we have immense store houses of prehistoric cloth preserved completely in the original forms and colors. Recent studies of museum collections by a textile expert have shown that the fineness of weave exceeds that of any other part of the world. As to forms of weave, we find the same techniques as in the Old World, even to pile and gauze."

Mr. W. H. Holmes,[6] speaking of the Maya-Quiche area says of textile art; "Few traces of the textile art have been spared, but judging by the sculptural and pictorial representations, the costumes of the people were among the most elaborate that the world has ever known." From this it would appear that weaving skill was not lacking among native races to produce even silk. Prescott in a foot note discussing the supposed knowledge of silk among the natives, says:

"It is doubtful how far they were acquainted with the manufacture of silk. Carli supposes that what Cortes calls silk was only the fine texture of hair, or down, mentioned in the text. (*Lettres Americ.*, tom. I. let. 71) But it is certain they had a species of caterpillar, unlike our silkworm, indeed which spun a thread that was sold in the markets of ancient Mexico." (*Conquest of Mexico*, Vol. I p. 117).[7]

Believing that this, with the indicated printed matter I send you covers the problems suggested in the notes of Mr. Couch.

I am most truly yours,

---

1. "Book of Mormon," in Book of Mormon, 9:32: "And now, behold, we have written this record according to our knowledge, in the characters which are called among us the reformed Egyptian, being handed down and altered by us, according to our manner of speech."

2. Marquis de Jean François Albert du Pouget Nadaillac, *Pre-Historic America*, trans. N. d'Auvers [pseud.] and ed. W. H. Dall (New York: G. P. Putnam's Sons, 1885). See also marquis de Nadaillac, *Pre-Historic America*, trans. by N. D'Auvers (New York: G. P. Putnam's Sons, Knickerbocker Press, 1893). The original French edition was published in 1882 by Masson.

3. John Fiske, *The Discovery of America*, 3 vols. (Cambridge, Mass.: Riverside Press, 1902). Volume 1 has two themes: to awaken Americans to the interest and importance of American archeology for the study of the evolution of human society and to describe

the discovery of America. The first volume is divided into four chapters: 1, "Ancient America"; 2, "Pre-Columbian Voyages"; 3, "Europe and Cathay"; and 4, "The Search for the Indies."

4. John Fiske, *Excursions of an Evolutionist*, 16th ed. (Boston: Houghton, Mifflin, 1894). Of the fourteen chapters in this book, Roberts was apparently particularly interested in chapter 5, "Was There a Primeval Mother-tongue?," which discusses the derivation of a dozen languages from a common ancestor as a temporary and local phenomenon in the history of human speech and not as a permanent or universal fact. According to Fiske, when one language produces several descendants of similar characteristics, it must have "a high degree of permanence and a wide extension. It must be spoken for a long time by large bodies of men spread over a wide territorial area."

5. Clark Wissler, *The American Indian* (New York: Douglas C. McMurtrie, 1917). This work was a general summary of anthropological research in North and South America. Wissler was a museum curator who became interested in classifying and "objectifying" the essential facts concerning aboriginal America. Of the thirty-one chapters, Roberts was apparently especially interested in Chapter 2, "Domestication of Animals"; Chapter 3, "Textile Arts"; Chapter 7, "Work in Stone and Metals"; Chapter 13, "Mythology"; Chapter 17, "Linguistic Classification"; Chapter 20, "Theories of Culture Origin"; and Chapter 21, "New World Origins."

6. William H. Holmes, *Handbook of Aboriginal American Antiquities*, Smithsonian Institution, Bureau of American Ethnology, Bulletin 60 (Washington, D.C.: Government Printing Office, 1919). This reference work or manual of thirty-six chapters attempts to assemble and present the antiquities of North and South America in a manner which would be understandable and usable for students interested in the evolution of cultures. The volume is specifically concerned with the scope of archeological science, the origins of race, migrations, chronology, cultural evolution, the development of arts, and the use of implements.

7. William H. Prescott, *History of the Conquest of Mexico*, 3 vols. (Philadelphia: David McKay, 1891). The first volume has an introduction that deals with the antiquities and origin of the Mexican nation. Book 1 of Volume 1 examines the geography and climate, primitive races, and the Aztec empire with a detailed look at Aztec culture and history. Book 2 discusses the discovery and conquest of Mexico by Cortes.

William E. Riter to B. H. Roberts

Logan Utah   Feb. 27-1921[1]

Dear Mr. Roberts:

I want to take this occasion to thank you for the answers to the Couch Book of Mormon questions which in my mind were very well answered. I have forwarded them to Mr. Couch at Washington D.C. I have another question in my mind which I would appreciate very much if you could favor me with an explanation.

"Why can not the Negro hold the Priesthood?" I understand that our church does not ordain a negro to the Priesthood on account of the curse put upon Caine. The question arises, "Why should this race suffer on account of Caine's sin?" On page 2 of "The Essentials of Church History" the following statement occurs. "It was therefore essential that a Redeemer be provided through whose atonement for the fall, all men, without regard to their belief, *race* or color, are entitled to come forth in the resurrection of the dead, to be judged according to their works."[2]

Through the atonement of Christ was not also the sins of Caine washed away and the heavens opened to all mankind? There has been some confusion in my mind on this subject and I would appreciate very much if you would clear it up for me.[3]

Respectfully
Wm. E. Riter

1. This date should read Feb. 27, 1922.
2. Joseph Fielding Smith, *Essentials in Church History* (Salt Lake City: Deseret News Press, 1922). Joseph Fielding Smith, a son of Mormon president Joseph F. Smith, was named an apostle on April 7, 1910, and served as president of the Church from January 23, 1970, until his death on July 2, 1972. His one-volume work, *The Essentials in Church History*, has gone through many editions and has been widely used as a textbook in the priesthood quorums, Church schools, and auxiliary organizations of the Mormon Church.
3. Riter died in 1953. And not until much later, in a Dec. 29, 1979, article reviewing momentous changes of the 1970s in the Mormon Church, did the *Deseret News* proclaim: "One of the major events of the 70's was a revelation announced June 9, 1978, extending the priesthood to all worthy males—thereby allowing black men to hold the priesthood."

B. H. Roberts to Heber J. Grant, Council, and Quorum of Twelve Apostles[1]

Salt Lake City, Utah, March, 15th 1923 [1922][2]

Dear Brethren:

You will perhaps remember that during the hearing on "Problems of the Book of Mormon" reported to your Council January, 1922, I stated in my remarks that there were other problems which I thought should be considered in addition to those submitted in my report. Brother Richard R. Lyman asked if they would help solve the problems already presented, or if they would increase our difficulties. My answer was that they would very greatly increase our difficulties, on which he replied, "Then I do not know why we should consider them." My answer was, however, that it was my intention to go on with the consideration to the last analysis. Accordingly, since the matter was already so far under my hand, I continued my studies, and submit herewith the record of them. I do not say my conclusions, for they are undrawn.

In writing out this my report to you of those studies, I have written it from the viewpoint of an open mind, investigating the facts of the Book of Mormon origin and authorship. Let me say once and for all, so as to avoid what might otherwise call for repeated explanation, that what is herein set forth does not represent any conclusions of mine. This report herewith submitted is what it purports to be, namely a "study of Book of Mormon origins," for the information of those who ought to know everything about it *pro et con,* as well that which has been produced against it, and that which may be produced against it. I am taking the position that our faith is not only unshaken but unshakable in the Book of Mormon, and therefore we can look without fear upon all that can be said against it.

While searching for the answers to the questions of Mr. Couch, submitted through Mr. William E. Riter, I came in contact with the material here used, and concluded that while the subject was fresh in my mind to make it of record for those who should be its students and know on what ground the Book of Mormon may be questioned, as well as that which supports its authenticity and its truth.

If it is impossible for the General Authorities to consider this whole matter together, then, I submit that it might be referred to the committee you appointed to consider with me the answers to be given Mr. Couch, namely, Elders Ivins, Talmage, and Widtsoe,[3] with a request that they report on the same. I am very sure that you will find the material herewith submitted of intense interest, and it may be of very great importance since it represents what may be used by some opponent in criticism of the Book of Mormon.

It is not necessary for me to suggest that maintenance of the truth of the Book of Mormon is absolutely essential to the integrity of the whole Mormon movement, for it is inconceivable that the Book of Mormon should be untrue in its origin or character and the Church of Jesus Christ of Latter-day Saints be a true Church.

All which is respectfully submitted.

Very truly your brother,

1. Roberts indicated to Richard R. Lyman in his letter of Oct. 24, 1927, that this letter was never sent.

2. The date should read 1922. See note 65 to the Introduction of the present volume.

3. John A. Widtsoe was born January 31, 1872, on the island of Froen in Norway and came to Utah in 1883 with his widowed mother and a brother. He received a B.A. degree from Harvard University and a Ph.D. from the University of Gottingen, Germany, and served as president of both the Utah State Agricultural College and the University of Utah, leaving the latter position in 1921 to become an apostle in the Church. During the 1920s he was probably the most noted scientist in the Church, being widely recognized for his research and writing in the fields of irrigation and dry-farming. He also wrote extensively about Mormon theology, including a treatise entitled *Seven Claims of the Book of Mormon.* He died in 1952. Salt Lake *Tribune,* Nov. 30, 1952.

B. H. Roberts to Richard R. Lyman

October 24, 1927

Dear Brother Lyman:

You perhaps will recall our conversation of a few days ago in relation to the inquiry we had before the Council of the Twelve Apostles on some problems associated with the Book of Mormon, just previous to my commencing my mission in the Eastern States,[1] and how I reminded you that on the former occassion here alluded to I announced that what I had presented did not constitute all our B. of M. problems, that there were others. You then asked, "Well, will these help solve our present problems or will it increase our difficulties?" to which I replied, "It would very greatly increase our problems." At which you said (and I thought rather lightly) "Well, I don't see why we should bother with them then." To this I answered that I should go on with my studies nevertheless. And the other day I told you, if you remember, that I had continued my investigations and had drawn up a somewhat lengthy report for the First Presidency and the Council of the Twelve. Then came my call to the Eastern States and the matter was dropped, but my report was drawn up nevertheless together with a letter that I had intended should accompany it, but in the hurry of getting away and the impossibility at that time of having my report considered, I dropped the matter, and have not yet decided whether I shall present that report to the First Presidency or not. But since I mentioned this matter to you the other day, and also because you took considerable interest on the former occasion of more than five years ago and wrote letter to Professor Chamberlain and Dr. Middleton and others about the subject, I thought I would submit in sort of tabloid form a few pages of matter pointing out a possible theory of the Origin of the Book of Mormon that is quite unique and never seems to have occurred to anyone to employ, largely on account of the obscurity of the material on which it might be based, but which in the hands of a skillful opponent could be made, in my judgment, very embarrassing.

I submit it in the form of a Parallel between some main outline facts pertaining to the Book of Mormon and matter that was published in Ethan Smith's "View of the Hebrews" which preceded the Book of Mormon, the first edition by eight years, and the second edition by five years, 1823-5 respectively.[2] It was published in Vermont and in the adjoining county in which the Smith Family lived in the Prophet Joseph's boyhood days, so that it could be urged that the family doubtless had this book in their possession, as the book in two editions flooded the New England States and New York.

In addition to this publication of such matter Josiah Priest published at Rochester, N.Y., twenty miles from Palmyra his first work on American Antiquities, under the title of "The Wonders of Nature and Providence."[3] This in 1824, six years before the publication of the Book of Mormon and within twenty miles of Palmyra. And in this book Mr. Priest quotes very copiously from the "View of the Hebrews" and quite extensively from Humboldt's "New Spain" which was published in translation into English, and largely circulated throughout the United States in 1811.

Necessarily the matter presented is rather large in volume, but I hope its interest will excuse its length, will ask you to consider it from this view point. Suppose it to be submitted to you as a question in this form:

"The Origin of the Book of Mormon:—Did Ethan Smith's *View of the Hebrews*, published eight and five years before Joseph Smith's Book of Mormon, Supply the Structural Outline and some of the Subject Matter of the Alleged Nephite Record?"

Such a question as that may possibly arise some day, and if it does, it would be greatly to the advantage of our future Defenders of the Faith, if they had in hand a thorough digest of the subject matter. I submit it to you and if you are sufficiently interested you may submit it to others of your Council. Let me say also, that the Parallel that I send to you is not one fourth part of what can be presented in this form, and the unpresented part is quite as striking as this that I submit.[4]

Very truly yours,

1. Roberts served as president of the Eastern States Mission from May 1922 to April 1927. The headquarters were located in New York City.

2. Ethan Smith, *View of the Hebrews* (Poultney, Vt.: Smith & Shute, 1823); Ethan Smith, *View of the Hebrews,* 2d ed. (Poultney, Vt.: Smith & Shute, 1825).

3. As Roberts indicates, the first edition of Josiah Priest's book, *The Wonders of Nature and Providence Displayed,* was published at Rochester, New York, in 1824. The *National Union Catalog* does not list this first edition but does include citations for the second and third editions: Josiah Priest, *The Wonders of Nature and Providence, Displayed* (Albany: Published by Josiah Priest, E. and E. Hosford, Printers, 1825), and Josiah Priest, *The Wonders of Nature and Providence, Displayed* (Albany: E. and E. Hosford, 1826). The book lives up to its title by including many things miraculous and supernatural plus about thirty-five pages of "proof" that the American Indians were descended from the ancient Hebrews, with a proper reference that much of this material was extracted from Ethan Smith's *View of the Hebrews,* "with some additional remarks."

Roberts's well-thumbed and extensively marked second edition copy (April 1, 1825) of the *View of the Hebrews* is now part of the B. H. Roberts Collection at the Marriott Library, University of Utah.

4. "A Parallel" consists of eighteen typed pages arranged in parallel columns on each page, citations from the Book of Mormon appearing on the left and quotations and notes from the *View of the Hebrews* on the right. Eighteen parallels are discussed. Although known to some scholars during the 1930s, as already indicated, "A Parallel" first became public knowledge on October 10, 1946, when Benjamin E. Roberts presented it in an address to the Timpanogos Club at the Hotel Utah in Salt Lake City.

"BOOK OF MORMON DIFFICULTIES:
A STUDY"

B. H. Roberts was not satisfied with his brief answers to the five questions propounded by Mr. Couch; he prepared a much more detailed analysis of the Book of Mormon, of 141 typed pages, which he submitted to President Heber J. Grant and Counsellors, the Quorum of the Twelve Apostles, and his own Council of Seventy in January 1922. This examination, compiled in the rather short period of about three months, from October 1921 to January 1922, raised so many questions for Roberts that he decided to seek help from Heber J. Grant, the Prophet, Seer, and Revelator of the Church, and from his brethren in the presiding councils. As the correspondence indicates, Roberts was not satisfied with what he conceived to be a rather superficial reaction to his report during the first two days of meetings with the First Presidency and the Twelve Apostles, although some of his colleagues were evidently quite shaken by his disclosures. When a third meeting with President Grant plus some evening sessions with a select few of the apostles were also unsatisfactory, Roberts then embarked upon a rather prolonged study and a new approach to a possible explanation of the origin of the Book of Mormon, comparing it with Ethan Smith's *View of the Hebrews*.

I

Linguistics

The following question is submitted by a Mr. Couch of Washington, D.C., as a result of his studies of the Book of Mormon:

"The 'Mormon' tradition states that the American Indians were the descendants of the 'Lamanites.' The time allowed from the first landing of Lehi and his followers in America to the present is about twenty-seven hundred years. Philologic studies have divided the Indian languages into five distinct linguistic stocks which show very little relationship. It does not appear that this diversity in the nature and grammatical constructions of Indian tongues could obtain if the Indians were the descendants of a people who possessed as highly developed a language as the ancient Hebrew; but indicates that the division of the Indians into separate stocks occurred long before their language was developed beyond the most primitive kind of articulations.

"Again: The time allowed from the landing of Lehi is much too short to account for the observed diversity."

The question is, how may all this be reconciled with the claims of the Book of Mormon respecting peoples and languages in America.

This question is a very fair and proper one. Also it understates rather than overstates the Book of Mormon difficulties by giving the arrival of Lehi's colony in America as the time element of the difficulties instead of a thousand years later as the questioner would be justified in doing, since the Hebrew language was spoken with only such variations as would arise in a thousand years, and when stabilized by being preserved in written form by Book of Mormon peoples as late as 400 A.D.

These peoples had a considerable written literature up to this time, 400 A.D., based upon a collected copy of the Jewish national books. These records consisted of the Five Books of Moses and a record of the Jews from the beginning down to the commencement of the reign of Zedekiah, King of Judah; also the prophecies of the holy prophets down to the commencement of the reign of Zedekiah, including many of the prophecies of Jeremiah.(1)

Precious parts from these books, especially portions of the prophecies of Isaiah, were copied by some of their inspired men into the Nephite books and records that were made, and frequent quotations

(1) I Nephi 5; 13:23, where, comparing the record of the Jews that would be had among the Gentiles, i.e., the Old Testament, with the records engraven upon the brass plates in possession of the Nephites, the latter is held to be a large and fuller record than that possessed by the Gentiles—our current Old Testament.

and citations are found in the records of the Nephites to such scriptures. That this written literature was considerable is evident from the Book of Mormon. Mormon in his abridgement of the Book of Helaman, speaking of the period about 46 B.C., says:

"And now there are many records kept of the proceedings of this people, by many of this people, which are particular and very large, concerning them;

"But behold a hundredth part of the proceedings of this people, yea, the account of the Lamanites, and of the Nephites, and their wars, and contentions, and dissensions, and their preaching, and their prophecies, and their shipping, and their building of ships, and their building of temples, and of synagogues, and their sanctuaries, and their righteousness, and their wickedness, and their murders, and their robbings, and their plundering, and all manner of abominations and whoredoms, cannot be contained in this work;

"But behold, there are many books and many records of every kind, and they have been kept chiefly by the Nephites;

"And they have been handed down from one generation to another by the Nephites, even until they have fallen into transgression."(2)

The Nephite prophets throughout their preaching appeal to scriptures had among the people, as if they were widespread and numerous. "Behold," one Alma is represented as saying about 82 B.C., when preaching to the people in the city of Ammonihah—"Behold, the scriptures are before you; if ye will wrest them, it shall be to your own destruction."(3) These people then began "to search the scriptures";(4) and a little later when a persecution arose against those who believed, their persecutors "brought forth their records which contained the holy scriptures and cast them into the fire also, that they might be burned and destroyed by fire."(5) The multiplication of records among the Nephites continued down to the days of Mormon and his son Moroni—400 A.D.—for Mormon it was who made the abridgement known as the Book of Mormon, from the extensive literature and many books of the Nephites, and his son Moroni, in addition to his personal writings consisting of the completion of his father's record and the ten chapters that make up the book which bears his name, wrote a condensed translation—with his comments—of the ancient record of the Jaredites—a people who had possessed the land before the arrival of the Nephites—under the title, "The Book of Ether." Nor were the branch of the people called Lamanites at this period without ability at least to read written language,

(2) See I Nephi 20-22 inclusive; also II Nephi 6-24 inclusive; Helaman 3:13-16.
(3) Alma 13:20.
(4) Ibid., 14:1.
(5) Ibid., 14:8.

as we have the statement of Mormon that just previous to the last battles between Nephites and Lamanites, that he "wrote an epistle unto the King of the Lamanites and desired him that he would grant unto them the opportunity to gather their people unto the land of Cumorah for the final struggle between the two peoples"; and the King of the Lamanites seems to have understood the epistle, for he granted the request.(6)

Thus throughout the entire Nephite period, from 600 B.C. to 420 A.D., the people inhabiting America according to the Book of Mormon had a written language, a considerable literature, a thing that may be an important factor bearing upon the subject to be considered.

Lehi's Colony referred to above was made up of people from Jerusalem. First his own family; himself, his wife Sariah, his four sons, Laman, Lemuel, Sam, and Nephi, six in all. Second, one Ishmael and his family; himself, his wife, two sons, evidently married, if they had children it is not known, five unmarried daughters; and to this number must be added one Zoram, a servant in the household of one Laban, who was induced to join the colony. This makes a total of sixteen souls. Adding the two wives of the sons of Ishmael, and what children they may have had, might increase the number of the colony to twenty-five, or possibly to thirty, certainly not more than that. They all lived in the city of Jerusalem during the reign of King Zedekiah, and in the midst of the civilization of that period. From the genealogical records connected with the Jewish scripture brought along by the colony, Lehi learned that he was a descendant of that Joseph, son of Jacob, who was sold into Egypt.

It should be remarked that there was contact with no other people or source of literature that would influence the character of Nephite and Lamanite language than this national literature of the Jews. For though there was a subsequent union of the Nephite people with another people, about 200 B.C., yet these were the descendants of a colony which had left Jerusalem at the time of the disasters which befell the Jews with the fall of King Zedekiah about 588 B.C. This colony, the number of which is unknown, but generally believed to be small, landed in the North American continent, most likely in the southern part of it, where some two hundred and fifty years later they were discovered by and united with the Nephites, becoming with them, thereafter, one people.

They are described by the Nephite historians as being "numerous," at the time they formed a junction with the Nephites, and their language had been so far corrupted that the Nephites, though a kindred people and coming from the same country and city, where the same language and civilization obtained, could not understand their speech. They had brought no records or books with them from Palestine, and though Jews

(6) Mormon 6:2, 3.

they denied the existence of God. The Nephites instructed them in their language, and from their oral traditions learned the above meager facts concerning them. It is clear that having a language of common origin with that of the Nephites — the Hebrew — this contact and continuance of association between the people of Zarahemla — for so their second people was called — and the Nephites would not greatly affect the language of the latter.

It should be noted also that this people of Zarahemla came in contact with the last survivor of the race which had previously occupied the region of what we now call Central America and northward for about sixteen centuries, that is, if we accept the Bible chronology, according to Usher, for the dispersion at Babel, which is placed at 2,247 B.C.; and the Jaredite destruction he regarded as taking place shortly after the arrival of Lehi's colony from Jerusalem, say in the first half of the sixth century B.C.

Two fragments of records came into the hands of the Nephites from this more ancient people. The first fragment was a round stone on which was engraved an account of the last survivor of the ancient people from Babel, one Coriantumr, who had been found by the second colony from Jerusalem, and who survived among them about nine months. Necessarily the record upon this stone was brief, merely giving an account of this sole survivor of the ancient people, of their destruction and of their origin. The engravings upon the stone were translated by one of the Nephite seers by means of Urim and Thummim (Mosiah, second century B.C.), from which the facts here noted were learned about Coriantumr and his people.

The second fragment was a record engraven upon twenty-four gold plates discovered by a detachment of Nephites who had wandered northward from Zarahemla and discovered the ruins of the civilization of the people from Babel, and the evidences of their destruction. This in the latter part of the second century B.C. This record was also translated by means of Urim and Thummim into the Nephite language, and proved to be an account of the people from Babel from the time of their departure from that place to the time when they had been destroyed. Also it gave an account of historical events from the dispersion at Babel to the creation of Adam.(7) Of this period of the record we have no translation. A synopsis of this record was made by Moroni — 400-420 A.D. — and became part of the Nephite record translated by Joseph Smith and known in the Book of Mormon as the Book of Ether. This slight contact between the people of Nephi and this more ancient people from Babel, yielding only these two fragments of historical literature, would not greatly affect

(7) Mosiah 28:11-17. Also Ether 1.

the language of the Nephite people. So that from the Book of Mormon viewpoint, the facts respecting the languages of the American native races are that they originate from two small Hebrew colonies, leaving Jerusalem about 600 years B.C., speaking the highly developed Hebrew language of the period of Jeremiah and King Zedekiah. This colony in the new home — America — perpetuated written language as well as the spoken Hebrew, with such changes as would naturally be made in a new environment in one thousand years — down to the destruction of the Nephites about four hundred years A.D. Then follows another thousand years from the destruction of the Nephite people and their civilization to the discovery of the western hemisphere by Columbus — 1492 — during which time there may have been immigrations to America either from European countries or from Asia. How far such immigrations may have influenced American race linguistics and cultural elements in the New World can only be conjectured, but they must necessarily be held as of uncertain extent and value, and of but slight influence since no positive trace of them or of their culture can be followed.

The question to be kept in mind in this study of linguistic problems, presented by Mr. Couch's questions, and, as necessarily associated with such problems — the origin of the American Indians — is, how may the foregoing Book of Mormon facts be reconciled with the facts now known respecting the languages of the native American Race. This requires a brief survey of the alleged state of knowledge concerning American linguistics and American race origin.

When America was discovered and its interior penetrated by Europeans, the greatest curiosity was excited as to the origin of its inhabitants. These speculations, many and various, were largely controlled at first by what are now called the "Hebrew Myths" of a universal deluge, in which the whole of the human species perished "except a few in western Asia," and the subsequent dispersion of the descendants of those survivors from Babel's Tower. Among the theories advanced and "defended with great display of erudition" was the theory that the Americans were "descendants of the ten lost tribes of Israel." This was based upon the idea that when, according to the testimony of the writer of the Second Esdras, Apochraphal Book of the Old Testament,[1] the "ten tribes" were carried away prisoners out of their own land in the time of Hosea (8th century, B.C.), they took counsel together in the land of their captivity and resolved that they would "leave the multitude of the heathen, and go forth unto a further country, where never man dwelt, that they might there keep their statutes, which they had never kept in their own land." To carry out this pious intent they performed a year and a half's journey from the land of their captivity, and ever since have been known as the "lost tribes." It has now for a long time been a matter of intense curiosity what became of these "lost tribes." The discovery of the inhabitants of America to some men furnished the solution, and much research was devoted to the task of proving the theory of an Israelitish migration to America.

Among earlier writers to support this theory was Gregario Garcia— 1560-1627—in his work *Origin of the Indians of the New World.*[2] He refers to the Esdras exodus of the Israelites as the foundation of the Hebrew theory of origin, and brings the wanderers to America via the Northwest—Bering's Strait—thence south and easterwardly to Mexico and central America. He depends upon similarities in character, dress, religion, physical peculiarities, and custom, to support the theory. The work is published in Spanish, but an abridgement of his argument is given in Bancroft's *Native Races.*(8)

Next to Garcia comes James Adair, in his *History of the American Indians,* published in England, 1775.[3] Adair was a trader among the Indians for about forty years. He confines the scope of his work to the north American Indians.

The magnificent works of Lord Kingsborough, consisting of nine imperial folio volumes are devoted to this Hebrew theory of origin for the American Indians. The work was published 1830-48.

A small volume, less than three hundred pages, was published in support of this theory, in Vermont, about 1820. I judge this to be the probable date of its first publication since a second edition was published in 1825.(9)

Henry R. Schoolcraft, whose six elaborate volumes were published under authority of Congress—Bureau of Indian Affairs, 1847-1857— may be quoted as among those tentatively favoring the "probability of a Shemitic origin for at least the northern stocks," of the American Indians. This he says "revives with the investigation of the principles of their languages. It is sought to place this study on a broader basis, by the accumulation of vocabularies and grammars—from all the leading stocks."(10) A number of those who wrote articles for Schoolcraft's volumes quite boldly adopted the theory of Hebrew origin of the Indian languages, among these the Rev. Thomas Hurlburt, in a *Memoir on the*

(8) 5:77-83.
(9) It is of interest to note that Ethan Smith, its author, lived at Poultney, Vermont, where he was pastor of a church, and here the book was published. Poultney is in Rutland County, the county which adjoins Windsor County on the west. It was in the latter county that Joseph Smith was born (at Sharon) and where his family resided until the Prophet was about ten years of age. (See *History of the Church,* 1:2.)
(10) *Schoolcraft's Reports,* Part I?

Inflections of the Chippewa Tongue, and Rev. William Hamilton in *Remarks on the Iowa Language.*(11)[4]

It should be remarked in this connection that Schoolcraft's works were made the subject of vigorous attacks, after official investigation under the direction of the U.S. Bureau of Ethnology. Col. Garrick Mallory, U.S. Army, reports the matter in a paper read before the Anthropological Society of Washington, D.C., in 1888, in which he said:

"The general character of his voluminous publication has not been such as to assure modern critics of his accuracy, and the wonderful minuteness, as well as comprehension, attributed by him to the Ojibwa hieroglyphs has been generally regarded of late with suspicion. It was considered in the Bureau of Ethnology an important duty to ascertain how much of truth existed in these remarkable accounts, and for that purpose its pictographic specialists, myself and Dr. W. J. Hoffman as assistant, were last summer directed to proceed to the most favorable points in the present habitat of the tribe, namely, the northern region of Minnesota and Wisconsin, to ascertain how much was yet to be discovered. The general results of the comparison of Schoolcraft's statements with what is now found shows that, in substance, he told the truth, but with much exaggeration and coloring. The word 'coloring' is particularly appropriate because, in his copious illustrations, various colors were used freely with apparent significance, whereas, in fact, the general rule in regard to the birch-bark rolls was that they were never colored at all; indeed, the bark was not adapted to coloration. The metaphorical coloring was also used by him in a manner which, to any thorough student of the Indian philosophy and religion, seems absurd. Metaphysical expressions are attached to some of the devices, or, as he calls them, symbols which could never have been entertained by a people in the stage of culture of the Ojibwa."(12)[5]

A number of other writers proposed and sustained this theory of Hebrew origin for both the American race and its languages, or else at

(11) *Schoolcraft's Reports,* Part I:385-97 et seq. Some writers mistakenly quote these enclosures in Schoolcraft's works as of Schoolcraft himself, as witness *Improvement Era* for December, 1921, where Schoolcraft is quoted as saying: "The idea that our Indians were descendants of the Jews, I always considered merely as a poetic one, and fit only for works of fiction. But in spite of my prejudices to the contrary, parts have developed themselves, and shown a resemblance between the Hebrew and Indian languages in general, which I cannot find between the Indian and any other language. I have no inferences but let the facts speak for themselves." (Schoolcraft, *Indian Tribes of the United States,* 5:387.) The facts are that this is not Schoolcraft at all, but Rev. Hurlburt referred to above. See *Schoolcraft's Reports,* Part I:385, 387.

(12) Powell's *Seventh Annual Report to the Bureau of Ethnology,* p. 156. The quotation is from the paper of W. J. Hoffman on the subject of the Mide-Wiwin or Grand Medicine Society of the Ojibwa. Schoolcraft is further discredited at p. 161, of the same work.

least an Hebrew infusion into them, but these named above were the earliest and the most important.(13)

The theory is altogether discredited by later writers. "No one at present," writes Daniel G. Brinton, quite generally conceded to be the very highest authority on American linguistics—"No one at present would acknowledge himself a believer in this theory." "But it has not proved useless," he adds, "as we owe to it the publication of several most valuable works"; and mentions in a footnote the works of Blair,⁶ and "Lord Kingsborough's Mexican Antiquities."(14)

In like summary manner he disposes of "The Lost Atlantis" theory which he characterizes with "the lost tribes" theory as "another equally vain dream." This theory, upon rather vague historical implications, assumes the existence of a land bridge between North Africa and South America, affording means of communication between the two continents, and the possible peopling of America from Africa, and also influencing the civilization of America from that quarter by an infusion of Egyptian or Phoenician culture.(15) "The account," remarks Brinton, "may have referred to the Canary Islands, but certainly not to any land-bridge across the Atlantic to the American continent. Such did exist, indeed, but far back in the Eocene period of the Tertiary, long before man appeared on the scene. The wide difference between the existing flora and fauna of Africa and South America proves that there has been no connection in the life-time of the present species."(16)

So too with the opinions that America was "peopled from Polynesia, or directly from Japan or China." He cites the map of a distinguished Ethnologist—supposedly De Quartrefages—showing the courses by which

(13) H. H. Bancroft gives a list of those who have written in support of the theory and those who have opposed it. This in *Native Races*, 5:95-97.

(14) *The American Race*, 1891, p. 18. Brinton was professor of American Archaeology and Linguistics in the University of Pennsylvania and also professor of General Ethnology at the Academy of Natural Sciences, Philadelphia, and officially connected with many learned societies in foreign countries. For a list of them see the title page of *The American Race*.

(15) There are not wanting those who reverse order of race and cultural movement by assuming that the origin of the world's civilization was in America, likely in Yucatan and thence moved eastwardly via the "Lost Atlantis." Among these, and chiefly, is Augustus Le Plongeon; see his *Queen Moo*, 1896, and also his *Sacred Mysteries Among the Mayas and the Quiches*. But few investigators, however, share his views. Remarking on this class of writers W. H. Holmes, author of *Handbook of Aboriginal American Antiquities* (Smithsonian Institution—1919) says: "Some students of the subject are satisfied that authentic evidence of man's presence during the glacial period has been obtained, others find sufficient reason for believing in man's existence in both North and South America far back in Tertiary times, while a single bold advocate of Autochthonic (indigenous) antiquity (undoubtedly referring to Le Plongeon) has promulgated the view that man originated in the western world, rather than in the eastern, and proceeds to identify his forebears among the American lower orders." *Aboriginal American Antiquities*—1919—p. 58.

(16) *The American Race*, p. 19.

he supposes the Japanese arrived in America. "He adds," says Brinton in a footnote, "the wholly incorrect statement that many Japanese words are found in American languages."(17) So far from being proved is the theory of America being peopled by migrations from Polynesia that, according to Mr. Brinton, "we have satisfactory proof that the eastern islands of Polynesia were peopled from the western island at a recent date, that is, within two thousand years."(18)

Baldwin in his *Ancient America*—1878[7]—very emphatically, and I may say vehemently, denounces this "ten lost tribes" theory, and with it all Israelitish theories of origin. "This extremely remarkable explanation of the mystery was devised very early, and it has been defended by some persons, although nothing can be more unwarranted or more absurd." He claims it was put forward by Spanish monks who first established missions in the country. "Lord Kingsborough," he writes, "adopted their views and gave up nearly the whole of one of his immense volumes on 'Mexican Antiquities' to an elaborate digest of all that had been written to explain and support these absurdities. Others have maintained this Israelitish hypothesis without deeming it necessary to estimate in a reasonable way what was possible to those Israelites." Baldwin then discusses what he considers the impossibility of such a journey as the theory would impose upon "the ten tribes," and how it would end in "utter barbarians rather than a notable phase of civilization, such as that found in America," and concludes his comment by saying: "This wild notion, called a theory, scarcely deserves so much attention. It is a lunatic fancy, possible only to men of a certain class, which in our time does not grow."(19)

Nadaillac, in his *Pre-Historic America*, classes among what he considers "the crude and imperfectly digested hypotheses, which have engaged the attention of untrained Ethnologists," this "ten lost tribes" and several other theories that would ascribe the origin of the Americans to full fledged races such as we know at present in other regions of the world. "Among those who have been claimed," he writes, "as the original or genuine ancestors of the Americans are the Chinese, the Japanese, the Maylays, the Egyptians, the Phoenicians, the Basques, 'the ten lost tribes of Israel,' the early Irish, the Welsh, the Norsemen, some unknown Asiatic free masons, and other equally unknown Buddhists. Volumes have been

(17) Ibid., p. 19.
(18) Ibid. This statement that the movement of peoples in Polynesia was from the eastward to the westward, and about 2,000 years ago, may prove strong support to Book of Mormon believers who hold that the Hawaiian Islands, and some other of the Pacific groups, were peopled from America by those who sailed out into the west sea—Pacific Ocean—in the ships of Hagoth, which to the mainland people became lost. This about 60 or 50 B.C. See Book of Mormon, Alma 63. For treatises on the theme see articles by D. M. McAllister in the June number of the *Improvement Era*, 1921.[8]
(19) *Ancient America*, pp. 166-67.

filled with the most enthusiastic rubbish by men upon whose ability and sanity in other matters, nothing has ever thrown a doubt. Fortunately the era of such speculations is passing away. (This remark in 1893.) The scientific treatment of anthropological subjects is no longer the exception. The 'ten lost tribes' still linger with us, and doubtless will continue to do so for sometime, probably becoming, in their time, the subject of investigation by psychologists interested in aberrant mental phenomena."(20)

Dellenbaugh, in his *North Americans of Yesterday*—1906—says that "because of certain similarities of physique, of words, or of myths, or of customs, however slight, the Amerinds (contracted from American Indians) have been identified with almost every people under the sun. . . . Some of the arguments advanced to uphold the so-called identifications are extraordinary. In language the Amerinds have been found to speak—or at least have been claimed to speak—Irish, Welsh, Norse, Chinese, and many other independent or inter-related tongues; yet with the exception of the Basque, the structure of all the Old World languages has little in common with the Amerind. Brinton has shown that a number of Maya words resemble our English words of the same meanings, as, 'bateel' and battle; 'hol' and hole; 'hun' and one; 'lum' and loam; 'pol' and poll; (head) 'potum' and pot; 'pul' and pull; and so on, but nobody has yet ventured to deduce from this that the Mayas are first cousins to the English."(21) Later on in his work Dellenbaugh says: "As for 'the lost tribe theory,' on which Kingsborough was wrecked, no Archeologists of today would be willing to give it a second thought." He then adds that which agrees with what the statement of our questioner, Mr. Couch says, and with the conclusions of all our more recent writers on American linguistics—say, viz.: "A multitude of stock languages differing from each other, yet forming a world-group by themselves, are found here (i.e., America). The people who speak them, from Panama to the Arctic, are

(20) *Pre-Historic America*, pp. 531-32. I quote from the translation of the French by N. D'Auvers published in 1893, G. P. Putnam's Sons, New York, and London, the Knickerbocker Press. The original French edition of the Marquis de Nadaillac's was published in 1882 by Masson, the translation here used was made with the sanction of the author, and also by his permission it was modified by the translator, "and revised to bring it into harmony with the results of recent investigation and the conclusions of the best authorities on the archaeology of the United States." See "note by the American editor," following title page of edition quoted.

(21) *North Americans of Yesterday*, pp. 25, 26. Dellenbaugh was through a number of years the close companion of Major Powell among the Indian tribes of the arid West. His really great work, *The Americans of Yesterday*—1906—published by the Knickerbocker Press, G. P. Putnam's Sons, New York and London, is dedicated to "Major Powell, whose courage solved the problem of the Colorado River, and whose foresight established the Bureau of American Ethnology. This Book is Affectionately Dedicated in Memory of Days Afloat and Afield."⁹

in their habits, customs, and physical characteristics wonderfully homogeneous, yet they appear to exhibit several types that have been moulded into a family resemblance by some strange circumstance."(22) Again he writes:

"By some powerful influence and long assocation they had, whatever their origin, been moulded into one race. Where had they come from? How did they come to be so much alike? Why did their highest development take place down by the Isthmus instead of the Great Lakes, or in the fertile valley of the Mississippi? These are pertinent questions. Attempts have been made to answer them by importing different people from different parts of the world and their recent culture with them. But the more the Amerinds are studied the more homogeneous do we find them and the more isolated from Old World influences. Culture, as mentioned, was not confined to one stock; it permeated through unrelated stocks. The languages, too, are totally different from all others. Thus the more the matter is investigated, the more are we confined to the western hemisphere for the origin of the American people, as we know them."(23)

With the remark above that the American languages "are totally different from all others" agree the deductions of Clark Wissler, in his work *The American Indian, An Introduction to the Anthropology of the New World*. This work is held generally as one of the most excellent upon the subjects of which it treats, as also one of the most recent — 1917. Mr. Wissler is also Curator of Anthropology of the American Museum of Natural History, New York City. In agreement with Dellenbaugh's remark that the American languages "are totally different from all others," Mr. Wissler writes:

"The discovery of New World origins is not merely a problem in culture. Language is also a reliable index to origin. So far, *no evidence has come to hand that would identify a single New World language with an Old World stock*. In fact, the only language found in both America and Asia is the speech of the Eskimo, represented in Asia by a small group of villages on the extreme coast of Siberia. This exception may be ignored in this instance. Then, though there is a great diversity of language within the New World itself, we have a right to expect that if colonies were planted here by an Old World culture, such colonization would have grafted-in Old World tongues."(24) "Yet so far, there is no trace of such intrusion. Hence, as the case stands today, in language, we must conclude that the separation of the New World man from the Old

---

(22) Ibid., pp. 429-30.
(23) Ibid.
(24) And especially would one think this true where there was such a grafting in as the Book of Mormon represents the use of the Hebrew to be; and which persisted until the closing period of the Nephite Era, viz., 420 A.D.

World was exceedingly remote, so remote that the existence of an advanced state of culture among the original stock is improbable."(25)

On the subject of infusions of Old World tongues and other elements of culture into America by reasons of migrations from the Old World, Bancroft has the following thoughtful passage:

"In the preceding pages it will have been remarked that no theory of a foreign origin has been proven, or even fairly sustained. The particulars in which the Americans are shown to resemble any given people of the Old World are insignificant in number and importance when compared with the particulars in which they do not resemble that people.

"As I have remarked elsewhere, it is not impossible that stray ships of many nations have at various times in various places been cast upon the American coast, or even that adventurous spirits, who were familiar with the old-time stories of a western land, may have designedly sailed westward until they reached America, and have never returned to tell the tale. The result of such desultory visits would be exactly what has been noticed, but erroneously attributed to immigration en masse. The strangers, were their lives spared, would settle among the people, and import their ideas and knowledge to them. This knowledge would not take any very definite shape or have any very decided effect, for the reason that the sailors and adventurers who would be likely to land in America under such circumstances, would not be thoroughly versed in the arts or sciences; still they would know many things that were unknown to their captors, or hosts, and would doubtless be able to suggest many improvements. This, then, would account for many Old World ideas and customs that have been detected here and there in America, while at the same time the difficulty which arises from the fact that the resemblances, though striking, are yet very few, would be satisfactorily avoided. The foreigners, if adopted by the people they fell among, would of course marry women of the country and beget children, but it cannot be expected that the physical peculiarities so transmitted would be perceptible after a generation or two of re-marrying with the aboriginal stock. At the same time I think it just as probable that the analogies referred to are mere coincidences, such as might be found among any civilized or semi-civilized people of the earth. It may be argued that the various American tribes and nations differ so materially from each other as to render it extremely improbable that they are derived from one original stock, but, however this may be, the difference can scarcely be greater than that which apparently exists between many of the Aryan branches.

"Hence it is that many not unreasonably assume that the Americans are autochthones (i.e., indigenous) until there is some good ground given for believing them to be of exotic origin."(26)

(25) *The American Indian*, p. 361; 2nd edition 1922, pp. 398-99.
(26) *Native Races*, 5:130-31.

All this will be recognized as important in our present study as it affects the relationship of American languages to the Hebrew which the Book of Mormon compels us to believe was the language brought to America by the colonies of Lehi and Mulek—and which, so far as we are informed by that record, was the only source of American languages; for so slight, as already pointed out in these pages, was the contact of the Nephite people with the Jaredites and their language, that the Jaredite influence may be ignored, since their language perished with their race.

On the subject of American Anthropology in general, definitions of language stocks, dialects, and time development of them Mr. Wissler writes:

"As applied to the New World, the sole objective of anthropology is to discover the origin and conditions which have produced the Indian and his culture. The questions of origin look simple enough," but Mr. Wissler expressed the opinion that they will "put the intellect of man and his scientific methods to a supreme test." "Positive and complete answers," he adds, "cannot now be given to any of these questions, yet anthropology has *something definite to offer on every point,* though so far this information lies hidden from the uninitiated reader in an accumulated mass of published data and special literature for the reason that no formal attempt has yet been made to summarize or to present a general review of the New World anthropology as a whole." It is to supply this need that his "handbook" on the subject was projected and published.(27)

Defining language stocks and dialects, our author writes:

"So long as the tongues of two or more groups do not diverge beyond the possibility of communication, they are usually considered as dialects, though the degree of mutual intelligibility connoted by that term may vary greatly. When mutual unintelligible tongues are found to possess consistent similarities in vocabulary or grammatical structure, particularly the latter, they are said to be of the same family, or stock. Thus, all the languages of the New World may be placed in stock groups, the conception of a stock being a group of related languages with their dialectic subdivisions."(28) And later: "The conception of a linguistic

_____

(27) *The American Indian,* introduction, p. 3.
(28) Ibid., pp. 280-81. Relative to the origin of this classification in the U.S. Mr. Wissler remarks: "The determination of these stocks for the native tribes of the U.S. was initiated by Galatin in 1836, and brought to a definite form in 1891 by J. W. Powell, who organized the Bureau of Ethnology at Washington. . . . Powell confined his classification to the tribes of the U.S. and Canada, which he grouped under fifty or more stocks and prepared a map showing their distribution. It is not too much to say that this classification and map is the very foundation of American anthropology. The work was so well done that very few changes have been made; and as it was, in the main, based upon mere vocabularies, its excellence stands as a worthy memorial to Powell and his able associates."

stock is a group of languages all the members of which have a common ancestor, and between whom it is possible to establish degrees of relationship. Hence, the moment we identify a language as belonging to a definite stock we automatically assert its genetic relationship."(29)

Making a distinction between unity in stock and identity of speech, Mr. Wissler at an earlier page says: "Though the English and German language are of the same stock, they are far from being mutually intelligible, and this well illustrates what we met with in Native American stocks."(30)

Reverting again to Wissler, and now on the relationship of stock languages he says: "It is quite probable that future investigation will result in the elimination of some of these stocks, and in any event establish some kind of historical relationship. When this comes to pass, we may find that languages have also a geographical grouping not unlike that for other cultural traits. Incidentally, we note that the existence of even such geographical affinities as have been so far established suggest long and permanent residence in one area."(31)

As to the present number of these stocks, he says in his summary on the next page —

"For the United States and Canada there are 56 stocks; for Mexico and Central America 29; for South America 84."

It will be recalled at this point doubtless that our questioner, Mr. Couch, represents that "philological studies have divided the Indian languages into five distinctive linguistic stocks which show very little relationship"; and it will be a matter of surprise to hear Dr. Wissler saying that in the United States and Canada alone there are fifty-six stocks; in Mexico and Central America, twenty-nine; and in South America eighty-four, making a total of 169. The apparent discrepancy arises from the fact that Mr. Couch had in mind, no doubt, a certain arbitrary geographical classification of all the American stocks, made chiefly for convenience of treatment, by Mr. Brinton; but really, Mr. Brinton is in substantial agreement with Mr. Wissler and the other authorities on this subject; for in discussing American stock languages he says: "Where we cannot find sufficient coincidences of words and grammar in two languages to admit of supposing that under the laws of linguistic science they are related, they are classed as independent stocks or families. Of such there are about eight in North and as many in South America. . . . For convenience of study I classify all the stocks into five groups, as follows: I. The North Atlantic Group. II. The North Pacific Group. III.

(29) Ibid., p. 283.
(30) Ibid., p. 332.
(31) Ibid., p. 285.

The Central Group. IV. The South Pacific Group. V. The South Atlantic Group."(32) With this explanation it will be seen that there is substantial agreement among those who may be considered authorities upon the subject of American language stocks and their number.

On the "lost tribes theory" of origin for the American race, and other theories of origin W. H. Holmes, author of a series of Hand Books for the Bureau of American Ethnology published by the United States Government (Smithsonian Institute) — 1919 — writes:

"Scientific research in the domain of American archeology did not begin until well along in the nineteenth century, and for a long time the meager disquisitions respecting the remains of antiquity were colored by speculative interpretations and handicapped by the point of view imposed by Old World conditions. Gradually, however, archeologists have broken away from the thrall of the past and have exposed many of the fallacies which had grown into settled beliefs, and now the records of prehistoric times are being interpreted in the light of their own testimony. The public, however, is slow to follow and the cloud is not fully lifted from the popular mind, which seems prone, perhaps from long habit, to find error more fascinating than truth."

On the notion that the presence of highly civilized nations is necessary to account for mounds and ruined temples and cities, he remarks:

"Among the fallacies which early took hold of the popular mind, appearing everywhere in the older literature, are those of the presence in America of civilized pre-Indian populations. The mound builders, so-called, were supposed to have reached a high stage of culture and to have disappeared completely as a race, a conclusion reached after superficial examination of the monumental remains of the Mississippi Valley. This idea had held with great tenacity notwithstanding the facts that many articles of European provenance (origin) are found in the mounds as original inclusions, indicating continuance of construction into post-Columbian times, and that the aborigines in various parts of the American continent, as in Mexico, Central America, and Peru, when first encountered by the Spanish invaders, were occupying a culture stage far in advance of anything suggested by the antiquities of the Mississippi Valley.

"A fallacy similar to that regarding the mound builders fastened itself upon the ancient cliff dwellers of the arid region when traces of their interesting culture first came to light, but more recent investigation has shown that the ancient occupants of the region who built and dug their dwellings in the cliffs were in general the immediate ancestors of the Pueblo tribes which occupy the same region to-day.

"Speculation has ever been rife regarding the origin of the aborigines

(32) *The American Race*, pp. 57-58.

and supposed significant analogies have been made out with nearly every race and people of the Old World. A favorite theory of the earlier students of the subject regarded them as descendants of the "lost tribes of Israel, and as a result, oddly enough, literature has been enriched by the publication of several valuable works on the habits and characteristics of the Indians, written with the view of establishing identities between the two races—works which otherwise would never have existed. Perhaps the most important of these works are Adair's *History of the North American Indians* (1775) and Lord Kingsborough's *Mexican Antiquities* (1830-48)."(33)

Of those who discredit the Israelitish origin of the American Indians, John Fiske ought not to be omitted. Dealing with the question "Whence came these Indians?" he proceeds to say:

"Since the beginning of the present century discoveries in geology have entirely altered our mental attitude towards this question. It was formerly argued upon the two assumptions that the geographical relations of land and water had been always pretty much the same as we now find them, and that all the racial differences among men have arisen since the date of the 'Noachian Deluge,' which was generally placed somewhere between two and three thousand years before the Christian era. Hence inasmuch as European tradition knows nothing of any such race as the Indians, it was supposed that at some time within the historic period they must have moved eastward from Asia into America; and thus there was felt to be a sort of speculative necessity for discovering points of resemblance between American languages, myths, and social observances and those of the oriental world. Now the aborigines of this continent were made out to be Kamtchatkans, and now Chinamen, and again they were shown with quaint erudition, to be remnants of the ten tribes of Israel. Perhaps none of these theories have been exactly disproved, but they have all been superseded and laid on the shelf."(34)

In a footnote he gives a summary of the Book of Mormon as one of the exhibits of the Israelitish theory of American Indian origin, and which he characterizes as a "curious piece of literary imposture."

(33) *Handbook of American Antiquities*—1919—pp. 13, 14. The fact that Mr. Holmes was for many years chief of the Bureau of American Ethnology, Smithsonian Institution, during which time Frederick Webb Hodges's *Handbook of America North of Mexico in Two Parts*—volumes—2,193 pages—[was published] as Bulletin 30—will be taken as sufficient to establish Mr. Holmes's standing as an authority upon the subjects on which he is quoted in this "study."[10]

(34) *The Discovery of America*, Three Volumes, Houghton, Mifflin Co., 1902 Edition, 1:2, 3. Fiske may be thought to be too general a writer and too superficial to be taken as an authority upon American Antiquities or any other special theme, but as presenting the current and authoritative opinion on the subjects of which he treats there can be no doubt of the reliability of his statements.

Of the time element in connection with this theory of American Indian origin and language Mr. Fiske writes:

"It is altogether probable that the people whom the Spaniards found in America came by migration from the Old World. But it is by no means probable that their migration occurred within so short a period as five or six thousand years. *A series of observations and discoveries kept up for the last half-century seem to show that North America has been continuously inhabited by human beings since the earliest Pleistocene times, if not earlier.*"(35)

As to the Pleistocene age, after a discussion of the pros and cons of the evidence of its antiquity, Mr. Fiske says: "If we adopt the magnificent argument of Dr. Croll which seems to me to hold its ground against all adverse criticism, and regard the Glacial epoch as coincident with the last period of high eccentricity of the earth's orbit, we obtain a result that is moderate and probable. That astronomical period began about 240,000 years ago, and came to an end about 80,000 years ago."(36)

It follows, of course, that if North America, as Mr. Fiske observes, "has been continuously inhabited by human beings since the earliest Pleistocene times, if not earlier," then man has been an inhabitant of North America from a period between 240,000 and 80,000 years ago.

"Whether the Indians are descended from this ancient population or not," he observes, "is a question with which we have as yet no satisfactory methods of dealing. It is not unlikely that these glacial men may have perished from off the face of the earth, having been crushed and supplanted by stronger races. There may have been several successive waves of migration, of which the Indians were the latest. There is time enough for a great many things to happen in a thousand centuries. It will doubtless be long before all the evidence can be brought in and ransacked, but of one thing we may feel pretty sure; the past is more full of changes than we are apt to realize. Our first theories are usually too simple, and have to be enlarged and twisted into all manner of shapes in order to cover the actual complication of facts."(37)

Further on our author remarks:

"As already observed, we can hardly be said to possess sufficient data for determining whether they (i.e., the American Indians) are descended from the Pleistocene inhabitants of America, or have come in some later wave of migration from the Old World. Nor can we as yet determine whether they were earlier or later comers than the Eskimos. But since we have got rid of that feeling of speculative necessity above

(35) Ibid., p. 50.
(36) Ibid., pp. 7, 8.
(37) Ibid., pp. 17-18.

referred to, for bringing the red men from Asia within the historic period, it has become more and more clear that they have dwelt upon American soil for a very long time. The aboriginal American, as we know him, with his language and legends, his physical and mental peculiarities, his social observances and customs, is most emphatically a native and not an imported article. He belongs to the American continent as strictly as its opossums and armadillos, its maize and its goldenrod, or any members of its aboriginal fauna and flora belong to it. In all probability he came from the Old World at some ancient period, whether pre-glacial or post-glacial, when it was possible to come by land; and here in all probability, until the arrival of white men from Europe, he remained undisturbed by later comers, unless the Eskimos may have been such. There is not a particle of evidence to suggest any connection or intercourse between aboriginal America and Asia within any such period as the last twenty thousand years, except in so far as there may perhaps now and then have been slight surges of Eskimo tribes back and forth across Bering Strait."(38)

In his Preface to the work here so extensively quoted, Mr. Fiske claims that the ancient society that Europeans were becoming acquainted with in that wonderful age of discovery of the fifteenth and sixteenth centuries — that ancient society in aboriginal America — "had pursued its own course of development, cut off and isolated from the Old World for probably more than fifty thousand years."(39)

Reverting to American language stocks again, and seeking to keep the investigation as near as may be to the line of Mr. Couch's questions, I call attention to the remarks of Dellenbaugh on the subject of American language stocks and the time element in their development.

"Even where a group of Amerinds (contraction of American Indians) speak related languages or dialects, there are, and were, such wide variations that the one is not understood by those speaking the other. Therefore we have in North America not only a large number of distinct languages, but within these separate languages an immense number of dialects or sub-languages, sometimes as many as twenty in one stock, varying from each other as much as, say, English and German. At least sixty-five of the separate stock languages are distinguished in North America which appear so radically separated from each other that it is believed impossible that they ever should have sprung from the same parent, unless it may have been at a time so remote as to be beyond the scope of present investigation. . . . Following the distribution of tribes as closely as possible at the time of the first contact with white men, Powell and his able associates of the U.S. Bureau of Ethnology in Wash-

(38) Ibid., pp. 23, 24.
(39) Ibid., preface, pp. xi, xii.

ington have produced a map, based on Gallatin's. The separate stocks north of Mexico are each represented by a different colour, every colour standing for a variation in language as great as that between Hebrew and English, not related as English and Spanish. . . . Continuous study may succeed in bringing some of the stocks into relationship or in dividing them still further. In their beginning, languages probably changed rapidly; memory was deficient, intercourse slight, and comparatively short separations of tribes speaking originally the same tongue were sufficient to establish entire new sets of words. These separations were apt to occur frequently when methods of subsistence were crude and difficult, migrations frequent, and population sparse. As races developed memory grew to better proportions, and after the introduction among the Amerinds of mnemonic records and other memory devices their languages became more crystallized, till within the later centuries changes have come about slowly. That many more languages once existed on the American continents than we have any trace of is, therefore, probable. By intercourse, by intermingling, by the crossing and absorbing of stocks was finally produced what we find to-day, or did find yesterday, a reduced number of different stocks, but still so many that the archaeologist views the field with amazement, and the layman looks upon it with incredulity. . . . Not only does the differentiation of the stock languages indicate antiquity, but that of the dialects adds strong testimony. Dr. Brinton cites Mr. Sthol's opinion that the difference which is presented between the Cakchiquel and the Maya dialects could not have arisen in less than two thousand years."(40)

The above, it must be remembered, is said of a difference between two American dialects, not between two stocks. The difference between stocks and dialects is this: So long as the tongues of two or more groups do not diverge beyond the possibility of communication — that is, being understandable between the tongues or groups — then they are dialects; when mutually unintelligible, say as between the German and the English would be, then they are stocks. Obviously it would take a very much longer time to produce the divergence represented by language stocks than by dialects. And if, as stated in the passage above, the difference between the Cakchiquel and Maya dialects could not have arisen in less than 2,000 years, how many thousand years would it require to produce language stocks — which are so much more widely divergent than dialects? And from the Book of Mormon standpoint, it should be remembered, all these stocks came into existence since the Nephite debacle at Cumorah 400 A.D.

Following the quotation last given, Mr. Dellenbaugh writes another

(40) *The North Americans of Yesterday,* pp. 19-22.

paragraph which greatly adds to our Book of Mormon difficulties, and which is not mentioned by Mr. Couch, but which, nevertheless, ought to be made part of this investigation, and which must be of concern to us. These difficulties are those which arise from the quality of a language to persist as well as to vary, and the isolation of the American languages from the languages of the Old World. Following is the passage:

"These Amerind languages are as remarkable for their separation in a body from the Old World languages, as they are in their separation from each other. This in itself seems to bestow upon the Amerind people a vast antiquity in their isolation from other peoples, and adding to it the testimony of their art works, their implements, and their pictographs and hieroglyphs, there seems to be no escape from granting them to be a division of mankind by themselves."(41)

And now how shall we answer these questions on this matter of American languages? Let us remember that there is both the tendency to alterations, resulting in the slow production of dialects and finally of stocks; and also the tendency to persist in the use both of words and of structure in languages.

Shall we deny the rather obvious slowness of change in language requiring long periods for the production of the dialects and of the stocks? If so, but only to a limited extent, we may have respectable authority for our position. Nadaillac, for instance, discussing the character of the American languages says:

"Their diversity may be accounted for by the constant crossing of races, migrations, and by the new customs and ideas which gradually become introduced even amongst the most degraded peoples; still more by the well recognized instability and mobility of many aboriginal languages." Then he adds that which seems most improbable: "Some missionaries say they have found the language of tribes revisited after an absence of ten years completely changed in the interim." (*Pre-Historic America*, pp. 6, 7.)

John Fiske says "the speech of uncivilized tribes when not subject to the powerful conservative force of widespread custom or permanent tradition, changes with astonishing rapidity."(42)

Referring to the case of a group small enough to use but one language, and then breaking up. Under such circumstances he notes that "the dialects," resulting from such a breaking up, "would change so rapidly as to lose their identity; within a couple of centuries it would be impossible to detect any resemblance to the language of the primitive tribe." He remarks further that "the facility with which savage tongues

(41) Ibid., pp. 22-24.
(42) *Excursions of an Evolutionist*, p. 155.

abandon old expressions for new has no parallel in civilized languages, unless it be in the more ephemeral kinds of slang. It is sufficiently clear, I think, under such circumstances that a language will seldom or never acquire sufficient stability to give rise to mutually resembling dialects. If the habits of primitive men were in general similar to those of modern savages, we need not wonder that philologists are unable to trace all existing languages back to a common origin."(43) In evidence of this tendency among savage tribes to changes in language quickly, he first cites the fact that in civilized speech "no words stick like the simple numerals; we use the same words today, in counting from one to ten that our ancestors used in central Asia ages before the winged bulls of Nineveh were sculptured; and the change in pronunciation has been barely sufficient to disguise the identity. But in the language of Tahiti, four of the ten simple numerals used in Captain Cooke's time have already become extinct:—

> Two was rua; it is now piti.
> Four was ha; it is now maha.
> Five was rima; it is now pae.
> Six was ono; it is now fene."(44)

Now if the above was said without limitations by the author, or without challenge by other authorities, it would be very valuable to our side in this discussion. It would justify and explain, somewhat, at least, the existence of a great variety of dialects and stocks in the American race languages, and also the changes that took place in Book of Mormon tongues according to that book. First, in the case of Mulek's colony which left Jerusalem about eleven years after Lehi's colony, and who were brought to the New World where they builded the city of Zara-hemla; and when found about two hundred or two hundred and fifty years afterwards, by a division of the people of Nephi, their language had been so changed that the Nephites, descendants from a colony of the same people, from the same city, using the same language, and from the heart of the same civilization, could not understand them. They had brought no written records with them; and, though Jews, they had become atheists.(45) Second, the changes in language by the Nephites referred to by Moroni, alluding, however, more especially to written language: "And now behold," he writes, "we have written this record (The Book of Mormon) according to our knowledge, in the characters which are called among us the reformed Egyptian, being handed down and altered by us, according to our manner of speech." This writing in

(43) Ibid., pp. 156-57.
(44) Ibid., p. 156.
(45) See Omni 1:12-19.

Egyptian character, however, seems to have been occasioned in the interest of economizing space upon the tablets used, rather than by any lack of ability to employ the Hebrew characters. This about 400 A.D., or a thousand years after Lehi's small colony left Jerusalem. "If our plates had been sufficiently large," writes Moroni, immediately following the remark quoted above, "we should have written in Hebrew; but the Hebrew hath been altered by us also; and if we could have written in Hebrew, behold we would have had no imperfections in our record. But the Lord knoweth the things which we have written, and also that none other people knoweth our language; therefore he hath prepared means for the interpretation thereof."(46) Which, of course, was Urim and Thummim.

The quoted remarks of Mr. Fiske, it should be observed, however, are not without limitations. In the languages where he speaks of the changes taking place so rapidly — in "uncivilized tribes" — he says: "Such languages usually contain but a few hundred words, and these are often forgotten by the dozen and replaced by new ones even in the course of a single generation." And then by way of illustration: "Among many South American Indians, as Azara tells us, the language changes from clan to clan, and almost from hut to hut, so that members of different families are obliged to have recourse to gesture to eke out the scanty pittance of oral discourse that is mutually intelligible."(47)

This I submit does not describe the conditions existing among the Book of Mormon peoples, neither of the people of Mulek nor of the people of Lehi. The former, despite such wars and contentions as had broken out among them, had become "very numerous," and had remained together and founded a city, and but one city, for we have reference to no other that they founded. The latter — the Nephites — in addition to being numerous, and closely associated in community life, were further preserved from such changes, at least as are spoken of by Mr. Fiske, by the stabilizing influence of a written language and the existence of a widespread literature, and this even down to the close of the Nephite period 420 A.D.(48)

Also Mr. Fiske's conclusions respecting the rapid changes in uncivilized languages are not unchallenged by other authorities. Dellenbaugh challenges them specifically. "It may be urged," he remarks, after dissenting from Fiske's conclusion, "that the Amerind languages are loose and shifting and that a few centuries would be sufficient to bring about on this continent a complete and total difference in a language from its

(46) See Mormon 9:31-34.
(47) *Excursions of an Evolutionist*, p. 156.
(48) See Ante.

mother tongue in, we will say, Siberia; but the more closely the matter is studied the more apparent is the tenacity with which each stock retains its special form."(49)

He then gives the following illustration of the tenacity of a native tongue, under circumstances most likely, one would think, to be conducive of change in or even the loss of the tongue altogether.

"Of this tenacity a modern example exists in the village of Tewa (or Hano) now forming one of the seven villages of the Moki, and situated on which is known as the 'First or East Mesa.' The people of this village are not Hopi (Moki) stock, Hopi being the Moki name for themselves, but belong to a Rio Grande stock, the Tanoan of Powell, and the Tehua of Brinton, having come from the Rio Grande country to their present location somewhere about 1680. The Moki, who are believed to belong to the Shoshonean stock (though they are probably composite), permitted them to repair and occupy old houses which stood on the site of the present village and there they have lived amicably ever since, to all appearances completely amalgamated with the Moki. The ordinary observer sees little to distinguish them from the other Amerinds of the locality, and they speak the Moki language like Mokis; but within their own village and by their own firesides they largely use the speech of their forefathers, and to all appearances will go on speaking it till the end. Here, then, is this little community separated for a long period and by many miles from their immediate kindred, mingling daily with people of another stock and another language, yet preserving their own language intact. And if this has happened once within historical times it may have happened before any number of times, and goes to prove that these various languages have in them elements of stability greater than has heretofore been admitted."(50)

After quoting Fiske's opinion from *Myths and Myth Makers* that "barbaric languages are neither widespread nor durable," and that "in the course of two or three generations a dialect gets so strangely altered as virtually to lose its identity," Mr. Dellenbaugh remarks in refutation, that the Algonquian languages were spread over an immense area, and the Shoshonean had an even greater range.(51)

To appreciate the overwhelming nature of this answer, reference to the language map by Major Powell is necessary. It is published in connection with his *Seventh Annual Report to the Bureau of Ethnology*—a government document. Reference to that map will show that the Algonquian stock language extends well nigh across the North American

(49) See *North Americans of Yesterday*, pp. 24, 25.
(50) Ibid., pp. 22-24.
(51) Ibid., p. 24.

continent from the interior of Labrador, to westward of Lake Winnepeg, in British America; then southward from Hudson's Bay past our own Great Lakes down the Mississippi valley to the junction of the Tennessee with the Mississippi, thence eastward—save for the intrusion of a division of the Iroquoian stock, around Lake Erie and Ontario, and in part of New York and of Pennsylvania—to the mouth of the Delaware; thence up the Atlantic coast to Nova Scotia and New Foundland. The Shoshonean stock already spoken of as having a greater range, occupying practically all of Mexico and extending in a wide strip running northwesterly and southeasterly from the western part of Texas through New Mexico, Colorado, Utah, Nevada, parts of California, Idaho, and Oregon.

Continuing his refutation of Fiske's opinion, Dellenbaugh adds:

"Brinton contradicts the assertion of Waldeck 'that the language (of the Mayas) has undergone such extensive changes that what was written a century ago is unintelligible to a native of today.' So far is this from the truth that, except for a few obsolete words, the narrative of the Conquest, written more than three hundred years ago by the chief, Pech, could be read without difficulty by any educated native. Thus it seems probable that the Amerind languages extant have been spoken nearly as we know them today for a great many centuries, and that modifications crept in slowly; so slowly that the language roots and grammatical construction of the various stocks are so distinct that they form the safest guide now available in the classification of the various branches of the Amerind race; and furthermore that, judged by these tests, these languages have no relationship to any other group."(52)

Again quoting Powell, Dellenbaugh represents him as saying that in his long study of savage tongues he has everywhere been "impressed with the fact that they are singularly persistent, and that a language which is dependent for its existence upon oral tradition is not easily modified."(53)

Now to quote Powell larger than Dellenbaugh's passage:

"There is an opinion current that the lower languages change with great rapidity, and that, by reason of this, dialects and languages of the same stock are speedily differentiated. This widely spread opinion does not find warrant in the facts discovered in the course of this research. The author has everywhere been impressed with the fact that savage tongues are singularly persistent, and that a language which is dependent for its existence upon oral tradition is not easily modified. The same words in the same form are repeated from generation to generation, so that lexic and grammatic elements have a life that changes very slowly. This is especially true where the habitat of the tribe is unchanged."(54)

(52) Ibid., pp. 24, 25.
(53) Ibid., p. 24.
(54) Powell's *Seventh Annual Report to the Bureau of Ethnology*—1886—p. 141.

Powell, it should be remembered, stands higher than John Fiske in the science of American Linguistics; and, moreover, the passage quoted from him has special reference to the American stocks and dialects, while Fiske's quoted remarks have reference to language in general.

Then, in addition to the time element in the producing of American language stocks, and the matter of rapid or slow changes in them, there is the further fact of the absence of any trace of Old World languages in them to be considered.

We have all seen that Wissler held that "so far no evidence has come to hand that would identify a single New World language with an Old World stock. . . . Then, though there is a great diversity of language within the New World itself, we have a right to expect that if colonies were planted here by an Old World culture, such colonization would have grafted in Old World tongues. Yet, so far, there is no trace of such intrusion. Hence, as the case stands today in language, we must conclude that the separation of the New World man from the man of the Old World was exceedingly remote."(55)

Dellenbaugh, we have seen also says, "No authentic trace of any Old World language thus far has been found on this (the American) continent." Again, "A multitude of stock languages, differing from each other, yet forming a world-group by themselves are found here. . . . The languages are totally different from all others. Thus the more the matter is investigated the more closely are we confined to the Western hemisphere for the Amerind people *as we know them*."(56)

"The culture of the native Americans strongly attests the ethnic unity of the race," remarks Brinton. "This applies equally to the ruins and relics of its vanished nations, as to the institutions of existing tribes. Nowhere do we find any trace of foreign influence of instruction, nowhere any arts of social system to explain which we must evoke the aid of teachers from the eastern hemisphere."(57)

John Fiske says: "The aboriginal American, as we know him, with his language and legends, his physical and mental peculiarities, his social observances and customs, is most emphatically a native and not an imported article. . . . There is not a particle of evidence to suggest any connection or intercourse between aboriginal America and Asia within any such period as the last twenty thousand years."(58) In his preface to the work here quoted he remarks that ancient society in America "had

(55) *The American Indian*, p. 361.
(56) *The North Americans of Yesterday*, pp. 429-30.
(57) *The American Race*, pp. 43-44.
(58) *The Discovery of America*, 1:24.

pursued its own course of development, cut off and isolated for probably more than fifty thousand years."(59)

"All the American Indian languages, which vary widely among themselves," remarks H. G. Wells,[11] "are separable from any Old World group. Here we may lump them altogether, not so much as a family as a miscellany."(60)

In his summary of deductions, after his prolonged discussion on American languages, Major Powell, recognized as an authority of American Ethnology, says:

"The North American Indian Tribes, instead of speaking related dialects, originating in a single parent language (as the Book of Mormon compels us to believe), in reality speak many languages belonging to distinct families, which have no apparent unity of origin."(61)

And again: "The conclusion which has been reached, therefore, does not accord with the hypothesis upon which the investigation began, namely, that common element would be discovered in all these languages, for the longer the study has proceeded the more clear it has been made to appear that the grand process of linguistic development among the tribes of North America has been toward unification rather than toward multiplication, that is, that the multiplied languages of the same stock owe their origin very largely to absorbed languages that are lost."(62)

After a hundred and thirty pages devoted to the origin of the American Indian — made up of synoptic theories of origin, including the Book of Mormon theory — H. H. Bancroft says:

"In the preceding pages it will have been remarked that no theory of a foreign origin has been proven, or even fairly sustained. The particulars in which the Americans are shown to resemble any given people of the Old World are insignificant in number and importance when compared with the particulars in which they do not resemble that people.

"As I have remarked elsewhere," he continues, "it is not impossible that stray ships of many nations have at various times and in various places been cast upon the American coast, or even that adventurous spirits, who were familiar with the old-time stories of a western land, may have designedly sailed westward until they reached America, and have never returned to tell the tale. The result of such desultory visits would be exactly what has been noticed, but erroneously attributed to immigration en masse. The strangers, were their lives spared, would settle among the people, and impart their ideas and knowledge to them. This

(59) Ibid., preface, p. xii.
(60) *The Outline of History,* 1:157-58. For the remark he cites Farrand, *The American Nation,* and E. T. Payne's *History of the New World, Called America.*
(61) *Seventh Annual Report to the Bureau of Ethnology,* p. 44.
(62) Ibid., pp. 140-51.

knowledge would not take any very definite shape or have any very decided effect, for the reason that the sailors and adventurers who would be likely to land in America under such circumstances, would not be thoroughly versed in the arts or sciences; still they would know many things that were unknown to their captors, or hosts, and would doubtless be able to suggest many improvements. This, then, would account for many Old World ideas and customs that have been detected here and there in America while at the same time the difficulty which arises from the fact that the resemblances though striking, are yet very few, would be satisfactorily avoided. The foreigners, if adopted by the people they fell among, would of course marry women of the country and beget children, but it cannot be expected that the physical peculiarities so transmitted would be perceptible after a generation or two of remarrying with the aboriginal stock. At the same time I think it just as probable that the analogies referred to are mere coincidences, such as might be found among any civilized or semi-civilized people of the earth. It may be argued that the various American tribes and nations differ so materially from each other as to render it extremely improbable that they are derived from one original stock, but, however this may be, the difference can scarcely be greater than that which apparently exists between many of the Aryan branches.

"Hence it is many not unreasonably assume that the Americans are autochthones, (i.e., indigenous) until there is some good ground given for believing them to be of exotic origin."(63)

And later in closing his review of theories of origin he writes:

"No one at the present day can tell the origin of the Americans; they may have come from any one, or from all the hypothetical sources enumerated in the foregoing pages, and here the question must rest until we have more light upon the subject."(64)

In an earlier volume of *Native Races,* Mr. Bancroft remarks:

"The researches of the few philologists who have given American languages their study have brought to light the following facts. First, that a relationship exists among all the tongues of the northern and southern continents; and that while certain characteristics are found in common throughout all the languages of America, these languages are as a whole sufficiently peculiar to be distinguishable from the speech of all the other races of the world."(65)

Again he remarks upon American languages:

"It is not at all improbable that Malays, Chinese, or Japanese, or

(63) *Native Races,* 5:130.
(64) Ibid., p. 132.
(65) Ibid., 3:553.

all of them, did at some time appear in what is now North America, in such numbers as materially to influence language, but hitherto no Asiatic nor European tongue, excepting always the Eskimo, has been found in America; nor have affinities with any other language of the world been discovered sufficiently marked to warrant the claim of relationship. Theorizers enough there have been and will be; for centuries to come half-fledged scientists, ignorant of what others have done or rather have failed to do, will not cease to bring forward wonderful conceptions, striking analogies; will not cease to speculate, linguistically, ethnologically, cosmographically and otherwise, to their own satisfaction and to the confusion of their readers. The absurdity of these speculations is apparent to all but the speculator."(66)

In opposition to all this, of course, it would be easy to make a compilation of testimony proving from it that American languages have a connection with other languages, and especially with the Hebrew. One might quote what in its day—1645—was regarded as the very great sermon of Rev. Thomas Thorowgood, entitled *Jews in America; or Probabilities that the Americans are Jews?* referred to by Rivero and Tschudi in their work *Peruvian Antiquities* (1855).(67)[12] But this was answered by Sir Hamon L'Estrange in his book *Americans no Jews* (1651).[13] "And, as we think," write Messrs. Rivero and Tschudi, "conclusively answered." "The hypothesis, however," they add, "has been revived at various periods since, but has not generally found favor among the best informed students of American antiquities."(68)

One could quote Squire whom Nadaillac in a footnote represents as asserting that out of the four hundred languages which he says exist in America; 187 words of these are common to foreign languages; 104 occur in Asiatic or Australian; 43 in European; and 40 in African. "This, however," adds Nadaillac, "requires further confirmation."

One might go on with such a compilation of testimony here referred to from the works of Garcia, or Adair. Even Brasseur de Bourbourg might be quoted as thinking that some Jews had reached America.(69) One could quote Kingsborough without limit, and Ethan Smith's *View of the Hebrews; or the Tribes of Israel in America;* also one might quote from the sympathetic treatment of the presence of Israelitish immigrants in America in Josiah Priest's work, *American Antiquities*—1833—to

(66) Ibid., pp. 559-60.
(67) See work named above, pp. 22-23.
(68) Ibid., pp. 22-23. And in their text, after a full statement of the theory, and especially in relation to supposed Hebrew words, they add: "At first view, the proofs produced by different authors in favor of an Israelitish immigration, may seem conclusive; but if closely examined, it will be seen that this hypothesis rests on no solid foundation." Ibid., p. 11. The date of this work *Peruvian Antiquities* bears date—the English translation—of 1855.
(69) See his *History of Native Civilization,* 1:17.

which he devotes twenty-eight pages.(70)[14] One could quote some of the contributors of Schoolcraft's *Reports to the Bureau of Indian Affairs,* making up as they do six massive volumes.

One could do that, but of what value would all that be in the presence of the more recent evidences and conclusions of our modern investigators? It would be like quoting the investigations and conclusions of medical authorities of one or two hundred years ago in relation to medicine and surgery against the men of that science today, enlightened as they are by the progress of their own and a number of other related sciences which clear their vision and give authority to their views.

So it might be urged as to our modern investigators, American Archeologists, whose assistants in the field are working under government patronage and supervision, and who are specialists in their lines and trained to the work. Can we deny the facts as they allege them to be? Can we successfully overthrow their deductions? If not then it is vain to quote those authors who are antiquated in this field of knowledge, and never had the opportunity of thoroughly investigating scientifically, but seized upon the reports of traders and travelers among the Indian peoples, seeking to uphold preconceived notions of origin concerning the American people,(71) the first and most universally accepted theory being this notion of an Israelitish origin.

The facts, then, developed up to this point seem to be —

1. That there are a large number of separate language stocks in America that show very little relationship to each other — not more than that between English and German.

2. That it would take a long time — much longer than that recognized as "historic times" — to develop these dialects and stocks where the development is conceived of as arising from a common source of origin — some primitive language.

3. That there is no connection between the American languages and the language of any people of the Old World. New World languages appear to be indigenous to the New World.

(70) *American Antiquities.* I cite the Fifth Edition, 1838.
(71) At this point it would be well to keep in mind what Dellenbaugh has so well said:
"In the first flush of the discovery of America, Europe was wild with the romance of it, and mystery was the order of the day. More wonderful things still were expected. Fables that had done good service for centuries were transported to the new lands, and there blazed up with the mysterious uncertainty of the ignis fatuus luring and deceiving, till the gold-thirsting Europeans struggled in the pursuit of such phantoms as the 'Seven Cities.' The most extraordinary tales appeared tame in the atmosphere of dazzling imagination. Exaggeration of one kind or another has ever since been the inheritance of the Amerind people, and it is only within a comparatively few years that these 'Americans of Yesterday' have been scientifically studied and their real character and attainments given proper places." *North Americans of Yesterday,* pp. 9-10.

4. That the time limits named in the Book of Mormon—which represents the people of America as speaking and writing one language down to as late a period as 400 A.D.—is not sufficient to allow of these divergencies into the American language stocks and their dialects.

5. That if there have been migrations from Asiatic, African, or European countries in the period from the destruction of the Nephites—400 A.D.—to the discovery of America by Columbus—a period of a thousand years—then such immigrations were sufficient in volume or frequency, as to affect the language or culture of American peoples.

And now the question: What is the answer to be to all this?

Can we in the face of the authorities here presented say that the independent language stocks and their inclusive dialects do not exist?

Can we say that it does not require long periods of time—much longer than that which may be derived from the Book of Mormon Nephite period of occupation of the New World—the only period that can be considered in connection with this subject—to develop the dialects and the language stocks of the American race?

Can we successfully affirm that the time limits represented in the Book of Mormon—a thousand years from the close of the Nephite period to the discovery of America and the advent of the Europeans—are sufficient in which to produce from one common source, viz., the Hebrew, the noted development of stocks and dialects?

Can we assert from any well grounded facts known to us or established by any authority that there is a connection between the American and some of the Old World languages, and especially with the Hebrew, as would seem to be required by the Book of Mormon facts?

In the present status of the case it seems to me that only one of four possible courses are open to us to follow; and each of them has its special and formidable difficulties, and for that reason I present them in the form of questions.

1. Can we answer that the Nephites and the people of Mulek—really constituting one people—occupied a very much more restricted area of the American continents than has heretofore been supposed, and that this fact (assumed here for the argument) would leave the rest of the continents—by far the greater part of them say—to be inhabited by other races, speaking other tongues, developing other cultures, and making, though absolutely unknown to Book of Mormon people, other histories? This might account for the diversity of tongues found in the New World, and give a reason for the lack of linguistic unity among them.

To this answer there would be the objection that if such other races or tribes existed then the Book of Mormon is silent about them. Neither the people of Mulek nor the people of Lehi or after they were combined, nor any of their descendants ever came in contact with any such people, so far as any Book of Mormon account of it is concerned. As for the Jaredites they are out of the reckoning in this matter, as we have already seen, since their language and their culture, as active factors, perished with their extinction. Any beyond them, so far as a more ancient possession of the American continents is concerned, by previous inhabitants, we are barred probably by the Book of Ether statement that the people of Jared were to go "into that quarter where there had never man been," and nowhere is there any statement or intimation in the Book of Mormon that the people of Jared ever came in contact with any other people upon the land of America, save for the contact of the last survivor of the race with the people of Mulek, which does not affect at all the matters here under discussion.

Then could the people of Mulek and of Lehi, being such a people as they are represented to be in the Book of Mormon—part of the time numbering millions and occupying the land at least from Yucatan to Cumorah, and this during a period of at least a thousand years—could such a people, I repeat, live and move and have their being in the land of America and not come in contact with other races and tribes of men, if such existed in the New World within Book of Mormon times? To make this seem possible the area occupied by the Nephites and Lamanites would have to be extremely limited, much more limited, I fear, than the Book of Mormon would admit of our assuming.

2. Can we answer that the period of a thousand years—from the destruction of the Nephites, 400 A.D., to the coming of the Europeans—is a sufficient length of time to allow of many—say enough—infusions of immigrants from other lands, from Europe, Asia, Africa, or Polynesia, to account for the diversity of language stocks and dialects in all the New World? If this is to be the answer where is the clear-cut, indubitable evidence of such infusion of other races with their languages and their culture within such time limits? All authorities could be quoted against such an assumption. For while nearly all authorities upon American Archaeology concede the possibility of such immigrations—except the few earlier writers who stand for Hebrew origin or infusion—they all insist that such infusions must have been so few in number, and so slight in their influence as to leave no trace of their presence upon American languages or culture.

3. Can we answer our questioner, Mr. Couch, and all others who question us upon the same lines—can we say to them, despite the seeming facts as set forth by those who are accepted as authorities upon American Antiquities, Ethnology, and philology—notwithstanding their testimony and their conclusions that there are many distinct language stocks among

the American Indians to produce which, together with the many dialects in each would require thousands of years—more time than is allowed for such development in the Book of Mormon—since the time when all the people spoke one tongue, and that the highly developed Hebrew language—despite all this, we say that the time limits of the Book of Mormon are sufficient to produce all these results as to American language stocks and their dialects. And further we say, despite what these same authorities record with reference to the absence of all trace of Old World tongues in American languages—nevertheless all the American stocks of language and their numerous dialects, had their origin in one common source and that the Hebrew language, the use of which prevailed up to 400 A.D., whether traces of it can be found or not in the present American languages. And we place our revealed truths in the Book of Mormon against the alleged facts resulting from the investigations of Ethnologists and Philologists and the deductions of their science, and calmly await the vindication we feel sure that time will bring to the Book of Mormon.

Much could be said for the boldness and perhaps for the honesty of such an answer, but is the reasonableness or wisdom of such an answer equally apparent? It certainly would have no effect upon the educated class throughout the world. It would only excite ridicule and contempt in them. It would be the answer of fanatics prompted by, and only possible because of ignorance, they would say.

What would be the effect of such an answer upon the minds of our youth? Our youth, already so willing to follow in so many other branches of learning the deductions of the sciences in their high school and college courses.

4. Is silence the best answer? Is silence possible in such a questioning age as ours—such an age of free inquiry? May the questions propounded to us be ignored? Would not silence be looked upon as a confession of inability to make an effective answer? Would not silence be a confession of defeat?

Is there any other answer to the questions propounded to us than some one of the four here proposed and briefly discussed? If so I shall hail it with very great satisfaction, especially if it is free from the serious difficulties that seem to attach to each of the answers above presented.

II

Were Domestic Animals—Horses, Asses, Oxen, Cows, Sheep, Swine; Iron and Steel; Swords and Scimeters; Silk, Wheat, Barley, and Wheel Vehicles Known to Native American Races in Pre-Columbian, and within Historic Times?

Mr. Couch presents as other Book of Mormon difficulties the existence of the horse in America within historic times; possession of a steel bow when it is doubtful if the Hebrews at the time of its being mentioned had knowledge of steel; the existence and use of cimeters—centuries before that word or form of weapon was known in the orient, to which both word and weapon was peculiar; and lastly the knowledge of silk—and I add wheat and barley—when silk and these grains were unknown in America. This list of problems at the head of this division of my study I have somewhat enlarged because the things I have added belong to the same category of difficulties mentioned by Mr. Couch, and hence should not be omitted. Thus to the question of the presence of the horse in America within recent, that is to say, within historic times, within Book of Mormon times, I consider the whole list of Book of Mormon-mentioned domestic animals—horses, asses, oxen, cows, sheep, goats; and to the incident of the steel bow I add the whole Book of Mormon complex of metals—its iron age—its peoples—employing iron, steel, copper, brass—the use of all these in manufactures both for agricultural implements, and weapons of war.

Here follows the second part of Mr. Couch's statement.

Statement of Mr. Couch.

2. The Book of Mormon states that when the followers of Lehi reached North America they found, among other animals, the horse here. Historical and paeleontological data shows that the horse was not in America at that time, nor did it arrive for 20 centuries afterward.

3. Nephi is stated to have had a bow of steel which he broke shortly after he had left Jerusalem, some 600 years B.C. There is no record that I know of which allows the Jews the knowledge of steel at such a period.

4. Reference is frequently made in the Book of Mormon to "sword and cimiters." The use of the word "cimeter" does not occur in other literature before the rise of the Mohammedan power and apparently that peculiar weapon was not developed until long after the Christian era. It does not, therefore, appear likely that the Nephites or the Lamanites possessed either the weapon or the term.

5. Reference is also made to the possession by the Nephites of an abundance of silk. As silk was not known in America at that time the question arises where did they get it?

First then as to domestic animals, the horses, asses, oxen, cows, sheep, swine, and even goats. The Book of Mormon thoroughly commits us to their presence in America within historic times—within Book of Mormon times, which in their utmost limits extend from soon after the dispersion from Babel—2,247 B.C., according to the Usher Chronology of the Bible, to 400 A.D., a period of 2,647 years. Within these limits the Book of Mormon repeatedly asserts the existence of the domestic animals named as being in existence and in use by the people. It represents the Jaredites as having these domestic animals in the land to which they had been led. This within the first century of their occupancy of it—the land of America.

"And in the space of sixty and two years [presumably from the time of their landing in North America] they had become exceeding strong, insomuch that they became exceeding rich. Having all manner of fruit, and of grain, and of silks, and of fine linen, and of gold, and of silver, and of precious things; and also all manner of cattle, of oxen, and cows, and of sheep, and of swine, and of goats, and also many other kind of animals which were useful for the food of man; and they also had horses, and asses, and there were elephants and cureloms, and cumoms; all of which were useful unto man, and more especially the elephants, and cureloms, and cumoms; and thus the Lord did pour out his blessings upon this land which was choice above all other lands."(1)

Then on the arrival of Lehi's colony in America, about 589 B.C., they found domestic animals in the land. The descriptive passage is as follows:

"And it came to pass that we did find upon the land of promise, as we journeyed in the wilderness, that there were beasts in the forests of every kind, both the cow and the ox, and the ass and the horse, and the goat, and the wild goat, and all manner of wild animals, which were for the use of men. And we did find all manner of ore, both of gold, and of silver, and of copper."(2)

Then later, between 554-521, one Enos writing of conditions among the Nephites in his day, said:

"And it came to pass that the people of Nephi did till the land, and raise all manner of grain, and of fruit, and flocks of herds, and flocks

(1) Ether 9:16-20.
(2) I Nephi 18:25.

of all manner of cattle of every kind, and goats, and wild goats, and also many horses."(3)

About 90 B.C., a certain petty King among the Lamanites making inquiry concerning the whereabouts of a certain Nephite named Ammon, who had rendered him and his household some service, he was answered —

"Behold, he is feeding thy horses. Now the king had commanded his servants, previous to the time of the watering of their flocks, that they should prepare *his horses* and *chariots,* and conduct him forth to the land of Nephi; for there had been a great feast appointed at the land of Nephi, by the father of Lamoni, who was king over all the land.

"Now when king Lamoni heard that Ammon was preparing his horses and his chariots, he was more astonished, because of the faithfulness of Ammon, saying, surely, there has not been any servant among all my servants, that has been so faithful as this man; for even he doth remember all my commandments to execute them. . . . And it came to pass that when Ammon had made ready the horses and the chariots for the king and his servants, he went in unto the king."(4)

"Now when Lamoni [the petty king in question] had heard this [an incident calling him to an adjoining jurisdiction] he caused that his servants should make ready his *horses and his chariots.*"(5)

After a hundred years had passed — one hundred and seven years from the above recorded incident, to be exact, bringing us to the year 17 A.D. — in giving an account of a Nephite preparation for battle the Book of Mormon writer says:

"And they had taken their *horses,* and *their chariots,* and their cattle, and all their flocks, and their herds, and their grain, and all their substance, and did march forth by thousands, and by tens of thousands, until they had all gone forth to the place which had been appointed, that they should gather themselves together to defend themselves against their enemies."(6)

Then within the same incident, reciting the advantages which the Nephites had over their robber enemies, it is written:

"Therefore there was no chance for the robbers to plunder and to obtain food, save it were to come up in open battle against the Nephites; and the Nephites being in one body, and having so great a number, and having reserved for themselves provisions, and horses, and cattle, and flocks of every kind, that they might subsist for the space of seven years,

(3) Enos 1:21.
(4) Alma 18:9-12.
(5) Ibid., 2:6.
(6) III Nephi 3:22.

in the which time they did hope to destroy the robbers from the face of the land. And thus the eighteenth year (i.e., A.D.) did pass away."(7)

Still under the same incident, but 26 A.D., giving an account of the happy return of the Nephites to their lands after the war, the writer says:

"And now it came to pass that the people of the Nephites did all return to their own lands, in the twenty and sixth year, every man, with his family, his flocks and his herds, his horses and his cattle, and all things whatsoever did belong unto them."(8)

The foregoing unequivocally commits the Book of Mormon to the existence and use of the horse and the other domestic animals mentioned above—horses, asses, oxen, cows, sheep, goats, swine (the last, however, only among the Jaredites).

And now what are the conclusions of those who speak with recognized authority of the fauna of the New World? Unhappily they are unanimously against us. Mr. Clark Wissler, whose standing as an authority in American antiquities and the curator of the Museum of Natural History, New York City, was noted in the first division of this "study," is against us. His work *The American Indian,* it will be remembered, was published in 1917, so that in addition to coming from the highest authority it is one of the most recent works on the subject. In his chapter devoted to "Domestication of Animals and Methods of Transportation," he says:

"The common domesticated animals (in the New World) were the dog, the llama, and the related alpaca. *There were no others.* It is true that we have on record instances of individual animals of other species being tamed, but in no case were they propagated."

Our author then mentions birds of which the Americans had the turkey of Mexico and the Pueblo tribes within the United States; cranes he says were bred in Carolina; and that the bee was domesticated in Mexico by the Aztec and Maya, as is still the case among some groups of natives in Central America and Northwest Brazil.

"The dog," he says, "appears in Paleolithic Europe [i.e., the old stone age period] in close association with the remains of man and was practically universal in aboriginal America." He says also that the dog was used for at least four purposes: "transportation, hunting, guarding, and companionship, or food according to locality. They varied greatly in size and form from the small pug-like type found in Peru and the hairless variety of the tropics, to the great hairy beasts reared in some parts of the Arctic."

(7) Ibid., 4:4.
(8) Ibid., 6:1.

Other authorities, as we shall see, mention dogs as being in possession of the native Americans as domestic animals, but strangely enough no mention is made of dogs in possession or use of the Book of Mormon peoples.

"Returning to our subject," he remarks [that is transportation], "we see that the prevailing mode of land transport in the New World was by human carrier. *The wheel was unknown in pre-Columbian times.* The wild fauna afforded nothing like the horse and ox of the Old World. The caribou has been found far less suitable for domestication than the closely allied reindeer; and the bison has proved rather too strenuous. . . . It is fair to assume that if the bison and the caribou had been available to the Peruvians the tale would be different. . . . Before the time of Columbus, *no tribe* had *an animal able to carry a man.* . . . The coming of the Spaniards made quick changes. The mule and donkey were soon in general use in the area of intense maize culture, though they have not yet entirely displaced the llama of Peru. Wild cattle soon overran Texas and southern California, and in the Pampas became almost as numerous as the bison in the north. Their presence greatly modified the food supply, but the most far-reaching change resulted from the spread of the horse. We know that the use of the horse spread much faster *than exploration,* so that in many cases our first actual view of a tribe is as a horse user."(9)

"The only place where a pastoral culture was noted was again in Peru. The Spaniards found the llama in great domestic herds, sometimes reaching to thousands. In addition to their use in transportation they were slaughtered for their flesh and sheared for their wool. The use of milk seems to have been *unknown here as well as in other parts of the New World.* In fact the Indians as a whole seem to be as deeply prejudiced against milk as the Chinese, for it is with the greatest difficulty that our reservation tribes can be led to care for milk cows."(10) Strange, this absence of the use of milk as a diet since the Book of Mormon peoples were immigrants into the New World from regions where the use of milk was a common diet, and came to a land of "cattle and cows," yet no mention is made of the use of milk as a diet in the Book of Mormon.

The conclusions of Mr. W. H. Holmes, of the Bureau of American Ethnology, and whose work *Handbook of Aboriginal American Antiquities* was published in 1919, is also against the Book of Mormon statements concerning the existence of domestic animals, that is the horse, cattle, sheep, and also on the existence of wheeled vehicles. He writes:

(9) *The American Indian,* pp. 32-39. A fine article on the horse and the spread of its use among the Indian peoples of the New World, after its introduction by Europeans, will be found in *Hand Book of American Indians* — Smithsonian Institute — 1912 — Art. "Domestication."
(10) *The American Indian,* p. 39.

"That the civilized nations of the Old World have never been in intimate relations with the tribes of the New World is apparent from the fact that so far as the material traces show pre-Columbian American culture was of strictly Stone Age types. The aborigines were without Old World beasts of burden, *wheeled vehicles,* and *sail-rigged craft*—essentials of the civilized state; *they had no cattle, sheep, or goats*—potent factors in the development of Old World sedentary life; they had little knowledge of iron or the smelting of ores—essentials in the development of civilization; no keystone arch—a principal requirement of successful building; no wheel or glaze in the potter's art; no well-developed phonetic alphabet—the stepping stone from barbarism to civilization. Cattle, a civilizing agency of much importance in the Old World, could not have survived a long voyage, and the calendar, a device of the priest-craft, might not readily be transferred from shore to shore by occasional or chance wayfarers, but it would appear that the wheel as a means of transportation might readily appeal to the most primitive mind. That no extended contact with the civilized peoples of the Old World occurred in pre-Columbian times is strongly suggested by the fact that this device was unknown in America, except possibly as a toy. It appears in no pictographic manuscript or sculpture, the highest graphic achievements of the race."(11)

He then mentions the toy chariots of terra cotta found by Charnay as follows:

"Charnay obtained from an ancient cemetery at Tenenepanco, Mexico, a number of toy chariots of terra cotta, presumably buried with the body of a child, some of which retained their wheels (fig. 7). The possibility that these *toys are of post-discovery manufacture* must be taken into account, especially since mention is made of the discovery of brass bells in the same cemetery with the toys."(12)

Nadaillac, speaking of these toy chariots discovered by Charnay, and of some bones of some gigantic ruminants (perhaps bisons)—the tibia of which were about one foot three inches long by four inches thick, the femur at the upper end about six inches by four inches—says:

"Admitting that there is no mistake, these facts are absolutely new, for previously it was considered that the early Americans did not know how to make either glass or porcelain, and that before the arrival of the Conquistadores none of our domestic animals were known in America, but that the oxen, horses, and sheep living there at the present day are all descended from ancestors imported from Europe.

"The excavations have also yielded some little chariots that Charnay

(11) *Aboriginal American Antiquities,* p. 20.
(12) Ibid., p. 20.

thinks were the toys of children. Now, supposing these toys to have been a reproduction in miniature of objects used by men, we must conclude that the Toltecs employed carriages, and that their use was not only given up, but absolutely unknown on the arrival of Cortes.

"The discoveries, we can but repeat, greatly modify the conclusions hitherto accepted. *But are these really original productions?* May they not have been imported? This is after all doubtful, and new proofs are needed to establish certainly that the objects discovered really date from the pre-Columbian period before we can admit that in the eleventh century the Toltecs possessed domestic animals, that they knew how to make and fashion porcelain, glass, perhaps even iron, for Charnay also collected in his excavations several iron implements. He himself expresses an idea that the material of which they were made dates from the Spanish period (i.e., after the coming of the Spaniards). He does not explain why he makes an exception on this point with regard to the glass and porcelain objects."(13)

Nadaillac says on his own account:

"The native Americans lived among mammalia, birds, fish, and reptiles mostly unknown in Europe. In the south the llama was their chief domestic animal; they used it as a beast of burden, ate its flesh, clothed themselves with its wool. Oxen, camels, goats, horses, and asses *were unknown to them.* The European dog, our faithful companion, also appears to have been a stranger to them. His place was very inadequately filled by the coyote, or prairie wolf, which they kept in captivity and had succeeded in taming to a certain extent."(14)

This statement will enable the reader to understand a reference by Nadaillac, in a later page, to the finding of "a horse, very similar to our own"; and again to the finding of "a horse by Sequin in connection with numerous bones of extinct animals, a bear larger than the cave bear. . . . the mastodon, and the megatherium." This "horse" was the horse of pre-historic times, back in the Pliocene period when it is conceded the horse existed in America—many thousand of years ago.(15)

John Fiske, discussing the matter of the founding of a colony by Northmen south of Davis Strait, says:

"The most convincing proof that the Northmen never founded a colony in America, south of Davis Strait, is furnished by the total absence of horses, cattle, and other domestic animals from the soil of North America until they were brought hither by the Spanish, French, and English settlers in the sixteenth and seventeeth centuries. If the Northmen

(13) *Pre-Historic America*, pp. 356-57.
(14) Ibid., pp. 3, 4.
(15) Ibid., pp. 25, 28, 535.

had ever settled in Vinland, they would have brought cattle with them, and if their colony had been successful, it would have introduced such cattle permanently into the fauna of the country. . . . That domestic cattle, after being supported on American soil during the length of time involved in the establishment of a successful colony (say, for fifty or a hundred years), should have disappeared *without leaving abundant traces of themselves, is simply incredible.* Horses and kine are not dependent upon man for their existence; when left to themselves, in almost any part of the world, they run wild and flourish in what naturalists call a 'feral' state."(16)

Referring to Pleistocene times, John Fiske speaks of the existence of "at least six or seven species of ancestral horses," this in connection with the mastodon, Siberian elephant, carrying us far beyond historic times. Speaking of domestic animals in America within historic times — say within the last five to ten thousand years — he remarks:

"The domestication of horses and asses, oxen and sheep, goats and pigs, marks of course an immense advance. Along with it goes considerable development of agriculture, thus enabling a small territory to support many people. It takes a wide range of country to support hunters. In the New World, except in Peru, the only domesticated animal was the dog. Horses, oxen, and the other animals mentioned did not exist in America, during the historic period, until they were brought over from Europe by the Spaniards. In ancient American society there was no such thing as a pastoral stage of development, and the absence of domesticable animals from the western hemisphere may well be reckoned as very important among the causes which retarded the progress of mankind in this part of the world."(17)

"It was a serious misfortune for the Americans," says Brinton, "that the fauna of the continent did not offer any animal which could be domesticated for a beast of draft or burden. There is no doubt but that the horse existed on the continent contemporaneously with post-glacial man; and some palaeontologists are of opinion that the European and Asian horses were descendants of the American species; but for some mysterious reason the genus became extinct in the New World many generations before its discovery. The dog, domesticated from various species of the wolf, was a poor substitute. He aided somewhat in hunting, and in the north as an animal of draft; but was of little general utility. The llama in the Cordilleras in South America was prized principally for his hair, and was also utilized for burdens, but not for draft. Nor were there any animals which could be domesticated for food or milk. The

(16) *The Discovery of America*, 1:252-54.
(17) Ibid., pp. 15, 32, 33.

buffalo is hopelessly wild, and the peccary, or American hog, is irreclaimable in its love of freedom."

The only evidence offered to the contrary of the above statements is found in Priest's *American Antiquities* — 1833. I give it at length:

"Among the subjects of antiquity, which are abundant on the American continent, we give the following, from Morse's *Universal Geography,* which in point of mysteriousness is not surpassed, perhaps, on the globe. In the state of Tennessee, on a certain mountain, called the enchanted mountain, situated a few miles south of Braystown, which is at the headwaters of the Tennessee river, are found impressed in the surface of the solid rock, a great number of tracks, as turkeys, bears, horses, and human beings, as perfect as they could be made on snow or sand. The human tracks are remarkable for having uniformly six toes each, like the Anakims of Scripture; one only excepted, which appears to be the print of a negro's foot. One, among those tracks, is distinguished from the rest, by its monstrousness, being of no less dimensions than sixteen inches in length, across the toes thirteen inches, behind the toes, where the foot narrows toward the instep, seven inches, and the heel ball five inches. One also among the tracks of the animals is distinguished for its great size; it is the track of a horse, measuring eight by ten inches; nearly the size of a half bushel measure, and perhaps the horse which the greater warrior led when passing this mountain with his army. That these are the real tracks of the animals they represent appears from the circumstance of this horse's foot having slipped several inches, and recovered again; the figures have all the same direction, like the trail of a company on a journey."(18)

Then after the manner of too many writers on American antiquities Priest proceeds to speculate:

"Not far from this very spot are vast heaps of stones, which are the supposed tombs of warriors, slain, in the very battle this big footed warrior was engaged in, at a period when these mountains which give rise to some branches of the Tugulo, Apalachiocola, and Hiwassee rivers, were in a state of soft and clayey texture. On this range, according to Mexican tradition, was the holy mountain, temple and cave of Olami, where was also a city and the seat of their empire, more ancient than that of Mexico. To reduce that city, perhaps, was the object of the great warrior, whose tracks with that of his horse and company, still appear.

"We are of the opinion that these tracks found sunk in the surface of the rocks, of this mountain, are indubitable evidence of their antiquity, going back to the time when men dispersed over the earth, immediately after the flood.

(18) *American Antiquities*, pp. 156-57.

"At the period when this troop passed the summit of this mountain, the rock was in a soft and yielding state; time, therefore, sufficient for it to harden to its present rocky consistency is the argument of the great distance of time elapsed since they went over it. It is probable that the whole of these mountains, out of which arise the branches of the rivers above alluded to, were, at the time when the deluge subsided, but a vast body of clay."(19)

Later Priest refers to the subject again, in these words:

"The horse, it is said, was not known in America till the Spaniards introduced it from Europe, after the time of its discovery by Columbus, which has multiplied prodigiously on the innumerable wilds and prairies of both South and North America; yet the track of a horse is found on a mountain of Tennessee, in the rock of the enchanted mountain, as before related, and shows that horses were known in America in the earliest ages after the flood."(20)

Recently, when speaking to brethren with reference to domestic animals in America, and more especially about the horse, I have been surprised to find almost invariably that reference would be made to recent finds in California of skeletons of horses and other animals, such as the mastodon, large species of deer, lions, etc., as having changed in some way the positive and well nigh universal testimony about the absence of the horse from America within historic times. The finds referred to are placed in the Museum of History, Science and Art, of Los Angeles County, Los Angeles, California. They were taken from asphalt pits, from Rancho La Brea, in the county above named, from 1913 to August 1915. Because these skeletons, among them some horses, are not "fossil," but "the bone itself, preserved in the asphaltum in which they were imbedded," it has apparently been concluded that the remains gave evidence of the existence of the horse in America within recent, that is to say within historic times. Having misplaced my own notes made on visiting the Museum a year or two ago, I recently wrote to President Joseph W. McMurrin for information, and he secured for me the printed handbook of the Museum containing all the information to be had on the subject of the Rancho La Brea finds. The title of the booklet is — *Notes on the Pleistocene Fossils obtained from Rancho La Brea Asphalt Pits*. This title itself at once puts the "finds" beyond all historic times. They are animals of the Pleistocene period, according to what is published concerning them by the Museum of History, Science and Art of Los Angeles; and that period terminated some twenty-five thousand years ago and extends back of that period indefinitely some two hundred thousand or five

(19) Ibid., pp. 157-58.
(20) Ibid., p. 263.

hundred thousand years. "The bones of these finds," says the Museum pamphlet, "were accumulated sometime during that period."

"The fossil-beds are a series of crater like pits, generally disconnected, filled with oil-soaked sand and earth in which the bones were embedded." "Large animals approaching these craters (in very ancient times) to drink (and when water was adjacent or covered them) would press unduly on the brittle and over-hanging edges, when a plunging fall would seal the victims' fate, their bones being gradually deposited beneath, as the bodies disintegrated or were devoured by carnivores."

The complete skeleton of the horse represented in the collection "is about the size of our western range horse, but with a relatively large head." Mr. L. E. Wyman, author of the handbook on the collections in question, and at present in charge of the Museum at Los Angeles, when asked if any authoritative estimate had been made as to when this horse of the Asphalt Pits had become extinct, answered "only that it was sometime in the Pleistocene age," which age has been already considered above. He was also asked if there was any evidence of the horse having been in the western hemisphere in historic times, previous to their introduction from Europe. He answered "none whatever." These questions and answers are given that there may remain no doubt as to the notion of those connected with these Asphalt finds, and in charge of them, as to their belonging to a pre-historic age, and therefore of no value as evidence of the horse being in America within Book of Mormon times.[15]

Since writing the above my attention has been called to an article in the *Saturday Evening Post* of December 24th, 1921, which had a subtitle "An Ancient Mystery Solved." My young friend thought it might be helpful to me in the collection of evidence—he knew me to be working on the existence of the horse in America—helpful as he thought in solving my present problem. But, alas, it does but confirm the reality of our difficulty as to the non-existence of the horse in America within historic times. I quote the part that is pertinent.

"An Ancient Mystery Solved"

"Geologists have collected with infinite pains a superb ancestral picture gallery of literal lithographs, or stone cuts, fossils of the rocks showing every stage of growth up to the modern wild horse—nothing like it anywhere in the world. For fully half a million years they grew and shot up and flourished in hundreds of thousands, then suddenly, only a short geologic period before the appearance of man, they disappeared as suddenly and completely as if they had been engulfed by an earthquake, and never reappeared again in America until brought over by the early Spanish explorers. It was not an earthquake or a southward push of a glacier ice sheet, for all the other families of animals went right on filling the records of the rocks with their fossil thumb prints.

"What could possibly have wiped out of existence one of the hardiest and most vigorous of all the creatures and spared all the rest? It was one of the most puzzling mysteries of geology.

"A short time ago the famous paleontologist—which is a terrible name to call an unoffending scientist, but only means student of ancient life—Dr. Henry Fairfield Osborn, puzzling over this mystery, noticed a report of the latest ravages of the tsetse fly among both horses and humans. The thought struck him at once, why might not some fly-borne plague solve the problem? He made inquiries among his scientific friends who were interested in fossil insects and was told that there was no known trace of any fly or other insect capable of such a spread in the rocks of that period, but they would keep a sharp lookout on the new material coming in.

"Within six months they reported the discovery of the lithograph of an insect which was clear and delicate enough not merely to be recognized as a fly but as a Glossina, or tsetse."(21)[16]

The suggestion is, that the extinction of the horse in those very ancient times was possibly due to some such plague as the tsetse fly—a mere guess, of course, but yet possible. Still that whole event is so remote in the past that it affects not our present problem at all. For note the statement, that while the horse flourished in America so abundantly for fully half a million of years—"hundreds of thousands" of them, then they suddenly disappear. But this was in "a short geological period before the appearance of man (i.e., on the earth) . . . and (they) never reappeared again in America until brought over by the early Spanish explorers." These statements establish the fact that this is dealing with an incident of very great antiquity, with an incident in a geological period, according to scientists before the existence of man on the earth at all.

It may be urged, however, that this account does point out a possible cause for the sudden disappearance of the horse in that very ancient time; and if such a cause did occasion the sudden and complete disappearance of the horse from the American continents, then may it not have been from such similar cause in more recent times—within say the time limits prescribed by the Book of Mormon for the existence of the horse, and other domestic animals in America—may it not have been from such a cause that the more modern horse has also disappeared from America? The possibility of that I think must be allowed, provided the horse in these more recent times was here. But it must be remembered

(21) This excerpt is from an article by Woods Hutchison, M.D., on the subject of "Insect-Borne Diseases," the paragraphs quoted above are a mere incident in the treatise.

that before one accounts for his disappearance, one must establish the fact of his existence in America in recent, that is to say, within historic times; and that is precisely what has not been done, and is what constitutes our embarrassing problems. From no tumuli or mounds or burial places where might be expected the evidence of equine existence; in no native sculpture on temple walls, or tablets, or monuments—which give us abundant evidence of other forms of native American animal life—yet no representation of the horse anywhere has been found. The same is true as to the preserved pictoglyphs; also as to native story, or legend, or tradition—nowhere has the evidence for the existence of the horse in America within historic times been found.

As to cattle and sheep and their existence in America within historic times being proven by the claim that the buffalo and mountain sheep are the descendants of the domestic cattle and sheep of the ancient native peoples of America run wild, each must form his own opinion. The bighorn, the mountain sheep of the mountainous area of the western part of the United States and Canada, was undoubtedly here; as also was the buffalo, spread over a wide area of the continent.

Iron and Steel: The Book of Mormon thoroughly commits us to the fact of the use of iron and steel among Book of Mormon peoples; also to copper and brass; and to the existence of a civilization which comports with the use of such metals, and this even among the Jaredites, the most ancient of Book of Mormon peoples. Speaking of conditions obtaining in the reign of their King named Kish, most probably the thirteenth in the line of their kings, it is said:

"And they built a great city by the narrow neck of land, by the place where the sea divides the land. And they did preserve the land southward for a wilderness, to get game. And the whole face of the land northward was covered with inhabitants. And they were exceeding industrious, and they did buy and sell, and traffic one with another, that they might get gain. And they did work in all manner of ore, and they did make gold, and silver, and iron, and brass, and all manner of metals; and they did dig it out of the earth; wherefore they did cast up mighty heaps of earth to get ore, of gold, and of silver, and of iron, and of copper. And they did work all manner of fine work. . . . And they did make all manner of tools to till the earth, both to plough and to sow, to reap and to hoe, and also to thrash. And they did make all manner of tools with which they did work their beasts. And they did make all manner of weapons of war. And they did work all manner of work of exceeding curious workmanship. And never could be a people more blessed than were they, and more prospered by the hand of the Lord.

And they were in a land that was choice above all lands, for the Lord had spoken it."(22)

And of the Nephites it is written — the First Nephi speaking — between 588-570 B.C. —

"And I, Nephi, did take the sword of Laban (brought by the colony from Jerusalem), and after the manner of it did make many swords, lest by any means the people who were now called Lamanites should come upon us and destroy us; for I knew their hatred towards me and my children, and those who were called my people. And I did teach my people, to build buildings; and to work in all manner of wood, and of iron, and of copper, and of brass, and of steel, and of gold, and of silver, and of precious ores, which were in great abundance."(23)

Again in the days of Jarom, about 200 B.C., this view is given of the Nephite use of iron and steel, and also a glimpse of their high state of civilization.

"And we (the Nephites) multiplied exceedingly, and spread upon the face of the land, and became exceeding rich in gold, and in silver, and in precious things, and in fine workmanship of wood, in buildings, and in machinery, and also in iron and copper, and brass and steel, making all manner of tools of every kind to till the ground, and weapons of war; yea, the sharp pointed arrow, and the quiver, and the dart, and the javelin, and all preparations for war."(24)

With reference to Nephi's steel bow we may quote in support of the Hebrews having this knowledge and use of steel in the exact form in which the Book of Mormon refers to it, viz., in the form of a steel bow — several passages from the Bible. David avers, as among his favors received of God: "He teacheth my hands to war; so that a bow of steel is broken in mine arms."(25) Also in Job it is written: "He shall flee from the iron weapon, and the bow of steel shall strike him through."(26) These are striking passages and directly in point, but it has to be admitted that it is very much questioned if the Hebrews had knowledge and use of steel in the times of David and Job. As high authority as Dr. William Smith's *Dictionary of the Bible* (Hackett Edition)[17] says, in its article on "Steel," mentioned in the Bible, that in all cases where the word "steel" occurs in the authorized version, the true rendering is "copper"; with the exception that in the passages I have just cited from Samuel, Job, and Psalms — there it is always translated "brass." Whether the ancient

(22) Ether 10:20-28.
(23) II Nephi 5:14, 15.
(24) Jarom 1:8.
(25) II Samuel 22:35; Psalms 18:24.
(26) Job 20:24.

Hebrews were acquainted with "'steel,'" continues Dr. Smith, "is not perfectly certain." Another eminent authority says:

"Steel: This word in the authorized version, 2 Sam. 22:35; Job 20:24; Psalms 18:34; Jeremiah 15:12, is translated from a Hebrew word meaning 'brass' or 'copper'; and in the Revised Version (the product of modern scholarship) is always rendered 'brass.' It is very doubtful if steel was known to the ancient Jews."(27)

The general subject of iron in America and its use by the Nephites is discussed at length in my third volume of *New Witnesses for God*, and every passage that I could find favorable to the existence and use of iron is there considered. Some of the writers cited, however, are scarcely competent, I have since learned, to speak with authority upon the subject. These are Priest, Conant,[18] DeRoo.[19] Baldwin, however, is cited to some effect where he says:

"Iron was unknown to them (i.e., the Peruvians) in the time of the Incas, although some maintain that they had it in the previous ages, to which belong the ruins of Lake Titicaca. [It] is impossible to conceive how the Peruvians were able to cut and work stone in such a masterly way, or to construct their great roads and aqueducts without the use of iron tools. Some of the languages of the country, and perhaps all, had names for iron; in official Peruvian it was called 'quillay,' and in the old Chilian tongue 'panilic.' 'It is remarkable,' observes Molina, 'that Iron, which has been thought unknown to the ancient Americans has particular names in some of their tongues.' It is not easy to understand why they had names for this metal, if they never at any time had knowledge of the metal itself. In the 'Mercurio Peruano' (tome 1, p. 201, 1791) it is stated that, anciently, the Peruvian sovereigns, 'worked magnificent iron mines at Ancoriames, on the west shore of Lake Titicaca'; but I cannot give the evidence used in support of this statement."(28)

As for the rest, the authorities are against the Native Americans having knowledge or use of iron: "There is no evidence," says Bancroft, "that the use of iron was known (i.e., among the Americans) except the extreme difficulty of clearing forests and carving stone with implements of stone and soft copper."(29)

Referring to some of the stones in the ruins of Peruvian buildings, Prescott[20] remarks: "Many of these stones were of vast size; some of

(27) This from the *Comphrehensive Bible Helps*, edited by Philip Schaff, D.D., LL.D., late Professor of Church History in Union Seminary, N.Y., editor of the Schaff-Herzog *Encyclopedia of Religious Knowledge*. The *Comprehensive Helps* quoted above are published in Wilmore's New Analytical Reference Bible—1918—by Funk & Wagnall Co., New York and London.[21] See also Jamieson-Faussett-Brown *Commentary* on Job 20:24, and Jeremiah 15:12.[22]

(28) *Ancient America*, pp. 248-49.

(29) *Native Races*, 4:779.

them being full thirty-eight feet long, by eighteen broad, and six feet thick. We are filled with astonishment when we consider that these enormous masses were hewn from their native bed and fashioned into shape by a people ignorant of the use of iron."(30)

But why could not the argument of Wilkinson be followed when confronted with a similar problem respecting the ancient Egyptian works in stone? He allowed that the achievements of that ancient people in quarrying and shaping huge blocks of stone to be an evidence of their knowledge and use of iron, but that its tendency to decomposition and oxidation prevented any specimens of it from being preserved.(31)

Whatever may be said for the value of this argument, however, we are confronted with the undeniable fact that everywhere when found by Europeans, native American races lived in the stone age of civilization. This is clearly set forth by the following passage from Brinton:

"We may say that America everywhere at the time of the discovery was in the polished stone age. It had progressed beyond the rough stone stage, but had not reached that of metals. True that copper, bronze and the precious ores were widely employed for a variety of purposes; but flaked and polished stone remained in all parts the principal material selected to produce a cutting edge. Probably three-fourths of the tribes were acquainted with the art of tempering and moulding clay into utensils or figures; but the potter's wheel and the process of glazing had not been invented. Towns and buildings were laid out with a correct eye, and stone structures of symmetry were erected; but the square, the compass, the plumb line, and the scales and weight had not been devised. Commodious boats of hollowed logs or of bark, or of skins stretched on frames, were in use on most of the waters; but the inventive faculties of their makers had not reached to either oars or sails to propel them, the paddle alone being relied upon, and the rudder to guide them was unknown."(32)

"The upper status of barbarism," remarks John Fiske, "insofar as it implies a knowledge of smelting iron, was never reached in aboriginal America. In the Old World it is the stage which had been reached by the Greeks of the Homeric poems and the Germans in the time of Caesar. The end of this period and the beginning of true civilization is marked by the invention of a phonetic alphabet and the production of written records. This brings within the pale of civilization such people as the ancient Phoenicians, the Hebrews after the exodus, the ruling classes at

(30) *Conquest of Peru*, 1:37.
(31) The argument is briefly stated by Prescott, and he cites Wilkinson's *Ancient Egypt*, 3:246-54.[23]
(32) *The American Race*, pp. 51-52.

Nineveh and Babylon, the Aryans of Persia and India, and the Japanese."(33)

Later Mr. Fiske remarks: "Dr. Draper expressed the opinion that the Mexicans and Peruvians were morally and intellectually superior to the Europeans of the sixteenth century. The reaction from the state of opinion in which such an extravagant remark was even possible has been attended with some controversy; but on the whole Mr. Morgan's main position has been steadily and rapidly gaining ground (i.e., a less extravagant view of the high quality of Peruvian civilization), and it is becoming more and more clear that if we are to use language correctly when we speak of the civilization of Mexico and Peru, we really mean civilizations of an extremely archaic type, considerably more archaic than that of Egypt in the time of the Pharaohs. A 'civilization' like that of the Aztecs, without domestic animals or iron tools, with trade still in the primitive stage of barter, with human sacrifices, and with cannibalism, has certainly some of the most vivid features of barbarism."(34)

To this may be added the conclusions of Clark Wissler on the same subject.

"It is frequently said that the whole of the New World was at the time of discovery still in the stone age. This is an unjust estimate of the metallurgic development in Mexico and Peru, but is true in a certain sense, since some stone tools were still in use even at the most advanced metallic centers. Outside the region of high culture the characterization holds and, even at the present moment, stone-age culture survives among a few outlying remnants of the aboriginal population."(35)

Also he says:

"The fine sculptures of the Maya were executed with stone tools. We can safely assume, therefore, that all the stone work of the New World belongs strictly to a stone age and was such as could, and in the main was, accomplished without the use of metal tools."(36)

Again:

"Their culture was essentially a stone age culture, which used copper and gold, particularly the latter, only for ornament. In the smelting and casting of gold they were very skillful. Thus we have in the ancient Maya a fine example of the height to which a people may rise with only tools of stone and wood. While the later Aztec culture was in foundation a stone culture, it went somewhat farther than the Maya in the development of copper tools, but not so far as did the Inca of Peru."(37)

(33) *The Discovery of America*, pp. 37-38.
(34) Ibid., p. 40.
(35) *The American Indian*, p. 115.
(36) Ibid., p. 118.
(37) Ibid., p. 228.

The statements of Mr. Couch with reference to the "cimeter" will have to be allowed, at least this far, namely, that frequent use is made of the word in the Book of Mormon; and that the use of the word does not occur so far as I can find, in other literatures before the rise of the Mohammedan power, which occurred long after the departure of the colony of Lehi from Jerusalem. The first mention made of the "cimeter" in the Book of Mormon is in the Book of Enos 1:20, where the writer, speaking of the Lamanites, says: "And their skill was in the bow, and in the cimeter, and the ax." This about the middle of the fifth century B.C.

The last use of the word is recorded in Helaman 1:14, 51 B.C. Here the Lamanites were represented as being armed "with swords and with cimeters and with bows and with arrows, and with breast-plates, and with all manner of shields of every kind." The use of the word occurs about ten times in the Book of Mormon between the first and the last time it is used. The word is of oriental and uncertain origin and appears in various forms. How it came to be introduced into the speech and writings of the Nephites, and how not used in the other Hebrew literature at an earlier date, is so far as I know, unaccountable. The earliest use of the word I have found is in Gibbon, where referring to the alleged incident of finding the sword of Mars for Attila, he there calls that sword of Mars "cimeter"(38); but that was about 450 A.D.

It has been suggested that granting the use of steel by the Nephites, and the manufacture of various kinds of swords by them they may have made a crescent shaped weapon of the sword type, and the Nephite name for this special form of sword, whatever it was, in the modern translation by Joseph Smith was rendered "cimeter," which would overcome the special difficulty raised by Mr. Couch. This still leaves us, however, with all the difficulties of the Book of Mormon iron age upon our hands when called upon to face the fact of the existence of an all-embracing stone age—and only a stone age, save for the use of metals in ornamental traits, and a slight and doubtful use of copper for tools, in a very limited area.

Mr. Couch's question in reference to "silk" is not so difficult. He states that reference is made in the Book of Mormon to the possession

---

(38) See *Decline and Fall*, 4:195—Murry's edition of 1887—where the story is told as follows: "It was natural enough that the Scythians should adore, with peculiar devotion, the god of war; but as they were incapable of forming either an abstract idea or a corporeal representation, they worshiped their tutelar deity under the symbol of an iron 'cimeter.' One of the shepherds of the Huns perceived that a heifer, who was grazing had wounded herself in the foot, and curiously followed the track of blood, till he discovered among the long grass the point of an ancient sword, which he dug out of the ground, and presented to Attila. That magnanimous, or rather artful, prince accepted, with pious gratitude, this celestial favour; and, as the rightful possessor of the sword of Mars, asserted his divine and indefensible claim to the dominion of the earth."[24]

by the Nephites of an abundance of "silk"; then, "as silk was unknown in America at that time, the question arises 'where did they obtain the silk?'"

The Book of Mormon makes reference to the Jaredites, early in their career in America as having "all manner of fruit, and of grain, and of silks and of fine linen, and of gold and of silver, and of precious things."(39) Reference is also made to this manufacture — "silk" — in the Nephite period about 90 B.C. (Alma 1:29; and 4:6).

The manufacture of silk is of great antiquity. It was an industry in China before the Empress Se-ling-she encouraged the cultivation of the mulberry tree in aid of it (2,640 B.C.), about which time also she invented the silk weaving loom. If this Chinese chronology be allowed then silk was known even before the Jaredites left the Old World for the New, and they may have brought knowledge of the fabric and its manufacture with them. Silk was also known to the Hebrews a thousand years before Christ. Of the good wife the writer of Proverbs says, "her clothing is silk and purple."(40) This, according to Usher in 1015 B.C.

It will be said, however, that silk is unknown among the Americans, and it must be conceded that generally that seems to be taken for granted, and chiefly for the reason, I would say, of the absence of the fabric from among the natives when discovered by Europeans, and for lack of evidences of its existence among their discovered antiquities. The absence of silk among the natives when discovered by the Europeans could be accounted for by the debacle which overtook the Nephite civilization at the close of the fourth century, A.D., when the art of producing silk, together with many other arts, may have been lost. And the lack of its existence in native American antiquities could be accounted for by the perishable nature of the fabric, as I am assured, by those competent to speak on the matter, that the chemical elements of silk are such that when compared with cotton, for instance, the former might perish while the latter would persist. Of this, however, I am not competent to speak from my own knowledge. On the high authority of Mr. Wissler, however, it may be claimed that the native Americans did not manufacture silk. With reference to it he writes:

"There seems to be but four classes of textile fiber in general use: wool, bast, cotton, and silk. Of these, aboriginal America used all but the last."(41) Later, however, he states that in Maya the natives wove cotton so fine "that the Spaniards took it for silk."(42) Of the excellence of weaving and the product in South America Wissler also remarks:

(39) Ether 9:17.
(40) Proverbs 31:22.
(41) *The American Indian*, p. 45.
(42) Ibid., p. 227.

"Taxes, fines, and tributes were levied in fine cloth. As to the qualities, we have not only the testimony of early observers, but in the desert burial grounds of Peru we have immense store houses of prehistoric cloth preserved completely in the original forms and colors. Recent studies of museum collections by a textile expert have shown that the fineness of weave exceeds that of any other part of the world. As to forms of weave, we find the same techniques as in the Old World, even to the pile and gauze."(43)

Mr. W. H. Holmes, speaking of the Maya-Quiche Area, says of textile art: "Few traces of the textile art have been spared, but judging by the sculptural and pictorial representations, the costumes of the people were among the most elaborate that the world has ever known."(44) From this it would appear that weaving skill was not lacking among native races to produce even silk, and Prescott, though somewhat doubtfully, in a footnote discussing the supposed knowledge of silk among the natives, says:

"It is doubtful how far they were acquainted with the manufacture of silk. Carli supposes that what Cortes calls 'silk' was only the fine texture of hair, or down, mentioned in the text. (*Lettres Americ.*, tom. i, let. 21). But it is certain they had a species of caterpillar, unlike our silkworm, indeed, which spun a thread that was sold in the markets of ancient Mexico. See the *Essai Politique* (tom. III, pp. 66-69), where M. de Humboldt has collected some interesting facts in regard to the culture of silk by the Aztecs. Still, that the fabric should be matter of uncertainty at all shows that it could not have reached any great excellence or extent."(45)

And here I leave the matter of the silk difficulty.

At the close of this review of the status of knowledge derived from works of authority on the subjects of domestic animals in America, iron and steel, the wheel, cimeters, and silk, we are again confronted with the question, as in the case of the difficulties about languages, what are to be our answers to the questions asked on these subjects.

Can we in the face of the statements and deductions of the authorities here presented, say that the domestic animals, the horse, the cow and the ox, sheep, goats, and swine, were known and used by Americans within historic times, previous to the discovery of America?

Can we successfully assert in the face of the statements of these authorities to the contrary, that it was an iron and steel age civilization,

(43) Ibid., pp. 59, 60. The report of the recent studies of the "textile expert" is the one published in *Harper's Magazine* for July, 1916, by Mr. M. D. Crawford, whose work was undertaken at the request of Mr. Wissler two years before.[25]
(44) *Aboriginal Antiquities*, Part I, p. 130.
(45) *Conquest of Mexico*, 1:117.

with its attendant higher culture of a written language, which obtained in America within historic times previous to the discovery of America by Columbus, rather than a stone age culture, with its lower stage of civilization?

There can be no question but what the Book of Mormon commits us to the possession and use of domestic animals by both Jaredite and Nephite peoples; and to the age and civilization of iron and steel and of the wheel, and of a written language, by both these peoples. And they, with their descendants, constitute all the inhabitants of the New World, so far as the Book of Mormon informs us, except as to the Gentile races which by the spirit of prophecy it was foreseen would come in later times.

What shall our answer be then? Shall we boldly acknowledge the difficulties in the case, confess that the evidences and conclusions of the authorities are against us, but notwithstanding all that, we take our position on the Book of Mormon and place its revealed truths against the declarations of men, however learned, and await the vindication of the revealed truth? Is there any other course than this? And yet the difficulties to this position are very grave. Truly we may ask "who will believe our report?" in that case. What will the effect be upon our youth of such a confession of inability to give a more reasonable answer to the questions submitted, and the awaiting of proof for final vindication? Will not the hoped for proof deferred indeed make the heart sick? Is there any way to escape these difficulties?

Again I ask, is silence our best answer? And again the question comes, can we remain silent in our age of free inquiry? Can we ignore such questions as are submitted by Mr. Couch, and which are also being asked by our youth? Will not silence in relation to these matters, as in the case of the language difficulties, be a confession of defeat?

These questions are put by me at the close of this division of the "study" not for self-embarrassment, surely, nor for the embarrassment of others, but to bring to the consciousness of myself and my brethren that we face grave difficulties in all these matters, and that if there is any way by which we may "find wisdom, and great treasures of knowledge, even hidden treasures"—for I am sure that neither an appeal to the books written by men, nor even to the books of scripture now in our possession, will solve our present difficulties—then a most earnest appeal should be made to that source of wisdom and knowledge, and with a faith and persistence that will admit of no denial.

III

The Question of the Origin of Native
American Races and
Their Culture

The question of the origin of American races is not brought up by Mr. Couch, but in considering his questions the matter of origin both of the American race and its culture — its civilization and the difficulties attendant upon those questions in their relations to the Book of Mormon have persistently intruded upon my attention, and hence I have concluded to place here the notes incidentally collected while pursuing my studies on the other matters treated in the foregoing divisions of the subject of Book of Mormon difficulties.

It has been assumed quite generally by writers in support of the Book of Mormon hitherto that there was wanting a reasonable accounting for the American race, and more especially an accounting for the monuments of civilization in the midst of which the native races lived when discovered by Europeans, and for which their status of mixed barbarism and semi-civilization appeared inadequate to account. It was this apparent inadequacy on the part of native races to account for themselves or what was about them which led to the development of the several theories about their origin, their European, or Asiatic, or Polynesian, or "Lost Tribes" theory of origin.

This felt need of finding foreign sources of origin for the native races and their culture, however, appears to have passed, at least to a very great extent; and the more satisfied do authorities become that both the origin of the native races and of their "civilization" may be accounted for on other grounds than that of a recent — that is to say, within historic times — immigration into America, with an attendant Old World civilization, such as is assumed by nearly all the theories of foreign origin, and more especially by the "Lost Tribes" theory; and the Book of Mormon account of race origin, or race culture, and the final loss of said civilization by the destruction of the people who founded it.

Let us have in our consciousness the Book of Mormon statement of origin. I say "statement of origin," because to those who accept the Book of Mormon as of divine origin, it gives more than a theory of origin — it tells of the origin of American peoples.

Previous to the departure of Jared's colony from the dispersion at Babel to the American continent as to a promised land — "a land choice above all other lands" — *the Book of Mormon postulates those lands as uninhabited.* It may be questioned if the command of the Lord to Jared's colony to go into an uninhabited land—"yea, into that quarter where there never had man been"—had reference to their ultimate destination in the land of promise, the American continents, or to some land *en route,* into which they immediately passed. But let that be as it may, when the Jaredites came to America the Book of Mormon account of them assumes throughout that there were no other inhabitants in all that land. Throughout their long occupancy of the land—about sixteen hundred years from their arrival a few years after their departure from Babel to the coming of Lehi's colony, early in the sixth century B.C.—there is no mention or assumption of their coming in contact with any other people, or of their being any other people in all the land. They are sole possessors of it. Here they lived and developed their peculiar culture uninfluenced by contact with other people, either by reason of finding primitive inhabitants in the land, or by reason of infusion of other people among them.

From those who have given attention to the Book of Mormon account of the Jaredites it is assumed that their seat of Government and center of civilization was in Central America; that their movements in occupying the land from first to last were confined to the North continent. That they became very numerous may be assumed from the record of Ether, since in their last great battles, which exterminated the race, "two millions of mighty men" were slain, "and also their wives and children." If even a conservative estimate of the population be made from this basis, it would bring their number to from ten to fifteen millions. Their civilization, according to the Book of Mormon account of it, was of a very high order. Not a civilization of the stone age new or old, but an *iron age of civilization far advanced,* as witness the following description of it:

"And they were exceeding industrious, and they did buy and sell, and traffic one with another, that they might get gain.

"And they did work in all manner of ore, and they did make gold, and silver, and iron, and brass, and all manner of metals; and they did dig it out of the earth; wherefore they did cast up mighty heaps of earth to get ore, of gold, and of silver, and of iron, and of copper. And they did work all manner of fine work.

"And they did have silks, and fine twined linen; and they did work all manner of cloth, that they might clothe themselves from their nakedness. And they did make all manner of tools to till the earth, both to plough and to sow, to reap and to hoe, and also to thrash. And they did make all manner of tools with which they did work their beasts. And they did make all manner of weapons of war. And they did work all manner of work of exceeding curious workmanship. And never could be a people more blessed than were they, and more prospered by the hand of the Lord. And they were in a land that was choice above all lands, for the Lord had spoken it."(1)

An earlier description of their civilization gave a pastoral coloring to the picture of it:

"And in the space of sixty and two years, they had become exceeding strong, insomuch that they became exceeding rich, having all manner of fruit, and of grain, and of silks, and of fine linen, and of gold, and of silver, and of precious things. And also all manner of cattle, of oxen, and cows, and of sheep, and of swine, and of goats, and also many other kind of animals ·which were useful for the food of man. And they also had horses, and asses, and there were elephants and curelooms, and cumoms; all of which were useful unto man, and more especially the elephants, and curelooms and cumoms. And thus the Lord did pour out his blessings upon this land, which was choice above all other lands."(2)

Their language was doubtless the oldest, and one must needs think the best, of all languages; for among other special favors granted to the family of Jared and his greater brother was that their language, the one in general use before the confusion at Babel, was not confounded, but was preserved unto them in its purity. Also the Jaredites had a literature. When the Nephite king Mosiah translated some of their records—the twenty-four plates of Ether, brought by Limhi's expedition from the land Desolation—it is stated that they gave an account not only of the people who were destroyed (the Jaredites) from the time they were destroyed back to the building of the great Tower, at the time the Lord confounded the language of the people and scattered them abroad upon the face of the earth, but they (the plates) also gave an account of events beyond that time even up to the creation of Adam. It is only reasonable to conclude that the record engraven on gold plates by the last Jaredite historian, the prophet Ether, was but one of many such records among the Jaredites; for since they came from the Euphrates valley with a knowledge of letters, there is nothing in their history which would lead us to suppose they lost that knowledge; but on the contrary everything to establish the fact that they continued in possession thereof; for not only was Ether, the last of their prophets, able to keep a record, but the last of their kings, Coriantumr, was able to write; for in the days of the Nephite king, Mosiah I, a large stone was brought to him with engravings on it which he interpreted by means of Urim and Thummim; and the record on the stone gave an account of Coriantumr, written by himself, and the slaying of his people; and it also recorded a few words concerning his fathers and how his first parents came out from the Tower

(1) Ether 10:22-28.
(2) Ibid., 9:16-20.

at the time the Lord confounded the language of the people. So that, from first to last, the Jaredites had a literature.

They also had a knowledge of God imparted unto them, a knowledge of the future mission of the Christ, and of human redemption through him. From time to time throughout their history God sent inspired men to them, but despite it all they dwindled into unbelief, and finally met with the extinction described in the Book of Ether.

The Nephite occupancy of the continents in succession to the Jaredites also assumes the presence of no other people upon the land except the Jaredites, and the second colony — Mulek's — which left Jerusalem shortly after Lehi's departure. It was Mulek's colony which met the last and only survivor of the Jaredites.

These are the only peoples that occupied the American continents, up to 420 A.D., according to the Book of Mormon; they speak of no other with whom they came in contact, or who immigrated into the land during their occupancy of it. If there was any infusion of other peoples into the American continents, such infusion, so far as the Book of Mormon is concerned, must have been subsequent to 420 A.D. Moreover, Lehi, in his day, declared it to be wisdom that the land to which he had been brought should be kept "as yet from the knowledge of other nations, for many nations would over run the land," that there would be no place for an inheritance and therefore Lehi obtained a promise that only those whom the Lord should bring should come to the land, and that they "should be kept from all other nations that they may possess this land unto themselves" (II Nephi 1:8, 9).

Nephite culture, or civilization, as well as the Jaredite, was also of a highly developed order. An iron and steel culture rather than a stone one, new or old. The first Nephi shortly after arriving on the promised land, America, and after separating from his elder brethren, and constituting a separate group of people, says:

"And we did observe to keep the judgments, and the statutes, and the commandments of the Lord in all things, according to the law of Moses. And the Lord was with us; and we did prosper exceedingly; for we did sow seed, and we did reap again in abundance. And we began to raise flocks, and herds, and animals of every kind. And I, Nephi, had also brought the records which were engraven upon the plates of brass; and also the ball, or compass, which was prepared for my father, by the hand of the Lord, according to that which is written. And it came to pass that we began to prosper exceedingly, and to multiply in the land. And I, Nephi, did take the sword of Laban, and after the manner of it did make many swords, lest by any means the people who were now called Lamanites should come upon us and destroy us; for I knew their hatred towards me and my children, and those who were called my people. And I did teach my people, to build buildings; and to work in all manner of wood, and of iron, and of copper, and of brass, and of steel, and of gold, and of silver, and of precious ores, which were in great abundance."(3)

Enos and Jarom, writing of the status of the Nephite culture in the 4th and 3rd century B.C., say:—the first writing of the Lamanites, "and their skill was in the bow and in the cimeter, and the ax." Then of the Nephites, he writes:

"And it came to pass that the people of Nephi did till the land, and raise all manner of grain, and of fruit, and flocks of herds, and flocks of all manner of cattle of every kind, and goats, and wild goats, and also many horses."(4)

Then Jarom, speaking of the Nephites:

"And we [the Nephites] multiplied exceedingly, and spread upon the face of the land, and became exceeding rich in gold, and in silver, and in precious things, and in fine workmanship of wood, in buildings, and machinery, and also in iron and copper, and brass and steel, making all manner of tools of every kind to till the ground, and weapons of war; yea, the sharp pointed arrow, and the quiver, and the dart, and the javelin, and all preparations for war."(5)

Helaman, speaking of conditions obtaining in the half century immediately before the coming of Christ, and describing the inter-continental movements of the Nephites about that time:—

"And it came to pass that they did multiply and spread, and did go forth from the land southward to the land northward, and did spread insomuch that they began to cover the face of the whole earth, from the sea south, to the sea north, and from the sea west to the sea east. And the people who were in the land northward, did dwell in tents, and in houses of cement, and they did suffer whatsoever tree should spring up upon the face of the land, that it should grow up, that in time they might have timber to build their houses, yea, their cities, and their temples and their synagogues, and their sanctuaries, and all manner of their buildings. And it came to pass as timber was exceeding scarce in the land northward, they did send forth much by the way of shipping. And thus they did enable the people in the land northward, that they might build many cities, both of wood and of cement. And it came to pass that there were many of the people of Ammon, who were Lamanites by birth, did also go forth into this land. And now there are many records kept of the proceedings of this people, by many of this people, which

(3) II Nephi 5:10-15.
(4) Enos 1:21.
(5) Jarom 1:8.

are particular and very large, concerning them. But behold a hundredth part of the proceedings of this people, yea, the account of the Lamanites, and of the Nephites, and their wars, and contentions, and dissensions, and their preaching, and their prophecies, and their shipping, and their building of ships, and their building of temples, and of synagogues, and their sanctuaries, and their righteousness, and their wickedness, and their murders, and their robbings, and their plundering, and all manner of abominations and whoredoms, cannot be contained in this work: But behold, there are many books and many records of every kind, and they have been kept chiefly by the Nephites. And they have been handed down from one generation to another by the Nephites, even until they have fallen into transgression."(6)

A little later (25 B.C.) this picture of cultural conditions is given:

"And behold, there was peace in all the land, insomuch that the Nephites did go into whatsoever part of the land they would, whether among the Nephites or the Lamanites. And it came to pass that the Lamanites did also go whithersoever they would, whether it were among the Lamanites or among the Nephites; and thus they did have free intercourse one with another, to buy and to sell, and to get gain, according to their desire. And it came to pass that they became exceeding rich, both the Lamanites and the Nephites; and they did have an exceeding plenty of gold, and of silver, and of all manner of precious metals, both in the land south, and in the land north. Now the land south was called Lehi, and the land north was called Mulek, which was after the sons of Zedekiah; for the Lord did bring Mulek into the land north, and Lehi into the land south. And behold, there was all manner of gold in both these lands, and of silver, and of precious ore of every kind; and there were also curious workmen, who did work all kinds of ore, and did refine it; and thus they did become rich. They did raise grain in abundance, both in the north and in the south; and they did flourish exceedingly, both in the north and in the south. And they did multiply and wax exceeding strong in the land. And they did raise many flocks and herds, yea, many fatlings. Behold their women did toil and spin, and did make all manner of cloth, and of fine twined linen, and cloth of every kind, to clothe their nakedness. And thus the sixty and fourth year did pass away in peace."(7)

Referring to the statement above, "they did raise grain in abundance," in an earlier day about 200 B.C., speaking of a branch of the Nephite people — the people of Zeniff — the record says: "And we began to till the ground, yea, even with all manner of seeds, *with seeds of corn,*

(6) Helaman 3:8-16.
(7) Ibid., 6:7-13.

and of wheat, and of barley, and with neas, and with sheum, and with seeds of all manner of fruits; and we did begin to multiply and prosper in the land." (Mosiah 9:9).

This status of civilization continued with the Nephites—hence with the American race—far into the period after the coming of Christ. Immediately following that marked event the people in America rebuilt their cities that had been destroyed by the cataclysms attending upon the crucifixion, burial, and the resurrection of the Christ, and for two centuries, and for the greater part of three, they had a veritable golden age. They had through two centuries their goods in common, but in the early part of the 3rd century A.D. that system of life was broken up. Pride began to make its appearance, manifesting itself in the "wearing of costly apparel, and all manner of fine pearls, and of the fine things of the world." Also the people "began to be divided into classes; and they began to build up churches to get gain."(8) At the close of that century "gold and silver did they lay up in store in abundance, and did traffic in all manner of traffic."(9) The art of writing continued with both Lamanites and Nephites; warfare was conducted on a large scale, involving the movement of opposing armies of more than two score thousand on a side;(10) and thirty thousand to fifty thousand.(11) In the last great battles which terminated the Nephite period, two hundred and forty thousand men were slain on the side of the Nephites alone.(12) And the Lamanites who wrought this destruction "with the sword, and with the bow, and with the ax, and with all manner of weapons of war"(13) must have lost nearly an equal number.

Thus throughout the Nephite period, as well as throughout the Jaredite period, an iron and steel culture with other traits that fittingly go with that complex is found.

The question before us is, can this Book of Mormon account for the origin of the American peoples, and of such a culture as the Book of Mormon postulates among them be maintained against other theories of origin and of cultural postulates.

Whatever the view of our recent authorities may be upon American archaeology in relation to the origin of the American Indians, they are pretty well agreed that the occupancy of the continents by them is of great antiquity. Brinton quoting Professor Frederick Wright, "who has studied the problem of the Niagara gorge with especial care," and who

(8) See IV Nephi.
(9) Ibid.
(10) Mormon 2:9.
(11) Ibid., 2:25.
(12) Ibid., 6.
(13) Ibid., 6:9.

"considers that a minimum period of twelve thousand years must have elapsed since its erosion began"—then quotes approvingly Professor Gilbert's remark, that "whatever the age of the great cataract may be, the antiquity of man in America is far greater, and reaches into a past for which we have found no time-measure."(14)

Closing a review of the evidence for man's existence in America in very ancient times, Mr. Brinton holds that such facts as he has considered "place it beyond doubt that man lived in both North and South America at the close of the glacial age." Then considering the possibility of the Ice Age in America being posterior to that in Europe, he adds—"In any case the extreme antiquity of man in America is placed beyond cavil. He was here long before either northern Asia or the Polynesian islands were inhabited, as it is well-known that they were first populated in Neolithic times."(15)

While holding that America may have been peopled from the Old World, but at a very early age when land bridges in the north linked the continents together, he discusses the question as to where it was on the American continent that "the Americans were moulded into an independent race," for such he holds the race to be.

"Can we discover the whereabouts of the area which impressed upon primitive American man—an immigrant, as we have learned, from another hemisphere—those corporeal changes which set him over against his fellows as an independent race?" I believe that it was in the north temperate zone. It is there we find the oldest signs of man's residence on the continent; it is and was geographically the nearest to the land areas of the Old World and so far as we can trace the lines of the most ancient migration, they diverged from that region. But there are reasons stronger than these. The American Indians cannot bear the heat of the tropics even as well as the European, not to speak of the African race. They perspire little, their skin becomes hot, and they are easily prostrated by exertion in an elevated temperature. They are peculiarly subject to diseases of hot climates, as hepatic disorders, showing none of the immunity of the African. Furthermore, the finest physical specimens of the race are found in the colder regions of the temperate zones, the Pampas and Patagonian Indians in the south, the Iroquois and Algonkins in the north; whereas, in the tropics they are generally undersized, short-lived, of inferior muscular force and with slight tolerance of disease.

"These facts, taken in connection with the geologic events I have already described, would lead us to place the 'area of characterization'

(14) *The American Race*, pp.31-32. Brinton cites Gilbert's *Sixth An. Rept. of the Committee of the N.Y. State Reservation*, p. 84, Albany, 1890.[26]
(15) *The American Race*, p. 28.

of the native American east of the Rocky Mountains, and between the receding wall of the continental ice sheet and the Gulf of Mexico. There it was that the primitive glacial man underwent those changes which resulted in the formation of an independent race. We have evidence that this change took place at a very remote epoch."(16)

Mr. Brinton holds that this race is "singularly uniform in its physical traits, and individuals taken from any part of the continent could easily be mistaken for inhabitants of numerous other parts." Cultural unity also contributes to the evidence of ethnic unity. On this he has the following passage:

"The culture of the native Americans strongly attests the ethnic unity of the race. This applies equally to the ruins and relics of its vanished nations, as to the institutions of existing tribes. Nowhere do we find any trace of foreign influence or instruction, nowhere any arts or social systems to explain which we must evoke the aid of teachers from the eastern hemisphere. The culture of the American race, in whatever degree they possessed it, *was an indigenous growth,* wholly self-developed, owing none of its germs to any other race, ear-marked with the psychology of the stock.

"Furthermore, this culture was not, as is usually supposed, monopolized by a few nations of the race. The distinction that has been set up by so many ethnographers between 'wild tribes' and 'civilized tribes,' *Jagervolker* and *Culturvolker,* is an artificial one, and conveys a false idea of the facts. There was no such sharp line. Different bands of the same linguistic stock were found, some on the highest, others on the lowest stages of development, as is strikingly exemplified in the Uto-Aztecan family. Wherever there was a center of civilization, that is, wherever the surroundings favored the development of culture, tribes of different stocks enjoyed it to nearly an equal degree, as in central Mexico and Peru. By them it was distributed, and thus shaded off in all directions.

"When closely analyzed, the difference between the highest and the average culture of the race is much less than has been usually taught. The Aztecs of Mexico and the Algonkins of the eastern United States were not far apart, if we overlook the objective art of architecture and one or two inventions. To contrast the one as a wild or savage with the other as a civilized people, is to assume a false point of view and to overlook their substantial psychical equality.

"For these reasons American culture, wherever examined, presents a family likeness which the more careful observers of late years have taken pains to put in a strong light. This was accomplished for governmental institutions and domestic architecture by Lewis H. Morgan; for

(16) Ibid., pp. 34, 35.

property rights and the laws of war by A. F. Bandelier; for the social condition of Mexico and Peru by Dr. Gustav Bruhl; and I may add for the myths and other expressions of the religious sentiment by myself."(17)

Of the character of this American culture, in direct opposition to the notion of our Book of Mormon iron and steel culture, he adds:

"We may say that America everywhere at the time of the discovery was in the polished stone age. It had progressed beyond the rough stage, but had not reached that of metals. True that copper, bronze, and the precious ores were widely employed for a variety of purposes; but flaked and polished stone remained in all parts the principal material selected to produce a cutting edge. Probably three-fourths of the tribes were acquainted with the art of tempering and moulding clay into utensils or figures; but the potter's wheel and the process of glazing had not been invented. Towns and buildings were laid out with a correct eye, and stone structures of symmetry were erected; but the square, the compass, the plumb line, and the scales and weight had not been devised. Commodious boats of hollowed logs or of bark, or of skins stretched on frames, were in use on most of the waters; *but the inventive faculties of their makers had not reached to either oars or sails to propel them,* the paddle alone being relied upon, *and the rudder to guide them was unknown.*"

The Book of Mormon, it will be remembered, represents its people — the Nephites — as possessed of the knowledge of the sail and also the rudder; and Mormon, writing of the state of the Book of Mormon people, represents them as being like "a vessel tossed about upon the waves, without sail or anchor or without anything with which to steer her."(18) A bit of comparison not likely to be used if Mormon and the Nephites were without knowledge of sail or anchors, or rudders.

With all that Mr. Brinton in the foregoing quotations says, Mr. Clark Wissler, whose standing as an authority on these matters has been noted in preceding pages — being Curator of Anthropology in the American Museum of Natural History, New York, and whose work here quoted bears the date of 1917 — is in substantial agreement. This will be seen by the following quotations, for the copiousness of which I shall make no apology. The subjects treated are important.

"Assuming, for the time at least, the single origin of all New World peoples, we may now turn to the question in which all are interested, viz., the relation of the Indians to mankind in general. As has often been stated, the affinities of the New World man are with Mongolians and to a less marked degree with Polynesians. With the former we have close

(17) Ibid., pp. 43-45.
(18) Mormon 5:18.

parallels in hair, form of eye, breadth of face, and bodily proportions. With the Polynesians the agreements are chiefly in pigmentation and to some extent the hair. Hrdlicka," he continues, "has formulated a convenient statement of the problem, which may serve as our point of departure.[27]

"The conclusions, therefore, are: The American natives represent in the main a single stem or strain of people, one homotype; this stem is identical with that of the brown-yellow race of Asia and Polynesia; and the main immigration of the American has taken place, in the main, at least, gradually and by the northwestern route in the earlier part of the recent period, after man had reached a relatively high stage of physical development and multiple secondary differentiations. The immigration, in all probability, was a dribbling and prolonged overflow, likely due to pressure from behind, or want, and a search for better hunting and fishing grounds in the direction where no resistance of man as yet existed. This was followed by multiplication, spread, and numerous minor differentiations of language due to isolation and other natural conditions, and by the development, on the basis of what was transported, of more or less localized American cultures. It is also probable that the western coast of America, within the last 2,000 years, was on more than one occasion reached by small parties of Polynesians, and that the eastern coast was similarly reached by small groups of whites, and that such parties may have locally influenced the culture of the Americans; but such accretions have nowhere, as far as we know today, modified the native population."

Thus far Hrdlicka, and, I judge, with large approval. Commenting on the above, however, Wissler remarks:

"Such conclusions must, in last analysis, rest upon a satisfactory classification of mankind as a whole, but as stated at the outset, this has proved a difficult problem, and the reader will find the literature of the subject very perplexing, each investigator proposing a different scheme."(19)

Still later Mr. Wissler comments: "Now, with the main facts before us (i.e., relative to man in the New World, and his cultural development considered), and recognizing that the differentiation of cultures is a historical phenomenon, we should be able to project the general outlines of man's career in the New World. Recalling our conclusion that the Indian came here from Asia at a relatively recent period, we find ourselves confronted with the question as to what elements of culture man brought with him when he crossed over to America. Recent efforts," he then points out, "have been made to show that all the higher culture complexes of the New World were brought over from the Old, particularly from China or the Pacific Islands." Most of these writings he holds may be

(19) *The American Indian*, pp. 310-12.

ignored as being merely speculative, still some of the facts cited for correspondence to Pacific Island cultures "have not been satisfactorily explained"; and he cites as common to America and the Pacific Islands such things as "blowguns, plank canoes, hammocks, lime chewing, head-hunting cults, the man's house, and certain masked dances common to the New World and the Pacific Islands," and there "appears the tendency to mass upon the Pacific side of the New World." "This gives these traits a semblance of continuous distribution with the Island culture. Yet it should be noted that these traits, as enumerated above, have in reality a sporadic distribution and that there are exceptions." "On the other hand, there is no great *a priori* improbability that some of these traits did reach the New World from the Pacific Islands. Satisfactory proof of such may yet be attained, but such *discoveries would not account for New World culture as a whole.* Then there is abundant data to show that the Polynesians are recent arrivals in the Pacific; *in fact Maya culture must have been in its dotage long before they were within striking distance of the American coast.*"(20)

So Wissler continues the pros and cons of more or less fine spun considerations bearing upon the subject, but the upshot of it all is that while the American race may have had its origin in Central Asia, a very long time ago, and then performed its great crescent formed movement northeasterly into America *via* Bering's Strait, thence southward into Alaska, and southeasterly through what is now British America, the United States, Mexico, Central America, Yucatan, the Isthmus and South America—yet the race arrived in America in such a primitive state of culture—if culture it may be said to have possessed—that the American culture has been developed by these people in America—is, therefore, the culture, indigenous to America, and but slightly, if at all, affected by later intrusions either from Europe or the Pacific Islands. Mr. Wissler then proceeds:

"We have found the highest centres of culture in Mexico and Peru to be not really unique growths, *but to possess many of the fundamental traits common to the wilder folk in the marginal areas of both continents.* New World culture is thus a kind of pyramid whose base is as broad as the two Americas and whose apex rests over middle America. *We have found no just ground for assuming that the culture of the Maya was projected into the New World from the Old,* where it rested as the replica of cultures beyond the Pacific. That influences of various kinds did reach the New World from the Old is apparent, but each of these must upon its own merits, particularly as to its chronology, be subjected to the most exacting investigation. . . . The centres of civilization in the New World

(20) Ibid., pp. 355-56.

were the highlands of Mexico and western South America which, as they developed, reacted to the stimulus of their more backward brothers in the other parts of the land in much the same fashion as did the different groups of Mongoloid peoples in Asia."(21)

Relative to chronology of Native American culture Mr. Wissler has some very enlightening conclusions. After a very fine introduction of his chapter on chronology he remarks:

"Mexico, Peru, and Yucatan have histories from which, as a vantage ground, respectable chronologies have been established. Of these, the last is the most extended, for the very good reason that the Maya have left to us a number of dated inscriptions. While these have come down to us in terms of the curious and highly original Maya calendar, yet modern scholars have been able to correlate them with our own reckoning. This correlation is, of course, not absolute, so the exact dates of one investigator do not quite agree with those of another, but still all have the same sequence. The following brief list based upon Morley's readings will give an adequate idea of the age of Maya culture."(22)

Mr. Wissler then quotes Morley to the effect that the earliest date for the Maya culture is fixed at 200 B.C.[28] Their period of sculpture is fixed at 50 A.D., the last of dated sculpture fixed at 600 A.D. The triple alliance of Chichen Itza, Uxmal and Mayapan—a native confederacy—and the period of architectural development (which now excites our wonder) is placed at 1,000 A.D. The breaking up of this triple alliance by the ruler of Chichen Itza, who was overcome by the ruler of Mayapan, aided by the Nahua—and which marks the beginning of the rise of the Nahua influence, is fixed at 1200 A.D., while the overthrow of Mayapan and the collapse of Maya culture is set down at 1450 A.D. A hundred years later—1517, to be exact—the first Spanish expedition came to Yucatan.

"Thus we see," Mr. Wissler remarks, "that fully two thousand years ago Maya art had already reached a high level of development, *implying far more remote beginnings*. No such series can be found in Peruvian antiquities, but they may be the older for all that. The history of the rise of the Inca is fairly well known, the succession of rulers being as follows."(23)

Then follows a table of the Incas beginning with Rocca the first definitely known, about 1200 A.D., to Huascar in 1532, when the Spaniards came on the scene.(24)

"For the career of the Aztec in Mexico we have a respectable historic

(21) Ibid., pp. 361-64.
(22) Ibid., p. 270.
(23) Ibid., p. 271.
(24) Ibid.

literature, but for the want of dated sculptures cannot estabish so remote a chronology as for the Maya." The table of the Mexican chronology is then given, the earliest dates being but crudely approximate, it is confessed. The Toltec cities of Tula, etc. are said to be founded 300 A.D. The founding of the city of Mexico, by the Aztecs, is set down at 1325 A.D., and the building of the great temple in the city of Mexico—famous for human sacrifices—is set down as 1487. Cortes in 1521 captures the city. A list of Aztec rulers is quoted from the native historian Sahagun extending from 1370 A.D. to 1521, when the Spaniards came.(25)

"The career of the Aztec rulers," remarks Mr. Wissler, "closely parallels both as to time and extent that of the Inca in Peru, but both were later than the rise of the Maya. The similar dominance of the rulers of Bogota in Colombia should be noted, though historians have been less successful in projecting their chronology."(26)

As to earlier periods of chronology for man's occupancy of America, Wissler concedes that Holmes has successfully combatted all claims to an inter-glacial man in America; "but this negative result," he claims, "is difficult to harmonize with the cultural career of the aborigines"; and this led Boas—1910—to formulate the dissenting view, viz., that man was an inhabitant of America in the inter-glacial age.[29] "Many investigators agree," continues Wissler, "that ten to twenty thousand years is all that can be allotted for the lapse of time since the last retreat of the ice in the New World. This, of itself," Wissler suggests, "might give time enough to account for the growth of American culture." "Reference to our chapter on chronology," however, he remarks, "will show that this leaves a very narrow margin for the development of aboriginal culture"(27)—ten to twenty thousand years.

This is here set down just to indicate the long periods of time these modern authorities demand for the occupancy of the New World by man, and for the development of his cultures.

Mr. W. H. Holmes is the author of a series of *Hand Books* on *Aboriginal American Antiquities,* published under government direction by the Smithsonian Institution, Bureau of American Ethnology. My quotations from him are from Bulletin 60—1919—and will be so indicated throughout.

On the sources of "mis-information" about American antiquities, his remarks are so illuminating, and so valuable as a warning against a too ready acceptance of sporadic and irresponsible reports of American Antiquities, that they are given here at length:—

(25) Ibid., p. 272.
(26) Ibid.
(27) Ibid., p. 317.

"While the resources enumerated (i.e., certain sources of information) are or may be drawn upon with gratifying results, the sources of misinformation are no less a subject of archeological concern. These comprise, referring especially to America, the misinterpretations and errors embodied in four centuries of literature, among which are the imperfect observations and erroneous deductions of a host of amateur explorers and would-be historians. Especially to be deprecated is the utilization of this class of observations by enthusiastic supporters of vague theories and preconceived views, and the demand for sensational matter by the public press, a large contingent of which is ready to accept for public consumption whatever is novel or sensational without serious regard for its verity.

"The diversity of invented and exaggerated statements which finds currency is, indeed, appalling. The world hears constantly of the discovery of skeletons of giants and of pygmies; of caverns filled with mummified bodies and rich plunder; of ruined cities abounding in marvelous works of art; of hardened copper; of walls and buildings of astonishing magnitude; of sunken continents; of ancient races associated with extinct species of animals; of inscribed tablets of doubtful origin and extraordinary import; of low-browed crania attributed to prehistoric races but which are mere local variations or pathological freaks; of fossil bones of animals parading as the bones of man; of reputed petrified human bodies which, on inspection, turn out to be of modern cement; of faked pottery, metal work, and the like, so well wrought and so insidiously brought to the attention of scholars as to have become in certain instances the types of antiquity; of learned readings of undecipherable inscriptions; and of the remains of man and his culture from formations of all ages, dating from the present back to the Carboniferous age. The output is so great and the public mind so receptive to error that the tide of misinformation keeps steadily on, hardly reduced in bulk by the never-ceasing efforts of science. The compilations of a Bancroft, a Winsor, or a Fiske, illumined as they are by exceptional genius, could not always rise above the vitiated records upon which they drew; and our best authorities in many cases are subject to the danger of combining the original errors into new fictions so compounded and difficult of analysis as to elude the vigilance even of the critical scientific world.

"From the first, potent agencies of error have conspired to obscure the aboriginal record. The attitude of the propaganda of Christianity at the period of discovery was such that the first impulse of the Spanish conquerors was to destroy at once all traces of the native religion, and a vast number of important sculptures, the 'idols' of the people, were mutilated or beaten to fragments, and the native books and paintings, the treasures of native learning and art, were ruthlessly destroyed. The impulse to destroy was perhaps not so strong on the part of the French and English when they reached North America, but this may have been due in part to the fact that there was little to destroy that could be regarded as dangerous to the cause of religious fanaticism.

"The loss to history through this policy of destruction is beyond compute. The thought of preserving a record of the native people and the strange cultures which they had developed seems to have entered the minds of but few until 300 years had passed, and even then it was only when questions of the geological antiquity of man came to the front in Europe that it was deemed worth while to inquire into the present or the past of the aborigines of America as scientific problems. The work of sifting the truth from the literature of this period is a task surpassed in difficulty only by that of the explorer who essays to dig his data from the ground."(28)

On the problems of American Archaeology he remarks: "Many of the problems of antiquity have been solved, but still others remain which must await fuller investigation than has yet been possible." Among these are the origin of the native race, the period or periods of arrival in America, the routes of migration, the areas occupied by the successive incoming groups, the character and relations of the cultures introduced, the influence of environments and of successive environments on the people and their culture, and the manner in which the stages of culture supervened one upon another, together with their general chronology. Indeed, some of the questions can never be fully answered, as the solutions are unrecorded in the objective forms of art with which archeology has principally to deal. However—this much he claims has been done—"the deep mystery which a short time ago enshrouded some of the greater problems is now dispelled, *and visions of mysterious races and lost civilizations haunt the minds of those only who failed to keep in touch with the progress of archeological research throughout America.*"(29)

Remarking on the progress of archeological research, Mr. Holmes gives the following account of it.

"Scientific research in the domain of America archeology did not begin until well along in the nineteenth century, and for a long time the meager disquisitions respecting the remains of antiquity were colored by speculative interpretations and handicapped by the point of view imposed by Old World conditions. Gradually, however, archeologists have broken away from the thrall of the past and have exposed many of the fallacies which had grown into settled beliefs, and now the records of pre-historic times are being interpreted in the light of their own testimony. The

(28) Bulletin 60, pp. 10-12.
(29) Ibid., preface, p. xv.

public, however, is slow to follow and the cloud is not fully lifted from the popular mind, which seems prone, perhaps, from long habit, to find error more fascinating than truth.

"Among the fallacies which early took hold of the popular mind, appearing everywhere in the older literature, are those of the presence in America of civilized pre-Indian populations. The mound builders, so-called, were supposed to have reached a high stage of culture, and to have disappeared completely as a race, a conclusion reached after superficial examination of the monumental remains of the Mississippi Valley. This idea had held with great tenacity notwithstanding the facts that many articles of European provenance (origin) are found in the mounds as original inclusions, indicating continuance of construction into post-Columbian times, and that the aborigines in various parts of the American Continent, as in Mexico, Central America, and Peru, when first encountered by the Spanish invaders, were occupying a culture stage far in advance of anything suggested by the antiquities of the Mississippi Valley."(30)

Remarking further on this subject of the mound builders, he says:

"During the second half of the century researches extending over a large part of the United States were rapidly initiated, and a vast body of substantial information was brought together and published by individuals, societies, and institutions, and by the government. During this period a gradual change took place in the views of students regarding the mound builders, and at the close of the century there was practical unanimity in the view that the builders of the great earthworks were the ancestors of the Indian tribes found in possession of the general region, and that the culture represented is not of a grade especially higher than that of the tribes first encountered by the whites in the lower Mississippi Valley and in some of the Gulf States to the east."(31)

He reaches the same conclusion with reference to the cliff dwellers of our arid and semi-arid regions.(32)

Concerning the theory of degeneracy of American culture, between the present and past, and the consequent implied notion that it required a highly civilized race to produce it, and now vanished, he writes:

"Among the varied misconceptions embodied in our literature is the belief that the native culture had reached before the Columbian discovery its highest development and had given way to a period of general decadence, conforming thus with the fate of certain Old World civilizations. Although frequently promulgated, this theory is not fully

(30) Ibid., p. 13.
(31) Ibid., pp. 15, 16.
(32) Ibid., p. 13.

sustained by facts with regard to the race as a whole; doubtless some advanced groups, as the Maya, had reached a climax of progress and had retrograded, but it would be difficult to prove that any of these cultures, represented as they are by important works of sculpture and architecture, were on the whole greatly superior to the culture achievement of the Aztec or the Incas at the period of discovery. Among the conciliatory offerings of Montezuma sent to the approaching conqueror of Mexico were certain works of art unsurpassed on the continent for technical perfection and esthetic refinement, and the culmination of Mayan culture development, even if decadent at the period of conquest, could not have been remote. The remarkable stucco embellishments of the city of Palenque, for example, exposed in a peculiarly destructive climate, on the pillars, roofs, and roof crests of the great buildings, are not entirely effaced today, and this evidence of recentness cannot be fully discredited by the chronological determinations of archeologists obtained through a study of the inscriptions, since these, so far as read, may not represent the later stages of the local development."(33)[30]

Respecting the origin of the American race Mr. Holmes holds to the biotic solidarity of the human race, which he represents as now meeting with "very general acceptance" (p. 18); also to the greater antiquity of man in the Old World, and hence to the migration of man to the New (in, to us, remote periods) though not necessarily confining it to one movement nor to the coming of one tribe or race. "Not only does America," he remarks, "furnish no tangible evidence of antiquity so great as to give the theory of autochthonic [indigenous] origin of the American race, but . . . it has failed so far to afford satisfactory evidence of the arrival of man on the continent in remote geologic time."(34)

Then on the subject of Asiatic origin and the probability that more than one tribe or race may have come into America, he writes:

"The student pursuing inquiries with regard to racial origins in America turns to the known aborigines and their somatic characteristics, historic and prehistoric, and seeks to discover significant suggestions of relationship with Old World races. Heretofore, knowledge of the peoples of northeastern Asia has been so meager that satisfactory comparisons with them could not be made, but recent researches have opened up this field and have demonstrated the marked similarity of certain of the northeastern Asiatic tribes to the American Indians. This fact, taken in connection with the geographical proximity of northeastern Asia and Arctic America, would seem to offer a satisfactory solution of the question of origin."(35)

(33) Ibid., pp. 14, 15.
(34) Ibid., p. 19.
(35) Ibid.

Later he remarks: "The aborigines are usually spoken of as a distinct race, but are more properly regarded as a subrace — an ancient off shoot of the yellow-brown race of Asia. Notwithstanding this, it is observed that the racial characters of the Americans are measurably distinctive and homogenous, differing more or less from those of the better-known typical Asiatics, and some students have reached the conclusion that a long period was required to bring about these results. Again, those who begin with the assumption that the arrivals in America were of a single or homogeneous stock marvel at the diversity in physical characters exhibited by the tribes, *and inquire whether a long period was not required to produce the differentiations;* but until the character of the incoming peoples with respect to homogeneity is determined, it is practically unavailing to attempt an estimate of the chronologic significance of present similarities and differences. Although the immigrants may have reached America through a single portal they were not necessarily a homogeneous people racially. Today the great region from which they are believed to have been derived contains tribes exhibiting marked physical differences, diversity being the rule among primitive tribes there as elsewhere. Arrivals along the Bering shores, whether during glacial, interglacial, or postglacial times, probably included numerous tribes, or even linguistic stocks presenting degrees of physical differences corresponding to those observed today among the tribes of Siberia, and Mongolia, or even those of central Asia. Considering these possibilities and the extent of the American Continent over which the immigrants wandered, the similarities of group characters are perhaps quite as much to be remarked upon as the differences, and are at present equally valueless as indexes of chronology."(36)

It is to be observed here that Mr. Holmes does not hold that radical diversity of languages among the Americans, such as Mr. Couch refers to in his question, does not require long periods of time to develop, but holds that there may have been "numerous tribes or even linguistic stocks that migrated to America," and that part of the differentiations in the languages of the migrating tribes took place in Asia. Then, again, it must always be remembered in speaking of chronology, or the time element in all these more recent authorities on American antiquities, there is an abandonment of the Biblical chronology as set forth by Usher, and hence that time element deals with much longer periods than runs with the popular conception of chronology in relation to these things. It must be conceded, however, that Mr. Holmes stands for a more recent date to be read into our American Archeology than other authorities on the subject, both as to the geological periods when man appears in the New

(36) Ibid., pp. 54, 55.

World as well as to the time element that is required for the development of American culture. He it was who assailed so vigorously the antiquity of man in America as indicated by the discovery of the Calaveras skull, alleged by Whitney[31] and other geologists to demonstrate that man occupied America in Tertiary times, perhaps more than a million years ago; and many have accepted the deductions of Holmes in this discussion on man's geological antiquity based upon this and other geological finds, as reasonable.(37)

On the subject of the time element in the discussion of cultural development Mr. Holmes holds the following conservative views:

"The diversified phenomena of material culture have been the subject of extended studies by chronologists. The evolution of the arts and industries of primitive peoples was naturally a process involving much time, but assuming that culture development in America began with an advanced hunter-fisher stage, progress toward the higher stages, observed by the European colonists, may have been comparatively rapid. Traces of geologically ancient man have not been found in America as in Europe, and investigations are proceeding with painful slowness and much halting along the various lines of research, and false leads have been followed in many cases, prolonging the investigations and impeding progress. Students have sought in many ways to establish a chronology of the occupation of the continent by man. The magnitude of the work accomplished in the building of mounds and other earthworks in the Mississippi Valley has been dwelt upon at length, and the time required for the growth and decay upon these works of a succession of forests has been computed. The vast accumulations of midden deposits in both North and South America and the fact that the beds composing them seem in cases to indicate a succession of occupancies by tribes beginning in savagery and ending in well-advanced barbarism have been considered by chronologists. Striking physiographic mutations, as changes of level in coast lines and alterations in river courses since man took possession, have been taken into account. Modifications of particular species of mollusks between the time of their first use on the shell-heap sites and the present time, and the development in one or more cases of new varieties, suggest hoary antiquity, but the highest estimate of elapsed times based on these evidences does not exceed a few thousand years. After carefully weighing the evidence collected by him in Alaska, Dall reached the conclusion that the earliest midden deposits on the Aleutian Islands are probably as much as 3,000 years old. It is possible that, considering the character of the evidences, other students utilizing the

(37) Holmes's discussion of the subject will be found in Chapter VIII, "Problems of Chronology," ibid., pp. 51-94.

same observations might have reached results differing from those of Dall.

"We view with wonder the massive ruins left by the more cultured peoples of Middle and South America and speculate on the time required for the evolution of stone-built cities, as Tiahuanaco or Cuzco, Chichen or Copan, from villages or primitive type. Referring, however, to Old World civilizations, we discover that many of the grandest culture developments matured quickly and were short-lived, being the product of some spasm of religious enthusiasm or some abnormal development of national power and enterprise. In India, for example, some of the most wonderful architectural creations of all time were built and abandoned within a few centuries. It is a well-ascertained fact that while the great architectural monuments of Java, Cambodia, and India were rising in their grandeur in the early centuries of the Christian era, the stone-built structures of America were also springing up in the forests of Yucatan and Central America. Centuries rather than millenniums have witnessed the accomplishment of the greatest material achievements of humanity. Shall we then be able to predicate great antiquity for the occupation of the American Continent on the testimony furnished by the achievements of human labor or even on the length of time required for the evolution of the American cultures from the Asia?"(38)

This would seem quite encouraging for those whose theories both for the origin of the American race and of its culture require a more recent time than is generally allowed by authorities for their claims, but so far as the time element for Book of Mormon statements is concerned, the next paragraph of Bulletin 60 ends all such encouragement. I quote it:

"As thus presented, the testimony of racial and cultural phenomena *dissociated from geological criteria does not serve* to indicate clearly an antiquity for the aboriginal occupancy beyond a few thousand years. *Through association with geological formations, the age of which can be determined with some degree of accuracy, both cultural and somatic remains combine to extend our vision with reasonable clearness well back toward the close of the last glacial occupation of middle North America, a period whose duration is estimated by some students at from eight to twenty thousand years.* Some students of the subject are satisfied that authentic evidence of man's presence during the glacial period has been obtained, others find sufficient reasons for believing in man's existence in both North and South America far back in Tertiary times, while a single bold advocate of autochthonic antiquity has promulgated the view

(38) Ibid., pp. 56-58.

that man originated in the western world rather than in the eastern, and proceeds to identify his forbears among the American lower orders."(39)

This estimate of from eight to twenty thousand years, leading back to the close of the last glacial occupation of middle North America, represents *the minimum of time for such occupancy,* save for the remark of Dellenbaugh in his Preface to *The North Americans of Yesterday* where he holds, in his belief, that there has been an error in considering the glacial period of the remote past. He declares that "it is probably less than 5,000 years since the ice front was at Lake Erie. Eminent geologists have estimated it as less than 7,000 based on the erosion at Niagara; but as the erosion immediately following the disappearance of the ice is extremely rapid, it seems safe to cut down the period."(40) Discussing this glacial age in the body of his work Dellenbaugh says:

"The period of time that has elapsed since the so-called disappearance of the ice was formerly believed to be very great, but latterly views on this point have been much modified. Gilbert has declared, after a study of the Niagara gorge, that the time since the ice left that region is not more than seven thousand years, perhaps less. More recent investigations have tended to confirm his suggestion of fewer years. Immediately after the recession of glacial ice, as may be seen in Alaska today, erosion is extremely rapid. I have not space to discuss this point at length, but it is apparent that the rate of erosion is variable, *and I doubt if more than five thousand years have passed since the ice left the vicinity of the Niagara gorge.* As it still lingers in the North, far down on the Pacific side, it is probably not more than a thousand years since its influence was powerful in affecting the climate of all the region southward. The north is undoubtedly growing warmer. Some five hundred years ago Alaska was still covered with glacial ice. Five hundred years from now there will scarcely be a glacier to be found there, except in the highest mountains. 'The next generation will find few of them with their fronts still in the sea,' says Henry Gannett."(41)

This passage, however, it must be remembered, has to do with the recession of the ice line of the glacial period from the middle regions of the United States, and not the fixing of the time of the American Race's occupancy of the continent. Dellenbaugh holds to a greater antiquity for man in America than the glacial period itself. His views are interesting, and important, and carry with them not a little evidential value. I quote:

"On this continent (i.e., North America) the chief centre of culture

(39) Ibid., p. 58.
(40) *North Americans of Yesterday,* preface, p. xi.
(41) Ibid., pp. 441, 443.

was the narrowest part; the population was packed there as in the narrow end of a funnel, leaving the whole broad top thinly peopled. The question immediately arises: 'Why was this so?' It is evident at a glance that there was some preponderating, irresistible influence which compelled the inhabitants to draw into these narrow, restricted regions, there to act and react one tribe on another, and this influence was constantly at work moulding them all. If the continent had been peopled within any comparatively recent time, it is not reasonable to suppose that the tribes would willingly have huddled together far down in the most limited area. It is also from this area apparently that all the arts have spread. The crowding and the culture development were coincident. What was the cause of it? If we can arrive at a satisfactory understanding of the cause, it seems to me that we have the solution of the whole matter. The explanation appears to be that the continent was *peopled before the beginning of the glacial epoch, and the crowding into the narrow regions, and consequently the development of culture there, were due to the encroachment from the north of the great cold.* Wright says: 'Just before the beginning of the ice age, a temperate climate corresponding to latitude 35 on the Atlantic coast [i.e., roughly, the line of Cape Hatteras on the Atlantic, Memphis, and Los Angeles] extended far up toward the north pole, permitting Greenland and Spitzbergen to be covered with trees and plants similar in most respects to those found at the present time in Virginia and North Carolina. Here indeed in close proximity to the north pole were then residing, in harmony and contentment, the ancestors of nearly all the plants and animals which are now found in the north temperate zone.' It is not unreasonable to suppose, then, that man was also here, though as yet the scientific evidence is perhaps not sufficient to prove it. If he circles the globe in the Northern regions at that time, and was also occupying Central portions, the cold drove all south, and together with changes of land levels, cut off the American division from the other world. *Migration legends are useless in determining the origin of the Amerinds, for they can only relate to the comparatively recent changes of location before which for a long period,* the people drifted up and down and across the continent under the influences I have suggested. However, man first originated, or where, he was doubtless distributed, like the flora and fauna, at some exceedingly remote period, over the whole world, by causes not now understood, but one of which was probably a greater continuity of land surfaces than exists today."(42)

Then later: "The people were driven southward [i.e., by the ice movement], and those most favorably situated developed the most. The people most favorably situated were all who were already in, or could

(42) Ibid., pp. 431-32.

fight their way to, the temperate lowlands of southern Mexico and Central America, which were rendered somewhat more extensive by the recession of the sea, caused by the withdrawal of the immense quantities of water that were heaped up in ice thousands of feet in thickness. This has been estimated to have lowered the waters of the ocean by from 500 to 1,000 feet. The lands thus laid bare were climatically inviting and probably were soon covered with vegetation. In South America the people were crowded northward, or held there by the cold coming from the south. It would be in the northern portions, particularly the lowlands, that we ought to find evidence of the highest development, especially on the side receiving warm currents, and there is where we do find it. We apparently have then a northern and a southern limit to the ancient inhabitants of this hemisphere within which climatic conditions during the period of great cold, and for some time thereafter, were most favourable to human development. This limit in the Northern continent is latitude 23° and in the Southern also 23°. Within these lines the great pre-Columbian development took place, and the heart of this development, on the Northern continent, seems to have rested between the isthmus of Tehuantepec and the present upper frontier of Honduras, chiefly on the lowlands, and probably also on lands now beneath the ocean.

"In North America, south of latitude 23°, then, most of the tribes of the continent were crowded by the great cold, and here they developed their chief characteristics, so that by the time the ice began its last recession they had become a homogeneous people, with the greatest advancement and the greatest similarities in the region where the population had been densest, with a diminishing scale outward, those tribes farthest from the culture centre varying most from the highest culture attained. The tribe on the extreme edge was, and is now, represented by the Eskimo. The development and the distribution of the arts were in the same order, and here apparently is the explanation of the superior excellence of Central American arts, and the seeming derivation of all the arts on the continent from this centre. Finally the recession of the ice caused renewed trouble. The melting of it and the return thereby of the locked-up waters to the ocean caused a submergence of lowlands that had been made habitable by their withdrawal. There were floods and floods. Tribes were overwhelmed or were driven to higher ground. There was a renewed shifting of populations over the whole continent. Those which had been held back toward the highlands and toward the ice, accustomed to the cool airs and to a particular food, readily followed the retrogression of the ice, impelled always by pressure of the tribes farther south. They were inured to cold. The most southerly tribes became inured somewhat to heat, and clung to their lands, impelled also to do this by the pressure of wilder tribes recoiling from contact with still other tribes. But heat being debilitating, and especially so to the Amerind constitution, the Yucatan peoples, who were those who had attained the highest development, gradually degenerated under its influence, and before the voyage of Columbus whole cities were depopulated. Some held their own for a longer period, but were already on the way to decline when the Spaniards appeared. In some cases their towns were occupied by an inferior tribe of perhaps the same stock, or an inferior tribe dwelt around them, and, not knowing the origin of the architectural works, attempted to account for them by fairy tales like the legend of the Dwarf's House, which Stephens learned. The people nearest the ice front are still represented by the Eskimo, and their next neighbours, as of yore, are the Athabascans, and Algonquins, and so on down in zones more or less distinct, but considerably deranged by subsequent migrations, to the builders of the Yucatan ruins."(43)

To this I add the testimony of Frederick Webb Hodge, author of *Handbook of American Indians, North of Mexico, in Two Parts*, published by Smithsonian Institution, Bureau of American Ethnology, Bulletin 30, 1912, 2,193 pages. The following is from the article on Archeology:

"In no part of America are there remains of man or his works clearly indicating the presence of peoples distinct from the Indian and the Eskimo, or having culture markedly different in kind and degree from those characterizing the aborigines of historic times. Archeological researches serve to carry the story of the tribes and their culture back indefinitely into the past, although the record furnished by the various classes of remains grows rapidly less legible as we pass beyond the few well-illumined pages of the historic period. It is now known that the sedentary condition prevailed among the aborigines to a much larger extent than has been generally supposed. The more advanced nations of Middle and South America have been practically stationary for long periods, as indicated by the magnitude of their architectural achievements, and even such primitive groups as the Iroquois, Algonquins, and others of northern America have occupied their general historic habitat for unnumbered generations. The prehistoric remains of the various regions thus pertain in large measure to the ancestors of the historic occupants, and the record is thus much more simple than that of prehistoric Europe. ... Efforts have been made to distinguish definite states of culture progress in America corresponding to those established in Europe, but there appears to be no very close correspondence. The use of stone was universal among the tribes, and chipped and polished implements appear to have been employed at all periods and by peoples of every stage of culture, although the polishing processes seem to have grown relatively

(43) Ibid., pp. 435-40.

more important with advancing culture, being capable of producing art works of the higher grades, while flaking processes are not. Some of the more advanced tribes of the South were making marked headway in the use of metals, *but the culture was everywhere essentially that of polished stone.* (See Stone-work, Metal-work.)

"The antiquity of men in America has been much discussed in recent years, but as yet it is not fully agreed that any great antiquity is established. Geological formations in the United States, reaching well back toward the close of the Glacial period, possibly ten thousand years, are found to include remains of man and his arts; but beyond this time the traces are so meager and elements of doubt so numerous that conservative students hesitate to accept the evidence as satisfactory."(44) This conservative estimate of 10,000 years, carries us far beyond the time limits fixed by the Book of Mormon.

Of John Fiske's views of the antiquity of man on the America continents I have already given quotations in the division on languages, and nothing further either from him or others will be necessary to get the modern viewpoint on these questions before us.

After the above had been written my attention was called by Professor Levi Edgar Young of the Department of History of the State of Utah University,³² to an article in *Science* for August 11th, 1915 (pp. 190-95) by G. Elliot Smith,³³ in which it was thought from recollection of the article, that evidence was adduced that would modify somewhat the more recent ideas as given in the foregoing respecting the origin, age, and source of American culture, and perhaps compel a return to the earlier idea of an Egyptian or Hebrew origin for the American race and its culture. Examination of this article, however, discloses nothing that covers any of these points in a way to affect the problems of our Book of Mormon difficulties. Mr. Smith's article is a protest against what he regards as the mischievous inclination to accept the precept of some of our recent writers who in accounting for similar cultural traits existing between the American race and Old World cultural traits, say that such likeness arises from the "similarity" of the workings of the human mind; that "similar needs and like circumstances will lead various isolated groups of men in a similar phase of culture, independently one of the other, to invent similar arts and crafts, and to evolve identical beliefs." Then Mr. G. Elliot Smith, having inveighed against dogmatism, rather dogmatically launches the opinion that there was about the 9th century B.C. a widely diffused culture from Egypt into all surrounding countries of the world. He turns to what he considers — "The positive evidence that establishes the reality of the migrations of culture-bearing peoples, it will be found

(44) Bulletin 30, Part I, pp. 74-76.

that there is now available a vast mass of precise and unquestionable testimony in substantiation of the conclusion that the curiously distinctive culture-complex which was gradually built up in Egypt between the years B.C. 4,000 and B.C. 900 began to be widely diffused, at some time after the latter date, west, south and east; and that the latter (the easterly migration), with many additions and modifications which it received on the way (in the Sudan, East Africa, and Arabia; in the eastern Mediterranean, Phoenicia, Armenia and Babylonia; in India, Ceylon, Burma and the Malay Peninsula; in Indonesia and China; and finally in Polynesia) ultimately reached the Pacific coast of the Americas and leavened the aboriginal population of the vast continent with the ferment of the ancient civilization of the Old World."

This averment that there may have been an Egyptian cultural infusion into America 900 years B.C. affords no solution to the Book of Mormon difficulties that require not the evidence of an infusion of this character to leaven "the aboriginal population of the vast continent with the ferment of the ancient civilizations of the Old World"—not this, but what is required is that evidence shall be produced that will give us an *empty America 3,000 years* B.C., into which a colony from the Euphrates valley (supposedly) may come and there establish a race and an empire with an iron and steel culture; with a highly developed language of that period; then, after an existence of about sixteen or eighteen hundred years, shall pass away, become extinct in fact, as a race and as a nation; this about 600 B.C., *leaving the American continents again without human inhabitants.*

Then into these second time empty American continents—empty of human population—we want the evidence of the coming of two small colonies about 600 B.C., which shall be the ancestors of all native American races as we know them; possessing as did the former race—domestic animals, the horse, ass and cow; with an iron and steel culture; and a highly developed written literature, the national Hebrew literature in fact.

Any one who will hold these needs of our Book of Mormon difficulties in mind will discover that they are not at all affected by the *Science* article of Mr. G. Elliot Smith.

Once more we face our problems—how shall we answer the questions that arise from these considerations of American archeology?

Can we successfully overturn the evidences presented by archeologists for the great antiquity of man in America, and his continuous occupancy of it, and the fact of his stone age culture, not an iron and steel culture? Can we successfully maintain the Book of Mormon's comparatively recent advent of man in America and the existence of his iron and steel and domestic animal, and written language stage of culture against the deductions of our late American writers upon these themes?

If we cannot, what is to be the effect of it all upon the minds of our youth? What is to be our general standing before the enlightened opinion of mankind? Is silence to be our answer? Again will occur to thoughtful minds the difficulties attendant upon silence. In the last analysis of things silence would be acknowledgement of defeat. Silence in an age of free inquiry is impossible. An appeal to the old writers is of little value. The recent accepted authoritative writers leave us, so far as I can at present see, no ground of appeal or defense—the new knowledge seems to be against us. To stand up and say to the modern world we place our revealed truth against all the evidence and deductions of your science, and await the vindication of new evidence yet to be discovered, is heroic; but is it, and will it be convincing? Most humbly, but also most anxiously, I await the further development of knowledge that will make it possible for us to give a reasonable answer to those who question us concerning the matters herein discussed.

But, of course, in the meantime there may have occurred to your more enlightened minds a solution to all these problems that will cause all our difficulties to disappear. Most humbly I pray it may be so, and I shall be happy to give that enlightenment welcome.

NOTES

1. Jacob M. Myers, *I and II Esdras* (Garden City, N.Y.: Doubleday & Co., 1974), prints the books of Esdras, together with notes and a preface. II Esdras is composed of three major parts: Chapters 1-2 discuss Ezra's commission from the Lord and the deliverance of the Jews from Egyptian bondage; Chapters 3-14 contain the original material of the book, the seven visions of Ezra, and Chapters 15-16 note the Lord's promises to deliver the Hebrew people from persecution. The entire book is a work of lamentation about the oppressions, sufferings, and torments of Ezra's people. Chapter 13 deals with the Lost Ten Tribes and their travels east into an uninhabited country.

2. Gregorio Garcia, *Origen de los Indios de el Nuevo mundo, e Indias Occidentales, averiguado con discurso de opiniones por el padre presentado Fr. Gregorio Garcia* (Madrid: En la imprenta de F. Martinez Abad, 1729).

3. James Adair, *The History of the American Indians* (London: E. and C. Dilly, 1775). A recent reprint adds further insight to this famous work: Samuel Cole Williams, ed., *Adair's History of the American Indians* (New York: Argonaut Press, 1966). Adair arrived in South Carolina in 1735 to engage, for a period of forty years, in the Indian trade among the Cherokee, Catawba, and Chickasaw. He then went to England, where his book appeared in 1775. His purpose was to give an account of the origin and history of the southern Indians and to examine their language, religion, methods of making war and peace, and other aspects of their culture. Adair was especially interested in the similarities of the customs and religious rites of these Indians with those of the Jews, and

he advanced twenty-three "arguments" to prove his thesis. His work has been used as a basic authority by many American ethnologists and historians.

4. Henry R. Schoolcraft, *Historical and Statistical Information Respecting the History, Conditions and Prospects of the Indian Tribes of the United States*, 6 vols., collected and prepared under the direction of the Bureau of Indian Affairs per Act of Congress of March 3, 1847 (Philadelphia: Lippincott, Grambo, 1851). The work attempted to examine all seventy tribes east of the Rocky Mountains as to their names, geographic positions, events, languages, and monuments, with language being considered as "the true key of their affinities." Volume 4 contains the two articles B. H. Roberts mentions: Thomas Hurlburt, "A Memoir on the Inflections of the Chippewa Tongue," 385-96; and William Hamilton, "Remarks on the Iowa Language," 397-406. Hurlburt thought that "the Indian languages seem naturally to fall into the track of the Hebrew," while Hamilton was of the opinion that "the principles of the language correspond more with the ancient than with the modern class of languages; with the Hebrew . . . more than with any other."

5. John Wesley Powell, *Seventh Annual Report of the Bureau of Ethnology to the Secretary of the Smithsonian Institution, 1885-86* (Washington, D.C.: Government Printing Office, 1891). Divided into two parts, the Powell *Report* examines explanations among the Indian mounds and stone villages in Part I and deals with office work in Part II. Three scientific papers accompany the reports, including Colonel Garrick Mallory's discussion of Schoolcraft's work.

6. The footnote referred to on page 18 of Daniel G. Brinton, *The American Race: A Linguistic and Ethnographic Description of the Native Tribes of North and South America* (Philadelphia: D. McKay, 1901), cites Adair's (not Blair's) *History of the North American Indians.* It is possible that the error was made because Roberts may have been aware of another early work on North American Indians: Emma Helen Blair, ed., *The Indian Tribes of the Upper Mississippi Valley and Region of the Great Lakes as Described by Nicolas Perrot, French Commandant in the Northwest*, 2 vols. (Cleveland: Arthur H. Clark Co., 1911). This work was written by Perrot about 1680.

7. John D. Baldwin, *Ancient America, in Notes on American Archaeology* (New York: Harper & Brothers, 1878). The author's aim in this handbook was to give a summary of what was known of American antiquities. Roberts owned a copy of the book, which is filled with his marginal notes. When he read the book, Roberts was attempting to use Baldwin's material to prove the authenticity of the Book of Mormon and noted such references as: p. 69—"Toltec-Nephite"; p. 125—of the origin of the word, Maya, "May not Maya come from Moroni"; p. 198—Baldwin mentions Colhuas who "came from the east in ships," and Roberts notes, "Were Colhuas the Muleks?"; and p. 264, Baldwin wrote that Montesinos listed four brothers as the first rulers of the Inca Empire, and the Roberts's note identifies the four as "Lamon, Lemuel, Sam—Nephi Nephi ruler." The above are typical as selected from Roberts's marginal notes in Baldwin's book.

8. Duncan M. McAllister, "Important Appeal to Native Hawaiians and Other Polynesians," 24 (June 1921):703-12. The author used material from Dr.

Abraham Fornander, *Collection of Hawaiian Folklore*, to prove that the American continent was the original home of the Hawaiian race and that certain Hebraic customs and traditions were common among the American Indians and Polynesians. In the B. H. Roberts collection in the Marriott Library, there is a six-page article entitled "Relationship of American Aborigines and Pacific Islanders," "compiled by D. M. McAllister" and with notes from Reverend William Ellis's "Polynesian Researches."

9. Frederick S. Dellenbaugh, *The North Americans of Yesterday: A Comparative Study of North-American Indian Life, Customs, and Products, on the Theory of the Ethnic Unity of the Race* (New York: G. P. Putnam's Sons, 1906). Dellenbaugh was a member of the second Colorado River voyage with J. W. Powell and held to the theory that the Amerind peoples of the Western Hemisphere had become a "world-race by themselves, existing in various stages of the same culture." Roberts's personal copy has many marginal notes, including the following: p. 14—"CONCLUSION: No evidence of out-side derivation of Am. Race"; p. 16—"Without domestic animals"; p. 30—Dellenbaugh wrote, "Outside of Yucatan and Mexico there were no native books," and Roberts noted, "Use this if you argue for restricted area for N. & Lamanites"; p. 429—Roberts underlined a portion of a sentence of Dellenbaugh's, "As for the Lost-Tribes-of-Israel theory, . . . *no archaeologist of today would be* willing to give it a second thought"; and among the notes on the back end sheets were: "Dialects: Some differences in dialects could not have arisen in less than 2,000 years"; "No old world languages in Am."; and "No *Iron* found among Mayas."

10. Frederick Webb Hodge, ed., *Handbook of American Indians North of Mexico,* Smithsonian Institution, Bureau of American Ethnology, Bulletin 20, in two parts (Washington, D.C.: Government Printing Office, 1907). In this famous work Hodge gives a descriptive list of the linguistic stocks, confederacies and tribes, and settlements north of Mexico, "together with biographies of Indians of note, sketches of their history, archaeology, manners, arts, customs, and institutions, and the aboriginal words incorporated into the English language."

11. H. G. Wells, *The Outline of History,* 1 (New York: Macmillan, 1920). The quotation which Roberts uses is from Chapter XIV of Book II, "The Languages of Mankind."

12. Johann Jakob von Tschudi and Mariano Eduardo de Ribero y Ustáriz, *Peruvian Antiquities,* trans. Francis L. Hawks (New York: A. S. Barnes & Co., 1854). The purpose of the book was to study the institutions of Peru, examine the archeological monuments, and obtain a knowledge of the languages, laws, customs, and empires. Tschudi also published *Travels in Peru* (New York: A. S. Barnes & Co., 1854), which consists of extracts from his journal of a trip through Peru.

13. Hamon L'Estrange, *Americans no Jewes, or Improbabilities that the Americans are of that race* (London: Printed by W. W. for Henry Seile, 1652). After reading Thomas Thorowgood, *Jewes in America, or Probabilities that the Americans are of that Race* (London: Printed by W. H. for Tho. Slater, 1650), L'Estrange, in his book, attacked the "error" of Thorowgood, concluding, "I

confesse I finde him a man of so sharpe an appetite, and strong and easie and Ostrich concotion, as I cannot sit at table any longer with him."

14. Josiah Priest, *American Antiquities and Discoveries in the West* (Albany, N.Y.: Printed by Hoffman & White, 1834). Priest postulates that America was settled by many different peoples before the flood, that it was the country of Noah, and that it was the place where the ark was built.

15. L. E. Wyman, *Notes on the Pleistocene Fossils Obtained from Rancho La Brea Asphalt Pits* (Los Angeles: Los Angeles County Museum of Natural History, 1915). The family of Henry Hancock worked the La Brea Tar Pits from the 1860s down into the early 1900s, selling tons of the asphalt for fuel. In 1913 the family presented the twenty-three-acre plot to the County of Los Angeles. During the next two years, from 1913 to 1915, L. E. Wyman and E. J. Fischer investigated the fossil beds in the Tar Pits, Wyman noting in his journal about Pit #61, "Bones are plentiful . . . and of splendid quality . . . in the first state of preservation."

In the B. H. Roberts collection in the Marriott Library, there is a copy of a letter from Joseph W. McMurrin to Roberts, accompanying the Wyman pamphlet, which indicates that McMurrin talked with Wyman. McMurrin reported: "From Mr. Wyman I received this statement: 'The horse originated in Western North America . . . and migrated to Asia by means of the Northern land bridge! In answer to the direct question, Is there any evidence of the horse having been in the western hemisphere in *historic* times previous to their introduction from Europe? he said: 'None whatever.'" Roberts underlined the word "historic."

Joseph W. McMurrin was a fellow member, with Roberts, of the First Council of Seventy as well as being president of the California Mission. He served as the head of the mission from 1919 until ill health forced his retirement on January 31, 1932. He died October 26, 1932.

16. Woods Hutchinson, "Insect-Borne Diseases," *Saturday Evening Post,* 194 (Dec. 24, 1921):14-15, 61-62. Hutchinson was the author of two books on the subject of communicable diseases: *Preventable Diseases* (Boston: Houghton Mifflin, 1909) and *Common Diseases* (Boston: Houghton Mifflin, 1913). Osborn had just authored two books in his field: *The Origin and Evolution of Life* (New York: Charles Scribner's Sons, 1918) and *Men of the Old Stone Age,* 2d ed. (New York: Charles Scribner's Sons, 1916).

17. William Smith, *A Dictionary of the Bible: Comprising its Antiquities, Biography, Geography, and Natural History, . . . also Archaeology and Literature* (Boston: Thomas Y. Crowell, n.d.). There were other editions besides the above and the Hackett printing, including one edited by the Reverend Samuel W. Barnum (New York: D. Appleton and Co., 1880).

18. Roberts is probably referring to Albon Jasper Conant, *Footprints of vanished races in the Mississippi valley—being an account of some of the monuments and relics of pre-historic races scattered over its surface, with suggestions as to their origin and uses* (St. Louis: C. R. Barnes, 1879).

19. This reference is probably to Peter DeRoo, *History of America before Columbus, according to Documents and Approved Authors* (Philadelphia: J. B. Lippincott, 1900).

20. William H. Prescott, *History of the Conquest of Peru,* ed. John Foster Kirk, 2 vols. (Philadelphia: J. B. Lippincott, 1890).

21. *Wilmore's New Analytical Reference Bible, Containing the following . . . aids to the Proper Study of . . . the Holy Bible . . . Comprehensive Bible Helps . . . revised and edited by Philip Schaff . . .* (New York: Funk & Wagnalls, 1918). *The Schaff-Herzog Encyclopedia of Religious Knowledge* was based on the work of Albert Hauck, edited in the 3rd ed. by Johann J. Herzog, and adapted for the American public by Philip Schaff. An edition edited by Samuel M. Jackson was published in New York City by Funk & Wagnalls in 1908.

22. Robert Jamieson, A. R. Fausset, and David Brown, *A Commentary: critical, practical and explanatory, on the Old and New Testaments . . . ,* 4 vols. (New York: F. H. Revell, 189[?]).

23. John Gardner Wilkinson, *The Manners and Customs of the Ancient Egyptians,* 5 vols. (London: John Murray, 1847). There were several other editions, but pages 247-54 in this one refer to the material Roberts was considering.

24. Edward Gibbon, *The History of the Decline and Fall of the Roman Empire . . . ,* 8 vols. (London: Murray's British Classics, 1887).

25. M. D. C. Crawford, "The Master Weavers of the Desert Empire," *Harper's Magazine,* July 1916, 287-96.

26. Grove Karl Gilbert, *Sixth Annual Report of the Committee of the New York State Reservation* (Albany, 1890).

27. Ales Hrdlicka's many works discounted the theory that "a man of distinctly primitive type and of exceptional geological antiquity" existed on the American continents. He argued "that America was peopled by immigration from the Old World, which could not have taken place until after great multiplication and wide distribution of the human species and the development of some degree of culture." Ales Hrdlicka, *Skeletal Remains Suggesting or Attributed to Early Man in North America,* Smithsonian Institution, Bureau of American Ethnology, Bulletin 33 (Washington, D.C.: Government Printing Office, 1907), 9, 98.

28. Sylvanus Griswold Morley, *An Introduction to the Study of the Maya Hieroglyphs,* Smithsonian Institution, Bureau of American Ethnology, Bulletin 57 (Washington, D.C.: Government Printing Office, 1915), 2, 3.

29. Franz Boas, *Handbook of American Indian Languages,* Smithsonian Institution, Bureau of American Ethnology, Bulletin 40, Part I (Washington, D.C.: Government Printing Office, 1911), 5-14; Franz Boas, *The History of the American Race,* Annals, volume 21 (New York: New York Academy of Sciences, 1912), 177-83.

30. In a marginal note, Roberts wrote "Introduce here Stephens conclusions." John L. Stephens, *Incidents of Travel in Central America, Chiapas, and Yucatan,* 2 vols. (New York: Harper & Brothers, 1871), 2:436-57. The author was of the opinion that there was nothing of Europe or Egypt in the ruins of Central America, that they were unique to the Western Hemisphere. He also was of the opinion that the monuments he observed in Yucatan were not of

great antiquity but had been built by the same people met by the Spanish conquerors "or of some not very distant progenitors."

31. J. D. Whitney, *Auriferous gravels of the Sierra Nevada of California,* vol. 6, no. 1 (Cambridge, Mass.: Memorial Museum of Comparative Zoology at Harvard, 1880), 51-94.

32. Levi Edgar Young, a grandnephew of Brigham Young, and a member of the First Council of Seventy in the Mormon Church from January 23, 1910, until his death on December 13, 1963, was educated as an historian and served as a faculty member at the University of Utah for forty years from 1899 to 1939. He was president of the First Council of Seventy for the last twenty-seven years of his life.

33. G. Elliott Smith, "The Origin of the Pre-Columbia Civilization of America," *Science,* 44 (1916):190-95.

"A BOOK OF MORMON STUDY"

After the disappointing sessions with the leaders of the Church as they discussed his "Book of Mormon Difficulties. A Study" during the winter of 1922, B. H. Roberts continued his search for possible explanations as to the origin of the Mormon scripture and seized the opportunities presented by his mission presidency in New England to examine early literature that could have been available to Joseph Smith during the time the Book of Mormon was being produced. His surprising conclusion was that *View of the Hebrews,* written by the Reverend Ethan Smith of Vermont and published in two editions of 1823 and 1825, predated the writing of the Book of Mormon and could have furnished the "ground plan" for Joseph Smith's authorship. Roberts's "A Book of Mormon Study" considers this approach in some detail, and he bolsters it by extensive reference to the latest scientific investigations available to him during the late winter and early spring of 1922 when he wrote the "Study." Not content with this examination, Roberts also spends the last part of his "Study" examining the "Imaginative Mind" of Joseph Smith, certain internal inconsistencies in the Book of Mormon, and, finally, the similarity of conversions in the book to Christian conversions of the period in the times and vicinity when and where the Book of Mormon was "translated."

LITERATURE AVAILABLE TO JOSEPH SMITH AS A
GROUND PLAN FOR THE BOOK OF MORMON

A number of years ago in my treatise on the Book of Mormon under the general title *New Witnesses for God,* I discussed the subject, "Did the Book of Mormon antedate works in English on American antiquities, accessible to Joseph Smith and his associates." The object in considering the question at that time was to ascertain whether or not the alleged historical incidents of the Book of Mormon, and its subject matter generally, were derived from speculations regarding the origin, migrations, customs, religion, language, or other lore of the American race, published previous to the coming forth of the Book of Mormon; or if the Book of Mormon truly indicated the source of those American Indian traditions and antiquities. Of course the discussion recognized the fact that such publications must not only exist before the coming forth of the Book of Mormon, but must also be accessible to Joseph Smith or his associates, in order to be of any force in the supposition that such publications might have furnished the material from which the Book of Mormon was constructed, or its general outlines suggested.

In that discussion it was pointed out how great the task would be for Joseph Smith to become sufficiently acquainted with the body of American antiquities as to make the alleged historical incidents, religion, and culture of the Book of Mormon peoples conform to all that—as far as it does conform to it. Also the improbability of Joseph Smith acquiring such knowledge, even if available through books, since it is conceded, on all hands, that he was not a reader of—much less a student of—books. But, most of all, it was insisted upon that books sufficient for a ground plan of the Book of Mormon, and accessible to Joseph Smith, did not exist. Books in Spanish were of course eliminated from consideration as being unavailable to Joseph Smith and his associates, for the obvious reason that neither himself nor his associates knew Spanish. It was also stated that the only available English source of information likely to be accessible to him or his associates would be:—
First, the publications of the "American Antiquarian Society, Translations and Collections" published in the *Archaeoligia Americana,* Worcester, Massachusetts, 1820. This information was held to be so fragmentary that it could not have suggested material for the Book of Mormon, even if it could be proven that Joseph Smith was familiar with the collection.
Second, the little book by Ethan Smith, *View of the Hebrews or the Tribes of Israel in America,* published in Vermont (first edition 1823),

second edition in 1825, which I pass for the present without comment, and reserve it for special consideration later.

Third, The History of the American Indians by James Adair, published in England 1775, and much quoted in America. Mr. Adair confines the scope of his work to the North American Indians among whom he was a trader for many years.

Fourth, the translation of some parts of Baron Von Humboldt's works on *New Spain,* published first in America and England, between the years 1806 and 1809; and later John Black's enlarged translation of it in New York, 1811. It was a work frequently quoted by American writers, both before and immediately following the publication of the Book of Mormon.

The writer at the time being considered did not take sufficiently into account the work of Josiah Priest on *American Antiquities,* since it was not published — the first edition of it — until 1833, several years after the publication of the Book of Mormon. It should then have been observed, however, that the material of Priest's book was much in evidence throughout New England and in New York before it was crystalized in his *American Antiquities* publication. For years such materials as were then found and discussed, theories as to the origin of the American Indians, including "the ten lost tribes" theory of Hebrew infusion into the American race, together with frequent mention of cultural traits favorable to this supposed Hebrew infusion — all this was matter of common speculation in the literature of America, before the publication of either Priest's *American Antiquities* or the Book of Mormon. Priest himself, indeed, published a book in which some of these matters were discussed, before the publication of his *Antiquities,* viz., *The Wonders of Nature and Providence,* copyrighted by him June 2nd, 1824, and printed soon afterwards in Rochester, New York, only some twenty miles distant from Palmyra, near which place the Smith family had resided there for some years. It will be observed that this book preceded the publication of the Book of Mormon by about six years. At the time I made for my *New Witness* the survey of the literature on American antiquities, traditions, origins, etc., available to Joseph Smith and his associates, this work of Priest's was unknown to me; as was also the work by Ethan Smith, *View of the Hebrews* — except by report of it, and as being in my hands but a few minutes.

In his book, by Josiah Priest, *The Wonders of Nature and Providence,* at page 228, Mr. Priest begins to argue at length that the Indians may be descendants of the Israelites. He quotes from Clavigero, a Catholic missionary, who advocated the idea in the 17th century; from William Penn, who advocated the same theory as early as 1774; from a sermon by Dr. Jarvis, preached before the "American Historical Society" in 1811.

Jarvis quotes from Rev. Samuel Sewall, fellow of Harvard College; and Samuel Willard, vice-president of the same institution; and from several New England historians; from Dr. Boudinot, and Dr. Jonathan Edwards; from Charlevoix; from Dr. Pratz's *History of Louisiana;* and, in brief, he quotes in all about forty writers, half of whom are Americans, who advocated in one way or another, that the American Indians are Israelites. "Most of these writers," one critic of the Book of Mormon urges, "lived and wrote before Joseph Smith was born." "Priest proves," he continues, "that it was the almost universal opinion of the ministers of New England and the Middle States, that the Indians were descendants of the Hebrews." It should be held in mind that the book containing all this — *The Wonders of Nature and Providence* — was published in 1824, six years before the Book of Mormon was printed, and within twenty miles from where the Smith family resided from about 1815 to 1830.

It is not, and could not be urged, of course, that such works as Adair's, Von Humboldt's, or the "Proceedings of the American Antiquarian Society" would be in the hands of Joseph Smith or his family, years before the publication of the Book of Mormon; but it is altogether probable that these two books — Priest's *Wonders of Nature and Providence,* 1824; and Ethan Smith's *View of the Hebrews* 1st edition 1823, and the 2nd edition 1825 — were either possessed by Joseph Smith or certainly known by him, for they were surely available to him, and of course, with all the collection of quoted matter from Humboldt, Adair, Boudinot,[1] and all the rest — some forty or fifty earlier authors in all being quoted.

That there was an intense and widespread public interest in this subject of American race origins, customs, religion, traditions, antiquities, etc., throughout New England and the Middle States before the publication of the Book of Mormon cannot be questioned, since Ethan Smith's book ran rapidly through two editions; Priest's *Wonders of Nature and Providence,* devoting a large section to the probable Israelitish origin of the American race, was followed a few years later by his *American Antiquities.* Of this later work three editions were published for subscribers within a year — 1833. A fourth was published the following year; the fifth edition in 1835. Of the fifth edition, the author says: "22,000 volumes of this work have been published for subscribers only." See title page of the eighth edition, 1838. For the history of this work, see Joseph Sabin's *Dictionary of Books Relating to America* (15:472).[2]

Moreover, on subjects widely discussed, and that deal in matters of widespread public interest, there is built up in the course of years, a community knowledge of such subjects, usually referred to as "matters of common knowledge" to which non-readers of books or of periodicals, and to which even the ignorant have more or less of access, through hearing such subjects discussed at the gathering places of the common people; the village store, the wheelwright's shop, the town meeting, and post office, the social meetings of the community, the gathering and dispersing throngs in attendance upon church services — in all such places the people hear and absorb knowledge of such subjects as are of general interest, until there is formed what I have referred to as "common knowledge" of things; and while not always accurate, or to any great extent reliable, and often wholly wrong, it does, however, register the prevailing opinions that have been created by such community discussions as have been had upon such subjects. Such "common knowledge" existed throughout New England and New York in relation to American Indian origins and cultures; and the prevailing ideas respecting the American Indians throughout the regions named were favorable to the notion that they were of Hebrew origin, with possession of cultures that sustained that theory, meaning by that the structure and vocabularies of languages; traditions respecting migrations to the country; creation and flood myths that seemed to reflect the Hebrew Bible account of these matters; religious conceptions and shadowy rituals, which also appeared to be colored with Hebrew ideas and ceremonies, with here and there the notion of a possible contact with Christian gospel ideas. All these notions were interwoven in the "common knowledge" of New England and New York, in the early decades of the nineteenth century, respecting the Indian race of America. And with the existence of such a body of knowledge, or that which was accepted as "knowledge," and a person of vivid and constructive imaginative power in contact with it, there is little room for doubt but that it might be possible for Joseph Smith to construct a theory of origin for his Book of Mormon in harmony with these prevailing notions; and more especially since this "common knowledge" is set forth in almost handbook form in the little work of Ethan Smith *View of the Hebrews,* and published from eight to five years before the Book of Mormon was published.

The question to be considered here, then, is: did such "common knowledge," supplemented by Ethan Smith's book respecting theories of "origin," and of "history" obtain in the vicinity where Joseph Smith spent his early youth and manhood, and was he a person of sufficiently vivid and creative imagination as to produce such a work as the Book of Mormon from such materials? It will appear in what is to follow that such "common knowledge" did exist in New England; that Joseph Smith was in contact with it; that one book, at least, with which he was most likely acquainted, could well have furnished structural outlines for the Book of Mormon; and that Joseph Smith was possessed of such creative imaginative powers as would make it quite within the lines of possibility that the Book of Mormon could have been produced in that way.

II

ETHAN SMITH'S BOOK, *VIEW OF THE HEBREWS,* AS STRUCTURAL
MATERIAL FOR THE BOOK OF MORMON; UNITY OF THE AMERICAN
RACE; AMERICAN LANGUAGE FROM ONE SOURCE—THE HEBREW

It is now time to consider the book, *View of the Hebrews*: or *The Tribes of Israel in America,* by Ethan Smith.

This book was published by Smith and Shute, Poultney, Vermont. The first edition was published 1823; the second edition in 1825.

Mr. Ethan Smith was a pastor of a church in Poultney, Rutland County, Vermont, in the county adjoining on the west the county of Windsor, in which the Prophet Joseph was born, and in which he lived with his parents until he was about ten years of age, when the family removed to the state of New York and settled at Palmyra, and a little later in the township of Manchester.

This study supposes that it is more than likely that the Smith family possessed a copy of this book by Ethan Smith, that either by reading it, or hearing it read, and its contents frequently discussed, Joseph Smith became acquainted with its contents. The date of the publication of the second edition would even make this possible. For though the Smith family left the state of Vermont before the publication of the *View of the Hebrews*—such was the universal interest in the subject, and being published in a locality near which for so long the family had resided—in the adjoining county—the Smiths would most likely have interest enough in the book to obtain it in their new home. The book, then, was in existence—first and second editions respectively—seven and five years before the publication of the Book of Mormon, and was written and published by a man residing in a county adjoining that in which the Smith family lived—not more than fifty miles from Sharon, as the crow flies. It had a wide circulation in New England and in New York, running through two editions in a few years. Contact with it, and knowledge of its contents, by the Smiths, is in every way a great probability. And even if that were not so, as to this particular book—if the Smiths never owned the book, never read it, or saw it, still its contents—the materials of which it was composed—would be, under all the circumstances, matter of "common knowledge" throughout the whole region where the Smiths lived from the birth of Joseph Smith in 1805, to the publication of the Book of Mormon in 1829-30.

I say this with great confidence because Ethan Smith's book is constructed of material that was largely of community knowledge and discussion before collected and published in Ethan Smith's book. This consisted of reports from missionaries and traders who had lived among the Indian tribes. They were a sort of people most interesting in those times, whose reports to periodicals of the day were gladly received by publishers, and eagerly read and discussed by the public. Indian origins, languages, customs, adventures among them—all this was "front page matter" throughout this period, and throughout New England, New York State, and Pennsylvania. Such matter appeared as reports to Indian missionary societies of the various Churches; to historical societies; to American antiquarian societies, in various states. All this even before the publication of Ethan Smith's book; and running through a period of fifty years before the publication of the Book of Mormon.

Ethan Smith, in his Index to the second edition of his *View of the Hebrews*, informs us that pages 114 to 225—one hundred and eleven pages—will be devoted to "promiscuous testimonies"; that is, promiscuous testimonies to the main fact for which his book stands, namely, the Hebrew origin of the American Indians; and at the same place he adds this—"*a few only of which* (testimonies) *shall be here noted*," indicating that many more existed. His testimonies for the Hebrew origin of the American Indians, however, really begin at page seventy-five; so that, in all, the space in his book devoted to that branch of the subject amounts to one hundred and fifty pages, or about one half of the book. This testimony consists of reports from missionaries to the Churches that sent them to the Indian tribes; and the reports of traders among the Indians.

Of this class Adair's work, *History of the American Indians,* published in England in 1775, but largely circulated in the United States, and devoted to upholding the theory of the Hebrew origin of the American Indians—is frequently referred to. Our author names twenty-three titles of arguments which Adair uses to prove that the native of the American continents are of the ten tribes of Israel, as follows:

"1. Their division into tribes. 2. Their worship of Jehovah. 3. Their notion of a theocracy. 4. Their belief in the ministration of Angels. 5. Their language and dialects. 6. Their manner of counting time. 7. Their prophets and high priests. 8. Their festivals, fasts, and religious rites. 9. Their daily sacrifice. 10. Their ablutions and anointings. 11. Their laws of uncleanness. 12. Their abstinence from unclean things. 13. Their marriages, divorces, and punishment of adultery. 14. Their several punishments. 15. Their cities of refuge. 16. Their purification and preparatory ceremonies. 17. Their ornaments. 18. Their manner of curing the sick. 19. Their burial of their dead. 20. Their mourning for their dead. 21. Their raising of seed to a deceased brother. 22. Their change of names adapted to their circumstances and times. 23. Their own traditions; the accounts of English writers; and the testimonies given by Spanish and other writers of the primitive inhabitants of Mexico and Peru" (pp. 147-48).

On these numerous headings Mr. Smith adduces both evidences and arguments, but necessarily the treatment is brief. At one point Mr. Adair's evidence is spoken of as "the main pillar," to a work by a Jew, Manasses Ben Israel, entitled *The Hope of Israel*, also written to show that the American Indians are the "ten lost tribes." At about the same place (pp. 79-80) our author notes that the "North American Reviewers" report a sermon by one Dr. Jarvis, delivered before the New York Historical Society — devoted to the same idea of the Hebrew origin of the Indians, and represents the "Reviewers" of this sermon as adding to the list of testimonies given by Dr. Jarvis, several "New England Historians, from the first settlement of the country." "Some," says our author, "they proceed to mention"; and then add the names of the Rev. Samuel Sewall, fellow of Harvard College, and Samuel Willard, vice-president of the same institution. These were of the opinion "that the Indians are the descendants of Israel." The "Reviewers" whom we here follow represent Dr. Jarvis as saying that regarding the Indians as descendants of Israel has been "an hypothesis which has been a favorite topic with European writers; and is a subject, to which it is hoped the Americans may be said to be waking up at last" (*View of the Hebrews*, p. 80).

Mr. Smith introduces us next to "Hon. Elias Boudinot, LL.D., President for some time, in those days, of the American Bible Society," and publisher of *Star of the West* largely devoted to this theory of the Hebrew origin of the American Indians, and which our author represents as being "most worthy of the perusal of all men." Mr. Boudinot gives a sympathetic account of the origin of Mr. Adair's work and confesses that in his own writings he had made "a free use" of the materials contained in it.

Mr. Smith proceeds from this point through a number of pages to quote from the reports of missionaries, travelers, and New England historians. Of the last, the *History of Vermont* by Dr. Williams, and Col. Smith's *History of New Jersey*; magazine articles, especially from the *Connecticut Magazine*; from government reports — such as that of the Rev. Dr. Morse, giving an account of his "Tour among the Indians of the West" — "made under commission of our (U.S.) Government, in 1820" (pp. 142-45). Schoolcraft's journals of *Travels among the Western Indians*, 1820, are quoted. Schoolcraft was then in the beginning of his work which would end in the production of his six elaborate volumes of Government reports 18 . Don Alonza de Ericilla's *Histori of Chile* is quoted (p. 158). Also Long's *Expedition to the Rocky Mountains*. Melvenda and Acasta, "authors noted in Boudinot's 'Star of the West,'" are quoted; also *Hunter's narrative of Manners and Customs of the*

Indians, printed in Philadelphia, 1823 (pp. 162-68). This is followed by quotations from a sermon of Rev. Mr. Cushman, preached at Plymouth, 1620; Governor Hutchinson of Mass. is quoted; so, too, William Penn, Charlevoix, and Dr. Pratz—author of a History of Louisiana. De Las Casas is quoted; and also Baron Von Humboldt's *Political Essays on the Kingdom of New Spain,* Black's translation of 1811—New York—of this last work is quoted at some length, and chiefly as to the native race origins, their computations of time, facts concerning their cities and monuments, government, and migrations (pp. 177-88). The *Archaeoligia Americana,* containing "Transactions of the American Antiquarian Society," published at Worcester, Mass., 1820, is quoted at some length; the quotations being intermixed with comments by Mr. Smith (pp. 188-216). From this source the story of Quetzalcoatl—sometimes referred to by later writers as the "Mexican Messiah"—is given at length (pp. 204-10).

The story is given of the Pittsfield Hebrew Manuscript Fragment for which Mr. Ethan Smith himself is largely responsible. The fragment was an alleged Hebrew parchment found in "Indian Hill," near Pittsfield, Mass., by a Mr. Joseph Merrick, in 1815. The find consisted of two pieces of thick raw-hide, "sewed and made water tight, with the sinews of some animal." In the folds of it were four folded leaves of old parchment, of a dark yellow color, containing "some kind of writing." One of these bits of parchment submitted to the neighbors—to whom the find was shown—was "torn in pieces." The remaining three pieces were delivered to a Mr. Sylvester Larned, a college graduate then in town, who took them to Cambridge (Mass.), and had them examined. They were written in Hebrew with a pen, in plain and intelligible writing. "After some time, and with much difficulty and assistance," Mr. Larned ascertained their meaning and certified the same in a signed report to Mr. Merrick. The writing was Hebrew and the translation was to be found as follows:

> "No. 1 is translated by Deut. VL. 4-9 verses inclusive.
> No. 2, by Deut. XI. 13-21 verses inclusive.
> No. 3, by Exod. XIII. 11-16 verses inclusive."
>
> (signed) Sylvester Larned.

(*View of the Hebrews,* pp. 219-20)

Mr. Smith, commenting upon these passages says that "The celebrated Calmet"—author of the Dictionary Vox Sagan (p. 151)—"informs us that these texts of Scripture (above cited) are the very texts of scripture which the Jews used to write on three out of four of their leaves of phylacteries." "From which it is presumable," he adds, "that the fourth leaf torn in pieces, contained the texts which belonged to the fourth leaf" (p. 220).

The local report of the matter was that some modern Jew might have left the manuscript in Pittsfield. This conjecture, it appears, had satisfied Rev. Dr. Holmes of Cambridge—"known to be a correct Hebrew scholar"—who had seen and "carefully read the three parchments." "His wonder (with that of others) had been laid to rest by the rumor of a Jew having been known to leave them in Pittsfield" (p. 222). Dr. Thomas, President of the "Antiquarian Society," at Worcester, Mass., with whom the parchments had been deposited for safe keeping, had also with them received the rumor of their Jewish origin, "and hence had not viewed it of great consequence." Mr. Merrick, the finder of this Hebrew parchment, and others in Pittsfield, did not accept this view of the fragments origin, nor did Mr. Ethan Smith, and the latter undertook with great zeal to solve the question of origin. With that end in view he first tried to find the parchments. He followed them from point to point where they were reported to have been, but failed to find them. Dr. Thomas, at Worchester, Mass., President of the Antiquarian Society of that place, acknowledged having received the parchment for safe keeping, but entertaining the view of its having been left in Pittsfield by some modern Jew, as stated above, he paid little attention to it, and knew not where he had placed it. A search conducted for several hours, in which Mr. Ethan Smith shared, failed to discover it, and it has remained "lost" to this day.

As a final item in this "promiscuous" list of testimonies Mr. Smith gives the following: "The Rev. Chauncy Cook of Chile, New York, at my house, gave the following information with liberty of inserting it with his name. He has lately been credibly informed by a minister (he cannot recollect his name, as several withn six months have called on him from New England) that Rev. Dr. West, of Stockbridge, gave him the following information: an old Indian informed him that his fathers in this country had not long since had a book which they had for a long time preserved. But having lost the knowledge of reading, it, they concluded it would be of no farther use to them, and they buried it with an Indian Chief. The minister spoke to Mr. Cook of this information of Dr. West *as a matter of fact*" (*View of the Hebrews*, p. 223).

Mr. Smith then couples these two items—the Hebrew parchment found in "*Indian Hill*," and this "lost book" of Dr. West's story—together. On the assumption that the native American race are descendants of Israel, then this Hebrew parchment with these passages of scripture written upon it, and brought with them in their migrations to the New World, might readily become very sacred to them. "They would most naturally become," says Mr. Smith, "some of the most precious contents in their holy ark [which he elsewhere reports some tribes of Indians to have, more properly "medicine bag"] as their nation formerly kept the holy law in the ark. Here such a phylactery would be safe through ever so many centuries." "This is so far from being improbable," Mr. Smith argues, "that it is almost a moral certainty. After their knowledge of reading had long been lost, some chief or high priest, or old beloved wise man (*keeping their tradition*), fearing these precious leaves might get lost, or parted, might naturally sew them in a fold of raw skins with the sinews of an animal (the most noted Indian thread), and keep this roll still in the ark; or carry it upon his belt. All this what might most naturally be expected in such a case. This thing might have been thus safely brought down to a period near to the time when the natives last occupied '*Indian Hill*' in Pittsfield; perhaps in the early part of the last century. Its owner then might lose it there; *or* (what is most probable) *it was buried with some chief, or high priest;* and hence was providentially transmitted to us" (p. 244).

So closes the testimonies for the Hebrew origin of the American Indians in Ethan Smith's book. This collection of "evidence," as before remarked, was published in this book by Ethan Smith, at least from seven and five years before the Book of Mormon was heard of. It was published and circulated in such proximity to Joseph Smith and his family as to be easily accessible to them. So far, then, as Hebrew origin of the American Indians contributes a cardinal trait of the Book of Mormon, the book by Ethan Smith might readily have supplied that suggestion, and the evidence of it is incontrovertible from the contents of the book itself, and the fact of its publication and circulation in the vicinity of the Smiths' places of residence. That the Ethan Smith book held that the American Indians were descendants of "the lost tribes of Israel" and the Book of Mormon theory is built upon the idea that they were descendants of the tribes of Ephraim and Manasseh, through the family of Ishmael and Lehi respectively, with an infusion from the tribe of Judah through the colony of Mulek, is a variation of slight importance, since the main idea is, so far as this particular matter is concerned, that the American Indians are descendants of the Israelites. The racial traits—language, traditions, customs, physical characteristics and the like—that would tend to prove the American race to be the "ten lost tribes," would be just as available to prove that they were of Israel through families of the tribes of Ephraim, Manasseh, and Judah. And hence I say the variations from being the "ten lost tribes," to being descendants from these three tribes of the same people, is of slight importance.

However, if Israelitish origin of the American race stated in Ethan Smith's book in such fashion that it might well be regarded as suggesting the Book of Mormon theory of origin for its peoples was all this book did, it would scarcely be worthwhile considering it as supplying material for the Book of Mormon; but in many ways, and at many points, as we shall see, Book of Mormon traits, in language, culture, the knowledge of and the use of metals, traditions, religion and even in the structure of the Book of Mormon — the material compiled in Ethan Smith's book, might well be taken as suggesting many things in the Book of Mormon.*

The stage which our task has now reached demands that we shall consider the question, does the book by Ethan Smith furnish any material for the ground plan of the Book of Mormon. Before that question is directly considered, however, it will be necessary to set forth, in outline, the main features of the Book of Mormon in structure and subject matter, in order that the contents of the two books may be better compared.

---

*Add also it would suggest the lost book buried in a Hill, by Prophet & High priest — lost art of reading etc.

III

OUTLINE OF BOOK OF MORMON FEATURES

The outstanding features in the Book of Mormon are first, the origin of its peoples; second, their migrations; third, their divisions after their arrival in the New World; fourth, their fate, and the fate of their civilization; fifth, their religion; sixth, the future of these people, as set forth in divine promises and prophecies.

Origin and migrations of the Book of Mormon peoples are so closely interwoven that they are best considered together.

The Jaredites

The oldest race of Book of Mormon peoples and their migration to the New World are the last to be dealt with in the Book of Mormon, viz., the Jaredites. The colony was not large. They came in eight small barges (see Ether 2:15 and ch. 6); all told they could not have exceeded one hundred. They came from the Tower of Babel at the dispersion following the confusion of tongues. While the colony is known as the "people of Jared," the real leader appears to have been "the Brother of Jared," a great prophet and seer, who under direction of the Lord, guided the colony in its journeyings to the New World.

As a special favor from the Lord the language of this colony was not confounded. Forewarned that the Lord would scatter the people "upon all the face of the earth" from Babel, Jared urged his prophet brother to plead with God to know whither they should go. "And who knoweth," said Jared, "but the Lord will carry us forth into a land which is choice above all the earth. And if it be so, let us be faithful unto the Lord, that we may receive it for our inheritance." And it was to be so. A divine commandment was given to make preparations for a migration to a distant land. Jared and his family, his brother's family, and the friends of these families were to be included in the company. The Lord promised to go before them into a land "which is choice above all the lands of the earth. And there will I bless thee, and thy seed," said the Lord to the Brother of Jared, "and raise up unto me of thy seed, and of the seed of thy brother, and they who shall go with thee, a great nation. And there shall be none greater than the nation which I will raise up unto me of thy seed, upon all the face of the earth" (Ether 1:41). The colony was brought to the New World and the prophetic promises of greatness realized in its development, according to the Book of Mormon.

Thorough preparations were made for the migration, including the collection of animals—male and female—and seeds of every kind to be taken with them. They journeyed northward from Babel into "the valley of Nimrod," named after the famous hunter. While yet in this valley the Lord commanded them that "they should go forth into the wilderness, *yea, into that quarter where there never had man been*" (Ether 2:5). And so the colony journeyed in the wilderness, and they crossed many waters in "barges" built for that purpose. "And the Lord would not suffer that they should stop beyond the sea in the wilderness, but he would that they should come forth unto the land of promise which was choice above all other lands"—i.e., the New World. At last they arrived on the shore "of the Great Sea, which divideth the lands," where they abode for four years. Here they became careless of the worship of God, for which they were reproved. Then followed preparations for the great voyage to the land they had been promised. Eight small barges were constructed to convey the colony and their animals, and their seeds, across the deep. Three hundred and forty and four days were they in transit. The place of their first landing was called by them "Moron," which, so far as may be ascertained, was somewhere in Central America (see the author's *New Witnesses for God*, vol. 2, ch. X, where the matter is considered at length). Here a great city was ultimately builded, which remained the capital of the Kingdom into which this colony grew, until the Jaredites were destroyed down to the last man of them, near the beginning of the 6th century, B.C. The kingdom founded by this colony endured about sixteen centuries, during which time it rose to great heights of civilization, and became numerous. Its culture was that of pastoral and agricultural and industrial peoples. They had "all manner of fruit, and of grain, and of silks, and of fine linen, and of gold, and of silver, and of precious things, and also all manner of cattle, of oxen, and cows, and of sheep, and of swine, and of goats, and also many other kind of animals which were useful for the food of man; and they also had horses, and asses, and there were elephants and cureloms, and cumoms; all of which were useful unto man, and more especially the elephants, and cureloms, and cumoms. And thus the Lord did pour out his blessings upon this land, which was choice above all other lands" (Ether 9:17-20). Also their culture was an iron and steel and other kind of metal culture, not a stone-age culture: "And they were exceeding industrious, and they did buy and sell, and traffic one with another, that they might get gain. And they did work in all manner of ore, and they did make gold, and silver, and iron, and brass, and all manner of metals; and they did dig it out of the earth; wherefore, they did cast up mighty heaps of earth to get ore, of gold, and of silver, and of iron, and of copper. And they did work all manner of fine work. And they did have silks, and fine twined linen; and they did work all manner of cloth, that they might clothe themselves from their nakedness. And they did make all manner of tools to till the earth, both to plough and to sow, to reap and to hoe, and also to thrash. And they did make all manner of tools with which they did work their beasts. And they did make all manner of weapons of war. And they did work all manner of work of exceeding curious workmanship. And never could be a people more blessed than were they, and more prospered by the hand of the Lord. And they were in a land that was choice above all lands, for the Lord had spoken it" (Ether 10:22-28).

In their last great war, which resulted in the extinction of the race, to the last man, it is stated that "two millions of mighty men had been slain; and also their wives and their children." With this as a basis of calculation, the late Orson Pratt[3] estimated the population of the Jaredite Kingdom at this time to be "from ten to fifteen millions" (see footnote "b" in 1914 edition, Ether 15). Their religion varied from the worship of the true God to idolatry.

The original colony came to the land—"into that quarter where there never had man been"; and they left the land, for a second time, as empty of human inhabitants as when they had found it. Nothing remained but the crumbling monuments of their ruined temples, altars, roads, and cities.

Such were the Jaredites. The last survivor, one Coriantumr, lived long enough to be found by the colony of Mulek, early in the sixth century, B.C., and died nine months later.

The existence of this Jaredite people, whence they came, their rise to power, and the fate which befell them became known partly from this sole survivor, and partly from a record by one Ether—the last of their prophets, who witnessed their utter destruction, and left his record where it was found by a detachment of a branch of the Nephite people. This record was brought to the Nephite prophet Mosiah, early in the century preceding the coming of the Christ; and it was translated by him into the language of the Nephites about 120 B.C. by means of the Urim and Thummim. Moroni, having charge of the sacred writings of the Nephites, about 400 A.D. found these plates of Ether among the other records and gave an abridged translation of them into the Nephite language, by means of Urim and Thummim, which abridgement was translated by Joseph and stands in the Book of Mormon as the Book of Ether.

The Nephites

The second migration to the New World, according to the Book of Mormon, was a colony made up of two families, one Lehi and his family, Israelites of the tribe of Manasseh (Alma 10:3); and the family of one Ishmael, supposed to be of the tribe of Ephraim (see *New Witnesses for God,* 3:172-73, where the matter is set forth at length in footnotes). These two tribes came of Joseph, Son of Jacob-Israel. They, directed of God, left Jerusalem about six hundred years B.C., and landed in the New World, by vessel, about twelve years later.

Briefly sketched, the chief events to be noted of this colony are that from the first there were disagreements in the colony arising largely from the differences in temperament among the sons of Lehi, of whom there were four. Nephi, the youngest of the sons, was a man of profound religious intuitions and fine spiritual instincts. He was thoroughly in sympathy with his father, Lehi's purpose in leaving Jerusalem, which was first to escape the impending doom of that city, denounced of God, and later executed by the Babylonians in the overthrow of King Zedekiah, and the captivity of the Jews; and second, to found a people in the New World, where there might be realized, as nowhere else there could be realized, certain promises made to the house of Israel through the descendants of the patriarch Joseph. Nephi shared in all the spiritual light and life, and revelations of his father Lehi, and influenced his next older brother, Sam, to accept his own and his father's and the Lord's guidance. The older pair of brothers, Laman and Lemuel, were of different temperament, worldly minded, with little or no faith in the mission of their father, and never in sympathy with their younger brother. They regretfully abandoned their estates and wealth in Jerusalem, for this wilderness journey to the New World. (See the writer's work *New Witnesses for God* where the matter is considered at length, 3:93-109.) Bickerings, complaints, unbelief, and rebellions on the part of these elder brothers and all they could influence in the little colony—the whole number of the colony leaving Jerusalem could not have exceeded thirty—marked the whole course of the journey, and the early years of occupancy of the New World. This disagreement led to an early division of the colony—within a period at least of thirty years. The division was drawn on religious lines, belief or unbelief in Lehi's mission, namely, the planting of a branch of the house of Israel in a larger land of promise than Israel had before known, to achieve divine ends.

Nephi, warned of God, separated from his brethren, taking with him all he could influence to his way of thinking, which from the partial enumeration given (II Nephi 5:6) must have been about half the colony—the whole colony by then could not have exceeded an hundred souls. "And all those," says Nephi, "who would go with me were those who believed in the warnings and the revelations of God; wherefore they did hearken to my words."

Sufficiently removed from the other half of the colony, this more righteous branch was taught and trained by their leader in the arts of peace. "I, Nephi, did cause my people to be industrious, and to labor with their hands." "Also," more in detail, "I did teach my people to build buildings, and to work in all manner of wood, and of iron, and copper and brass, and of steel, and of gold and of silver and of precious ores, which were *in great abundance.*" Also Nephi constructed a temple "after the manner of the temple of Solomon, save it were not built of so many precious things; *for they were not to be found upon the land*(!) But the manner of the construction was like unto the temple of Solomon, and the workmanship thereof was exceeding fine" (II Nephi 5:16).

Though loving peace, and desirous of living in peace, Nephi knew how deep was the hatred of his brethren towards himself and those who followed him, and therefore preparations for defense were made by the manufacture of "many swords," after the pattern of one brought from Jerusalem. Nephi was made "king" of this righteous branch of Lehi's colony, the succession of kings to carry his name (see II Nephi 5:18; and Jacob 2:9-11).

The anticipated conflict between the followers of Nephi — and they were called Nephites — and the other branch of Lehi's colony was not long delayed, for before forty years has passed away, counting from the time Lehi left Jerusalem, "we had already had wars and contentions with our brethren" writes Nephi (II Nephi 5:34); and Nephi is spoken of immediately after his death as having "wielded the sword of Laban" — (brought from Jerusalem) — in the defense of his people (Jacob 1:10).

The Lamanites

The other branch of Lehi's colony, following the leadership of Laman and Lemuel were called Lamanites, and were a people devoted to hunting and living upon the natural products of a fruitful wilderness. They were idle and headed towards barbarism, which ultimately became their state. Also they were "cut off" from the presence of the Lord, and that they might not be enticing to the Nephites, they were cursed of God with a skin of blackness, that whereas before the curse "they were white and exceeding fair, and delightsome," they were now dark skinned and repulsive (II Nephi 5:21-23). They became the very antithesis, then, of the Nephites — the one civilized, the other barbarian. One of the Book of Mormon writers referring to the status of the two peoples, in the closing decades of the second century, after Lehi left Jerusalem, says of the Lamanites: "They were led by their evil nature that they became wild, and ferocious, and a blood thirsty people, full of idolatry and filthiness; feeding upon beasts of prey; dwelling in tents, and wandering about in the wilderness, with a short skin girdle about their loins and their heads shorn; and their skill was in the bow, and in the cimeter, and the ax, and many of them did eat nothing save raw meat; and they were continually seeking to destroy us"—that is, the Nephites (Enos 1:20).

And of the Nephites he writes: "And it came to pass that the people of Nephi did till the land, and did raise all manner of grain, and of fruit, and flocks of herds, and flocks of all manner of cattle of every kind, and goats, and wild goats, and also many horses." Yet, notwithstanding this civilized manner of life and the existence of many prophets among them, and a literature—for they had brought with them from Jerusalem the national literature of the Jews extant in the reign of Zedekiah, King of Judah, when Lehi left Jerusalem, including the five Books of Moses and the writings of many of the prophets including the writings of Isaiah and some of the prophecies of Jeremiah—notwithstanding all these advantages, the Book of Mormon represents the Nephites as a stiff necked people, slow to understand, and manageable only through the severity of God, "continually reminding them of death, and the duration of eternity, and the judgments and power of God . . . stirring them up continually to keep them in the fear of the Lord" (Omni 1:21-24).

These traits of the two people, in the main, continued to be their distinguishing characteristics throughout their history, *until the barbarous entirely overcame the civilized, and destroyed them,* as we shall have occasion to see later, and which event is very remarkably set forth in Ethan Smith's book as being an event which likely happened among his lost tribes in America, and by which he accounts for the apparent existence of two kinds of people in the New World, one civilized, and the other barbarous.

The Colony of Mulek

A separation also took place among the Nephites, some time in the third or second century B.C. The more righteous part of the people of Nephi took their departure from the others, by now occupying what had come to be called "the land of Nephi," and made a considerable remove through the wilderness, under the leadership of one Mosiah, who subsequently became their King. Beyond the wilderness through which he led his following, Mosiah found a people inhabiting a city, known as "Zarahemla." They were descendants of a colony of Jews which had left Jerusalem about eleven years after Lehi's colony had departed from the same ill fated city. They are known in the Book of Mormon parlance and history as the colony of Mulek, that being the name of the leader of the colony, a son of King Zedekiah of Judah, who escaped at the time his father was overthrown and taken captive into Babylon. The colony had grown to be very numerous by the time Mosiah and his people found them, but they were without records or the art of writing and deprived of these stabilizing influences. Their language had become so far corrupted that although of the same racial stock, and speaking originally the same tongue with the Nephites, they could not understand the language of these kinsfolk so strangely met. Mosiah had the people of Zarahemla instructed in the Nephite tongue; also he was chosen king of the two people thus united; and hence forth known in Book of Mormon annals as Nephites.

The peoples from whom Mosiah and his following had separated, lapsed into barbarism, or semi-barbarism, united with the people of the wilderness previously known as Lamanites, and formed the "Lamanites" of the period of history following this separation, to the coming of Christ.

Between these two peoples, who were soon again in contact, there were almost continuous wars. The periods of peace were brief, and always uncertain; the battles were bloody, and the toll of death such as must have checked materially the growth of population. I feel safe in saying that among no other people of history do wars appear to have been so frequent, so long continued, or so sanguinary.

The remaining outstanding feature to be noted in the account of these Book of Mormon Peoples are: 1. The knowledge these people had of the scattering of Israel, and the future gathering of Israel, and their restoration to the lands of their fathers and the glory that shall be theirs when so restored. In both the scattering and the gathering of Israel, these peoples regard themselves as participating in; and also as participating in the promised future glory that is to be Israel's. These things are elaborately and laboriously set forth in the Book of Mormon. 2. The prophetic knowledge they had of the coming of the Messiah in the flesh, and of his mission of atonement. All this stated frequently in the language of accomplished fact, with admonition, and exhortation given in phraseology reminiscent of camp meeting hysterical pleadings, and attended by "swoonings" and "fallings," of the period immediately preceding, and at the time of the coming forth, of the Book of Mormon, as will be shown in its proper place. 3. Knowledge of great signs and wonders to precede the coming of the Son of God in the flesh — signs in the heavens and in the earth, the appearance of a new star and of three day and night periods — but all blended into one period of continuous light, as of one unbroken day.

Then at the crucifixion and the three day's entombment of the Christ, more terrible signs than these in heaven and earth — storm and tempest, attended by three days of awful darkness, during which earthquakes rocked the continents, raised valleys, submerged mountains, changed the coastlines, destroyed cities — burying some beneath new, uprising mountains, and submerging others by great tidal waves; then the voice of God, universally heard, reproving the people that remained. 4. The climax of New World experience is reached by the wonderful physical appearance of the resurrected Lord Jesus, followed by a rather elaborate ministry among the Nephites, surviving from the disastrous judgment which attended the crucifixion and the entombment of the Christ. The ministry of the risen Messiah resulted in the founding of an American Church of the Christ, all done very largely by repetition of New Testament sermons, paralleled — though exceeded — miraculous incidents, couched in English New Testament phraseology and peculiarities. 5. A golden age of peace and good will among the people of America followed the appearing and ministry of the Christ. A period in which the people had all things, as to material wealth in common. A veritable golden age, this, continuing without interruption through two hundred, and part of three hundred years. Then the gradual rise of pride, selfishness and decline; the revival of old distinctions of Nephite and Lamanite, with the bitterness and wars attendant upon such distinctions and divisions. 6. The war that began at the close of the fourth century A.D., resulting in the overthrow of the Nephite civilization, leaving the Lamanites and their barbarism everywhere triumphant.

Finally, the period of a thousand years of barbarism, to the coming of the Europeans in 1492. Such, in almost headline fashion, is the ground plan and chief things of the Book of Mormon.

IV

VIEW OF THE HEBREWS, AND THE GROUND PLAN OF THE BOOK OF
MORMON: TIME, PLACE AND RACE, SUBJECT MATTER—DESTRUCTION OF
JERUSALEM AND THE SCATTERING OF ISRAEL; RESTORATION OF JUDAH
AND ISRAEL; QUOTATIONS FROM ISAIAH

It should be remembered that the *View of the Hebrews* was published
a sufficient number of years before the publication of the Book of
Mormon to allow of its being the ground plan of that work, so far as
time element is concerned, if only in its contents the material is found
for such plan. This would be true even if only the second edition be
considered—1825. It becomes increasing true if the first edition—issued,
of course, several years earlier—be considered, as well as the second.*

It was published in such proximity to the home of the Smiths, where
Joseph Smith spent his boyhood, that it is scarcely conceivable that he
would escape having his attention called to it, though his family had in
the meantime removed to the state of New York. *View of the Hebrews*
represents the American race to be "the lost tribes of Israel," hence of
Hebrew origin. The variation in the Book of Mormon, from "the ten
lost tribes" theory, to their being descendants of two of the lost tribes—
Ephraim and Manasseh—with an infusion from the tribe of Judah through
the people of Mulek, as before remarked, is not of sufficient importance
to affect the main idea, namely, that the American Indians are of the
family of Israel, and hence heirs to the promises of God to that peoples.
And whatsoever would make for the proof of the American Indians being
"the ten lost tribes" would also make for proof of their being descendants
through the three fragments of tribes as represented in the Book of
Mormon.

The first chapter of *View of the Hebrews* opens with a treatise on
the "Destruction of Jerusalem," and the scattering of Israel—"until (quoting Isaiah 6:11-12) the cities be wasted without inhabitant; and the houses
without men; and the land be utterly desolate; and the Lord have removed
man far away, and there be a great forsaking in the midst of the land."
To this 46 pages are devoted.

The first chapter of the Book of Mormon also deals with the destruction of Jerusalem, and this scattering of Israel. The impending destruction of Jerusalem, prophetically made known to Lehi, the first of
Book of Mormon prophets, becomes the incentive for his departure,
with his family, from the doomed city, Jerusalem, and their ultimate
arrival in the New World.

Not only is the destruction of Jerusalem and the scattering of Israel

---

* The first edition was published in 1823.

an early discussed subject in *View of the Hebrews* and also in the Book of Mormon; but the heading of Chapter II in *View of the Hebrews*, is as follows: "THE CERTAIN RESTORATION OF JUDAH AND ISRAEL." This, then, becomes a subject early, and somewhat extendedly, discussed in Ethan Smith's book, as also it does in the first part of the Book of Mormon. (See these references in Index of 1921 edition—pp. 16-3, 17-14, 46-3, 63-11, 71-6, 90-15; in *View of the Hebrews*, see ch. I.) Ethan Smith quotes six different passages from Isaiah in support of the gathering of Israel and their restoration to their own lands, including among these passages the justly celebrated eleventh chapter of Isaiah, which was one of the passages quoted by the angel Moroni to Joseph Smith on that night of his three visits to the young prophet, September 23rd, 1823,[4] when making known to him the existence of the Book of Mormon, and the events of which it would be precursor: "The Lord shall set his hand the second time to recover the remnant of his people which shall be left from Assyria and from Egypt . . . and from the islands of the sea . . . and he shall set up an ensign for the nations, and shall assemble the outcasts of Israel and gather together the dispersed of Judah from the four corners of the earth. The envy also of Ephraim shall depart and the adversary of Judah shall be cut off. . . . And there shall be an highway for the remnant of his people which shall be left from Assyria, like as it was to Israel in the day when he came up out of Egypt" (Isaiah 11:11-16).

Mr. Ethan Smith also quotes Paul as referring to the restoration of Israel as a great event; and notes *"Their being again grafted into their own olive tree, as a notable event of the last days"* (Smith, p. 63, and Romans 11).

He also quotes many other passages on this gathering and the restoration of the house of Israel, this among them: "For the Lord will have mercy on Jacob, and will yet choose Israel, and set them in their own land. And the stranger shall be joined with them, and they shall cleave to the house of Jacob" (Isaiah 14:1; *View of the Hebrews*, p. 63). Then concludes his survey with this remark:

"Thus the prophetic writings do clearly decide, that both Israel and the Jews, *shall in the last days*, before the Millennium, be literally restored to their own land of Palestine, and be converted to the Christian faith" (Id., p. 64).

The last page or two of the chapter is devoted to a protest against the array of scriptural evidence on the subject being given a mystical meaning, *the prophecies are to be literally fulfilled.*

The early chapters of the Book of Mormon make frequent reference to the restoration of Israel to their lands, and also to the favor of Jehovah. Beginning at page sixteen of the current (i.e., 1921) edition, after speaking of the destruction of Jerusalem and of the Jews being carried away captive into Babylon, then Lehi is represented as saying that, "according to the own due time of the Lord, they should return again, yea, even be brought back out of captivity; and after they should be brought back out of captivity they should possess again the land of their inheritance."

Then follows his prediction of the coming of the Messiah in the flesh; of his rejection by the Jews; of his being slain by them; of his resurrection from death; of his being preached unto the Gentiles; and then of Lehi's exposition concerning "the gentiles and also concerning the house of Israel, that *they should be compared like unto an olive tree* whose *branches* should be *broken off* and *should be scattered* upon all the face of the earth. . . . And after the house of Israel should be scattered they should be gathered together again; or, *in fine,* after the gentiles had received the fulness of the Gospel, the natural branches of the *Olive tree,* or the remnants of the house of Israel, should be grafted in, *or come to the knowledge of the true Messiah, their Lord and their Redeemer"* (I Nephi 10:2-14).

The history of events, concerning the Messiah and of his mission, are given in greater detail to the first Nephi, son of Lehi, than to Lehi himself, and afterwards expounded at length to the somewhat skeptical elder sons of Lehi (I Nephi 11-15 inclusive. See also Chs. 19-21 inclusive, which ends the first Book of Nephi).

In the second Book of Nephi the prophetic history of events concerning Messiah is continued. In the book following this—the Book of Jacob—occurs the figure of Israel *as a tame olive tree whose branches are broken off and grafted into other stocks;* then how they are brought back and grafted again into the native stock is expanded into an elaborate allegory, occupying with Jacob's exposition of it, two chapters, one of 76, the other of 13 paragraphs. In Nephi's prophetic history of the Christ and of his mission, and events connected therewith—and these chiefly concerning the fortunes of Israel—their calamities and redemptions, and final triumph—the prophetic chapters and parts of chapters of Isaiah are freely drawn upon. From page 43, in the Book of Mormon, to page 95 *twenty-one chapters, nearly all complete, are quoted* from Isaiah, and all this quite generally in the exact phraseology of the authorized version of the English Bible!

Since it is represented in the Book of Mormon that the colony of Lehi brought with them the Hebrew national literature—the Old Testament scriptures, engraven in Egyptian characters on brass plates—comprising, as enumerated by Nephi himself, "the five books of Moses, . . . and also a record of the Jews from the beginning, even down to the commencement of the reign of Zedehiah, King of Judah, and also the prophecies of the holy prophets from the beginning, even down to the commencement of the reign of Zedekiah; and also many prophecies which have been spoken by the mouth of Jeremiah" (I Nephi 5:11-13)— since, I say, the Nephite writers had all this national literature to draw upon, is it not surprising that they limited themselves so largely to the writings of Isaiah, at least until the coming of Christ? Especially is it a matter of wonder that the quotations should be largely limited to Isaiah, since it is stated that the collection of the Hebrew literature, which was brought to the New World by Lehi's colony, was larger in volume than the Old Testament, prophetically seen circulating among the Jews and the gentiles (I Nephi 13:20-23)? *But may not this be accounted for by the fact that Mr. Ethan Smith practically does the same thing in his View of the Hebrews?* That is, he quotes chiefly from Isaiah in support of his views concerning Israel, their dispersion, their restoration, and their glorification—and the author of the Book of Mormon, following him, *does the same thing.*

We have already noted that in his second chapter, dealing with "THE CERTAIN RESTORATION OF JUDAH AND ISRAEL," that Mr. Ethan Smith quoted from six different chapters of Isaiah. In his fourth chapter, and in the few pages he devotes to a "Conclusion," he returns to the subject of the restoration and glorification of Israel, and in those two rather brief subdivisions of his work, he quotes from *twenty chapters of Isaiah,* while only quoting about half as many passages from all other scripture writers combined.

Even the Christ when referring to the Old Testament quotes chiefly from Isaiah. Jacob, the brother of Nephi, quotes almost complete chapters 48, 49, 50 and 51. Is there no significance in this preponderance of references to, and lavish quotations from Isaiah, when the Nephite writers had just as easy access to the other divisions of the Hebrew national literature as to Isaiah—is there no significance between this fact and the fact that Ethan Smith had a like preference for Isaiah, and quoted him in about the same proportion of preponderance as the author of the Book of Mormon does? And many passages quoted by Ethan Smith are identical with passages from Isaiah quoted in the Book of Mormon.

V

VIEW OF THE HEBREWS, AND THE GROUND PLAN OF THE BOOK OF
MORMON; THE EIGHTEENTH CHAPTER OF ISAIAH; AN ADDRESS TO
"CHRISTIAN" AMERICA? RELATION OF GENTILE AMERICA TO HEBREW
AMERICA

Isaiah eighteenth chapter is quoted in full by Ethan Smith in his final
chapter. He regards it as an address to the Christian people of the United
States. His chapter heading in this division of his work (4:227) stands as
follows:

"*An address of the Prophet Isaiah Relative to the Restoration of His
People.*"

This eighteenth chapter of Isaiah Ethan Smith then proceeds to
interpret, as a prophetic address to America and her people, a call to
the Christians of America to come to the rescue, and to aid in the
restoration of the house of Israel, and more especially to that division
of Israel occupying the New World. Mr. Smith was greatly affected by
this passage when writing his *Dissertation of the Prophecies*, published
some years before his *View of the Hebrews*. He found it then, as he
believed, a prophetic address to some Christian people, most probably,
as he then thought, applying to the people of Britain, notwithstanding
some geographical difficulties. But when he wrote his *View of the Hebrews*, he came to the conclusion that it was "far more probable that
the Christian people of the United States are the subjects of the address,"
or at least are "specially included in it." "Some of the greatest and best
of the divines," he adds, "have thought it strange, if nothing should be
found in the prophetic scriptures having a special allusion to our western
world, which by propitious heaven was destined to act so distinguished
a part both in the religious and political world *in the last days.*"

They have felt as though it might be presumed that some special
allusions would be had in some of the prophetic writings to so distinguished a community of *Zion* and of men under this impression Mr.
Edwards [i.e., Rev. Jonathan Edwards of early New England fame] apprehended this passage in Isaiah might allude to America: "*So shall they
fear the name of the Lord from the West*" (Isaiah 59:19). Almost all other
parts of the world are noted in prophecy. It is, therefore, not incredible
that our land [i.e., America] should be manifestly noted.

"This address in the 18th Chapter of Isaiah to be contemplated,"
he continues, "is clearly an address *to some people of these last days;*
and concerning events intimately connected with the battle of that great
day of God, which is now future, and not far distant, and is to introduce
the Millennium. . . . The address then cannot have been to any ancient

people or nation. This appears with certainty, from their being contemporary with the events of that great battle, and the restoration of the Jews. The call, then, must be to a people of the last days; a nation now on earth; and a nation to be peculiarly instrumental in the restoration of the Hebrews in the last days. For this is the very object of the address, to go and collect the ancient people of God; because in that time shall the present be brought unto the Lord of hosts of a people scattered and peeled (the very people of the ancient covenant in manifest descriptions repeatedly given) to the place of the name of the Lord of Hosts, *the Mount Zion. . . .* Should it be proved a *fact,* that the aborigines of our [the American] continent are the descendants of the ten tribes of Israel, it would heighten the probability to a moral certainty, that we are the people [i.e., of the U.S.] especially addressed, and called upon to restore them; *or bring them to the knowledge of the Gospel,* and to do with them whatever the God of Abraham designs shall be done. The great and generous Christian people, who occupy so much of the land of those natives," he argues, "and who are on the ground of their continent, and hence are the best prepared to meliorate their condition, and bring them to the knowledge and order of the God of Israel, must be the people to whom this work is assigned."

This view our author maintains with elaborate argument and many scripture references, including the notable passages on the subject from Jeremiah, 30 and 31st chapters, where the majestic gathering of Israel is represented as coming to pass in the last days. Also he changes the translated version of the first verse in Isaiah XVIII, to make it conform to his purpose: namely, that whereas in our common English version it begins with a denunciatory phrase—"*Wo to the land shadowing with wings"*—he changes the "Wo" to a particle of friendly calling—"*Ho land shadowing with wings,* which is beyond the rivers of Ethiopia," and justifies the change on the ground that the "whole connection and sense decide, that the word is here a friendly call, or address; as in this passage: "*Ho, every one that thirsteth, come ye to the waters,*" etc. The argument is continued throughout the chapter, and part of the subdivision called the "Conclusion," that the Christian nation of the United States will be the rescuing and preserving power to Israel in the New World.

The "land shadowing with wings," according to Mr. Smith (Isaiah 18:1), refers to the western continents of America, "where the two great wings of North and South America meet as at the body of a great eagle."

Also this land "sendeth ambassadors by the sea, even in vessels of bulrushes upon the face of the waters, saying, go ye swift messengers, to a nation scattered and peeled [i.e., to the house of Israel inhabiting America] . . . a nation meted out and trodden down hitherto" (Id., ver. 2).

And then, after "the land shadowing with wings is underway in fulfillment of the divine requirement, an apostrophe is made by the Most High to all nations, to stand and behold the banner of salvation now erected for his ancient people; and to hear the great Gospel trumpet, the blessed Jubilee, now to be blown for their collection and their freedom —

"*All ye nations of the world, and dwellers on the earth, see ye when he lifteth up an ensign on the mountains, and when he bloweth a trumpet, hear ye*" (Id., ver. 3).

And, finally, "At that time shall the present be brought unto the Lord of Hosts of a people scattered and peeled. . . . A nation meted out and trodden under foot (the state of ancient Israel) . . . to the place of the name of the Lord of hosts the Mount Zion" (Id., ver. 7). Then, in concluding his appeal to this strong Gentile nation in America, the United States, to fulfill their mission to the outcasts of Israel in America, he makes this remarkable address:

"Ho thou nation of the last days, shadowing with thy wings of liberty and peace; pity, instruct, and save my ancient people and brethren; especially the outcast branch of them, who were the natives of your soil. Pity that degraded remnant of a nation so terrible in ancient times, but who have been now so long wretched. Bring a present of them, ye worshippers of Jehovah, to the God of Abraham. Give not sleep to your eyes, till a house be builded to your God, from those ancient and venerable materials. Were not your fathers sent into that far distant world, not only to be (in their posterity) built up a great protecting nation; but also to be the instruments of gathering, or recovering the miserable remnant of my outcasts there, in the last days? Rejoice, then, ye distinguished people in your birthright, and engage in the work by Heaven assigned. Let not those tribes of my ancient people, who I have borne as on eagles' wings for so many ages; let them not become extinct before your eyes; let them no longer roam in savage barbarism and death. My bowels yearn for Ephraim, my first-born. 'For since I spake against him, I do earnestly remember him still.' 'I have seen his ways, and will heal him. I will restore peace to him, and to his mourners; peace in the renewal of my covenant. I will again bear him on eagles' wings, and bring him to myself. For you (my suppliants in the west), this honour is reserved' (Zeph. 3:10). The wings of your continent have long borne in his banishment. Let now the wings of your liberty, compassion, and blessed retreat, bear him from his dreary wilds to the temple of God.

"Look at the origin of those degraded natives of your continent, and fly to their relief. Send them the heralds of salvation. Send them the word, the bread of life. You received that book from the seed of Abraham. All your volume of salvation was written by the sons of Jacob. And by them it was transferred from Jerusalem to the lost heathen world, and to you; otherwise you had now been heathen, and eternally undone. Remember then your debt of gratitude to God's ancient people for the word of life. Restore it to them, and thus double your own rich inheritance in its blessings. Learn them to read the book of grace. *Learn them its history and their own.* Teach them the story of their ancestors; the economy of Abraham, Isaac and Jacob. Sublimate their views above the savage pursuits of the forests. Elevate them above the wilds of barbarism and death, by showing them what has been done for their nation; and what is yet to be done by the God of their fathers, in the line of his promise. Teach them their ancient history; their former blessings; their being cast away; the occasion of it; and the promises of their return. Tell them the time draws near, and they must now return to the God of their salvation. Tell them their return is to be as life from the dead to the Gentile nations. Tell them what their ancient fathers the prophets were inspired to predict in their behalf; and the charge here given for their restoration. Assure them this talk of an ancient prophet is for them, and they must listen to it and obey it. That the Great Spirit above the clouds now calls them by you to come and receive his grace by Christ the true star from Jacob, the Shiloh who has come, and to whom the people must be gathered. Inform them that by embracing this true seed of Abraham, you and multitudes of other Gentiles have become the children of that ancient patriarch; and now they must come back as your brothers in the Lord. Unfold to them their superlative line of the entail of the covenant; that 'as touching this election, they are beloved for the fathers' sakes'; that they were for their sins excluded for this long period, until the fulness of the Gentiles be come in, and so all Israel shall be saved.

"Go, thou nation highly distinguished in the last days; save the remnant of my people. Bring me a present of them 'to the place of the name of the Lord of hosts, the Mount Zion'" *(View of the Hebrews,* pp. 247-50).

Thus ends his appeal and all this is important, *because this is the very mission assigned by the Book of Mormon prophets to the Christian people of the United States:* Namely, in the language of Ethan Smith's book, "that we are the people [meaning the people of the U.S.] especially addressed [i.e., in Isaiah 18] and called upon to restore them [the American Indians — the lost tribes of Israel]; *or bring them to the knowledge of the Gospel,*" and to do with them whatever the God of Abraham designs shall be done"; or, in the language of the Book of Mormon, when proclaiming the purpose for which the Book of Mormon was written, and which is "to come forth in due time by way of the Gentile . . . *to show unto the remnant of the house of Israel what great things the Lord*

hath done for their fathers; and that they may know the covenants of
the Lord, and that they are not cast off for ever—and also to the
convincing of the Jew and Gentile that Jesus is the Christ, the Eternal
God, manifesting himself to all nations." This is from the title page of
the Book of Mormon, but it is a transcript from the plates of the Book
of Mormon, being Moroni's preface, to the Book of plates he delivered
to Joseph Smith, and hence part of the Book of Mormon itself. In the
body of the book the same purpose is stated. (See especially Mormon
4:12-15; and the writer's *New Witnesses for God,* vol. 2, ch. III.)

On the part that the great Christian nation of America shall take
in the restoring the Israel of God in America to a knowledge of their
place in God's scheme of things, and bringing them "to the knowledge
of the Gospel"—to use Ethan Smith's phraseology—the Book of Mormon is very explicit. The first Nephi, having read that portion of Isaiah's
writings, now found in chapter 49, a chapter dealing with the glorious
restoration of Israel to favor with God and to possession of their lands,
says: "Behold I will lift up mine hand unto the Gentiles, and set up a
standard unto the people; and they shall bring thy sons (Israel's sons) in
their arms, and thy daughters shall be carried upon their shoulders. And
kings shall be thy nursing fathers and their queens their nursing mothers"
(I Nephi 21:22, 23). Nephi was asked by his brethren if the things he
had read concerning the restoration of the house of Israel were to be
understood "according to things which are spiritual which shall come
to pass according to the Spirit and not the flesh"?—a question, strangely
enough, raised in the discussion by Ethan Smith in his book, and the
same conclusion reached as in the answer given, as we shall see, by Nephi.
"Thus the prophetic writings," says Ethan Smith—after quoting copiously on this subject from Isaiah and other scriptures—"Thus the prophetic writings do clearly decide, that both Israel and the Jews shall, in
the last days, before the Millennium, be *literally restored to their own
land of Palestine, and be converted to the Christian faith.* To give a mystical
import to all these prophecies, and say they will be fulfilled only in the
conversion of these ancient people of God to Christianity is to take a
most unwarrantable liberty with the word of God. Some have made such
pretense; but far be it from me to follow them! Why not as well apply
a mystical sense to every prediction to future events? to the prediction
of the battle of that great day, of the Millennium; of the resurrection
of the bodies of men; of the final judgment; of the conflagration of this
world; of heaven; of hell? Why may not those as well all be fulfilled, not
by a literal, but by some mystical accomplishment?" (*View of the Hebrews,*
p. 64.) Thus he argues for a literal fulfillment of Isaiah's prophecies
respecting the restoration of Israel to their own lands, and their return
to their own lands.

And now Nephi's answer as to whether the prophecies on the same subject in Isaiah are to be *literal,* or *spiritual* only:

"Behold, they were manifest unto the prophet, by the voice of the Spirit; for by the Spirit are all things made known unto the prophets, which shall come upon the children of men according to the flesh. Wherefore, the things of which I have read, are things pertaining to things both temporal and spiritual; for it appears that the house of Israel, sooner or later, will be scattered upon all the face of the earth, and also among all nations, and behold there are many who are already lost from the knowledge of those who are at Jerusalem. Yea, the most part of all the tribes have been led away; and they are scattered to and fro upon the isles of the sea; and whither they are, none of us knoweth, save that we know that they have been led away. And since they have been led away, these things have been prophesied concerning them, and also concerning all those who shall hereafter be scattered and be confounded, because of the Holy One of Israel; for against him will they harden their hearts; wherefore, they shall be scattered among all nations, and shall be hated of all men.

"Nevertheless, after they shall be nursed by the Gentiles, and the Lord has lifted up his hand upon the Gentiles, and set them up for a standard, and their children have been carried in their arms, and their daughters have been carried upon their shoulders, behold these things of which are spoken, *are temporal* [i.e., literal]; for thus is the covenant of the Lord with our fathers; and it meaneth us in the days to come, and also all our brethren who are of the house of Israel. And it meaneth that the time cometh that after all the house of Israel have been scattered and confounded, *that the Lord God will raise up a mighty nation among the Gentiles, yea, even upon the face of this land;* and by them shall our seed be scattered. And after our seed is scattered, the Lord God will proceed to do a marvelous work among the Gentiles, which shall be of great worth unto our seed; wherefore, it is likened unto their being nourished by the Gentiles, and being carried in their arms and upon their shoulders" (I Nephi 22:2-8).

Jacob, the brother of Nephi, also expounded the writing of Isaiah to the people of Nephi, especially chapters 48, 49, 50, and 51; all of which are given at length, and deal with the scattering and gathering and glorification of Israel. Commenting on these things in Isaiah 49:22, 23, and having more especially in mind the relationship of the Gentiles to the work of restoring Israel, and again more especially having in mind the Gentiles in the New World, he says—speaking of Israel:

"But behold, saith the Lord God; when the day cometh that they shall believe in me, that I am Christ, then have I covenanted with their fathers that they shall be restored in the flesh, upon the earth, unto the lands of their inheritance. And it shall come to pass that they shall be gathered in from their long dispersion, from the isles of the sea, and from the four parts of the earth; and the nations of the Gentiles shall be great in the eyes of me, saith God, in carrying them forth to the lands of their inheritance. Yea, the kings of the Gentiles shall be nursing mothers; wherefore, the promises of the Lord are great unto the Gentiles, for he hath spoken it, and who can dispute? But behold, this land, saith God, shall be a land of thine [the Nephites'] inheritance, and the Gentiles shall be blessed upon the land. And this land shall be a land of liberty unto the Gentiles, and there shall be no kings upon the land, who shall raise up unto the Gentiles; and I will fortify this land against all other nations; and he that fighteth against Zion shall perish, saith God; for he that raiseth up a king against me shall perish, for I the Lord, the king of heaven, will be their king, and I will be a light unto them forever, that hear my words. . . . For I will fulfill my promises which I have made unto the children of men, *that I will do unto them while they are in the flesh* [again, literally]; wherefore, my beloved brethren, thus saith our God, I will afflict thy seed by the hand of the Gentiles; nevertheless I will soften the hearts of the Gentiles, that they shall be like unto a father to them; wherefore the Gentiles shall be blessed and numbered among the house of Israel" (II Nephi 10:7-18).

Something of variation and enlargement will be observed in this from Ethan Smith's idea of the mission of the nation of the United States in its relation to Israel in America; but it can only be regarded as a very natural variation and development; namely, a more complete identification of the rescuing Gentile nation with Israel than is contemplated in the views of Mr. Smith.

There is yet another reference in the Book of Mormon to this idea of the mission of the American Gentile nation in its relation to the restoration and glorification of Israel in the New World. The importance of that reference arises from the fact that it is the resurrected Christ who is represented as making it. That passage also marks off still another variation in this mission, viz., the destruction of the Gentile nation if it fails in its mission with reference to the house of Israel in America.

The risen Christ is expounding to the Nephite disciples the passage in St. John 10th Chapter and 16th verse, to the effect that he had said to the disciples at Jerusalem that he had other sheep not of that fold at Jerusalem, them also he must bring, they must hear his voice, there must be one fold and one shepherd—then the risen Christ, speaking to the Twelve Special Nephite disciples, said:

"Ye are my disciples; and ye are a light unto this people, who are a remnant of the house of Joseph. And behold, this is the land of your inheritance; and the Father hath given it unto you. . . . And verily, I say unto you, that ye are they of whom I said, other sheep I have which are not of this fold; them also I must bring, and they shall hear my voice; and there shall be one fold, and one shepherd. And they understood me not, for they supposed it had been the Gentiles; for they understood not that the Gentiles should be converted through their preaching" (III Nephi 15:12, 13, 21, 22).

And again, the Christ still speaking: "And I command you that ye shall write these sayings, after I am gone, that if it so be that my people at Jerusalem, they who have seen me, and been with me in my ministry, do not ask the Father in my name, that they may receive a knowledge of you by the Holy Ghost, and also of the other tribes whom they know not of, that these sayings which ye shall write, shall be kept, and shall be manifested unto the Gentiles, that through the fulness of the Gentiles, the remnant of their seed who shall be scattered forth upon the face of the earth, because of their unbelief, may be brought in, or may be brought to a knowledge of me, their Redeemer. And then will I gather them in from the four quarters of the earth; and then will I fulfill the convenant which the Father hath made unto all the people of the house of Israel. And blessed are the Gentiles, because of their belief in me, in and of the Holy Ghost, which witness unto them, of me and of the Father. Behold, because of their belief in me, saith the Father, and because of the unbelief of you, O house of Israel, in the latter day shall the truth come unto the Gentiles, that the fulness of these things shall be made known unto them" (III Nephi 16:4-7).

But terrible "woe" is denounced against the Gentile nation if they fail of their mission to rescue and uplift Israel in America. The Gospel will be, in that event, taken from among them; "and I will suffer my people, O house of Israel," said the risen Lord of Israel, "I will suffer my people . . . that they shall go through among them and shall tread them down, and they shall be as salt that hath lost its savor, which is hence forth good for nothing but to cast out, and to be trodden under foot of my people, O house of Israel" (III Nephi 16:8-16).

There is much more to the same effect in the 20th and 21st chapters of III Nephi, only that the judgments denounced against the American Gentile nation are more terrible than those set forth in the quotations already given—and on the other hand, the blessings pronounced are more definitely stated, amounting in the end to this: That if the Gentiles "will repent, and hearken unto my words, and harden not their hearts, I will establish my church among them, and they shall come in unto the covenant, and be numbered among this the remnant of Jacob, unto whom I have given this land for their inheritance, and they shall assist my people, the remnant of Jacob, and also, as many of the house of Israel as shall come, that they may build a city, which shall be called the

New Jerusalem; and then shall the power of heaven come down among them; and I also will be in the midst" (III Nephi 21:22-25).

The variation from Ethan Smith's views of the mission of the Christian people in relation to the house of Israel in America is seen again to be a closer union of the Gentile Christians with the house of Israel than he contemplates, and a terrible judgment denounced against them if they fail in their part of the assigned privileges and duties.

In relation to these terrible judgments against the Gentile nation in the event of their not going to the rescue of the remnants of Israel in the land, and participating in the work assigned to them — the Messiah declares in that event — that:

"My people who are a remnant of Jacob, shall be among the Gentiles, yea, in the midst of them as a lion among the beasts of the forest, as a young lion among the flocks of sheep, who, if he go through both treadeth down and teareth in pieces, and none can deliver. . . . And I execute vengeance and fury upon them, even as upon the heathen, such as they have not heard" (III Nephi, 21:12, 21).

All this, it could be said by one disposed to criticize the Book of Mormon — all this might have seemed possible to men living in the early decades of the 19th century, 1820-1830, when Indian tribes of unknown strength but well attested ferocity occupied the greater part of the land over which the United States now extends its jurisdiction, but it is scarcely possible now to entertain such conceptions of native race terror, triumph, and domination over the Gentile nation of the United States. All reasonable expectation of such an event has passed.

The likelihood, therefore, is that either the Gentile nation has fulfilled its part with reference to Israel in the New World, has been as the nursing fathers and mothers to Israel in America, or else that the prophecies denouncing "woe" upon them for not doing it, are of no effect — are no true prophecies, and the book containing them no true scripture, a human document merely, not of divine origin. For as the Lord hath said, "When a prophet speaketh in the name of the Lord, if the thing follow not, nor come to pass, that is the thing which the Lord hath not spoken, but the prophet hath spoken it presumptuously; thou shalt not be afraid of him" (Deut. 18:22).

VI

MIGRATIONS OF ETHAN SMITH'S "TEN LOST TRIBES OF ISRAEL," AND THE
BOOK OF MORMON PEOPLES TO THE NEW WORLD; JOURNEY TO THE
LAND "WHERE NEVER MAN DWELT" PARALLELS; "ETHAN"—"ETHER"

Both the Book of Mormon and Ethan Smith's *View of the Hebrews*
bring their people to the New World by migrations from the old. Their
way of coming, however, is different. Ethan Smith, accepting the general
idea extant in his day that America was peopled via Bering Strait, thought
it possible that "the lost tribes" of Israel might as well have come that
way as any other people from Asia (*View of the Hebrews*, p. 168). The
Book of Mormon peoples, both Jaredites and Nephites, are brought by
way of the sea. In one respect, however, the migrations of the Jaredites
and of Ethan Smith's "lost tribes" are strikingly similar, and the fact is
mentioned in both cases in language nearly identical—both people are
brought into a land "*where never man dwelt.*" Ethan Smith adds "since
the flood." But, to be more specific, Ethan Smith, in working out his
theory that the American Indians are the "ten lost tribes" of Israel, takes
his account of the migration of that people from the Apocryphal book
of Esdras (II Esdras 13). Here in vision is shown a people who are declared
to be "the ten tribes of Israel" carried away prisoners in the days of
Hosea, king of Israel, by the king of Assyria, "and he carried them over
the waters, and so came they into another land." But these captives "took
counsel among themselves, that they would leave the multitude of the
heathen, and go forth into a further country, *where never man dwelt;*
that they might there keep their statutes which they never kept (i.e.,
uniformly, as they ought) in their own lands."

"*There was a great way to go, namely, of a year and a half*" The
Italics are Mr. Smith's, as if he would emphasize the length of the journey.
Then he continuing:

"The writer (meaning Esdras) proceeds to speak of the name of the
region being called Arsareth, or Ararat. He must allude here to the region
to which they directed their course to go this year and a half's journey.
This place where no man dwelt must, of course, have been unknown by
name. But Ararat, or Armenia, *lay north of the place where* the ten tribes
were planted when carried from Palestine. *Their journey then was to the
north,* or northeast. This writer [Esdras] says, "*They entered into the
Euphrates* [i.e., *valley,* of course] by the narrow passage of the river." He
must mean, they repassed this river in its upper regions, or small streams,
away toward Georgia; and hence must have taken their course between
the Black and Caspian Seas. This set them off *northeast* of the Ararat,
which he mentions (*View of the Hebrews*, p. 75).

Finally they reach the New World.

Mr. Smith then proceeds to argue that as God had determined to make "outcasts of these tribes," though little confidence may be placed in the Book of Esdras as a book of inspired prophecy, yet what is here described as happening to these people "seems just such an event as might be expected, had God indeed determined to separate them from the rest of the idolatrous world, and banish them by themselves, in *a land where no man* dwelt since the flood." And if they took counsel with themselves, as they naturally would do, "they certainly could not have taken counsel to go into Hindostan, or any of the old and long crowded nations of Asia."

This reference to "the ten tribes" *not* going to Hindostan etc., really refers to a theory mentioned in Mr. Smith's Appendix to his book, about the possibility of "the ten tribes" having migrated to Hindostan or Afghanistan, since "black Jews" are found there, and exhibit in their racial characteristics, and religions and domestic customs, it is alleged, many of the Hebrew race. Mr. Smith attempts an earnest refutation. (See pp. 271-85.) Such a place they would naturally have avoided. And to such a place the God of Israel would not have led them, to keep them in an outcast state distinct from all other nations as *his lamb in a large place.*" (See Appendix *View of the Hebrews.*)

Let us now turn to the Book of Mormon account of the Jaredite migration to the New World. Reference to chapter III of this writing will give the necessary facts about the Jaredites to be considered here.

It is to be noted first of all that a consultation is had among those to whom the journey is proposed, in both cases. Among the supposed Israelites, they "took counsel among themselves" as to the journey. Among the Jaredites the Brother of Jared urged his brother to "go and inquire of the Lord, to cry unto him" whither they should go.

That in both cases the motive of removal was a religious one. "Who knoweth," said Jared to his Brother when urging him to inquire of the Lord for a way of deliverance from the impending disaster at Babel, the confusion of tongues —"Who knows" said he, "but the Lord will carry us forth unto a land which is choice above all the earth? And if it so be, let us be faithful unto the Lord, that we may receive it for our inheritance" (Ether 1:38).

In the case of Mr. Smith's "lost tribes" the motive was a religious one. Quotes Mr. Smith: "They took this counsel among themselves, that they would leave the multitude of the heathen, and go into a further country; . . . that they might there keep their statutes which they had never kept (i.e., uniformly, as they ought) in their own land." (*View of the Hebrews,* pp. 74, 75.)

The journey in both cases was to the north. Ether describes the

Jaredite movement: the Brother of Jared had been commanded to gather the proposed colony together, then: "When thou has done this, thou shalt go at the head of them down into the valley which is *northward,* and there will I meet thee, and I will go before thee into a land which is choice above all the lands of the Earth" (Ether 1:41, 42). "And it came to pass that Jared and his brother" and their people "went down into the valley which was northward (and in the name of the valley was Nimrod, being called after the mighty hunter) with their flocks. . . . And it came to pass that they did travel in the wilderness, and did build barges, in which they did *cross many waters,* being directed continually by the hand of the Lord. And the Lord would not suffer that they should stop *beyond the sea* in *the wilderness,* but he would that they should come forth even to the land of promise which was choice above all other lands" (Ether 2:1, 6, 7). At last the colony came to "the great sea which divideth the lands" (i.e., some ocean). Here they pitched their tents and dwelt by the sea shore "for the space of four years." Here eight small barges were built, and in these the colony finally reached the land that had been promised them — to us the New World — America.

Mr. Ethan Smith, drawing his description of the supposed journey of his "lost tribes," and following Esdras, says: "The writer proceeds to speak of the region (i.e., to which they directed their course) being called Arsareth, or Ararat. He must allude here to the region to which they directed their course. . . . But Ararat, or Armenia, lay *North* of the place where the ten tribes were planted when carried from Palestine. Their journey then was, to the north or northeast. This writer [Esdras] says 'They entered into the Euphrates (i.e., into the valley of it, of course) by the narrow passage of the river.' He must mean, they *passed* this river in its upper regions, or small streams, away toward Georgia; and hence must have taken their course between the *Black and Caspian sea.* This set them off northeast of the Ararat, which he mentions." Finally they reached the New World. The journey then is northward in both cases. The valley of the Euphrates and the valley of Nimrod mutually suggest each other.

The "many waters" of the Jaredites ("the sea in the wilderness"), which they crossed in barges, correspond fairly well with the passing and repassing of the river Euphrates, and the course taken by the "ten tribes" between the "Black and Caspian Seas."

In each case the journey of the two people was to be a long one. In the case of Ethan Smith's Israelites it was "of a year and a half's" duration. In the case of the Jaredites, it required 344 days to cross the great sea; and how long to make the land journey from the valley of the Euphrates to the "Great Sea" is not known.

After mentioning these more or less corresponding and parallel things between the Jaredites and Ethan Smith's Israelites, I am not unmindful of the fact that one people—the Israelites of Ethan Smith—belong to the seventh century, and the other—the Jaredites—some two thousand years earlier, and therefore the comparison drawn is not between the same people, nor of people belonging to the same age. All that is freely granted. But let us here be reminded that what is sought in this study is not absolute identity of incidents, and absolute parallel of conditions and circumstances all down the line; but one thing here and another there, that may suggest another but similar thing in such a way as to make one a product of the other, as in the above parallel between the journey of the Jaredites and Ethan Smith's Israelites. Such as the motive for their journey being the same; the direction of the journey in both cases being northward; both peoples entering a valley at the commencement of their journey; both of them encountering many bodies of water in their journey; the journey in both cases being an immense one; and to a land, in the one case, "where never man dwelt" (Smith's book); and in the other case, "into a quarter where there never had man been" (Ether 2:5). Where such striking parallels as these obtain, it is not unreasonable to hold that where one account precedes the other, and if the one constructing the later account has had opportunity of contact with the first account, then it is not impossible that the first account could have suggested the second; and if the points of resemblance and possible suggestion are frequent and striking, then it would have to be conceded that the first might even have supplied the ground plan of the second.

Also let it be borne in mind, that the facts and the arguments employed here are cumulative and progressive, and that we have not yet reached the end of the story.

It is conceded that this infusion of the Jaredite people and their migration to the New World and their history there is a unique thing, and without direct parallel in Ethan Smith's book, though he does make inference to Babel, and its people in one of two places. In one case referring to the knowledge of mechanic arts being possessed in early times, and then lost. "Noah and his sons," he remarks, "must have known considerable of these arts, as appears in the building of the ark. And his early posterity must have known something considerable of them as appears in their building of Babel. But how many of the descendants of those ancient mechanics lost this knowledge" (p. 171). And again at page 179, Mr. Smith speaks of the pyramid at Cholula, Mexico, described by Humboldt as being constructed of alternate strata of brick and clay; and of various other pyramids described by the same author, that "suffice to prove the great analogy between these brick monuments and the temple of Belus at Babylon." But it is not claimed that there is anything in these references that suggest the Jaredites and their place in the Book of Mormon.

Ethan = *Ether*

In taking leave of the Jaredites and this Book of Ether, one word more, this name "*Ether*." Rather an unusual name, is it not? I do not find it among Bible names nor in any list of proper names of the unabridged dictionaries so far consulted. Could it be that it was a variation made from the "*Ethan*" of Mr. Smith's name-author of the *View of the Hebrews? Ethan = Ether!* Not impossible, at least; and the more likely since Mr. Ethan Smith in his *View of the Hebrews*, in the very pages describing the journey of his Israelites uses such a changing in words to get the northward journey of his Israelites established—as might readily suggest a change from "*Ethan*" to "Ether," as follows: "The writer" (Esdras) proceeds to speak of the region being called "*Asrareth*," or "*Ararat*." . . . "But *Ararat*, or *Armenia*, lay north of the place where the ten tribes were planted" (p. 75), which amounts to this:

"*Arsareth*" changed to "*Ararat*."

"*Ararat*" changed to "*Armenia*."

Why not someone else, influenced by such a suggestion, have it—

"*Ethan*" changed to "*Ether*"?

Do not take the idea too seriously, however, it is merely a passing suggestion of a bare possibility.

VII

VIEW OF THE HEBREWS; AND THE GROUND PLAN OF THE BOOK OF
MORMON; STRUCTURAL MATERIAL. THE AMERICAN RACE SEPARATED
INTO TWO DIVISIONS—CIVILIZED AND BARBAROUS IN BOTH BOOKS

I come now to more specific structural material for the Book of Mormon
to be found in the book of Mr. Ethan Smith.

Mr. Smith finds objection made to his theory of the American Indians
being the lost tribes of Israel, because of their ignorance of "the mechanic
arts, of writing, and of navigation." He points out that from Noah's time
and from Babel's tower many people had doubtless lost knowledge of
mechanic arts no less than these "lost tribes of Israel." Then wishing to
account for the loss of such arts among the tribes of Israel in America,
he advances the supposition that the tribes when arriving in America had
knowledge of, and used the mechanic arts, but having possession of a
vast continent filled with an abundance of game of all sorts, they were
lured to the life of hunting and its indolence.

He assumes a division of the people, an adherence on the part of
our division to maintain knowledge of and the use of the mechanic arts,
to found cities, build temples, mounds, fortifications, pyramids, and other
traits of civilization, the ruined monuments of which were found by the
Europeans upon their arrival in the New World. The other division
degenerated to savagery, with the result that a series of "tremendous
wars" ensued between the savage and the civilized divisions resulting in
the *annihilation of the latter* by the savage division, the destruction of
civilization together with the people who produced it, thus leaving the
continent in the grip of savagery, until the coming of the Europeans.

One acquainted with Book of Mormon historical events will recognize in all this an outline of Book of Mormon "history," what else
there is would be merely detail. The account of this matter is so important
to our inquiry that it deserves to be given in full from Mr. Smith's work,
and accordingly it is quoted here at length:

"That the people who first migrated to this western world did possess
some knowledge of the mechanic arts (as much doubtless, as was possessed by Israel when they disappeared in the east) appears from incontestable facts, which are furnished in Baron Humboldt, and in the *American Archaeology,* such as the finding of brick, earthenware, sculptures,
some implements of iron, as well as other metals, and other tokens of
considerable improvement; which furnish an argument in favour of the
Indians having descended from the ten tribes. For the ancient Scythians,
and people of the northeast of Asia, had no such degree of civilization

at the time the Indians must have reached this land. Hence they could not have been from them.

"The probability then is this: that the ten tribes, arriving in this continent with some knowledge of the arts of civilized life; finding themselves in a vast wilderness filled with the best of game, inviting them to the chase; most of them fell into a wandering, idle, hunting life. Different clans parted from each other, lost each other, and formed separate tribes. Most of them formed a habit of this idle mode of living, and were pleased with it. More sensible parts of this people associated together, to improve their knowledge of the arts; and probably continued this for ages. From these the noted relics of civilization discovered in the west, and south, were furnished. *But the savage tribes prevailed; and in process of time their savage jealousies and rage annihilated their more civilized brethren.* And thus, as a holy, vindictive Providence would have it, and according to ancient denunciations, all were left in an 'outcast' savage state. *This accounts for their loss of the knowledge of letters, of the art of navigation, and of the use of iron.* And such a loss can no more operate against their being of the ten tribes, than against their being of any other origin. Yea, we cannot so well account for their evident degeneracy in any other way, as that it took place under a *vindictive Providence,* as has been noted, *to accomplish divine judgments denounced against the idolatrous ten tribes of Israel.*

"It is highly probable that the more civilized part of the tribes of Israel, after they settled in America, *became wholly separated from the hunting and savage tribes of their brethren;* that the latter lost the knowledge of their having descended from the same family with themselves; *that the more civilized part continued for many centuries; that tremendous wars were frequent between them and their savage brethren, till the former became extinct.*

"This hypothesis accounts for the ancient works, forts, mounds, and vast enclosures, as well as tokens of a good degree of civil improvement, which are manifestly very ancient, and from centuries before Columbus discovered America. These magnificent works have been found, one near Bewark in Licking County, Ohio; one in Perry County, Ohio; one at Marietta; one at Circleville; one on Paint Creek; one on the eastern bank of the Little Miami river, Warren County; one on Paint creek near Chillicothe; one on the Scioto river; and other places.

"These works have evinced great wars, a good degree of civilization, and great skill in fortification. And articles dug from old mounds in and near those fortified places clearly evince that their authors possessed no small degree of refinement in the knowledge of the mechanic arts.

"*These partially civilized people became extinct.* What account can be given of this, *but that the savages extirpated them, after long and dismal wars?* And nothing appears more probable than that they were the better part of the Israelites who came to this continent, who for a long time retained their knowledge of the mechanic and civil arts, while the greater part of their brethren became savage and wild. No other hypothesis occurs to mind, which appears by any means so probable. The degrees of improvement, demonstrated to have existed among the authors of those works, and relics, who have ceased to exist, far exceed all that could have been furnished from the northeast of Asia, in those ancient times." (*View of the Hebrews*, pp. 171-73.)

A few pages later on, he further remarks:

"In the *Archaelogia Americana*, containing 'Transactions and Collections of the American Antiquarian Society', published at Worcester, Mass., in 1820, are found antiquities of the people who formerly inhabited the western parts of the United States. Of some of these I shall give a concise view, as additional arguments in favour of my theory, that some of the people of Israel who came into this western continent maintained some degree of civilization for a long time; but that *the better part of the outcast tribes of Israel here finally became extinct,* at least in North America, under the rage of their more numerous savage brethren." (Id., p. 188.)

Let us trace as far as they exist this outline in the Book of Mormon.

From the beginning in the colony of Lehi there existed the elements of such a division in the colony as finally took place. This was the "jealous rage" of the two older brothers in Lehi's family towards the two younger brothers. This led to the contentions and the divisions which separated the colony into two parties, and finally led to the creation of two peoples, the one civilized, the other barbarous. The first separation took place within the lifetime of the first Nephi, when the colony was not more than thirty years removed from the time it departed from Jerusalem. The colony divided about equally as to numbers, and as the colony did not exceed above thirty, when it left Jerusalem, each group into which they divided, must have been small. (II Nephi, 5:5, 6. See also the introduction to the book of I Nephi at the head of chapter I, 1921 Edition.)

The group led by the first Nephi at once took on the characteristics of the civilized group of Ethan Smith's book. "All those who would go with me," writes Nephi, in describing this first removal from the companionship of the two older brothers and their following, "were those who believed in God." They made a journey of "many days" into the wilderness, and called the place where they halted "Nephi," and thereafter called themselves "Nephites," after their leader. They observed "to keep the judgments, and the statutes and the commandments of the Lord in all things according to the law of Moses." They brought with them in the separation from their brethren the Jewish national literature that had been secured before leaving Jerusalem, and which was engraven on plates of brass. Not only so, but Nephi, commanded of God, made two sets of metallic plates on which to make a record of his people, one set for sacred, and the other for secular things, and thus perpetuated the art of writing among his people (II Nephi 5:29-34).

Nephi also took the sword of Laban, brought from Jerusalem, and from it fashioned many swords for defense, should his people be attacked by their brethren. "And I did teach my people," writes the first Nephi, "to build buildings, and to work in all manner of wood, and of iron and of copper, and of brass and of steel and of gold, and of silver and of precious ores, *which were in great abundance.*" Nephi also built a temple, and caused his people "to be industrious, and to labor with their hands." Over his protest Nephi was made "King" by his people; and he consecrated his two younger brothers to be "priests and teachers over the land of his people" (II Nephi 5).

As to the other division of the original colony, who by the way, took upon the name of the oldest son of Lehi, Laman, and hence were called "Lamanites," they as rapidly developed the traits of savagery as Nephi and his following developed the arts of civilization protected by government.

They were cursed of God with a skin of blackness, that whereas they had been "white and exceeding fair and delightsome," the "Lord God did cause a skin of blackness to come upon them," that they might be loathsome to Nephi's people. The curse was extended also to all those who should "mix with their seed." And because of the cursing which was upon them, "they did become an idle people, full of all mischief and subtlety, and did seek in the wilderness for beasts of prey." And the Lord revealed it to Nephi thus early, that the descendants of his brethren should be a "scourge" to his seed, if the latter should fail to remember the Lord, yea, they should "scourge them, even unto destruction" (II Nephi 5:25).

Considering that Ethan Smith's suggestion, as to the division of his "ten tribes" into two branches, one retaining, for some time at least, and perhaps for some centuries, civilization; and the other degenerating into barbarism, and finally utterly destroying both civilization and the civilizer—considering, I say, that this suggestion was made by Mr. Ethan Smith to account for the loss of the "mechanic arts," for the loss of "the use of iron," "loss of the knowledge of letters," by having the barbarous division destroy the civilized division to extinction, the author of the Book of Mormon laid the foundation in this chapter of II Nephi and here quoted—it could be said, with good reason—for such a scheme of things and events. Surely it will be observed that he has provided for the mechanic arts—"to build buildings, to work in all manner of wood, and of iron, and of copper, and of brass, and of steel, and of gold and of silver, and of precious ores, which were in great abundance." Also he has provided for the perpetuation of letters in both having the Jewish national literature with the civilized folk and the perpetuation of writing. Also for agriculture, for "we did sow seeds," says Nephi, "and we did reap again in abundance." "And we began to raise flocks and herds, and animals of every kind" (II Nephi 5:11). Also, as we have seen, that government and religion were provided for among the Nephites. A "King" chosen, what though his people could not exceed fifty at the time, and a priesthood was also founded.

On the other hand, the elements of savagery and ferocity were provided in this first division of the people. The curse of a black skin, hardened hearts against God, hatred towards their brethren, "idle, mischievous, full of all subtlety," are their outstanding characteristics, and already they are threatening to be an instrument in the hands of what Ethan Smith twice speaks of in the passage above quoted, as a "vindictive Providence"—a scourge to the good people—to the civilized—an instrument that "shall," in certain eventualities, "*scourge them even unto destruction*"!

Could an investigator of the Book of Mormon be much blamed if he were to decide that Ethan Smith's book with its suggestion as to the division of his Israelites into two peoples; with its suggestion of "tremendous wars between them"; and of the savages overcoming the civilized division led to the fashioning of chiefly these same things in the Book of Mormon?

These characteristics assigned above to Nephites and Lamanites, respectively, continued throughout Book of Mormon "history" to the bitter end, to the time of the Nephite destruction. One Enos, a Nephite writer speaking of conditions prevailing among these two people towards the close of the first century after Lehi's colony left Jerusalem, says:

"And I bear record that the people of Nephi did seek diligently to restore the Lamanites unto the true faith in God. But our labours were vain; their hatred was fixed, and they were led by their evil nature that they became wild, and ferocious, and a bloodthirsty people; full of idolatry and filthiness; feeding upon beasts of prey; dwelling in tents, and wandering about in the wilderness with a short skin girdle about their loins and their heads shaven; and their skill was in the bow, and in the cimeter, and the axe. And many of them did eat nothing save it was raw meat; and they were continually seeking to destory us."

Of the Nephites he said:

"And it came to pass that the people of Nephi did till the land, and raise all manner of grain, and of fruit, and flocks of herds, and flocks of all manner of cattle of every kind, (*sic!*) and goats, and wild goats, and also many horses."

"And there were exceeding many prophets among us" (the Nephites), says this writer and even as he speaks he appears to be anxious to bear witness that the elements exist in his people that will afford the future justification of their destruction—as if keeping it in mind, saying: "And the people were a stiff-necked people, hard to understand. And there was nothing save it was exceeding harshness, preaching and prophesying of wars, and contentions, and destructions, and continually reminding them of death, *and the duration of eternity,* and the judgments and the power of God; and all these things stirring them up continually to keep them in the fear of the Lord. I say there was nothing short of these things, and exceeding great plainness of speech, would keep them from going down speedily to destruction. And after this manner do I write concerning them" (Enos 1:20-24).

In the third century from the time Lehi's colony left Jerusalem, there was a second notable separation among the Nephites. This time the leader was one Mosiah, a prophet, and he, "warned of God," led a division of the people away, the more righteous part of them, of course, into the wilderness; there to nurture the righteous in the fear of the Lord. These are the people who found the descendants of the colony of Mulek at the city of Zarahemla. The effect of a people being without letters is emphasized at the meeting of these two peoples. The people of Mulek had brought no records with them in their flight from Judea, neither had their descendants kept records, or cultivated letters in any form, with the result that their language had become so far corrupted, that Mosiah's followers—though of the same stock-language and people—could not understand them; and though Jews, "they denied the being of their creator." Could not this be regarded—having in mind now Ethan Smith's book as suggesting outlines of the Book of Mormon—as forming a prophecy of what would be the conditions when Ethan Smith's civilized Israelites should be overcome by his Israelite savages? In the present case, however, the people of Mulek were instructed in the language of the Nephites, absorbed by them into one community, choosing one king—and this Mosiah, leader of the Nephites who had come to them—becoming one people hence forth, the Nephite, up to the coming at least of the Christ.

On the other hand, the people of the wilderness, existing before this separation under Mosiah's leadership, augmented by the Nephites left by Mosiah and his following, who, lapsing into barbarism, became the Lamanites unto the coming of the Christ.

In this interval, between the finding of the people of Mulek at

Zarahemla, in the third century B.C., to the coming of the Christ was a period of "tremendous" warfare between these two people. There was invasion after invasion on the part of the Lamanites into Nephite lands. Often the invaders were aided by traitors from among the Nephites, themselves ambitious of leadership. Some of the wars were protracted, and the battles were always sanguinary, the numbers slain being appalling. Intermittently, however, there were periods of peace, and these were fruitful of advancement in wealth and the progress of civilization.

VIII

VIEW OF THE HEBREWS; AND THE GROUND PLAN OF THE BOOK OF
MORMON; STRUCTURAL MATERIAL—DID THE SUGGESTED TRAITS OF
CIVILIZATION OF ETHAN SMITH'S BOOK SUGGEST THE TRAITS OF THE
NEPHITE CIVILIZATION? MECHANIC ARTS, LETTERS, NAVIGATION,
USE OF IRON

A period of peace that made for progress, such as was referred to in the closing remarks of the last chapter, followed a protracted war closing about sixty years B.C. "And they had had wars and bloodsheds, and famine, and affliction for the space of many years" (Alma 62:39). Then came the peace referred to and its attendant prosperity. There was a great movement northward from Zarahemla in this period. And as if to give assurance that there should be nothing lacking in the Book of Mormon to fill up the outline suggested by Ethan Smith's book—if that book *did* suggest the ground plan of the Book of Mormon—the Nephites entered upon an era of ship building and sea-going navigation. One Hagoth, descibed as "an exceedingly curious man," built an exceeding large ship and launched it forth into the west sea, "by the narrow neck [i.e., of land, and generally supposed to be the Isthmus of Panama], which led into the land northward. And behold, there were many of the Nephites who did enter therein and did sail forth with much provisions, and also many women and children; and they took their course northward. And in the thirty and eighth year (corresponding with 54 B.C.), this man built other ships. And the first ship did also return, and many more people did enter into it; and they also took much provisions, and set out again to the land northward. And it came to pass that they were never heard of more. And we suppose that they were drowned up in the depths of the sea. And it came to pass that one other ship also did sail forth; and whither she did go we know not. And it came to pass that in this year, there were many people who went forth into the land northward" (Alma 63:6-9).

A later reference to "shipping" and the "building of ships" is made in the Book of Mormon, but it deals with this same period, that is between sixty and forty years B.C. (Helaman 3:14). And again, but in the same chapter, it is written: "And it came to pass as timber was exceeding scarce in the land northward, they did send forth much by the way of shipping; and thus they did enable the people in the land northward that they might build many cities, both of wood and of cement" (Helaman 2:10, 11).

This is the last reference to "navigation" by ships in the Book of Mormon. Although there were fifty years yet in this period to the coming of Christ, and four hundred years afterward before the civilized people of the Book of Mormon shall pass away, yet during all this time, wherein is described "the golden age" of peace and of great prosperity; of their widespread occupancy of the land, how "they were spread upon all the face of the land," in the north as in the south; but there is no more mention of ships or of ship-building or of sea navigation. It seems to have been a trait which like Jonah's gourd, sprang up in a night, and perished in a night.[5]

What is meant by reference to this ship-building and ship-using-period—"navigation," to use Mr. Smith's phrase—is this: Reference to the extended quotation from Mr. Ethan Smith's work in the preceding chapter, and to another passage at page 171 of his book, will disclose the fact that objection was made to his theory that the American Indians are "the ten lost tribes" of Israel, on the ground of the Indians being "*ignorant of mechanic arts, of writing, and of navigation*" and, later, of "*the use of iron*" is added. It was held in opposition to his theory that if the Indians were Israelites they must have had knowledge of these several things—as migrating from a part of the world where they were known—and "being once known could never be lost." Smith's answer to this objection, let the student be reminded, is the supposed division of his Israelites into savages on the one hand, and civilized peoples on the other; "dismal wars" ensue between them, "and in process of time their savage *jealousies and rage* [i.e., of the uncivilized] annihilated their more civilized brethren. . . . This accounts for their loss of the art of navigation, and of the use of iron" (pp. 171-72).

How well the author of the Book of Mormon has followed the ground plan suggested by Mr. Smith as to mechanic arts may be seen in those Book of Mormon passages which represent the first Nephi as saying "And I did teach my people to build buildings, and to work in all manner of wood, and of iron, and of copper, and of brass, and of steel, and of gold and of silver, and of precious ores, which were in great abundance." And speaking at the same place of the temple which he and his people had just then completed, he says, "The workmanship thereof was exceeding fine" (II Nephi 5:15-16).

Later by some two hundred years, the same thing is practically repeated. The Nephites "multiplied exceedingly, and spread upon all the face of the land, and became exceeding rich in gold and in silver, and in precious things *and in fine workmanship* of wood, in buildings, and in machinery, and also iron and copper, and brass and steel, making all manner of tools of every kind, to till the ground, and weapons of war— yea, the sharp-pointed arrow, and the quiver, and the dart, and the javelin, and all preparations for war" (Jarom 1:8). In each of these references to industrial conditions it will be noted that there is a very great similarity in the materials enumerated that enter into mechanic arts, and also in the manner of referring to them. A similar enumeration, but made nearly three hundred years later, is given but extended to include fabrics: "The church began to be exceeding rich. . . . Having abundance of grain, and of gold and of silver, and of precious things, and abundance of silk, and fine-twined linen, and *all manner of good homely cloth*" (Alma 1:29).

It will be thought by some, let it be said in passing, that "good homely cloth" will be reminiscent of New England phraseology.

Ninety years after this the following occurs: "Behold, their women did toil and spin, and did make all manner of cloth of every kind, to clothe their nakedness" (Helaman 6:29).

Then what seems more remarkable than all is an enumeration of all these things, and substantially in the same phrases, in the record of the Jaredites, and speaking of conditions existing some eighteen hundred years before the Christ:

"And they were exceeding industrious, and they did buy and sell, and traffic one with another, that they might get gain. And they did work in all manner of ore, and they did make gold, and silver, and iron, and brass, and all manner of metals; and they did dig it out of the earth; wherefore they did cast up mighty heaps of earth to get ore, of gold and of silver, and of iron and of copper. And they did work all manner of fine work. And they did have silks, and fine-twined linen; and they did work all manner of cloth, that they might clothe themselves from their nakedness. And they did make all manner of tools to till the earth, both to plough and to sow, to reap and to hoe, and also to thrash. And they did make all manner of tools with which they did work their beasts. And they did make all manner of weapons of war. And they did work all manner of work of exceeding curious workmanship" (Ether 10:22-27).

And now, I submit, having shown how provision has been made to introduce the mechanic arts, letters, and the use of iron among the Book of Mormon people in harmony with the tentative suggestion of Ethan Smith's book—being the ground plan of the Book of Mormon—I submit, I say, that in order that there might be nothing lacking in the striking things numerated by Mr. Smith as entering into the ancient civilization of the native races of the New World, a period of ship-building and of navigation seems to have been inaugurated among Book of Mormon peoples. It is at least singular that this thing of ship-building and navigation should appear so suddenly, and disappear as suddenly; and to be, so far as one can see, so little associated with the life and civilization of the Book of Mormon peoples.

The same may be said as to the mention of "iron and steel" in the Book of Mormon, both among the Jaredites and the Nephites. It is mentioned as existing and in use (II Nephi 5:15; Jarom 1:8; and Ether 10:23-27), but it seems as if just mentioned, and not to be interwoven in the life and work of the peoples. On every hand is the evidence of a stone age civilization and not the evidence of an iron and steel age culture. And so as to domestic animals mentioned in the Book of Mormon—"the horse, the ass, the ox, the cow, the goat and the wild goat." All these are repeatedly mentioned as existing and in use by both Jaredites and Nephites (Ether 9:18, 19; I Nephi 18:25; Enos 1:21), yet they nowhere seem to be interwoven in the movements of the people; such, for instance, as horses aiding these peoples in travels, in migrations from place to place, or used in war—as giving advantage in battles, or their absence from battles occasioning defeat, or preventing or aiding pursuit after victory. None of these things, then, *seem to belong*. They are just intruded into the narrative, and do not seem to rise from it. Could it be that the author of the Book of Mormon, taking note of Ethan Smith's explanation to account for the "absence of mechanic arts," the art of writing, the knowledge of letters, the art of navigation, and of "the use of iron," proceeded arbitrarily to thrust into his alleged history the mention of these materials and the art of using them among his Nephites in order to comply with the supposed knowledge outlined in Ethan Smith's book? There is good ground for thinking so from the manner in which they are intruded into the Book of Mormon narrative.

Could it be that Ethan Smith, influenced and misled by the reported discovery of the evidence of iron and its uses among the native Americans in ancient times, was innocently followed into this error by the author of the Book of Mormon? For there is nothing on which the later investigators of our American antiquities are more unanimously agreed upon than the matter of the absence of the knowledge of, and hence the non-use of, iron or steel among the natives of America.

"We may say that America everywhere at the time of the discovery," says Daniel G. Brinton, "was in the polished stone age. It had progressed beyond the rough stone age, but had not reached the age of metals. True that copper, bronze and the precious ores were widely employed for a variety of purposes; *but flaked and polished stone remained in all parts the principal material to produce a cutting edge*" (*The American Race*, pp. 51-52).

"The upper status of barbarism," remarks John Fiske, "in so far as it implies a knowledge of smelting iron, was never reached in aboriginal America" (*The Discovery of America*, pp. 37-38). Later he speaks of the civilization of the Aztecs, as being "without domestic animals or iron tools" (Ibid., p. 40). One might continue to quote authorities upon this subject, but I judge it to be unnecessary, since the conclusion is unanimous on the part of those competent to speak upon the subject; and this after a long time of investigation, by experts under government direction. No such skilled research work had been done in the days of Ethan Smith. Certain reported finds in ancient mounds and ruined cities in America, and chiefly enumerated in his book, were accepted as indicating the use of iron and steel by ancient races in America, and the existence of "swords" and other war weapons was taken for granted. These are frequently referred to in Ethan Smith's pages. As, for example, in the extended quotation from his book in the preceding chapter, he refers to the "American Archaeology as furnishing the evidence of the existence of brick, earthenware, sculptures, *some implements of iron,* as well as other metals" (p. 172). Again he says: "Unless it can be proved that they (the ancient American race) had intercourse with Asia or Europe, we now see that they possessed the art of working with metals. . . . They probably must have *derived* their art of working metals from the commonwealth of ancient Israel. *They* possessed something of this knowledge" (Id., p. 190).

"Tools of iron not being found in these works (ancient mounds, etc.)," he remarks, "is no sign the authors did not possess them. For had they been there, they would no doubt long since have been dissolved by rust. Some remains of iron articles, however, are found as will be seen." He then describes how "the handle of a small *sword,* or large knife, made of an Elk's horn," was found in a mound at Circleville, Ohio. "A silver ferrule encompassed the end containing the blade; which silver ferrule, though black, was not much injured by rolling ages. The blade was gone by rust. But in the hole of the handle, there was left the oxide, or rust of the iron, of a similar shape and size of the shank formerly inserted" (Id., pp. 193-94). From near Newark, Ohio, he reports finds in tumuli with human bones—and emphasizes—"urns, *ornaments* of *copper, heads of spears,* and etc., *of the same metal,* as well as of medals of copper. . . . This fact shows that these ancient American inhabitants were not wholly unacquainted with the use of metals" (Id., p. 196).

Of another find at Marietta, Ohio, in connection with human bones, he speaks of "three large circular bosses, or ornaments, for a sword belt; or a buckler." Also of a plate of silver "which appears to have been the upper part of a sword scabbard." Then of three pieces of "broken copper tube . . . filled with iron rust." "These pieces . . . composed the lower end of the scabbard, near the point of the sword. No sign of the sword itself was discovered except the appearance of the rust above mentioned" (Id., p. 197). Also at this place he describes a find in one of the mounds near Chillicothe reported by Rev. Dr. Wilson of that place, reminiscent of the Urim and Thummim described by Joseph Smith. In this mound was a skeleton on a platform of twenty feet, formed of bark; and over it a mat formed of some bark. On the breast lay a piece of copper, which, with certain accessories to be described later (Chapter IX), he says "appeared to have been designed to wear upon the neck as a kind of breast plate" (Id., p. 195). In other places also our author refers to "breast plates" in connection with mound finds (Id., p. 150). Also on this page (195) Mr. Smith describes a semi-circular ditch, near one of the tumulus, about six feet deep, when first discovered. "At the bottom lay a great quantity of human bones. These are supposed to be the remains of men slain in some great battle. They were all of the size of men, and lay in confusion, as though buried in a pile, and in haste. Here might have been about the last of those civilized people who inhabited that station" (Id., p. 195).

May one venture without sacrilege to say that all this is strongly reminiscent of a certain Book of Mormon find, now to be noted? First, however, let one other element be added to what is quoted above from Ethan Smith—the item of numbers in population in the region described by Mr. Smith. Right in these pages carrying the description of iron traits among ancient American peoples, with the sword hilts that remain and the blades of which have perished, and objects taken for "breast plates," Ethan Smith refers to the reports made of numerous cities and extensive populations in the Ohio and Mississippi valleys, as follows:

"These ancient works continued all the way down the Ohio river to the Mississippi, where they increased and were far more magnificent. . . . The number of tumuli on that river exceeds three thousand. I have been sometimes induced to think" (this is the one who reports this matter to the *Archaelogia Americana* from which Ethan Smith quotes it) "that at the period when these were constructed, there was a population as numerous as that which once animated the borders of the Nile or of the Euphrates, or Mexico. Brackenridge circulates that there were 5,000 cities at once full of people. I am perfectly satisfied that cities similar to those of ancient Mexico of several hundred thousand souls have existed in this country" (Id., p. 199).

Now let the student, having in mind the last two or three pages of descriptive matter including reference to "hilts of swords, the blades of which have perished in rust"; to objects referred to as "breast plates"; to the existence of ruins that suggest thousands of cities with "immense populations"; to "the bones of great numbers, evidently slain in battle"— hold all this in clear vision and then read the following description of a numerous Book of Mormon people who had been destroyed, but whose remains and ruined cities had been found by a detachment of Nephites, about 120 B.C., and reported by those who found them in the following manner:

"And they [the aforesaid detachment of Nephites] were lost for the space of many days . . . having traveled in a land among many waters;

having discovered a land which was covered with bones of men, and of beasts, &c., and was also covered with ruins of buildings of every kind; having discovered a land which had been peopled with a people who were as numerous as the hosts of Israel. And for a testimony that the things that they have said are true, they have brought twenty-four plates which are filled with engravings, and they are of pure gold. And behold, also, they have brought breast-plates, which are large, and they are of brass and of copper, and are perfectly sound. And again, they have brought swords, the hilts thereof were cankered with rust; and there is no one in the land that is able to interpret the language or the engravings that are on the plates" (Mosiah 8:8-11).

This is the description of the finding of the ruins of the Jaredite people by the Nephites. The record on the twenty-four plates was afterwards translated. The question is, could the descriptions in Ethan Smith's book, quoted above, have suggested the Book of Mormon description of the Jaredite ruins. And also, to refer, in conclusion, to the other question that was suggested a few pages back, viz., did the author of the Book of Mormon innocently follow Ethan Smith into the error of supposing that the civilized part of the ancient inhabitants of America had an "iron and steel culture," and boldly ascribe it to his Nephites, and amplify, and emphasize both its existence and its extent? And did the author of the Book of Mormon also innocently follow Ethan Smith in relation to the whole category of civilized traits respecting mechanic arts, the knowledge of letters, and of navigation, as well as in the knowledge and uses of iron and steel, as herein set forth?

IX

THEORY OF TEN LOST TRIBES SUSTAINED BY ARGUMENT: UNITY OF RACE;
EXTENT OF OCCUPANCY OF THE NEW WORLD; SAMENESS OF LANGUAGE;
HEBREW ORIGIN; TRANSLATION; WHENCE URIM AND THUMMIM

Mr. Ethan Smith announces at page eighty-five that "from various authors and travelers among the Indians the fact that the American Indians are 'the Ten Tribes of Israel' will be attempted to be proved by the following arguments:

"1. The American natives have one origin.

"2. Their language appears to have been Hebrew.

"3. They have had their imitation of the Ark of the convenant in ancient Israel.

"4. They have been in the practice of circumcision.

"5. They have acknowledged one and only one God.

"6. The celebrated William Penn gives accounts of the natives of Pennsylvania, which go to corroborate the same point.

"7. The Indians having one tribe, answering in various respects to the tribes of Levi, sheds further light on this subject.

"8. Several prophetic traits of character given to the Hebrews do accurately apply to the aborigines of America.

"9. The Indians being in tribes, affords further light.

"10. Their having something answering to the ancient cities of refuge, seems to evince their Israelitish extraction.

"11. Their variety of traditions historical and religious, do wonderfully accord with the idea, that they descended from the ancient ten tribes."

After setting forth the eleven points of argument that he intends to follow, Mr. Smith proceeds through a number of pages to quote passages from the reports of missionaries, travelers, New England and other histories in support of them. It is not so much for the purpose of following Mr. Smith seriatim in his extended production of evidence and argument on these eleven points that are enumerated here—not so much that, as it is to call attention to the fact that from eight to five years before the Book of Mormon was published, there was in existence a book that contained an enumeration of particulars that enter into the Book of Mormon, and become its peculiar characteristics. This will the more appear as we proceed with our treastise.

Our author informs his readers that his argument upon the last member of his series, viz., that "the variety of traditions historical and religious, do wonderfully accord with the idea that they descended from the ancient ten tribes"—will exceed that upon all the rest put together.

These "evidences" he then proceeds with, and with the arguments, but I shall not follow him, only to note these which do most concern the study here being conducted.

Relative to the first item—"the natives have one origin"—our author depends upon sameness of language among the various tribes—these, however, chiefly of New England, Canada, and the Mississippi valley. The Indian language is conceded to have "a variety of dialects," but "all are believed to be the same radical language."

In proof of this Charlevoix, a French writer of the period, who came from France to Canada, is quoted. So, too, is Dr. Jonathan Edwards, son of President Edwards who lived in his youth among the Indians, as his father was a missionary among them before he became President of Princeton College. Dr. Edwards is said to have been familiar with the Mohegan dialect "as with his mother tongue." Dr. Boudinot is responsible for asserting that Dr. Edwards held that the language of the Delawares in Pennsylvania; of the Penobscots, bordering on Nova Scotia; of the Indians of St. Francis, in Canada; of the Shawnees, on the Ohio; of the Chippewas and other tribes in Michigan and New England—speak a language that is "radically the same," and that "the variations" are to be "accounted for from their want of letters and of communication." Dr. Boudinot is also quoted much to the same effect. He was devoted for forty years to the opinion that the Indians were "the lost tribes." It is said that "he sought and obtained much evidence on the subject." He it was who made so much of the supposed Hebrew words among the Indians—"Yo-be-wah (Jehovah) and Hal-le-lu-jah." These words he holds to be used through the Indian nations for thousands of miles, especially in their religious songs and dances. "With beating and an exact keeping of time, they begin a religious dance thus: 'Hal, hal, hal'; then 'le, le, le,' next 'lu, lu, lu'; and then close 'yah, yah, yah.'" This, it is claimed, is the Indian's traditional song of praise to the great spirit, and "is sung in South, as well as in North America" (*View of the Hebrews*, pp. 85-87).

Sameness of custom among the Indians is also appealed to as evidence of unity of race. Du Pratz, author of a *History of Louisiana*, is quoted to this effect. So, too, is Boudinot. The latter holding that the same color of the Indian generally is evidence of unity of race. So, too, Adair. Dr. Williams in his *History of Vermont* is quoted as saying: "In whatever manner this part of the earth was peopled, the Indians appear to have been the most ancient, or the original men of America. They had spread over the whole continent, from the fiftieth degree of north latitude [a line just south of Hudson's Bay] to the southern extremity of Cape Horn (about 55 degrees south latitude), and these men everywhere appeared to be the same race, or kind of people. In every part of the continent, the Indians are marked with a similarity of color, features, and every circumstance of external appearance" (Id., p. 88).

Pedro de Cicca de Leon, one of the conquerors of Peru and "who had traveled through many provinces of America," is quoted as saying of the Indians: "The people, men and women, although there are such a multitude of tribes or nations, in such diversities of climates, appear, nevertheless, like the children of one father and mother" (Id., p. 88).

The people in the extreme north part of America, the Esquimaus, are held by Mr. Smith to be of a different race than the Indians of North and South America; they may have come, he says, from North Europe *via* Norway, Iceland, Greenland hence to Labrador; but they do not enter into the reckoning of Mr. Smith.

With these ideas of the unity of the American race, and its widespread occupancy of the American continents; with the idea of the race springing from a small group, until they "appear like the children of one father and mother"; with the idea of the same language prevailing throughout, and that colored largely by the Hebrew from which it sprang originally, but now greatly changed by such mutations as a long lapse of time and a new environment would bring—all this is so in consonance with the Book of Mormon structural features that it may be said to be the very fabric of it; and since it is all found in Mr. Smith's book, published before the Book of Mormon was, it may well be thought to have suggested these features of the Book of Mormon. But let us consider these things more nearly, though briefly, and not necessarily in Mr. Smith's order of presentations.

Respecting the extent of the occupancy of the land of America by the Nephites, about B.C. the Book of Mormon says: "And it came to pass that they did multiply and spread, and did go forth from the land southward to the land northward, and did spread insomuch that they began to cover the face of the whole earth, from the sea south to the sea north, from the sea west to the sea east" (Helaman 3:8). Mr. Orson Pratt in his marginal footnotes on this verse[6] interprets "the land southward," to mean "South America"; "the land northward," to mean "North America." "The sea south," he interprets to mean the "Atlantic, south of Cape Horn"; and "the sea north" is the "Arctic, north of North America"; the "sea west" and the "sea east" are the "Pacific" and the "Atlantic," respectively. See edition of 1914. Pratt's interpretations are omitted from the edition of the Book of Mormon of 1921; but the verse in Helaman admits of such interpretation as Orson Pratt gives it, and his interpretation has been, and doubtless is, the general understanding of the Mormon people, respecting the passage; and for Pratt, it may be said, as against those who eliminate all his comments from the marginal notes, that he had the advantage of personal association with Joseph

Smith, translator of the Book of Mormon through many years, and hence would be more likely than they to know his idea of the meaning of the Book of Mormon on any given point such as that here considered.

It may be remarked with reference to what is said of the unity of the American race, that unity of race holds, notwithstanding what may be claimed about the Book of Mormon representing that two races occupied America in ancient times, the Jaredites and the Nephites. The Jaredites do not count in matters of the American race, as Europeans came to know it, for the reason that the Jaredite race passed out of existence, was utterly annihilated about the time the Nephites and the people of Mulek reached the new world in the sixth century B.C. These colonies henceforth came to an empty America, as far as human inhabitants are concerned, and they and their descendants are the only ones that have to be considered in the race question; and as these colonies of Lehi and Mulek were Hebrew people, unity of the American race, so far as it relates to Book of Mormon peoples, as they became known to Europeans at the time of discovery, is obvious.

In relation to the language of the Indians being Hebrew, or at least containing Hebrew elements, Mr. Ethan Smith relies upon and quotes Adair, Dr. Jonathan Edwards, and Boudinot. Edwards he represents as saying that both the Indian and the Hebrew "are found without prepositions; and are formed with prefixes and suffixes, a thing probably known to no other language." And he shows that not only the words, but the construction of phrases, in both have been the same; and that "their pronouns as well as nouns — are manifestly the same" (Id., p. 89). Mr. Adair is quoted to the effect that the Indian's "laconic, bold, and commanding figures of speech" exactly agree with the genius of the Hebrew. From Adair, Boudinot "and others of good authority," a table of words and phrases are given from the Indian language, with their equivalents from the Hebrew, and the interpretations in the English. A vocabulary of twenty-seven words are given, and seven phrases. "Some of these Indian words are taken from one tribe, and some from another. Any language in a savage state, destitute of all aid from *letters, must roll and change.* It is strange that after a lapse of 2,500 years, *a single word should, among such a people, be preserved the same.* But the hand of providence is strikingly seen in this, perhaps to bring that people to light" (Id., p. 90, also p. 93).

Governor Hutchison of Massachusetts is quoted as expressing his doubt upon the subject of the Indian language being Hebrew, "on account of the dissimilarity of the language of the natives of Massachusetts to the Hebrew." Whereupon our author, Mr. Ethan Smith, instantly remarks: *"Any language in a savage state, must in the course of 2,500 years, have rolled and varied exceedingly. This* is shown to be the case in the different dialects, and many new words introduced among those tribes, which are acknowledged to have their language radically the same" (p. 93).

The Italics in the above passages are mine, and are meant to emphasize the fact that the changes here recognized as likely to take place in a language under the circumstances noted above are the very changes, as I shall show noted in the languages of the Book of Mormon peoples, as having taken place. That is to say, a people "in a long savage state, destitute of all aid from letters," that is from written language—under such circumstances—" a language must roll and change." This represents exactly what happened in the case of what is called the people of Mulek in the Book of Mormon. This people is represented as being descendants of a small colony which fled from Jerusalem at the time King Zedekiah was taken captive by Nebuchadnezzar. This colony ultimately reached the New World, where they founded a city, known later as the city of Zarahemla; and there they were found some two and three hundred years later, by a division of the Nephites under a leader named Mosiah. And when so discovered, although they were men of the same race and language as the Nephites, both coming from the same city Jerusalem, from the heart of the same civilization, and leaving that city only about eleven years after the departure of Lehi's colony, yet in the course of some two hundred, or two hundred and fifty years, their lanugage "had become so corrupted," that is changed, that neither Mosiah nor his people, though descendants of the same Hebrew race-stock and language "could understand them." This people of Zarahemla had brought no records with them from Jerusalem, therefore they were "destitute of all aid from letters" to preserve their language forms, and hence the rolling and changes which Ethan Smith held to be inevitable under these given conditions.

Also the Book of Mormon affirms change in language among Book of Mormon peoples even when aided "by letters," that is to say, when written languages conserve the spoken forms of speech. In the closing years of the Nephite period, about 400 A.D., where one Moroni, preparing to give an abridgment of an ancient document had among the Nephites respecting the Jaredites, deplores the "faults" that may be found in his writings and remarks that could the Nephites have written in Hebrew, there would have been no imperfections in their records; but their plates were not sufficiently large to admit of this, and hence they had written their records in "characters which are called among us," says Moroni, "reformed Egyptian, being handed down and altered by us according to our manner of speech." Then follows his remark about their plates being too small to admit of their writing in Hebrew. Then as a further reason for not writing in Hebrew, Moroni adds—"but the Hebrew hath been altered by us, also"; hence the implication that there could have been no advantage in writing the Nephite records in this "altered Hebrew," with a view to having the records understood when found by future generations of men, since they could no more understand this record had it been written in such changed Hebrew, than in the Nephite changed or "reformed Egyptian" characters. "But the Lord knoweth the things which we have written," says Moroni, in connection with mentioning these changes in their written language he is explaining, and also that "none other people knoweth our language; therefore he hath prepared means for the interpretation thereof" (Mormon 9:31-34), meaning, of course, its translation by the miraculous means of "Urim and Thummim." (On the fact of the mutation of languages there is a fine treatise by Prof. Rafinesque in Priest's *American Antiquities* — Edition of 1838 — 5th Edition, pp. 315-22.)

All this leads one to the reflection, that if the purpose of the author of the Book of Mormon — let him be whom he may — was to place beyond the reach of modern knowledge the ancient language in which this book is said to have been written, and thereby place its translation beyond ordinary means of translation known to men; or when translated by the extraordinary means by which it is said to have been translated, beyond the possibility of criticism, or detection of fraud, then no more adroit scheme could have been invented by the wit of man, than the scheme disclosed in the passages considered above. It takes all beyond their depth, and the learned man is as helpless as the ignorant one in trying to solve this very sphinx of language problems.

Dealing here with language, it may be fitting to inquire if Ethan Smith's book affords any material that would suggest the Urim and Thummim to the author of the Book of Mormon, and the strange part it took in the alleged translation.

There certainly is such material in Mr. Smith's book where he discusses the 7th argument of the tabulated list, viz., and quoting Adair:

"In conformity to, or after the manner of the Jews, the Indian Americans have their prophets, high priests, and others of a religious order. . . . The Indian tradition says, that their fathers were possessed of an extraordinary divine spirit, by which they foretold things future; and this they transmitted to their offspring, provided they obeyed the sacred laws annexed to it. *Ishteallo*" (Mr. Adair says of those Indians) "is the name of all their priestly order; and their pontifical office descends by inheritance to the eldest. There are some traces of agreement, though chiefly lost, in their pontifical dress. Before the Indian Archimagus officiates in making the supposed holy fire for the yearly atonement for sins, the *Sagan* (waiter upon the high priest) clothes him with a white Ephod, which is a waistcoat without sleeves. *In resemblance of the Urim and Thummim, the American Archimagus wears a breast plate made of a white conch-shell, with two holes bored in the middle of it through which he puts the end of an otter skin strap, and fastens a buck horn white button to the outside of each, as if in imitation of the precious stones of the Urim"* (*View of the Hebrews,* p. 150).

At page 166, and quoting now Hunter's *Narrative of the Manners and Customs of the Indians* printed at Philadelphia, 1823, he says (speaking of the dress of the Indian high priest): "'His robe was a buffalo skin, singularly decorated with various colored feathers and procupine quills. And he wore on his breast, suspended upon his neck, a dressed beaver skin stretched on sticks, on which were painted various *hieroglyphic figures,* in different colors. The Indians speak of similar characters being among other tribes.' Here, as in Mr. Adair's account," says Mr. Smith, "is their high priest's robe, and breast plate." And also on the "breast plate," one may add, from the above description, "hieroglyphic figures," as if breast plate and the conch-shell and buck horn white button fastened to the outside of each, "in imitation of the precious stones of Urim," as Mr. Smith describes it, had something to do with the translation of these hieroglyphics.

Again, at page 195, Mr. Smith describes a find that was made in a mound on the Scioto river, near Chillicothe, reported by Rev. Dr. Wilson. The mound contained human bones: "Under its base in the center lay *a skeleton* on a platform of twenty feet, formed of bark; and over it a mat formed of some bark. On the breast lay *a piece of copper;* also a *curious stone* five inches in length, two in breadth, with two perforations through it, containing a string of sinews of some animal. On this string were many beads of ivory or bone. *The whole appeared to have been designed to wear upon the neck as a kind of breast plate."*

Take now the prophet Joseph's description of the Urim and Thummim found with the Book of Mormon:

"With the records was found a *curious instrument,* which the ancients called 'Urim and Thummim,' which consisted of two transparent stones set in the rim of a bow fastened to a breast plate. Through the medium of the Urim and Thummim I translated the record by the gift and power of God." Joseph Smith in the letter to Mr. John Wentworth, March 1st, 1842 (*History of the Church,* 5:537).[7]

Can there be any doubt, but what the things said in Ethan Smith's book, on the matter of "Urim and Thummim," "breast plates," and "curious stones" and "attchments to breast plates" — all published from eight to five years before the Book of Mormon was, are sufficient to suggest the Urim and Thummim as described by Joseph Smith?

The above described *"curious stone"* (suggesting perhaps, Joseph Smith's *"curious instrument"*) "five inches in length, two in breadth, with two perforations through it" — two holes — is a perfect description of such a stone once owned by W. W. Phelps, an early Mormon convert, from New York State, and which is traditionally among early Church members known as "Phelps' Urim," or "Peep Stone."[8] There is no knowledge of Church tradition that this man attempted to use this as a "Seer Stone," so far as results are concerned; but seership purposes is what the Phelps' "Curious Stone" was designed for. The *bright stones* of Urim and Thummim were for the purpose, no doubt, of fixing the gaze of the seer for purposes of concentration of mind. Taking this stone in one's hand—I did so with the Phelps' perforated stone—and drawing it toward the eyes until it reaches the right focus, the two holes become, of course, in appearance but one, and this a single bright spot of light, with all else excluded, which becomes the bright field in which the vision of the seer—the modern "Crystal Gazer"—appears. A glass of clear water is said to answer at times the same purpose. In a bit of seership in action described in chapter XIII, Joseph Smith makes use of a glass of water as a Urim, in his vision of, and his description of, the Rocky Mountain valleys—which he had never seen but in vision—as the habitat of the Latter-day Saints.

Phelps's "Seer Stone" was in the Salt Lake Museum at one time. I do not know where it now is but here is a photograph of it which I obtained:[9]

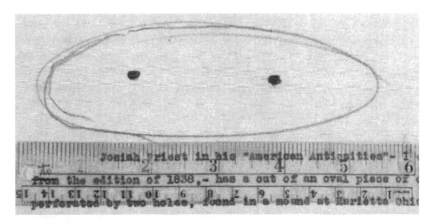

Josiah Priest in his *American Antiquities*—I refer to the edition of 1838—has a cut of an oval piece of copper perforated by two holes, found in a mound at Marietta, Ohio. The cut is included with cuts of numerous other objects, described having "been designed, in part, for ornament, and, in part, for superstitious ceremonies" (*American Antiquities;* see Frontispiece, and pp. 270, 180-82).

X

THE TRAIT OF THE WORSHIP OF ONE GOD—IDOLATRY AND HUMAN
SACRIFICE; REGARD FOR THE POOR; POLYGAMY AND CHASTITY—
PARALLELS

At page 98 of Ethan Smith's book, the statement already quoted in the
summary of things to be proven by argument is repeated: "They have
acknowledged one, and only one God." Then it is expanded by adding—
"And they have general views concerning the one Great Spirit, of which
no account can be given, but that they derived them from ancient revelation in Israel." Then again: "Other nations destitute of revelation have
had their many Gods. . . . But here is a New World of savages chiefly,
if not wholly free from such wild idolatry. Dr. Boudinot (being assured
by many good witnesses) says of the Indians who had been known in
his day: 'They were never known (whatever mercenary Spanish writers
may have written to the contrary) to pay the least adoration to images
or dead persons, to celestial luminaries, to evil spirits, or to any created
beings whatever.'" Mr. Adair is quoted somewhat to the same effect,
saying that "none of the numerous tribes and nations, from Hudson's
Bay to the Mississippi, have ever been known to attempt the formation
of any image of God" (*View of the Hebrews*, p. 98). Quite generally this
idea of the conception of one God under the title of "The Great Spirit"
is insisted upon by Mr. Smith, and beyond all question is over insisted
upon to get as much evidence out of it as possible for Israelitish origin;
yet the fact of idolatry existing among some Indian tribes is reluctantly
conceded, and is spoken of as a "degeneracy" of recent years among
some Indians of the far west reported in the Journals of a Mr. Giddings,
who is represented as saying that these Indians of the far west "differed
greatly in their ideas of the Great Spirit; one supposes that he dwells in
a buffalo, another in a wolf, another in a bear, another in a bird, another
in a rattle snake. On great occasions, such as when they go to war, and
when they return they sacrifice a dog, and have a dance. On these
occasions they formerly sacrificed *a prisoner taken in war;* but through
the benevolent exertions of a trader among them they have abandoned
the practice of human sacrifice" (Id., pp. 102-3). Again and quoting
Giddings Journal: "As you ascend the Missouri and proceed further west,
the nearer to the state of nature the savages approach, the more savage
they appear." "This may account," says our author, "for verging nearer
to idolatry in their views of the Great Spirit, viewing him as embodied
in certain animals" (Id., pp. 103-4). Further on Mr. Smith remarks: "It
is probable that while most of the natives of our land (America) had
their one Great Spirit, some of this wretched people talked of their

different gods. Among the natives on Martha's Vineyard, in the beginning of Mayhew's Mission among them, we find Mioxo in his conversation with the converted native Hiaccomes speaking of *his thirty-seven Gods;* and finally concluding to throw them all away to serve the one true God. We know not what this insulated native could mean by his *'thirty-seven Gods.'* But it seems evident from all questers, that such were not the sentiments of the body of the natives of America" (Id., p. 106).

This may be conceded here without reference to the absolute truth of it, although it is now known that idolatry together with the sacrificing of prisoners taken in war by them existed among many divisions of the American race. Enough, however, is said in this book of Ethan Smith's to suggest to the writer of the Book of Mormon, provided he came in contact with it, the idea of the existence of idolatry and the offering of human sacrifice to their gods. And that is precisely what is found in the Book of Mormon (See Alma 17:15, 31:1; and Mormon 4:15, 21). Alma, speaking of the Lamanites, says of them: "Thus they were a very indolent people, many of whom did worship idols, and the curse of God had fallen upon them because of the traditions of their fathers" (Alma 17:15). And again: One Zoram "was leading the hearts of the people to bow down to dumb idols," etc. (Alma 31:1). Of idolatry, coupled with human sacrifice of those taken in war — the thing we have seen above mentioned by Mr. Smith — it is said in the Book of Mormon — speaking of the Lamanites — "and [they] did take many prisoners, both women and children, and did offer them up as sacrifices unto their idol gods" (Mormon 4:14, 15, 21). The matter is referred to in several other places.

Query: Did the notion of idolatry existing among the natives of America — even though existing to a limited extent — and there found accompanied by sacrificing prisoners of war, as set forth in this book by Ethan Smith, suggest to the author of the Book of Mormon these traits of idolatry and human sacrifice among its peoples? The possibility of it, on the theory of a merely human origin for the Book of Mormon, is quite thinkable.

Again: Ethan Smith recounts the visit to a chief of the Delaware Indians by Messrs. Dodge and Bright, from the Union Mission, January, 1824, from whom they received the two following items:

1. *Regard for and care of the Poor.* "'Long ago' said the Chief, 'before ever a white man stepped his foot in America, the Delawares knew there was one God; and believed there was a hell, where bad folks would go when they die; and a heaven where good folks would go. . . . He believed there was a devil, and he was afraid of him.' These things he said were handed down by his ancestors long before William Penn arrived in Pennsylvania. He said he also knew it to be wrong if a poor man came to his door, *hungry and naked, to turn him away empty.* For

he believed God loved the poorest of men better than he *did proud rich men*" (*Views of the Hebrews*, p. 104).

Query: Did this suggest the mental attitude toward the rich and poor, and human pride among Book of Mormon teachers?

"Wo unto the rich, who are rich as to the things of the world," said Jacob, brother of the first Nephi, when teaching the people. "Because they are rich they despise the poor . . . and their hearts are upon their treasures; wherefore their treasure is their God. And behold their treasures shall perish with them. . . . They that are rich, who are puffed up because of their learning . . . and their riches — yea, they are they whom he [God] despises" (II Nephi 9:30, 42). And so Jacob: "Ye will seek them (i.e., riches) for the intent to do good — to clothe the naked, and to feed the hungry, and to liberate the captive, and administer relief to the sick and the afflicted" (Jacob 2:19). "And ye will not have a mind to injure one another . . . And also ye yourselves will succor those that stand in need of your succor; ye will administer of your substance unto him that standeth in need; and ye will not suffer that the beggar putteth up his petition to you in vain, and turn him out to perish" (Mosiah 4:13, 16).

Of the blessed condition that at one time obtained among Book of Mormon people a teacher said: "They did not send away any who *were naked*, or that *were hungry*, or that were athirst, or that were sick, or that had not been nourished; and they did not set their hearts upon riches; therefore they were liberal to all, . . . whether out of the Church or in the Church, having no respect to persons as to those who stood in need" (Alma 1:30); and so throughout.

Pride is equally condemned, as also contempt for the poor. "Because of pride . . . their churches have become corrupted. . . . Because of pride they are puffed up. . . . They rob the poor because of their fine sanctuaries. . . . They persecute the meek and the poor in heart; because of their pride they are puffed up. . . . O the wise, and the learned, and the rich that are puffed up in the pride of their hearts, . . . wo,wo,wo be unto them saith the Lord God Almighty, for they shall be thrust down to hell" (II Nephi 28:12-15). This in many places.

2. *Sanctity of Marriage and of Chastity: Polygamy Condemned.* This Delaware Indian Chief further reported that a "long time ago, it was a good custom among his people *to take but one wife, and that for life.* But now they had become so foolish, and so wicked, that they would take a number of wives at a time; and turn them away at pleasure!" (*View of the Hebrews*, p. 104).

Query: Did that passage suggest to the author of the Book of Mormon, the following incident? Jacob, the brother of the first Nephi, is instructing his people — reproving them, in fact, for their wickedness. He has reproved them for their pride, then this:

"And now I make an end of speaking unto you concerning this pride. And were it not that I must speak unto you concerning a grosser crime, my heart would rejoice exceedingly, because of you. But the word of God burthens me because of your grosser crimes. For behold, thus saith the Lord, this people begin to wax in iniquity; they understand not the scriptures; for they seek to excuse themselves in committing whoredoms, because of the things which were written concerning David, and Solomon his son. Behold, David and Solomon truly had many wives and concubines, which thing was abominable before me, saith the Lord; wherefore, thus saith the Lord, I have led this people forth out of the land of Jerusalem, by the power of mine arm, that I might raise up unto me a righteous branch from the fruit of the loins of Joseph. Wherefore, I the Lord God, will not suffer that this people shall do like unto them of old. Wherefore, my brethren, hear me, and hearken to the word of the Lord; for there shall not any man among you have save it be one wife; and concubines he shall have none; for I, the Lord God, delight in the chastity of women. And whoredoms are an abomination before me; thus saith the Lord of Hosts" (Jacob 2:22-28).

That the passage in Ethan Smith's book could have suggested such a lesson as this as chastity and marriage is quite within possibility. Strangely enough, also, Jacob places in contrast with this special wickedness of the Nephites the opposite traits of the Lamanites, which leads to the naming of virtues which Ethan Smith accredits to his "lost tribes" in America—the American Indians. Observe: "Behold," said Jacob, continuing to reprove the Nephites for their sin of unchastity—"Behold the Lamanites your brethren, who ye hate, because of their filthiness and the cursings which hath come upon their skins, are more righteous than you; for they have not forgotten the commandment of the Lord, which was given unto our fathers, that they should have, save it were one wife, and concubines they should have none; and there should not be whoredoms committed among them. And now this commandment they observe to keep; wherefore, because of this observance, in keeping this commandment, the Lord God will not destroy them, but will be merciful unto them; and one day they shall become a blessed people. Behold, *their husbands love their wives,* and their wives love their husbands; and their husbands and their wives love their children; and their unbelief and their hatred towards you is because of the iniquity of their fathers; wherefore, how much better are you than they, in the sight of your Creator?" (Jacob 3:5-7).

Mr. Ethan Smith devoted several pages to describing the virtues of the American Indians, as reported from various sources, wherein occurs the following; first as to constancy: "They rarely deviate from certain maxims and usages founded on good sense alone, which holds the place of law. They manifest much stability in the engagements they have entered upon, patience in affliction, as well as submission in what they apprehend to be the appointment of providence. In all this (he adds) they manifest a nobleness of soul, and constancy of mind, at which we rarely arrive with all our philosophy and religion" (*Views of the Hebrews,* pp. 174-75). This is quoted from Charlevoix, a Frenchman, who had made a journey from Quebec to New Orleans, and thus reported on the tribes through whose country he had passed in his more than two thousand miles journey. And one Bartram, who had spent "considerable time" among the Indians, thus reports upon their domestic virtues: "Joy, contentment, love, and friendship without guile or affectation, seem inherent in them, or predominant in their vital principle. . . . They are just, honest, liberal, hospitable to strangers, *considerate, loving, affectionate to their wives and relations, fond of their children,* frugal and perservering; charitable and forbearing" (Id., p. 175); and a Col. Smith is spoken of as referring to the Indians as "living in love and peace, and friendship without disputes, and in this respect being an example to many who profess Christianity" (Id.).

There is more to the same effect, but is not this sufficient? Can it be that it is mere coincidence that these special virtues of Jacob's Lamanites, and Ethan Smith's Indians should run so closely parallel in such a relationship? Might not Ethan Smith's Delaware Chief easily have suggested the Nephite Jacob's reproof of unauthorized polygamy and its attendant whoredoms among his people; and Ethan Smith's recounted Indian virtues be ascribed to the Lamanites by the author of the Book of Mormon in the antithesis drawn?

XI

MISCELLANEOUS TRAITS COMMON TO ETHAN SMITH'S *VIEW OF THE HEBREWS* AND THE BOOK OF MORMON: THE LOST BOOK OF GOD; THE CULTURE OF A WRITTEN LANGUAGE; MIGRATIONS; A TOUCH OF EGYPT

Before coming to the climax of the things to be mentioned in connection with this study of Ethan Smith's book as supplying structural material for the Book of Mormon, there are a number of less important items that should be mentioned at least. For while not equal to some of the things already mentioned, and certainly not equal to a special chapter that will immediately follow this one, they are by far too important to be omitted. And this more especially when their cumulative effect is considered. For while each item by itself might not be of so very much value yet when woven into the fabric of what is here being presented, and considered as part of what has gone before and what is to follow, the several items considered in this chapter will be found to be of importance, though considered hurriedly.

The story of "A Lost Book" — "A Book of God"

Of this character is the tradition among the Indians mentioned by Mr. Ethan Smith of a "Lost Book." He says: "Dr. Boudinot gives it as from good authority that the Indians have a tradition 'that the book which the white people have was once theirs. That while they had this book things went well with them; they prospered exceedingly; but that other people got it from them; that the Indians lost their credit; offended the Great Spirit, and suffered exceedingly, from the neighboring nations; and that the Great Spirit then took pity on them and directed them to this country'" (p. 115). Mr. Smith refers to this tradition again saying: "The Indians have a tradition that as they once, away in another country, had the old divine speech, *the Book of God*; they shall at some time have it again, and shall then be happy" (p. 130).

A variation of what is doubtless the same tradition begins at page 223: "Rev. Dr. West of Stockbridge gave the following information. An old Indian informed him that his fathers in this country had not long since had *a book* which they had *for a long time preserved*. But having lost the art of reading it, they concluded it would be of no further use to them; and they buried it with an Indian Chief."

Mr. Smith connects this "Lost Book" with a certain alleged find of a Hebrew manuscript at Pittsfield, Mass., already considered at length in chapter II of this writing. He thinks this "Lost Book" of the Indians might have reference to some such fragments of the word of God as this Hebrew parchment of the alleged "Indian Hill" Pittsfield find. "This is so far from being improbable," he remarks, "that it is *almost moral certainity*. After their knowledge of reading had long been lost, some chief or *high priest*, or old beloved wise man (*keeper of their traditions*), fearing their precious leaves would get lost, or parted, might naturally sew them in a fold of raw skins with the sinews of an animal (the most noted Indian thread) and keep this roll still in the ark; or carry it upon his belt. All this is what might most naturally be expected in such a case. This thing might have been thus safely brought down to a period near to the time when the native last occupied *Indian Hill*, in Pittsfield; perhaps in the early part of last century. Its owner then might lose it there; or what is more probable, *it was buried with some chief or high priest*; and hence was providentially transmitted to us" (Id., pp. 223-24).

Mr. Smith also alludes to this "Book of God" in the Appendix to his *View of the Hebrews*, where he defends the probable Hebrew origin of said traditional book, against the criticism of a "Reviewer," who insists that the ancestors of the Indians might have had *a book* without its being Hebrew. To which Mr. Smith sarcastically replies—"How strange it must be that none beside the Indians of America, and the 'Reviewer,' have any knowledge of such a book of God" (!) (p. 280). Of course with the merits of this controversy we have no concern beyond what structural material the tradition and the comments upon it might have furnished to the author of the Book of Mormon, if in contact with Mr. Smith's book. These are:

1. The existence of a "Book of God" had among the ancestors of the Indians.

2. The preservation of it for a long time among them.

3. That while they had this book things went well with them— they prospered exceedingly.

4. But the Indians "lost their credit," i.e., offended the Great Spirit.

5. That apparently in consequence of this offense they suffered greatly from neighboring nations.

6. That then the Great Spirit took pity on them and brought them to the New World.

7. This book at some time they will have again, and then shall they be happy.

8. This book they either lost or buried; in the latter case because they could no longer read it.

9. They buried it with some chief, "beloved old man," or "*high priest*"; "*keeper of the tradition*."

10. Mr. Smith, identifying this "Book of God" with certain Hebrew parchments, represents them as buried for their preservation in "*Indian Hill*."

This "Book of God" tradition among the Indians might have suggested the idea of having Lehi's colony bring with them from Jerusalem the collection of the Hebrew scripture, extant at the time of his departure from Jerusalem; also the Book of the Lamb of God, "seen in vision by the first Nephi," or some of the sacred writings among the Nephites known to exist, and some of them seen in vision, as the Book of Mormon was (cf. for this whole subject; I Nephi 13:20-42; also II Nephi 29:1-14; 30). It may have suggested the Book of Mormon custom of keeping and transmitting from hand to hand their sacred records by their "prophets" and "seers"—"the keepers of their tradition" who also were "high priests," and this through a long time—many centuries.

It may have suggested the Book of Mormon idea that departure from the law of God—the teaching of the scriptures—the "Book of God"—occasioned the loss of blessing, their loss of "credit with God"—among the Book of Mormon peoples.

It may have suggested the Book of Mormon idea that the "Lost Book," or the divine scriptures, will again come to the descendants of this ancient people, and then shall they "again be happy," or again "be blessed of the Lord" (see Book of Mormon passages cited above).

Ethan Smith's suggestion that the sacred Hebrew parchments buried by ancestors of the Indians in "Indian Hill" may have suggested the burial of Nephite records in the Hill Cumorah for their preservation until the time came for them to be brought forth. Who shall say it nay since the Indian tradition is so rich in suggestions of Book of Mormon traits.

Smith's "Lost Tribes," like the Book of Mormon Nephites, are accorded the art of writing

Following this matter of the "lost book of God," account of which is preserved in the tradition of the American Indians, is the important fact that Ethan Smith represents his "lost tribes" in America as possessing, in ancient times, the art of writing. They are represented as a people of letters. Quoting Mr. Humboldt, Mr. Smith asks: "How is it possible to doubt that a part of the Mexican nation had arrived at a certain degree of cultivation, when we reflect *on the ease with which their hieroglyphical books were composed and kept*" (*View of the Hebrews*, p. 182)? The Italics are mine in the above, because they emphasize two things in addition to the fact of according to the ancient Mexicans—part of this greater American race of which we have hitherto been speaking—the art of writing, it is suggested that "*a part*" of the nation had this culture of written language; and that their "hieroglyphical books" were kept with great care—two things prominent in Book of Mormon represented facts. Only the Nephites kept records—part of the people—of ancient America; and these records were written in Egyptian hieroglyphics and kept with very great care by them. Moreover, the fact that *hieroglyphical writing originated in Egypt* is stated in Ethan Smith's book, which may have suggested to the author of the Book of Mormon the idea of making Nephite records in his "reformed (or altered) Egyptian characters," i.e., hieroglyphics.

Mr. Smith represents Humboldt as saying that some tribes in New Mexico came from the northwest coast, where they left some of their half civilized brethren. Among these the hieroglyphical painting of *a harp* is found. The harp was an Israelitish musical instrument he notes. "The Jews in Babylon hung their harps upon willows," Mr. Smith urges. "And it is as natural an event that their brethren in the wilds of America, should place them in their silent hieroglyphical painting. *Whence could they have derived the knowledge of the accurate hieroglyphical paintings, which this most learned author exhibits as found among some of the Indians, unless they had learned them from people to whom the knowledge of hieroglyphics had been transmitted from Egypt, its original source"* (*View of the Hebrews,* p. 185)?

Is there not enough suggestion here to have Nephite records made in "reformed Egyptian characters"?

Hieroglyphical writing among the Mexicans is referred to again by Humboldt and quoted by Mr. Smith: "To give an accurate idea of the indigenous (native) inhabitants of New Spain . . . we must go back to a remote period when, governed by its own laws, the nation could display its proper energy. And we must consult the *hieroglyphic paintings,* buildings of hewn stone, and works of sculpture still in preservation, which, though they attest the infancy of the arts, bear however a striking analogy to several monuments of the more civilized people" (p. 182).

"*We know by our books* (said Montezuma in his first interview with that Spanish general [i.e., Cortes]) that myself and those who inhabit this country are not natives, but strangers who came from a great distance" (pp. 205-6). "We know by our Books" contains sufficient suggestion to make the ancient civilized nations of America a people possessed of letters—a culture of written language, as the Book of Mormon makes its Nephites.

Migrations

The remark above quoted from Montezuma's first interview with Cortes—"We know by our books that myself and those who inhabit this country are not natives, but strangers who came from a great distance"—is sufficient to suggest an origin by migrations for the inhabitants of America. But here and there throughout the work of Mr. Smith, the migrations are mentioned. As, for instance: "M'Kenzie gives the following account of the Chepewyan Indians: . . . They have also a tradition among them, that they originally came from another country, inhabited by very wicked people, and had traversed *a great lake*" (*View of the Hebrews*, p. 114). He also quotes Dr. Boudinot as speaking of this same tradition among the Indians—"Some of them call that obstructing water a *river* and some a lake." And he assures us the Indian tradition is "that nine parts of their nation out of ten passed over the river, but the remainder refused and stayed behind" (Id.). On the assumption that *View of the Hebrews* formed the ground plan of the Book of Mormon, we see in the above material for the migration of the Nephites, the departure of Lehi from Jerusalem, on account of the wickedness of the Jews, and the impending destruction of their chief city, Jerusalem, because of that wickedness; and the obstruction of waters variously referred to as a "*great lake*" or "river." In the Book of Mormon with the Nephites it is the "Red Sea." Then they "beheld the sea," doubtless, judging from the description of their travels, the Arabian Gulf opening to the Indian Ocean. This Lehi's colony called "Irreantum," which being interpreted is, "many waters." The Jaredite colony also had their "obstructing waters." To cross these "many waters" they built barges. In their journey in the wilderness they encountered a "sea"; this, too, was passed. At last they were brought "to the *great sea*, which divideth the lands." Maybe "the great lake" of the Indian tradition.

Quoting Adair Mr. Smith represents him as saying: "The Indian tradition says that their forefathers in very remote times came from a far distance country, *where all the people were of one color;* and removed *eastward* to their present settlements" (Id., p. 152, also p. 88). The *Italics* in the above are mine. In addition to the suggested migrations, did this passage suggest also *more than one color* among the ancestors of the Indians—the curse of a dark skin for the Lamanite; the preservation of a white skin for the Nephite who finally became extinct, and left us in America only the "Red Man"?

Did the passage also determine the course of Lehi's colony eastward?

Mr. Smith supposes in his book that the migrations of his "lost tribes" was northeastwardly from the land where they were held in captivity, northern Syria, from which they escaped, thence went over the immense land stretches a year and a half's journey to northwest America, via Bering Strait, thence southward in quest of suitable climates. "Those who dissent from my opinion of the Indian American origin," says Ethan Smith, "ought to inform us how the natives came here," says Mr. Smith. This suggests an alternative, and the author of the Book of Mormon evidently accepts it and sends both his Jaredites and Nephites—as also the colony of Mulek—by immense ocean voyages. And if one was free from the notion that the Book of Mormon was of divine origin, and could accord it a mere human origin, he would say that these ocean migrations were conceived and worked out by one deeply ignorant of the problems involved in such a passage from the Old World to the New—as would be the case of a man living throughout his boyhood and young manhood in the entirely inland state of Vermont, and the inland portions of the State of New York, and Pennsylvania, never coming in contact with the sea until after the Book of Mormon was published.

This, however, will be considered in another division of this study.

A Touch of Egypt

There is a touch of Egypt in Mr. Smith's book, though that comes through the mention of the pyramids of the New World, that are thought to resemble those of Egypt, with which the ancient Israelites were familiar, and which perhaps they helped to build, and hence their descendants in America, influenced by that traditional race remembrance, reproduced something like them in the New World (see pp. 180, 202, 204, 207). It must be conceded, however, that the only Egyptian cultural trait referred to in the Book of Mormon is that of the Egyptian hieroglyphics, in which the record of the Jews—the writings of the Old Testament up to about six hundred years B.C.—was engraven, and which Lehi's colony brought from Jerusalem to the New World, and in which characters they continued to record their own books (see I Nephi 1:2; Mosiah 1:4; and Mormon 9:32-34).

XII

MISCELLANEOUS TRAITS COMMON TO ETHAN SMITH'S *VIEW OF THE HEBREWS* AND THE BOOK OF MORMON: MILITARY AND SACRED TOWERS; FROM MONARCHIES TO REPUBLICS; OPPOSITION IN ALL THINGS;* THE HUNTERS FEAST AND LAYING THE FOUNDATION OF ZION

Military Watch Towers

At various places in the Book of Mormon watch towers are spoken of as having been erected, chiefly as connected with military uses. One such tower was built by a certain King Noah about 160 or 150 B.C. One near a temple, another on a hill north of a land called Shilom (Mosiah 11:12, 13). An account is given of an army of Lamanites being seen approaching the land of Shimlom from this tower, which discloses the uses of it (Mosiah 19:5, 6). A like use of it is again described in the chapter next following (Mosiah 20:7, 8). Again at the commencement of a protracted war which began between the Nephites and Lamanites, about 72 B.C. The Nephite leader directed his people in "digging up heaps of earth round about all their cities throughout all the land which was possessed by the Nephites. And upon the top of these ridges of earth he caused that there should be timbers; yea, works of timbers built up to the height of a man, round about the cities. And he caused that upon those works of timbers, there should be a frame of pickets built upon the timbers round about; and they were strong and high; and he caused *towers* to be erected that overlooked those works of pickets, and he caused places of security to be built upon those towers, that the stones and the arrows of the Lamanites could not hurt them. And they were prepared, that they could cast stones from the top thereof, according to their pleasure and their strength, and slay him who should attempt to approach near the walls of the city. Thus Moroni did prepare strongholds against the coming of their enemies, round about every city in all the land" (Alma 50:1-6).

Did Ethan Smith's book supply material that would suggest fortifications such as these throughout the Nephite lands and cities? Let us see: Mr. Smith describes certain notable remains of ancient earthworks as existing near Newark, in Licking County, Ohio. These he represents as being described "with their drawing or plates in the publication of the American Antiquarian Society, at Worcester, Mass., 1820." They have been many times reproduced in works on American antiquities—these drawings of the fortifications, but I limit my quotations to Ethan Smith's

---

*The subsection "Opposition in All Things" did not appear in the original typed copy, despite this heading.—Ed.

book because that is known to have been published from eight to five years before the publication of the Book of Mormon, and in the vicinity where Joseph Smith lived, previous to the publication of the Book of Mormon:

"Between two branches of the Licking river, at their junction, is one of the most notable remains of the ancient works. There is a fort including forty acres, whose walls are ten feet high. It has eight gateways, each of the width of about fifteen feet. Each gateway is guarded by a fragment of a wall, placed *before,* and about nine feet *within* the gate, of the bigness of the walls of the fort, and about four feet longer than the width of the gateway. The walls are as nearly perpendicular as they could be made with earth. Near this fort is another round fort containing twenty-two acres, and connected with the first fort by two parallel walls of earth about the size of the other walls. At the remotest part of this circular fort, and just without a gateway, is *an observatory so high as to command a view of the region to some distance.* A secret passage was made under this *observatory* to an ancient water course." Near this fort is another similar in character but enclosing about twenty-six acres. "All these works," referring to the whole group of "forts" he has described, continues Mr. Smith, "stand on a large plain, the top of which is almost level, but is highland by a regular ancient form near the two branches of the river, to a height of forty or fifty feet above the branches of the river. At four different places at the ends of the internal communications between the forts and down to the river, *are watch towers, on elevated ground,* and surrounded by circular walls. And the points selected for *these watch towers* were evidently chosen with great skill, to answer their design. These forts and chains of communications between them were so situated as nearly to enclose a number of large fields, which it is presumed were cultivated, and which were thus far secured from hostile invaders."

He describes two parallel walls leading off from these forts to others at a distance. "They have been traveled a mile or two," he observes, "and are yet clearly visible. . . . I should not be surprised if these parallel walls are found to extend from one work of defense to another for the space of thirty miles — such walls have been discovered at different places, probably belonging to these works, for ten or twelve miles at least." "He" — the writer to the Archaelogy — "apprehends this was a road between this settlement and one on the Hocking river. And he says: the planning of these works of defense 'speaks volumes in favor of the sagacity of these nations'" (*View of the Hebrews,* pp. 190-92).

And so he continues through a number of other pages with these descriptions of ancient works of fortifications, extending both up and down the Ohio and in the Mississippi valleys. But we need not follow him further. We can now as well as at the conclusion of his more elaborate descriptions ask — is it not quite possible that such a description of a succession of forts, linked together in the manner described, might well have suggested the fortifications described as the work of Moroni "who did prepare strongholds against the coming of their enemies, *round about every* city in all the land," and also built military *watch towers* overlooking these his fortifications such as are described also in this work of Ethan Smith?

Sacred Towers

Nor is this all on the subject of "Towers." Mr. Smith discusses at some length in the same connection certain sacred towers. The author he quotes from, of two tumuli, in a stone fort which he describes, as "a sacred enclosure," or "high place." This leads Mr. Smith a few pages further on to discuss "the high places" mentioned in the Old Testament scripture, as places built sometimes for the purpose of true worship, at other times for the practice of idolatry. "These ancient works of native Americans," he goes on to say, "may well remind us of what is said in the Old Testament writings of the ancient 'high places' of Israel. 'For they provoked him to anger with their high places' (Ps. 78:58). How abundantly are these noted through their sacred writings. In scores of text we read them. Such a king built their high places. Such a reformer destroyed them. Such a *vile king* rebuilt them. Such a good king again destroyed them, and so on. Here was a train of most common events. The hearts of Israel were long and most perfectly inured to the religious use of their high places, though it was forbidden. Scott (Bible commentator) remarks that then '*high places* were both for idolatry; and for the regular worship of Jehovah.' Solomon had used these high places (I Kings 3:3, 4). 'And Solomon loved the Lord, walking in the statutes of David his father; only he sacrificed and burned incense in *high places*.' And the King went to Gideon to sacrifice there; for that was the *great high place*." And so the discussion goes on at great length.

In the Book of Mormon we have this same trait of sacred tower building, and for the purpose of both true worship and idolatry. The wicked and Idolatrous King Noah built a high tower near the temple overlooking the land of Shilom. Also he caused a "*great tower* to be built on the hill north of the land Shilom, which had been a resort for the children of Nephi at the time they had fled out of the land" (Mosiah 11:12, 13; also Omni 1:12, 13). These were doubtless for observation and idolatrous purposes. In Helaman we have an account of a sacred tower in a garden of one of the Nephite prophets, by the highway which led to the chief marketplace in the city of Zarahemla. And here Nephi—

the prophet referred to—"had bowed himself upon the tower which was in his garden, which tower also was near the garden gate by which led the highway." And here he had prayed and attracted the attention of the people. "I have got upon my tower that I might pour out my soul unto my God," he said to the inquiring multitude, "because of the exceeding sorrow of my heart, which is because of your iniquities," he explained to the people (Helaman 7:10-14).

Is it not significant of one suggesting the other when we find both these kinds of towers—military and sacred—mentioned in Ethan Smith's book, and then find them also produced in the Book of Mormon published some years later?

Think what this would mean to proponents of the Book of Mormon if the terms of this evidence and argument were reversed. That is, suppose that if Ethan Smith's book had been published eight or five years after the publication of the Book of Mormon instead of that long a time before its publication—then what an importance would be accredited to his confirmation of "*towers*," military and sacred, mentioned in the Book of Mormon! Should not the evidence be as strong standing as it does now for the likelihood of the material in Ethan Smith's book suggesting what we now find in the Book of Mormon?

From Monarchy to Republic

Mr. Ethan Smith represents Humboldt as saying: "We have examples of *theocratic forms of government* in South America. For such were those of Zac, of Bogota and the Incas of Peru—two extensive empires in which despotism was concealed under the appearance of a gentle and patriarchal government." Then after discussing the mysterious founder of this form of government, and concluding that their traditions go back to Moses as the giver of such government system, he writes: "Our author," meaning Humboldt, "proceeds: 'But the Mexican small colonies, wearied of tyranny, gave themselves republican constitutions.' Now it is only after long popular struggles that these constitutions can be formed. The existence of republics does not indicate a very recent civilization. Here like a wise politician, he was showing that the Mexicans from ancient date were a civilized people, at least, in good degree" (*View of the Hebrews,* pp. 181-82). Again: "The form of their government indicated that they were the descendants of a people who had experienced great vicissitudes in their social state" (p. 183). Later, Humboldt quoting one Mozino is represented as saying that there was a "*Union of the civil and ecclesiastical power in the same persons of the princes*" (p. 186).

This is very remarkable, and may have really been, supposing that Ethan Smith's book was in the hands of Joseph Smith before the publication of the Book of Mormon, the source of some very important suggestions—structural material for the Book of Mormon. Book of Mormon peoples—both Jaredites and Nephites, and also the Lamanites—are given kingly forms of government. Then, in the case of the Nephites, with whom the Book of Mormon has most to do, after the lapse of about five hundred years from the time Lehi left Jerusalem, change from the monarchial form of government to a republican form— to a reign of judges, where the rulers are chosen by the voice of the people. In effecting this change the tyranny and evils of kingly rule and authority are pointed out in great detail, and the advantages of free government—government "by the voice of the people"—are extolled, and that form is finally adopted.

But kingly authority and ecclesiastical power had frequently been united in one person under the monarchy, and now, under the "reign of the judges," this union of civil and ecclesiastical authority was not forbidden. On the contrary the first chief judge of the land, elected under the new order of things, *was also* the *presiding high priest of the Church,* one Alma—one of the greatest prophets and religious teachers of the Book of Mormon characters; and also, as I have said, the first chief judge of the land under the constitution of the Nephite republic.

The evils of monarchy are discussed at length, and the advantages of free government expounded in Mosiah the 29th chapter. The Book of Alma, immediately following, is introduced to us by the Nephite compiler, in part as follows:

"The account of Alma, who was the son of Alma the first, and Chief Judge over the people of Nephi, and also the High Priest over the Church. An account of the reign of the Judges, and the wars and contentions among the people."

Two later Chief Judges appear also to have united the ecclesiastical and civil functions in their administration, viz., Nephi, son of Helam (see Helaman 3:37; 4:14) the seventh in the line of Judges, and Lachoneus, the eleventh in the line of Judges (III Nephi 3). But better yet this peculiar trait is expressly avowed as an established policy of the Nephites, and not only in respect of their civil magistrates but as to their military leaders as well:

"Now the chiefest among all the captains, and the great commander of all the armies of the Nephites, was appointed, and his name was Gidgiddoni. Now it was the custom among all the Nephites, to appoint for their chief captain save it were in their times of wickedness, some one that had the Spirit of revelation, and also prophecy; therefore this Gidgiddoni was a great prophet among them, and also was the Chief Judge."

And so in the Book of Mormon we have men warned against the

tyranny of monarchy—they grew weary of it—and changed from the kingly government to a republican form; and conspicuously unite civil and ecclesiastical powers, at times, in the same person, was the idea suggested by Ethan Smith's passage—"The Mexican small colonies wearied of tyranny gave themselves republican constitutions" and in their government there was "the union of the civil and ecclesiastical power in the same persons of the princes" (pp. 181, 185)? But Ethan Smith also says in this connection: "Now it is only after long popular struggles that free constitutions can be formed" (pp. 181-82); and again, speaking of the "Tanltees" (Tallees): *The form of their government indicated that they were descendants of a people who had experienced great vicissitudes in their social state.*" Was this the reason the Nephite republic—assuming for the sake of the inquiry that the author of the Book of Mormon was Joseph Smith—was given so stormy a career? Founded about 90 B.C. the republic continued down to about thirty A.D., when all government was overthrown and anarchy prevailed until the reconstruction occurred following the glorious appearing of the Christ in the New World after his resurrection.

In that period, from 90 B.C. to 30 A.D., the republic had a stormy career. Out of the Twelve Chief Judges or executives, of the republic in that period of one hundred and twenty years, three were murdered, and an attempt was made upon the life of another. There were three civil wars prompted by desires to re-establish kingly government, one of them a tremendous war, extending through thirteen years, and also combined with a war with the Lamanites, who fought on the side of the Nephite "King men" in this war. There were besides four Nephite-Lamanite wars, and two great uprisings of robber organizations, the last of which destroyed the government. Also there was one interregnum between the election of Chief Executives, besides a number of lapses or apostasies within the Church. So great was the tendency of the people to wickedness that two of the Chief Executives left the civil office to function as priests, to cry repentance to the people. Truly this record represents a stormy career for the Nephite republic and if this career was created to fit the suggestion of Ethan Smith's book, viz.— "It is only after long and popular struggles that these free constitutions can be formed," then the experience given the Nephite republic demonstrates the truth of his statement. And if the Nephites survived in descendants they would undoubtedly bear the marks "of a people who had experienced great vicissitudes in their social state."

The Indian Hunter's Feast and Laying the Foundation of Zion

An incident outside the Book of Mormon it is true but significant withal may as well be mentioned here. Speaking of preparations for the Indian "Hunter's feast," he briefly describes it as follows: "They choose twelve men who provide twelve deer. Each of the twelve men cuts a sapling; with these they form a tent, covered with blankets. They then choose twelve stones for an altar of sacrifice. Some tribes . . . choose but ten men, ten poles, and ten stones. Here seems an evident allusion to the twelve tribes; and also some idea of the ten separate tribes of Israel" (pp. 116, 117).

When Joseph Smith and the Colesville branch of the Church arrived at Independence in 1831, for the purpose of beginning the foundation of Zion—the city which the Book of Mormon declares shall be built upon this western land—and be in very deed a "New Jerusalem"—into which shall be gathered the remnants of Israel—he thus in his journal history records what happened:

"On the second day of August (1831), I assisted the Colesville branch of the Church to lay the first log for a house, as a foundation of Zion, in Kane Township, twelve miles west of Independence. The log was carried and placed by twelve men, in honor of the twelve tribes of Israel. At the same time, through prayer the land of Zion was consecrated" (*Hist. of the Church*, 1:196).

It is conceded that there are differences in the two incidents, but is there not also enough resemblance in the one to suggest the other?

XIII

THE MESSIAH IN THE NEW WORLD—QUETZALCOATL

Did the ancient American Indians know of the Christ?

Reference has already been made to a conversation had, according to Ethan Smith's book, by Messrs. Dodge and Blight—Indian Missionaries—in January, 1824, with a Delaware Indian Chief, respecting the treatment of the poor, and the idealized notions of chastity among his people anciently. Here we take up the remaining and most important part of that conversation, which relates to the question at the opening of this chapter. This Delaware Chief "was asked to state what he knew of Jesus Christ, the Son of God. He replied that 'he knew but little about him. For his part, he knew there was one God. He did not know about two Gods'" (*View of the Hebrews,* p. 104).

It is, as is well known, *the* great feature of the Book of Mormon, that Jesus Christ visited the land of America after his resurrection, and ministered unto the people here. Did this incident connected with the Delaware Chief suggest to the author of the Book of Mormon the bringing of the Christ to America and giving him a ministry among the ancient American Indians? Remember that the account of this conversation is given in a book published from eight to five years before the Book of Mormon was published; and it was published in a county adjoining the one in which the Smith family lived so long, and was easily within their reach and knowledge.

The idea of possible suggestion from Smith's book becomes more emphatically probable when in a later passage is found quoted from the *Political Essays of New Spain,* by Baron Humboldt, the following passage about "the Gospel" among the ancient peoples of Mexico: "It seems the Spanish missionaries found such traces of resemblance between some of the rites of the religion of the natives of Mexico, and the religion they wished to introduce (Catholicism) that our author (Humboldt quoted by Smith) says that they persuaded them *that the Gospel had, in very remote times, been already preached in America.* And they investigated its traces in the Aztec ritual with the same ardour which the learned who in our day engage in the study of Sanscrit." Then Ethan Smith's comment: "It is a noted fact that there is a far greater analogy between much of the religion of the Indians, and Christianity, than between that of any other heathen nation on earth and Christianity. The aged Indian, noted in the preceding pages, testified to this, when the children from the missionary school came home and informed what instruction they had received. The old Indian said: 'Now this is good talk. This is such as we used to hear when we were children from the old people, till some of the white people came among us, and destroyed it. We thank the Great Spirit that he has brought it back again'" (*View of the Hebrews*, p. 187).

These two passages of Ethan Smith's book, taken together, and with the question submitted to the Delaware Chief might well have suggested to the author of the Book of Mormon the introduction of the Christ and of the Gospel among the ancient Americans, a possibility that will be emphasized when we consider later in this study, as we shall, what the profane would consider an awkward attempt to expound the idea of two Gods—God the Father, and God the Son—and yet in such a manner as to have but one God—a problem raised by the remarks of our Delaware Chief on that very subject.

This idea of a ministry of the Christ among the ancient American Indians being possibly suggested by Ethan Smith's book is further emphasized when it is learned that the tradition of the culture hero Quetzalcoatl, sometimes referred to as the "Mexican Messiah," is also given in Ethan Smith's book from a writer who gives it from the *Transactions and Collections of the American Antiquarian Society,* published at Worcester, Mass., 1820. This contributor to the *Collections and Transactions* speaks of Quetzalcoatl as "the most mysterious being of the whole Mexican mythology." "An account is given of this person," says Mr. Smith, "sufficiently indeed intermixed with fables. . . . I will sketch the leading points of the picture."

Of these, however, I shall only present those which may have acted in connection with incidents from the New Testament—as suggestions to the creation of the Book of Mormon Messiah. "The name Quetzalcoatl," explains Mr. Smith, "signifies 'the serpent of green feathers.'"

The Book of Mormon Messiah, as also the New Testament Messiah, connects the Christ with the "serpent." "As Moses lifted up the serpent in the Wilderness, even so must the Son of Man be lifted up" (St. John 3:14). In the Book of Mormon the connection of the Christ with this incident of the serpent is given by the first Nephi, prophetically as follows:

"According to the words of the prophets, the Messiah cometh in six hundred years from the time that my father left Jerusalem. . . . and as the Lord God liveth that brought Israel up out of the land of Egypt, and gave unto Moses power that he should heal the nations, after they had been bitten by the poisonous serpents if they would cast their eyes unto the serpent which he did raise up before them. . . . behold I say unto you, that as these things are true . . . there is none other name given under heaven, save it be this Jesus Christ . . . whereby man can be saved" (II Nephi 25:20).

The same thing is referred to by a later Book of Mormon writer (Helaman 8:14, 15), and elsewhere.

Quetzalcoatl "was a bearded *White man*," according to Ethan Smith's account. In vision to the first Nephi (600 B.C.) was shown prophetically incidents connected with the birth and life of the Messiah. Among others the following: "And I beheld the city of Nazareth; and in the city of Nazareth I beheld a Virgin, and she was *exceeding fair and white*." His angel interpreter of the vision said to Nephi, "Behold the virgin whom thou seest is the mother of God" (*sic,* in the first edition, p. 25). It has been changed in later editions — but without improvement — to "Mother of the Son of God." If Quetzalcoatl suggested a "white" Messiah, it was of course fitting that his mother should be a virgin, "*exceedingly fair and white*," beautiful *and fair* above all other virgins," though scarcely of the racial type of the daughters of Judah. The traditional pictures of the Christ as a full "bearded man" would but accord with Quetzalcoatl as mentioned by Mr. Smith, and hence would not be specially noted in the Book of Mormon.

Quetzalcoatl "was high priest, of Tula, legislator, chief of a religious sect"; who, it is said, "inflicted upon themselves the most cruel penance." The Messiah of the Book of Mormon may be said to be "featured" strangely as first of all an "high priest" with all others deriving the high priesthood from him. "The Lord God ordained priests, after his holy order, *which was after the order of his son*," i.e., the Christ. "This high priesthood (conferred upon certain men) being after the order of his Son (the Messiah) which order was from the foundation of the world" (Alma 13).

"As legislator" the Book of Mormon Messiah repeats, and practically in the identical language of the New Testament, all that body of Christian legislation found in Matthew 5th, 6th and 7th chapters (c.f. III Nephi, 12th, 13th, and 14th chapters). As "Chief of a religious sect," or religious leader, the Messiah of the Book of Mormon is proclaimed the head of the Church of the New World and that Church was commanded to take upon it the name of Christ, and its members became known as "Christians." This even before the coming of Christ in the Flesh (see Alma 46:15) and also after his appearing in the flesh. To his disciples the Book of Mormon Messiah said: "Ye must take upon you the name of Christ, which is my name, for by this name shall ye be called in the last day. Therefore whatsoever ye shall do, ye shall do it in my name; therefore ye shall call the church in my name; and ye shall call upon the Father in my name, that he will bless the church for my sake; and how be it my church, save it be called in my name? for if a church be called in Moses' name, then it be Moses' church; or if it be called in the name of a man, then it be the church of a man; but if it be called in my name, then it is my church, if it so be that they are built upon my gospel" (III Nephi 27:5, 7, 8).

This very emphatically places that Book of Mormon Messiah at the head of the Church — corresponding to the tradition respecting Quetzalcoatl as "being the Chief of a religious sect."

The closing part of the passage respecting, viz., that his following "inflicted upon themselves the most cruel penance," is somewhat out of character with the Book of Mormon Messiah, unless the strictness of the life of self-denial enjoined upon his following by the repetition of the Christian legislation of III Nephi 12th, 13th and 14th chapters be regarded as fulfilling the characterization.

Quetzalcoatl "appeased by his penance divine wrath." Prophetically speaking of the Book of Mormon Christ, and of his suffering "to appease divine wrath," Mosiah writes: "God himself shall come down among the children of men, and shall redeem his people." He, God, "suffered temptation and yieldeth not to the temptation, but suffereth himself to be mocked, and scourged, and cast out, and disowned by his people. And after all this, after working many mighty miracles among the children of men, he shall be led, yea, even as Isaiah said, As a sheep before the shearer is dumb, so he opened not his mouth; Yea, even so he shall be led, crucified, and slain, the flesh becoming subject, even unto death, the will of the Son being swallowed up in the will of the Father and thus God breaketh the bands of death, having gained the victory over death; giving the Son power to make intercession for the children of men; having ascended into heaven; having the bowels of mercy; being filled with compassion towards the children of men; standing betwixt them and justice; having broken the bands of death, taken upon himself their iniquity and their transgressions; having redeemed them, and satisfied the demands of justice" (Mosiah 15:1-9). Also, as announced by the Book of Mormon Messiah himself, when he appeared to the Nephites:

"Behold I have given unto you my gospel, and this is the gospel which I have given unto you, that I came into the world to do the will of my father, because my Father sent me. And my Father sent me that I might be lifted up upon the cross; and after that I had been lifted up upon the cross, that I might draw all men unto me; that as I have been lifted up by men, even so should men be lifted up by the Father, to stand before me, to be judged of their works, whether they be good or whether they be evil; and for this cause have I been lifted up; therefore, according to the power of the Father, I will draw all men unto me."

"The Great Spirit offered Quetzalcoatl beverage" which, while it rendered him immortal, inspired him with a taste for traveling, and with an irresistible desire of visiting a distant country called Tlapallan." On the appearing of the Christ to the Nephites in the New World after his resurrection and departure from Jerusalem the first words he addressed to them were:

"Behold, I am Jesus Christ, whom the prophets testified shall come into the world; and behold, I am the light and the life of the world. *And I have drunk out of that bitter cup which the Father hath given me, and have* glorified the Father in taking upon me the sins of the world, in the which I have suffered the will of the Father in all things from the beginning" (III Nephi 11:10, 11).

Relative to "his taste for traveling," and "an irresistible desire of visiting a distant country," did it inspire the following incident in the life of the Book of Mormon Messiah:

He represents to his disciples in the New World that when he stated to his followers in Judea that "other sheep" he had which were not of the fold at Jerusalem—them also he must bring, and they should hear his voice, and "there should be one fold and one shepherd" (St. John 10:16)—he had in mind the people he would visit in the New World, the Nephites. Then to the Nephite disciples, after the above explanation, he said:

"And verily, verily, I say unto you, that I have other sheep, which are not of this land; neither of the land of Jerusalem; neither in any parts of that land round about, whither I have been to minister. For they of whom I speak, are they who have not as yet heard my voice; neither have I at any time manifested myself unto them. But I have received a commandment of the Father, that I shall go unto them, and that they shall hear my voice, and shall be numbered among my sheep, that there may be one fold, and one shepherd; therefore I go to show myself unto them" (III Nephi 16:1-3). All this indicated intention of movement on the part of the Book of Mormon Messiah might well arise from Quetzalcoatl's "taste for traveling," and his "irresistible desire of visiting a distant country."

"Quetzalcoatl *preached peace to men*, and would permit no other offering to the Divinity than the first fruits of the harvest."

The golden words of one of the beatitudes, "Blessed are all the peace makers, for they shall be called the children of God," the Book of Mormon Christ repeated to the Nephites in his ministry in the New World (III Nephi 12:9). Also there is the often iterated and re-iterated declaration of the Book of Mormon, that its Messiah came to fulfill the law of Moses, to put an end to its ever-recurring bloody sacrifices, and to substitute once for all Messiah's own sacrifice, in their stead. The voice of Jesus in a revelation to the people of the New World is represented as saying: "I am the light and the life of the world, I am Alpha and Omega, the beginning and the end. And ye shall offer up unto me no more the shedding of blood; yea, your sacrifices and your burnt offerings shall be done away, for I will accept none of your sacrifices and your burnt offerings; and ye shall offer for a sacrifice unto me a broken heart and a contrite spirit. . . . Behold, I have come unto the world to bring redemption unto the world, to save the world from sin; therefore whoso repenteth and cometh unto me as a little child, him will I receive; for of such is the kingdom of God. Behold, for such I have laid down my life, and have taken it up again; therefore repent, and come unto me ye ends of the earth, and be saved" (III Nephi 9:18-22).

Later, in person, the resurrected Messiah said to the Nephites: "Behold I say unto you that the law is fulfilled that was given unto Moses. Behold, I am he that gave the law, and I am he who covenanted with my people Israel; therefore, the law in me is fulfilled for I have come to fulfill the law; therefore it hath an end" (III Nephi 15:4, 5). And again the Book of Mormon, speaking of the disciples of the Messiah in the New World, after his departure from among them: "And they did not walk any more after the performances and ordinances of the law of Moses, but they did walk after the commandments which they had received from their Lord and their God, continuing in fasting and prayer, and in meeting together oft, both to pray and to hear the word of the Lord" (IV Nephi 1:12).

"The reign of Quetzalcoatl was a golden age of the people of Anahuac (Mexico). The earth brought forth without culture the most fruitful harvests. But the reign was not of long duration" (*View of the Hebrews*, p. 205).

Following the appearances of the Book of Mormon Messiah to the people of the New World there was a veritable "golden age." It is thus described: "And they had all things common among them, therefore they were not rich and poor, bond and free, but they were all made free, and partakers of the heavenly gift. . . . And there were great and marvelous works wrought by the disciples of Jesus, insomuch that they did heal the sick, and raise the dead, and cause the lame to walk, and the blind to receive sight, and the deaf to hear; and all manner of miracles did they work among the children of men; and in nothing did they work miracles save it were in the name of Jesus. . . . And the Lord did prosper them exceedingly in the land; yea, insomuch that they did fill cities again where there had been cities burned. . . . And now behold it came to pass that the people of Nephi did wax strong, and did multiply exceeding fast, and became an exceeding fair and delightsome people. And they were married, and given in marriage, and were blessed according to the multitude of the promises which the Lord had made unto them. . . . And it came to pass that there was no contention in the land, because of the love of God which did dwell in the hearts of the people. And there were no envyings, nor strifes, nor tumults, nor whoredomes, nor lyings, nor murders, nor any manner of lasciviousness; and surely there could not be a happier people among all the people who had been created by the hand of God; there were no robbers, nor murders, neither were there Lamanites, nor any manner of ites; but they were in one, the children of Christ, and heirs to the kingdom of God" (IV Nephi 1:3-17). This blessed state continued without interruption for about two hundred years, then pride, which so generally follows continued prosperity, asserted itself; class distinction arose, the people no longer had "their goods and their substance in common"; schisms arose in their Church, and the "golden age" began to decline, and within three hundred years had wholly passed away (IV Nephi 1:24-49). The reign of Quetz-alcoatl — doubtless having reference to his personal residence with the people as distinct from the "golden age" following his advent and de-parture — quite agrees with the briefness of Messiah's stay with the Ne-phites.

Quetzalcoatl dissappeared, "rather mysteriously after he promised the Cholulans (with whom he had lived for a time) that he would return and govern them again, and renew their happiness." So the Messiah of the Book of Mormon disappeared and in effect so promised to return and establish the people of this land in a veritable kingdom of peace and of righteousness. Ethan Smith points out the fact that it was this tradition held by the people of Mexico, and by Montezuma the reigning Emperor at the time of the Spanish invasion that made possible so easy a conquest of the country; for the Mexicans mistook the white bearded invaders from the east for the descendants of their long cherished culture-hero, Quetzalcoatl. The Book of Mormon Messiah foretells his disciples of the coming of Gentile races to this land of promise, to America (III Nephi 16:6-8); and if the Gentiles brought to the New World should turn to the Lord, then are they to be greatly blessed and numbered with the house of Israel who shall be on the land (Id., ver. 13); and shall assist these native Americans with others of the house of Israel to be gathered in upon the land to build "a city which shall be called the New Jerusalem." "And then shall they (the Gentiles) assist my people," the Book of Mormon Messiah is represented as saying, "the remnant of Jacob, and also as many as shall come, that they may build a city, which shall be called the New Jerusalem. And then shall they assist my people that they may be gathered in, who are scattered upon all the face of the land — in unto the New Jerusalem — and then shall the power of heaven come down among them; *and I also will be in the midst*" (III Nephi 21:22-25). All of chapters from 16 to 21 inclusive — and with many repetitions — deal at length with this subject. See also Ether 13:1-12. The establishment of this "New Jerusalem" in America is the beginning of that reign of peace in the land promised throughout the Book of Mormon. If the Gentiles on the land of America become converts to this scheme of things, and wholeheartedly join in with it, then blessed shall they be, and they shall have full participation in its achievements and its glory; but if not, if this program is not acquiesced in, then terrible judgments are denounced against them. "And I will execute vengeance and fury upon them," the Christ is represented as saying, "Even as upon the heathen, such as they have not heard" (III Nephi 21:21). See also the chapters cited in parentheses above where the judgments are threatened at length and the threats often repeated.

In offering the suggestion that the remarks found in Ethan Smith's book about the closer relationship between Christianity and the religion of other heathen peoples; and the story, as he relates it, of the culture-hero Quetzalcoatl, furnishing a rough outline of traits manifested in the career of the Book of Mormon Messiah—let the reader be reminded that identity of incident, or order of events, is not necessary to the fact of one thing suggesting another. It will be sufficient if it is proven (first) that there is priority of publication, a priority of sufficient duration for the subject matter to become known in the vicinity where both circumstances come into existence. (Second), where the likelihood is very great that the person producing the later circumstance, incident or book has been in contact with the earlier circumstance, incident or book. And (third), where the earlier circumstance, incident or book has subject matter within it of sufficient resemblance to suggest the later product, incident or book.

As to the first consideration, in this case, priority of production of Ethan Smith's book, and priority of sufficient duration for it to become generally known in the vicinity where both books were produced, there is absolute certainty. For Ethan Smith's book ran through two editions in New England before the Book of Mormon was published. As to the second consideration, in this case, the likelihood of Joseph Smith coming in contact with Ethan Smith's book is not only very great, but amounts to a very close certainty. For being published in an adjoining county to the one in which their home had been for so long, and the interest in the subject being very general, not only in New England but in New York also, it would be little short of miraculous if they did not know of Ethan Smith's book.

As to the third consideration, viz., had the Ethan Smith book subject matter of sufficient resemblance to Book of Mormon Messiah incidents to suggest the latter. Of this each may judge for himself, for the matter is before him from the two books.

There is in Ethan Smith's book, for instance, the question that was put to the Delaware Indian Chief—"What did he know of the Christ." It so happened that he knew nothing. But the question suggested the *possibility* of the Indians knowing something of the Christ, and that was reason for the question being asked. Then there follows the statement quoted from Humboldt by Smith that the Catholic fathers in Mexico found such traces of resemblances between some of the rites of the religion of the natives of Mexico, and the religion the fathers wished to introduce, that they persuaded the natives "that the gospel had in very remote times been already preached in America"; which would necessarily involve some knowledge of the Christ. This, with the story of Quetzalcoatl—given in outline—with his name in some way symbolizing the serpent, his being a bearded white man, the mystery of his coming, his being a legislator, the chief of a religious sect, the strictness of life and the penance he imposed on his following, his appeasing the divine wrath by his own penance, the golden age that followed his advent and instruction, the brevity of his personal reign, the beverage given him by the Great Spirit which rendered him immortal, but gave him also an irresistible desire for visiting a distant country, his abolishing the severity of cruel offerings to the Deity, and permitting only offerings of the first fruits of the harvests, his preaching peace to men, his strange departure from among his following, his promise to return and renew their happiness—all this, I submit, supplies subject matter overwhelmingly sufficient to suggest the visit of the Christ to the Book of Mormon people and his career among them.

Only in one particular, perhaps, will there be disappointment in the material found in Ethan Smith's book for suggesting Book of Mormon incidents. That will be in the very spectacular and dramatic matter of the signs given among Book of Mormon peoples as to the birth, crucifixion, death, and resurrection of the Christ. There is a total absence of anything in the work of our Vermont author on these very remarkable incidents. It should be remembered, however, that while it may be claimed with much force that many of the Book of Mormon traits were supplied by *View of the Hebrews*, it does not follow that every one should be supplied from that source. There are other sources whence might come suggestions, and equally available to Joseph Smith if he was the merely human author of the Book of Mormon. The signs of the birth of Christ as given in the Book of Mormon are striking and beautiful. They are given as prophecy and also as recorded fact—prophecy fulfilled; and, of course, in both cases, are essentially the same. Five years B.C. came a Lamanite prophet, one Samuel and predicted the signs to attend upon Messiah's birth:

"And behold, he said unto them, Behold, I give unto you a sign; for five years more cometh, and behold, then cometh the Son of God to redeem all those who shall believe on his name. And behold, this will I give unto you for a sign at the time of his coming; for behold, there shall be great lights in heaven, insomuch that in the night before he cometh there shall be no darkness, insomuch that it shall appear unto man as if it was day, therefore there shall be one day and a night, and a day, as if it were one day, and there were no night; and this shall be unto you for a sign; for ye shall know of the rising of the sun, and also of its setting; therefore they shall know of a surety that there shall be two days and a night; nevertheless the night shall not be darkened; and it shall be the night before he is born. And behold there shall a new star arise, such a one as ye never have beheld; and this also shall be a sign unto you."

The fulfillment of this prophecy — the historical events — are told in III Nephi 1:15-21. "And it had come to pass, yea, all things, every whit, according to the words of the prophets."

But while this is unique, it is not all original. The Gospel according to St. Matthew, tells us of the star-led magi, the three wise men of the East, who came inquiring "Where is he that is born king of the Jews? For we have seen his star in the East and have come to worship him." After their conversation with Herod, and learning that it was in Bethlehem of Judea that the Jews expected their Messiah would be born — then lo! the star they had seen in the East appeared "and went before them, till it came and stood over where the young child was," and there they found him, and "worshipped him" (Matt. 2:1-12). For the rest of the sign, "a day and a night and a day, as if it were one day, and there were no night," that is found substantially, in the writings of Zechariah. Not, however, as connected with the birth of Messiah, be it said but rather, connected, one would think, with his coming in glory, and with his resurrected Saints; for the description of the wonderful day is immediately preceded by these words: "And the Lord my God shall come, and all the Saints with thee." But it is with the marked similarity of the description of the "day" made up of two days and a night between as one day, that I am concerned with here, the application of the event as a sign of the birth of Messiah, instead of his glorious coming with his Saints, is merely a matter of transition of application, easily made:

"And it shall come to pass in that day, that the light shall not be clear nor dark; but it shall be one day, which shall be known to the Lord, not day, nor night; but it shall come to pass, that at evening time it shall be light" (Zech. 14:6, 7). Matthew and Zachariah, then, could well be thought of as furnishing material for the Book of Mormon signs of the Birth of Messiah.

So also as to the Book of Mormon signs of Messiah's death and resurrection. These events in the Book of Mormon are described as being attended with great terrors — with storm and tempest, and three hours of tremendous earthquakes which caused mountains to rise from plains, and mountains to sink to valleys; which buried cities beneath new raised mountains, and sank others beneath tidal waves of the sea. Other cities were destroyed by fire, and the whole face of the land was changed by tremendous upheavals of the land. There followed intense darkness through three days while the Christ was entombed. Darkness so intense that the vapor of it was felt by the people. No light could be kindled by any art known to those who survived tempest and earthquake. The sun was not seen nor moon nor stars. Absolute blackness brooded over the land, and meanwhile, throughout the land the penetrating voice of God was heard, proclaiming the extent of the destruction which had befallen the great and notable cities which had fallen; and the cause of this awful judgment which had come upon the land was announced — the sins of the people! Then came, at last, the return of the light, and subsequently the visit of the risen Christ. (The account of these tremendously dramatic things are recorded in the 8th, 9th, and 10th chapters of III Nephi.) I know of no more dramatic bit of writing in human literature than this account of the signs of Messiah's crucifixion, burial and resurrection given in the Book of Mormon; and yet the germ of it, the suggestion of it may well be said to be found in the New Testament scriptures. Matthew in his story of the crucifixion tells us that while the Christ was hanging upon the cross and the very thieves mocked him, behold, "From the sixth hour there was darkness over all the land unto the ninth hour" — three hours of darkness. And when he "yielded up the ghost," "the vail of the temple was rent in twain from the top to the bottom; and the earth did quake, and the rocks rent," and when the Roman centurion "and they that were with him watching Jesus, saw the earthquake, and those things which were done, they feared greatly, saying 'Truly, this was the Son of God!'" (Matt. 27). The items of the Book of Mormon story are practically all here; the darkness, the earthquake, the renting of the rocks, the fear of men impressed with these things — with all this in hand, it becomes a matter of expanding the several items to the required limits of the Book of Mormon story. The three hours darkness, expanded to three days of darkness; the evidently momentary earthquake of Matthew, to three hours of earth quaking; the local rending of rocks in Matthew, to the rending of a continent; and the fear of a Roman centurion and those that were with him, to the terror of a whole people.

With these things as suggestions as to signs for Messiah's birth and death and resurrection, and one of conceded vivid, and strong and constructive imaginative powers to work them all out, need not be regarded as an unthinkable procedure and achievement.

Of like character are one or two other items in New Testament and Book of Mormon connection, in which the New Testament might well be thought to supply the suggestions and the Book of Mormon a kind of elaboration, or enlargement of the incidents.

In St. John's Gospel is given that conversation between St. Peter and the risen Lord which led to the tradition that St. John would not die, but would remain in the earth until Messiah would come in glory. "What shall this man do," inquired St. Peter, referring to St. John. "If I will that he tarry till I come, what is that to thee," replied the Lord. "Then went this saying abroad among the brethren that that disciple should not die" (St. John 21:20, 23). This matter was taken up by the Christ in his New World ministry according to the Book of Mormon, and to three of the Twelve disciples chosen from among the Nephites was granted this same power and privilege to remain on the earth unto the coming of the Lord in glory. While in the New Testament there is left an element of doubt as to just what might be meant by the remark of the Christ concerning John — for "Jesus said not unto him, he shall not die; but, if I will that he tarry till I come; what is that to thee?" — in the Book of Mormon all doubt is swept away, both as to John and also as to the three Nephite disciples. They are to remain in the earth without tasting death, till the Lord come. It is quite possible that the New Testament incident suggested the larger one of the Book of Mormon (see III Nephi 28).

The Christ said to the New Testament disciples: "If ye have a faith as a grain of mustard seed, ye shall say unto this mountain, remove hence, to yonder place; and it shall remove" (Matt. 17:20). In the Book of Mormon such an incident is related as having actually, that is physically occurred! "The brother of Jared said unto the mountain Zeria *remove — and it was removed* (Ether 12:30)!

Moses of the Bible made a mysterious departure from Israel after being their leader above forty years. He died away from his people, over in the land of Moab, and while he was buried of the Lord, "No man knoweth of his sepulcher to this day" (Deut. 34). Elijah also mysteriously disappeared at the close of his mission in Israel. He was taken into heaven in a whirlwind, according to the Bible (II Kings 2). The Book of Mormon also had this element of mystery about the departures of some of its prophets. Of Alma, the prophet — about three quarters of a century B.C. — it is written: after blessing the Church

"He departed out of Zarahemla, as if to go into the land of Melek, And it came to pass that he was never heard of more; as to his death or burial we know not of. Behold, this we know, that he was a righteous man; and the saying went abroad in the church, that he was taken up by the Spirit, or buried by the hand of the Lord, even as Moses. But behold, the scriptures saith the Lord took Moses unto himself; and we suppose that he has also received Alma in the Spirit, unto himself; therefore, for this cause, we know nothing concerning his death and burial."

So also another prophet — Nephi, son of Helaman — about the time of the birth of Messiah strangely departed from his people. He gave the sacred records of which he had been made custodian unto his son— "Then he departed out of the land, and whether he went, no man knoweth" (III Nephi 1:2, 3). Were these departures of Book of Mormon holy men suggested by the similar incidents of the Bible? Really in imitations of the Bible incidents?

But now to return from this momentary divergence to the main theme of this writing—viz., did Ethan Smith's *View of the Hebrews* furnish structural material for Joseph Smith's Book of Mormon? It has been pointed out in these pages that there are many things in the former book that might well have suggested many major things in the other. Not a few things merely, one or two, or a half dozen, but many; and it is this fact of many things of similarity and the cumulative force of them that makes them so serious a menace to Joseph Smith's story of the Book of Mormon's origin. Let us consider in summary the chief things pointed out in this study.

The priority of publication by several years of Ethan Smith's *View of the Hebrews* is established, and referred to many times.

The likelihood of Joseph Smith and his family's contact with Ethan Smith's book and other books dealing with American antiquities has been insisted upon.

The material in Ethan Smith's book is of a character and quantity to make a ground plan for the Book of Mormon: It supplies a large amount of material respecting American antiquities—leading to the belief that civilized or semi-civilized nations in ancient times occupied the American continents.

It not only suggests, but pleads on every page for Israelitish origin of the American Indians.

It deals with the destruction of Jerusalem and the scattering of Israel, as the Book of Mormon does.

It deals with the future gathering of Israel, and the restoration of the Ten Tribes, as the Book of Mormon does.

It emphasizes and uses much of the material from the prophecies of Isaiah, including whole chapters, as the Book of Mormon does.

It makes a special appeal to the Gentiles of the New World—having in mind more especially the people of the United States—to become the nursing fathers and mothers unto Israel in the New World—even as the Book of Mormon does, holding out great promises to the great Gentile nation that shall occupy America, if it acquiesces in the divine program.

It holds that the peopling of the New World was by migrations from the Old, the same as does the Book of Mormon. It takes its migrating people into a country where "never man dwelt," just as the Book of

Mormon takes its Jaredite colony into "that quarter where there never had man been."

In both cases the journey was to the northward; in both cases the colony entered into the valley of a great river; they both encountered "seas" of "many waters" in the course of their journey; in both cases the journey was a long one. The motive in both cases was the same — a religious one; *Ethan* is prominently connected with the recording of the matter in the one case, and *Ether* in the other.

Ethan Smith's book supposes that his lost tribes divide into two classes, the one fostering the arts that make for civilization, the other followed the wild hunting and indolent life that ultimately led to barbarism, which is just what happens to the Book of Mormon peoples.

"Long and dismal" wars break out between Ethan Smith's civilized division and his barbarous division. The same occurs between Nephite and Lamanite, divisions drawn on the same lines of civilized and barbarous in the Book of Mormon.

The savage division utterly exterminates the civilized in Ethan Smith's book; the Lamanites, the barbarous division of the Book of Mormon, utterly destroy the civilized division — the Nephites.

Ethan Smith's book assumes for the ancient civilized people a culture of mechanic arts; of written language; of the knowledge and use of iron and other metals; and of navigation. The Book of Mormon does the same for its civilized peoples.

Ethan Smith's book assumes unity of race for the inhabitants of America — the Hebrew race, *and no other.* The Book of Mormon does the same.

Ethan Smith's book assumes that this race (save perhaps, the Eskimo of the extreme north) occupied the whole extent of the American continents. The Book of Mormon does the same for its peoples.

It assumes the Indian tongue to have had one source — the Hebrew; the Book of Mormon makes the same assumption for the language of its peoples.

Ethan Smith's book describes an instrument among the mound finds comprising breast plate with two white buckhorn buttons attached, "in imitation of the precious stones of the Urim," says Ethan Smith. Joseph Smith used some such instrument in translating the Book of Mormon, called Urim and Thummim.

Ethan Smith's book admits the existence of idolatry and human sacrifice; the Book of Mormon does the same.

Ethan Smith's book extols generosity to the poor and denounces pride, as traits of the American Indian; the Book of Mormon does the same for its peoples. Ethan Smith's book denounces polygamy, the Book of Mormon under certain conditions does the same as to David and Solomon's practices.

Ethan Smith's book quotes Indian traditions of a "Lost Book of God" and the promise of its restoration to the Indians, with a return of their lost favor with the Great Spirit. This is in keeping with the lost sacred records to the savage Lamanites of the Book of Mormon.

Ethan Smith's sacred book was buried with some "high priest," "keeper of the sacred tradition"; the Book of Mormon sacred records were hidden or buried by Moroni, a character that corresponds to this Indian tradition in the Hill Cumorah.

Ethan Smith's book describes extensive military fortifications linking cities together over wide areas of Ohio and Mississippi valleys, with military observatory or "watch towers" overlooking them; the Book of Mormon describes extensive fortifications erected throughout large areas with military "watch towers" here and there overlooking them.

Ethan Smith's book also describes sacred towers or "high places," in some instances devoted to true worship, in other cases to idolatrous practices; the Book of Mormon also has its prayer or sacred towers.

Part of Ethan Smith's ancient inhabitants effect a change from monarchial governments to republican forms of government; Book of Mormon peoples do the same.

In Ethan Smith's republics the civil and ecclesiastical power is united in the same person; this was a practice also with the Book of Mormon people.

Some of Ethan Smith's peoples believed in the constant struggle between the good and the bad principle, by which the world is governed; Lehi, first of Nephite prophets, taught the existence of a necessary opposition in all things—righteousness opposed to wickedness—good to bad; life to death, and so following.

Ethan Smith's book speaks of the gospel having been preached in the ancient America; the Book of Mormon clearly portrays a knowledge of the gospel had among the Nephites.

Ethan Smith gives, in considerable detail, the story of the Mexican culture-hero Quetzalcoatl—who in so many things is reminiscent of the Christ; the Book of Mormon brings the risen Messiah to the New World, gives him a ministry, disciples and a church.

Can such numerous and startling points of resemblance and suggestive contact be merely coincidence?

XIV

THE IMAGINATIVE MIND OF PROPHET JOSEPH SMITH: EVIDENCE OF ITS
EXISTENCE—EXAMPLES OF ITS FORCE

One other subject remains to be considered in this division of the "study" here conducted, viz.—was Joseph Smith possessed of a sufficiently vivid and creative imagination as to produce such a work as the Book of Mormon from such materials as have been indicated in the preceding chapters—from such common knowledge as was extant in the communities where he lived in his boyhood and young manhood; from the Bible, and more especially from the *View of the Hebrews*, by Ethan Smith? That such power of imagination would have to be of a high order is conceded; that Joseph Smith possessed such a gift of mind there can be no question.

The fact of it is first established by the testimony of the mother who bore him, Lucy Smith. Speaking of the days immediately following the revelation making known the existence of the Book of Mormon to her son—the ever memorable 23rd day of September, 1823—Lucy Smith in her *History of the Prophet Joseph Smith,* recounts how in the evening of that day, the young prophet sat up late detailing to the family the wonderful conversations he had with the angel; until the elder brother, Alvin, noting how exhausted the youthful prophet was suggested an adjournment of the story being related until the following evening. And this was done. This seems to have been the inauguration of a long series of such evenings according to the *History* by "Mother Lucy Smith" for she writes:

"From this time forth, Joseph continued to receive instructions from the Lord, and we continued to get the children together every night evening, for the purpose of listening while he gave us a relation of the same. I presume our family presented an aspect as singular as any that ever lived upon the face of the earth—all seated in a circle, father, mother, sons and daughters, and giving the most profound attention to a boy, eighteen years of age, who had never read the *Bible through in his life;* he seemed much less inclined to the perusal of books than any of the rest of our children, but far more given to meditation and deep study. . . . During our evening conversations, Joseph would occasionally give us some of the most *amusing* recitals that could be imagined. He would describe the ancient inhabitants of this continent, their dress, mode of traveling, and the animals upon which they rode; their cities, their buildings, with every particular; their mode of warfare; and also their religious worship. This he would do with as much ease, seemingly, as if he had spent his whole life among them." (*History of the Prophet*

Joseph, 1901 edition, Salt Lake City, Utah. Published under the sanction and direction of the late President Joseph F. Smith).[10]

It must be remembered that the above took place before the young prophet had received the plates of the Book of Mormon: these were the evenings immediately following the first interviews with Moroni. Whence came his knowledge for these recitals of "the dress," "the mode of the ancient inhabitants of America of traveling," "the animals on which they rode," "their cities," "their buildings," "their mode of warfare," "their religious worship"? And all this given "with as much ease, seemingly, as if he had spent his whole life among them"? Whence indeed, since all this happened *before* even *the second interview with Moroni* had taken place, and between three and four years before the translation of the Book of Mormon began. And yet it must be from that book that he would get his knowledge of the ancient inhabitants of America, unless he has caught suggestions from such common knowledge, or that which was taken for "knowledge," as existed in the community concerning ancient American civilization, and built by imagination from this and possible contact with Ethan Smith's *View of the Hebrews* his description of the ancient inhabitants of the land, their life, religion and customs. A year later he will be helped by Josiah Priest's book, *The Wonders of Nature and Providence,* published only twenty miles away, and it will have much to say about the Hebrew origin of the American Indian, and his advanced culture and civilization. Whence comes the young prophet's ability to give these descriptions "with as much ease as if he had spent his whole life" with these ancient inhabitants of America? Not from the Book of Mormon, which is, as yet, a sealed book to him; and surely not from Moroni, since he had had but one day and night of interviews with him, during which there had been several interviews, it is true, but these had been occupied with other subject matter than the things enumerated by Lucy Smith. These evening recitals could come from no other source than the vivid, constructive imagination of Joseph Smith, a remarkable power which attended him through all his life. It was as strong and varied as Shakespeare's and no more to be accounted for than the English Bard's.

Parley P. Pratt, one of Joseph Smith's most gifted followers, himself a poet, and wonderful preacher—perhaps the best voice Mormonism ever had—he said of the prophet, after giving the best pen-portrait of him on record—he said:

"He possessed a noble boldness, and independence of character; his manner was easy and familiar . . . his intelligence universal, and his language abounding in original eloquence peculiar to himself—not polished—not studied—not smothered and softened by education and refined by art; but flowing forth in its own native simplicity, and profusely abounding in variety of subject and manner. He interested and edified while, at the same time, he amused and entertained his audience; and none listened to him that were ever weary with his discourse. I have known him to retain a congregation of willing and anxious listeners for many hours together, in the midst of cold or sunshine, rain or wind, while they were laughing at one moment and weeping the next. Even his most bitter enemies were generally overcome if he could once get at their ears" (*Autobiography of Parley P. Pratt*, p. 47).[11]

One must indeed have vision to answer to and live up to such a characterization as that; and what is vision, for the most part, but vivid imagining? And what is Parley P. Pratt's description of Joseph Smith's power over a congregation—and over his very enemies, "if he could but once get at their ears"—but an expansion of the fireside exercise of those powers of imagination—as described by Lucy Smith—to the public forum?

Joseph Smith, himself, though perhaps unconsciously, supplies evidence of being betrayed by this, his unusually powerful faculty of imagination. When Oliver Cowdery started the publication of a series of historical letters in the *Saints' Messenger and Advocate*—1834—under the title, "Early Scenes and Incidents of the Church," the prophet thought the occasion a proper one to make an explanation in relation to certain charges being circulated about the boyhood, and the early manhood period of his life. This he did by a personal letter to Cowdery. The period to which his letter more particularly refers is from the family's arrival at Palmyra until he was twenty-one—about eleven years.[12]

"During this time," he writes, "as is common to most, or all youths, I fell into many vices and follies; but as my accusers are, and have been forward to accuse me of being guilty of gross and outrageous violations of the peace and good order of the community, I take the occasion to remark that, though as I have said above . . . I fell into many vices and follies, I have not, neither can it be sustained, in truth, been guilty of wronging or injuring any man or society of men; and those imperfections to which I allude, and for which I have often had occasion to lament, *were a light, and too often, a vain mind, exhibiting a foolish and trifling conversation.*" And whence came these manifestations of human weakness—especially manifested in youth—but from that fruitful source of both folly and strength, the over strong faculty of imagination? Even so it was with the prophet—he was unconsciously betrayed by that faculty into these exhibitions of boyhood folly to which he so admirably and frankly confesses.

Another testimony concerning the vividness and impressiveness of Joseph Smith's imaginative powers is from a very unimaginative person as I can witness, since he was a boyhood and manhood remembrance of mine through personal acquaintance, this was the late Anson Call, an early Utah pioneer and personal friend of Joseph Smith, honest man and devout disciple of the Prophet. The time of the incident to be related is July 14th, 1843, when the mind of the Prophet was much occupied with the thought of removing his people to the regions of the Rocky Mountains. A company of the brethren in company with the Prophet and his brother Hyrum, with other leading men from Nauvoo have arrived in Montrose, a small village on the west bank of the Mississippi opposite Nauvoo. The occasion of the gathering is to install some officers of the "Rising Sun" lodge of the Masonic order. Judge George Adams, one of the highest authorities in the Masonic fraternity in Illinois, had been sent to attend to this business of installing officers of the lodge. It appears that while Judge Adams was engaged with this business in the lodge, quite a large number of men were gathered on the outside of the building, whose advancement — or lack of it — in Masonic orders did not warrant their attendance upon the ceremonies. In the shade provided was a barrel of ice water, of which the brethren were drinking. The Prophet cautioned them against a too free use of it. The Prophet himself tasting of the water, held the glass and water in his hand, declared that the Latter-day Saints would yet go to the Rocky Mountains, "and, said he," according to Anson Call's narrative, "this water tastes much like that of the crystal streams that are running from the snow-capped Mountains." "I had before seen him in vision," says Mr. Call, "and now saw while he was talking his countenance change to white; not the deadly white of a bloodless face, but a living, brilliant white. He seemed absorbed in gazing at something at a great distance, and said: 'I am gazing upon the valleys of those mountains.' This was followed by a vivid description of the scenery of these Mountains (Mr. Call's narrative was given some years after the settlement of the Saints in Salt Lake Valley) as I have since become acquainted with it. Pointing to Shadrack, Roundy and others, he said, 'there are some men here who shall do a great work in that land.' Pointing to me he said, 'There is Anson, he shall go and shall assist in building up cities from one end of the country to the other; and you,' rather extending the idea to all those he had spoken of, 'shall perform as great a work as has been done by man, so that the nations of the earth shall be astonished, and many of them will be gathered in that land and assist in building cities and temples and Israel shall be made to rejoice.' It is impossible to convey in words," continues Mr. Call, "this scene which is still vivid in my mind, of the grandeur, of Joseph's appearance, his beautiful descriptions of this land, and his wonderful prophetic utterances as they emanated from the glorious inspirations that over-shadowed him. There was a force and power in his exclamations of which the following is but a faint echo: 'Oh the beauty of those snow-capped mountains.

The cool refreshing streams that are running down through those gorges!'
Then gazing in another direction, as if there was a change of locality:
'Oh, the scenes this people will pass through! The dead that will lie
between here and there.' Then, turning in another direction as the scene
had again changed, 'Oh, the apostacy that will take place before my
brethren will reach the land! 'But,' he continued, 'the priesthood shall
prevail over all its enemies, triumph over the devil and be established
upon the earth, never more to be thrown down.'" (The statement of
Mr. Call is to be found in "Tullidge's *Histories, Vol. II Southern Idaho,
Biographical, Supplement*, p. 271.)[13]

A vivid imagination in action would be a proper descriptive title to
Mr. Call's narrative of this incident in the Prophet's mental processes.

A superabundance of evidence of Joseph Smith's power of imagination exists outside the Book of Mormon. If the Book of Mormon be
regarded as of merely human origin, then, of course, to those so regarding
it, the rest of Joseph Smith's work falls to the same plane. His revelations
also become merely human productions; with no other source of origin
for them than the genius of the Prophet, and the chief source of that
genius would be the imaginative faculty of the Prophet. The revelations
of the Prophet regarded from this standpoint would supply well nigh
unlimited evidence for the possession of an imaginative faculty by him,
that is truly phenomenal. I find evidence enough to establish all this in
a single communication from the Prophet to the Saints, written by him
from Liberty Prison, where he, with a number of other brethren were
imprisoned, in the winter of 1838-39, while the Latter-day Saints in a
body, to the number of some twelve thousand souls, were being driven
from their homes in the State of Missouri, some parts of this communication were afterwards selected as the word of the Lord to the Prophet,
in Liberty Prison, and appear now as sections 121, 122, and 123, of the
Book of Doctrine and Covenants. I shall regard the document from
which these selections are taken, as a letter from the Prophet to the
Saints, for such it purported to be when written from Liberty Prison,
and it will sufficiently supply the illustration I seek for the demonstration
of the point here presented—the possession of a vivid, and strong, and
creative imagination by Joseph Smith. The whole document in its letter
form appears in *History of the Church*, vol. III, pp. 289-305.

The letter opens as follows:

"Your humble servant, Joseph Smith, Jun., prisoner for the Lord
Jesus Christ's sake, and for the Saints, taken and held by the power of
mobocracy, under the exterminating reign of his excellency, the governor,
Lilburn W. Boggs, in company with his fellow prisoners and beloved
brethren."

Then follow the names of his fellow prisoners, and the story and cause of their imprisonment—the injustice and cruelty of it. Then the soul-moving, and agonized question of the Prophet addressed to God:

"Oh God! where art Thou! And where is the pavilion that coverth thy hiding place? How long shall thy hand be stayed, and thine eye, yea thy pure eye, behold from the eternal heavens, the wrongs of thy people, and of thy servants, and thy ear be penetrated with their cries? Yea, O Lord, how long shall they suffer these wrongs and unlawful oppressions, before thine heart shall be softened towards them, and thy bowels be moved with compassion towards them?

"O Lord God Almighty, Maker of Heaven, Earth and Seas, and of all things that in them are, and who controllest and subjectest the devil, and the dark and benighted dominion of Sheol! Stretch forth thy hand, let thine eye pierce; let thy pavilion be taken up; let thy hiding place no longer be covered; let thine ear be inclined; let thine heart be softened, and thy bowels moved with compassion towards us, let thine anger be kindled against our enemies; and in the fury of thine heart, with thy sword avenge us of our wrongs; remember thy suffering Saints, O our God! and thy servants will rejoice in thy name forever."

To this appeal God is represented as answering:

"My son, peace be unto thy soul; thine adversity and thine afflictions shall be but a small moment; and then if thou endure it well, God shall exalt thee on high; thou shalt triumph over all thy foes; thy friends do stand by thee, and they shall hail thee again, with warm hearts and friendly hands; thou art not yet as Job; thy friends do not contend against thee, neither charge thee with transgression, as they did Job; and they who do charge thee with transgression, as they did Job; and they who do charge thee with transgression, their hope shall be blasted and their prospects shall melt away as the hoar frost melteth before the burning rays of the rising sun. . . . How long can rolling waters remain impure? What power shall stay the heavens? As well might man stretch forth his puny arm to stop the Missouri river in its decreed course, or to turn it upstream, as to hinder the Almighty from pouring down knowledge from heaven, upon the heads of the Latter-day Saints" (pp. 293, 297). Further:

"The ends of the earth shall inquire after thy name, and fools shall have thee in derision, and hell shall rage against thee, while the pure in heart, and the wise, and the noble, and the virtuous, shall seek counsel, and authority and blessings constantly from under thy hand, and thy people shall never be turned against thee by the testimony of traitors; and although their influence shall cast thee into trouble, and into bars and walls, thou shalt be had in honor, and but for a small moment and thy voice shall be more terrible in the midst of thine enemies, than the fierce lion, because of thy righteousness; and thy God shall stand by thee forever and ever.

"If thou art called to pass through tribulations; if thou art in perils among false brethren; if thou art in perils among robbers; if thou art in perils by land or by sea; if thou art accused with all manner of false accusations; if thine enemies fall upon thee; if they tear thee from the society of thy father and mother and brethren and sisters; and if with a drawn sword thine enemies tear thee from the bosom of thy wife. . . . and thou be dragged to prison, and thine enemies prowl around thee like wolves for the blood of the lamb; and if thou shouldst be cast into the pit, or into the hands of murderers, and the sentence of death passed upon thee; if thou be cast into the deep; if the billowing surge conspire against thee; if fierce winds become thine enemy; if the heavens gather blackness, and all the elements combine to hedge up the way; and above all, if the very jaws of hell shall gape open the mouth wide after thee, know thou, my son, that all these things shall give thee experience, and shall be for thy good. The son of Man hath descended below them all; art thou greater than he?

"Therefore, hold on thy way, and the Priesthood shall remain with thee, for their bounds are set, they cannot pass. Thy days are known, and thy years shall not be numbered less; therefore, fear not what men can do, for God shall be with you forever and ever."

So far these quotations are from parts of the communication afterwards incorporated in and accepted as revelations; but other parts of the letter, not so included, are as rich in imaginative elements as these above given. For example:

"Dearly beloved brethren, we see that perilous times have come, as was testified of. We may look, then, with most perfect assurance, for the fulfillment of all those things that have been written, and with more confidence than ever before, lift up our eyes to the luminary of day, and say in our hearts, Soon thou wilt veil thy blushing face. He that said 'Let there be light,' and there was light, hath spoken this word."

And this:

"What is Boggs (Governor of Missouri, who had persecuted the Saints) or his murderous party, but wimbling willows upon the shore to catch the flood-wood? As well might we argue that water is not water, because the mountain torrents send down mire and roil the crystal stream, although afterwards render it more pure than before; or that fire is not fire, because it is of a quenchable nature, by pouring on the flood; as to say that our cause is down because renegades, liars, priests, thieves and murderers, who are all alike tenacious of their crafts and creeds, have poured down, from their spiritual wickedness in high places, and from their strongholds of the devil, a flood of dirt and mire and filthiness and vomit upon our heads. No! God forbid. Hell may pour forth its rage like the burning lava of Mount Vesuvius, or of Etna, or of the most terrible of the burning mountains; and yet shall 'Mormonism' stand. Water, fire, truth and God are all realities. Truth is 'Mormonism.' God is the author of it. He is our shield. It is by Him we receive our birth. It was by His voice that we were called to a dispensation of His Gospel in the beginning of the fullness of times" (Id., pp. 291, 297).

Of the Constitution of the United States he said:

"Hence we say, that the Constitution of the United States is a glorious standard; it is founded in the wisdom of God. It is a heavenly banner; it is to all those who are privileged with the sweets of its liberty, like the cooling shades and refreshing waters of a great rock in a thirsty and weary land. It is like a great tree under whose branches men from every clime can be shielded from the burning rays of the sun" (Id., p. 304).

In the light of this evidence, there can be no doubt as to the possession of a vividly strong, creative imagination by Joseph Smith, the Prophet, an imagination, it could with reason be urged, which, given the suggestions that are to be found in the "common knowledge" of accepted American antiquities of the times, supplemented by such a work as Ethan Smith's *View of the Hebrews*, would make it possible for him to create a book such as the Book of Mormon is.

PART II

INTERNAL EVIDENCE THAT THE BOOK OF MORMON IS OF HUMAN ORIGIN — CONSIDERED

I

THE WANT OF PERSPECTIVE AND CONSISTENCY IN THE ALLEGED HISTORICAL INCIDENTS OF THE BOOK OF MORMON. PARALLEL BETWEEN NEPHITE AND JAREDITE MIGRATIONS. SPECIAL DIFFICULTIES OF THE JAREDITE SEA VOYAGE

If from all that has gone before in Part I, the view be taken that the Book of Mormon is merely of human origin; that a person of Joseph Smith's limitations in experience and in education, who was of the vicinage and of the period that produced the book—if it be assumed that he is the author of it, then it could be said there is much internal evidence in the book itself to sustain such a view.

In the first place there is a certain lack of perspective in the things the book relates as history that points quite clearly to an undeveloped mind as their origin. The narrative proceeds in characteristic disregard of conditions necessary to its reasonableness, as if it were a tale told by a child, with utter disregard for consistency. For example, there is the story of Lehi's departure from Jerusalem with his small colony; its landing in America; and its early movements in the land of promise. Let us note a few of its difficulties:

The first part of the journey is a three days' travel from Jerusalem to "near the shores of the Red Sea" (I Nephi 2:4-6). It may be thought a small matter, but the nearest point from Jerusalem to the Red Sea is about one hundred and seventy miles, and even if allowance is made for some change in the Red Sea's extension northward, in ancient times, the distance could scarcely be covered in three days.

The manner of the colony's traveling appears to have been on foot, carrying their "tents and provisions" with them. If they were helped in this three days' journey by the use of domestic animals common to the country and in general use at the time—the ass, the ox, the camel, the horse—singularly enough, *no mention is made of the fact*. Neither at the beginning of the trek nor at any time through their eight years' journey in the wilderness of Arabia, until coming to the shores of the Arabian Sea, nor at the time of embarking on the sea for the journey to the promised land, is there any mention made of the use of domestic animals. It is always, when making their several removals towards the land of promise, "and we did take our tents and depart into the wilderness," etc. In the second removal, after leaving Jerusalem, however, it is said they they "did gather together whatsoever things they should carry into the wilderness, and all the remainder of our provision which the Lord had given unto us, and we did take seed of every kind, that we might carry into the wilderness." But how this was conveyed, by beasts of burden, or on the backs of the people, nothing is said.

At this point it may be well to note that Lehi's colony was a very small one. All told it could not have numbered more than thirty souls and part of these were children of tender age, and several were people well advanced in life, so that the amount of "provisions," "seeds of every kind" together with their "tents," that they could carry in this journey could not be very considerable without the use of beasts of burden. Yet if they were employed no mention is made of that fact, and the general impression of the story is that they were without beasts of burden in their whole eight years' journey. No mention is made of such animals, either of taking them along or leaving them behind when beginning the sea voyage; but as soon as they arrive "to the promised land" (I quote the first edition of the Book of Mormon), they speak of finding "beasts in the forests of every kind." And then proceed to enumerate the *domestic animals,* "the cow and the ox, and the ass and the horse, and the goat and the wild goat, and all manner of wild animals which were for the use of man" (I Nephi 18:25). And all this without reference to how they got there in the wilderness of the New World; and how they happened to be domesticated, and already for the use of the New Colonists (cf. II Nephi 5:11)!

Lehi's colony, it must be remembered, came to an empty America, so far as human inhabitants were concerned—according to the Book of Mormon accounting of things. And if it should be urged that the Jaredite people had previously possessed the land, and the claim made that these domestic animals found by Lehi's colony were left in the continent by that people, then it should be remembered that the Nephite people never came in contact with the Jaredite race, that the latter was annihilated to the last man somewhere in the North Continent, while the Nephites, according to the general belief, landed in South America, in Chile about thirty degrees south latitude—[An alleged revelation to Joseph Smith on the subject of the course of Lehi's travels from Jersualem to America, says: "They traveled nearly a south, southeast direction, until they came to the nineteenth degree of north latitude; then, nearly east to the sea of Arabia, then sailed in a southeast direction, and landed on the continent of South America, in Chile, thirty degrees south latitude" (Richards & Little, *Compendium,* Art., "Gems from the History of Joseph Smith," p. 289).[14]

There is some ground for doubting if this item is a revelation (see this writer's *New Witness for God,* 3:501-3); but the compendium statement has the support of a very similar passage in the writings of Orson Pratt (see Pratt's *Works,* edition of 1851, "Remarkable visions," p. 7).[15] And these two passages may be said to represent the views of the Mormon People.] and from three to four thousand miles south of any lands occupied by the Jaredites! So that the likelihood of the domestic animals found by the Nephites in the "forests" of South America, having come from previously owned Jaredite stock, is exceedingly remote. Besides there is the problem of any domestic animals left over from the Jaredite occupancy—the length of time considered since these were under the control of man—the problem of their having become utterly wild— thoroughly undomesticated; where as these animals found by the Nephites in South America are spoken of in such fashion as to lead one to think they were at once available for use (cf. I Nephi 18:25; and II Nephi 5:11).

The Jaredite trek is very much of the same color as the Nephite. Each is undertaken because of impending disaster to the cities wherein the two peoples dwelt. The prophet Lehi warned of the destruction of Jerusalem, takes his flight, with his family and the family of Ishmael— a few friends—into the wilderness, to a land of promise. The prophet, Moriancumr, brother of Jared, warned of the destruction of Babel and the confusion of languages, with his brother's family and a few of the friends, of each, take their flight into the wilderness, and ultimately arrive in a land of promise—in both cases to "a land choice above all other lands." In both cases the colonies are small. Lehi's could not have exceeded thirty; the Jaredite colony could not have been more than one hundred in number. In both cases the colonies are promised that they should become a mighty people—great nations. There is in both cases a long journey through a wilderness. Both are miraculously led by prophesyings, by alternating divine reproofs and favors. Then as to things miraculous: If Lehi's colony had its wonderful "Liahona," the round ball with its spindles pointing the way the colony should travel and the direction in which the hunter would find game; and also had reflected upon its surface ever changing written instructions to meet changing conditions, and working according to the faith of those rightfully in possession of it—if the Nephites had this marvel, the Jaredites had the equal marvel of the sixteen small stones "molten out of a rock," by Moriancumr, and rendered self-luminous by the touch of God's visible finger, to give light to what, but for them, would have been a voyage of nearly a year's duration in continuous darkness (I Nephi 16:30-31). Also the Lord gave to Moriancumr two other stones, which were Urim and Thummim, for the purpose of seership, by which all things were revealed to him who rightly possessed them and rightly used them. And they were also designated to be used in translating languages (see Ether 4:23, 28).

Both Nephite and Jaredite colonies are brought through a wilderness to the sea shore, where a residence of considerable time is had before embarking for the New World. Both colonies had a long sea voyage; and both, strangely enough, seem to have almost prohibited the use of fire. In the case of the Nephites after the wilderness journey, when Nephi was preparing to build his ship "and it came to pass that I Nephi, did make a bellows wherewith to blow the fire. . . . And after I had made a bellows wherewith to blow the fire (first edition p. [43]) I did smite two stones together that I might make a fire. For the Lord had not hitherto suffered that we should have much fire, as we journeyed in the wilderness; for he said: I will make thy food become sweet, that ye cook it not; and I will also be your light in the wilderness; and I will prepare the way before you" (I Nephi 17:10-13). In the case of the Jaredites, it was also in connection with the sea voyage that fire became prohibitive. The Lord in discussing the problem of light for the barges said: "Ye cannot have windows, for they will be dashed in pieces. Neither shall ye take fire with you, for ye shall not go by the light of fire, for behold, ye shall be as a whale in the midst of the sea" (Ether 2:23, 24).

The prophet leaders of both colonies had clear vision of the Christ; and both equal pre-vision of his life and mission as the savior of the world. Both came to an empty America, and both people had remarkable wars of extermination. In the case of the Jaredites a war of extermination to the last man of the whole race; in the case of the Nephites, the annihilation of the Nephite people by their opponents, the Lamanites.

Both colonies had a long and miraculous sea voyage to the promised land. In the case of the Nephites the "ship" was not after the order of ships built by men, "but I did build it," remarks Nephi, "after the manner which the Lord had shown me; wherefore, it was not after the manner of men" (I Nephi 18:2). No description of this evidently unique vessel is given, beyond that from the context it is to be inferred that it was wind-driven, by means of sails, and had means of "steering," presumably by some sort of rudder; but in what the peculiarities of the ship consisted we are not told. The vessel was driven forth before the wind toward the promised land for the space of many days. The voyage was a long one, the distance covered being from the head of the Arabian Sea to the coast of Chile in South America, a journey of at least halfway round the earth. On the duration of the voyage we are not informed beyond the statement that they were driven forth "for the space of many days." On the way there was revelry and lewdness—dancing and singing on the part of the older sons of Lehi and their wives; as also by the sons of Ishmael, and their wives. And when Nephi protested against this course he was bound with cords and even his life threatened. The admonitions of Lehi and his pleadings for Nephi were in vain. He was now well stricken in years, and had suffered greatly on account of his rebellious sons, and both he and his wife, we are told, "were brought down, yea, even upon their sick-beds." And "because of their grief and much sorrow, and the iniquity of my brethren," says Nephi, "they were brought near even to be carried out of this time to meet their God; yea, their grey hairs were about to be brought down to lie low in the dust." Then, as if remembering that the colony was upon the high seas, the narrator adds to the stock phrase—"yea, even they were near to be cast with sorrow into the watery grave" (I Nephi 18:18)!

Under these circumstances "Liahona," the wonder compass, which had directed the journey of the colony through the wilderness, that worked by the faith, of those rightfully in charge of it, and that had directed the course of the sea voyage hitherto, as well as the wilderness journey, "did cease to work." A tremendous storm arose, and for three days they were driven from their course, and seemingly were "about to be swallowed up in the depths of the sea." Fear-stricken, the revelers relented, ceased their reveling and unbound Nephi. Under his faith the storm died away, the miraculous compass worked, and all was again well with the colony, until they reached the land of promise.

Continuing consideration of the parallelism in the two colonies, it can be said that for the great sea voyage of the Jaredites vessels, called barges, were also prepared under divine instructions, but manifestly of different type from that which Nephi was directed to build; for the Jaredite barges had neither sails nor means of steering, but evidently were to wallow their way through the sea, sometimes submerged and sometimes atop of the sea. Yet they were built "according to the instructions of the Lord, *and they were small,* and they were light upon the water, even like unto the lightness of a fowl upon the water." And yet, later, and after the barges had been prepared, "according as thou hast directed me" (Ether 2:18), said Moriancumr, it was found that they "were tight like unto a dish" (Id., ver. 17). There was no means of lighting, ventilating, or steering them (Id., verses 17-18). All these problems were submitted in great anxiety on the part of the prophet, to the Lord; in which submission further facts are developed concerning these barges and the manner in which they were intended to convey the colony to the promised land. When appealed to respecting the problem of light, the Lord said: "What will ye that I should do that ye may have light in your vessels? For behold, ye cannot have windows, for they will be dashed in pieces; neither shall ye take fire with you, for ye shall not go by the light of fire. *For behold, ye shall be as a whale in the midst of the sea;* for the mountain waves shall dash upon you. Nevertheless I will bring you up again out of the depths of the sea." The arrangement as to providing light in the barges for the voyage was, as above stated, by making the sixteen stones prepared by Moriancumr luminous, by the touch of God's finger, and placing two of them in each barge — "one in each end thereof; and behold, they did give light unto the vessel thereof." Ventilation was provided by cutting a hole in the top and bottom of each barge, so that one or the other of them — which ever happened to be the upper one at a given time — might be opened for admitting air. Apparently no arrangements were made as to steering, or for sailing; but when the voyage was begun "the Lord God caused that there should a furious wind blow upon the face of the waters, towards the promised land; . . . And it came to pass that the wind did never cease to blow towards the promised land while they were upon the waters" (Ether 6:5, 8); and so they were brought to their destination.

A fuller description of these barges, given in the exact language of the first edition of the Book of Mormon[16] — the phraseology has been changed somewhat in the 1921 edition, but for the full flavor of the description, the exact text of the first edition should be used. The time had come for the Jaredite colony to start their ocean voyage, so the Lord said:

"Go to and build, after the manner of barges which ye have hitherto built. And it came to pass that the brother of Jared did go to work, and also his brethren, and built barges after the manner which they had built, according to the instructions of the Lord. And they were small, and they were light upon the water, even like unto the lightness of a fowl upon the water; and they were built after a manner that they were exceeding tight, even that they would hold water like unto a dish; and the bottom thereof was tight like unto a dish; and the sides thereof were tight like unto a dish; and the ends thereof were peaked; and the top thereof was tight like unto a dish; and the length thereof was the length of a tree; and the door thereof, when it was shut, was tight like unto a dish. And it came to pass that the brother of Jared cried unto the Lord, saying: O Lord, I have performed the work which thou hast commanded me, and I have made the barges according as thou hast directed me. And behold, O Lord, in them there is no light, whither shall we steer. And also we shall perish, for in them we cannot breathe, save it is the air which is in them; therefore we shall perish. And the Lord said unto the brother of Jared, Behold, thou shalt make a hole in the top thereof, and also in the bottom thereof; and when thou shalt suffer for air, thou shalt unstop the hole thereof, and receive air. And if it so be that the water come in upon thee, behold, ye shall stop the hole thereof, that ye may not perish in the flood. And it came to pass that the brother of Jared did so, according as the Lord had commanded. And he cried again unto the

Lord, saying, O Lord, behold I have done even as thou hast commanded me; and I have prepared the vessels for my people, and behold, there is no light in them. Behold, O Lord, wilt thou suffer that we shall cross this great water in darkness?" (First Edition pp. 542-43).

Then followed the consideration of lighting as already described. Continuing the description of these barges when on the journey, it is said:

"And it came to pass that when they were buried in the deep there was no water that could hurt them, their vessels being tight like unto a dish, and also they were tight like unto the ark of Noah; therefore when they were encompassed about by many waters they did cry unto the Lord, and he did bring them forth again upon the top of the waters. And it came to pass that the wind did never cease to blow towards the promised land while they were upon the waters; and thus they were driven forth before the wind. And they did sing praises unto the Lord; yea, the brother of Jared did sing praises unto the Lord, and he did thank and praise the Lord all the day long; and when the night came, they did not cease to praise the Lord" (Current edition Ether 6:7-9).

In the wilderness journey the Jaredite colony are represented as carrying with them "their flocks which they had gathered together, male and female of every kind," also "fowls of the air"; and they did also prepare a vessel in which they did carry with them the "fish of the waters," and "deseret," which interpreted means "honey bee," and thus they did carry with them "swarms of honey bees"; "and seeds of every kind" (Ether 2:1-3). All this, under fair presumption, to be taken to the distant promised land, and hence carried on the ocean voyage. And although some of these things are not specifically enumerated as being taken along when "they got aboard of their vessels or barges," yet enough are enumerated to make it fair presumption that all these things above named were also taken "aboard," and that they were "gathered" for that purpose. Speaking of the colony embarking, it is written:

"And it came to pass that when they had prepared all manner of food, that thereby they might subsist upon the water, and also food for their flocks and herds, and whatsoever beast, or animal, or fowl that they should carry with them. And it came to pass that when they had done all these things, they got aboard of their vessels or barges, and set forth into the sea, commending themselves unto the Lord their God" (Ether 6:4).

Speaking in the reign of Emer, the fourth of the kings of the Jaredites, an enumeration is made of the things that enter into Jaredite culture, all manner of fruit and grain; of silks, and fine linen; of gold and silver and precious things; also all manner of cattle, oxen, cows, sheep, swine and goats, "and also many other kinds of animals which were useful for the food of man. . . . They also had horses and asses, and there were elephants and cureloms and cumoms; all of which were useful unto man, and more especially the elephants, and cureloms, and cumoms" (Ether 9:17-19).

There can be no doubt but what under the terms of *their flocks and herds,* and whatsoever beast, or animal or fowl that they should carry with them, that are said to have been loaded on to the barges, and for which also they carried food, was included the well known domestic animals named above. But did they also bring in the barges elephants, and the animals with the curious names of "cureloms" and "cumoms," said to be so "useful unto man"—apparently even more useful than oxen or horses, since their usefulness is so emphasized—did they transport these from the Old World to the New?

The trouble with bringing these animals—as well as "the flocks and herds, and whatsoever beast or animal or fowl they should bring with them"—and which they surely did load onto the barges—is that it very greatly increases the difficulties of the migration of this colony. It is emphasized that the eight barges "were small"; that "they were light upon the water, even like unto the lightness of a fowl" (Ether 2:16). The only suggestion of their size is very indefinite—"the length thereof was the length of a tree"; but the length of what tree? Nothing is said of the width, so we know nothing definitely of the barges save that they were small, and in addition to provisions, including of course water for all the animals brought over in the small barges, there are about one hundred colonists—estimated.

Added to the difficulty of the smallness of the barges for such a company of human souls and these animals, seeds and provisions and water for all is the duration of the voyage. "Three hundred and forty and four days" were they upon the water (Ether 6:11)! Only twenty-one days short of a whole year! Now, if the "elephants" and "cureloms" and "cumoms"—evidently animals somewhat of the same type as the elephants—are included in the list of animals brought over in the barges, and there is no reason for excluding them, then it is quite clear that the problems of conveying such a colony, in such vessels, and occupying such a length of time—is very greatly increased. And under all the circumstances is it much to be wondered at if intelligent people to whom the Book of Mormon is presented for consideration, should ask: "Do we have here a great historical document, or only a wonder tale, told by an undeveloped mind, living in a period and in an environment where the miraculous in 'history' is accepted without limitations and is supposed to account for all inconsistencies and lapses that challenge human credulity in the thought and in the easy philosophy *that all things are possible with God?*

II

PARALLELS IN NEPHITE AND JAREDITE TRAITS AND INCIDENTS AFTER ARRIVAL IN THE NEW WORLD: THE PROBLEM OF SOLOMON'S TEMPLE; KINGS, NEPHITE AND JAREDITE; THINGS MIRACULOUS THAT TEST CREDULITY

The same lack of perspective and of consistency is also manifest in the early movements of both Jaredite and Nephite colonies after arriving "to the promised land." Also the same tendency to parallel incidents and characteristics as we have noted in the formation of the two colonies, and the incidents of their wilderness journey and sea voyage. It may be asked, what of this parallelism? What does it amount to? If such a question should be asked the opponent of the Book of Mormon would answer with emphasis—"This of it. It supplies the evidence that the Book of Mormon is the product of *one mind*, and that, a very limited mind, unconsciously reproducing with only slight variation its visions." And the answer will be accepted as significant at least, if not conclusive.

In our examination of these matters let the smallness of Lehi's colony be constantly borne in mind. It could not have exceeded thirty, all told, who came out of Jerusalem. About thirty years later, that would be 570 B.C., the colony divided, and Nephi led away the more righteous part of it—say one half of the colony (see II Nephi 5:6). How many would there be in this righteous branch? Not more than a hundred; under the most liberal allowance for increase, and of these, many would be children. Yet we have Nephi saying, and he writes it with his own hand—for this part of the narrative is not within the part of the book that is an abridgement—we have him saying that his division of the colony has prospered exceedingly, they sowed seed and reaped again in abundance; they began to raise "flocks and herds, and animals of every kind." Nephi brought with him, in his separation from his brethren, the sacred records the colony had brought from Jerusalem; also he made plates on which to engrave the annals of his own people, both large and small plates for both sacred and secular chronicles, and thus prepared to perpetuate letters, and also he brought with him the sword of Laban which he used as a pattern in manufacturing other swords, for defense against the anticipated attacks of his brethren and their following. "And I (Nephi) did teach my people to build buildings, and to work in all manner of wood, and of iron, and of copper and of brass, and of steel, and of gold, and of silver, and of precious ores, *which were in great abundance*. And I, Nephi did build a temple; and I did construct it after the manner of the temple of Solomon, save it were not built of so many precious things; for they were not to be found upon the land; wherefore, it could not be built like unto Solomon's temple. But the manner of the construction was like unto the temple of Solomon; and the workmanship thereof was exceeding fine" (I Nephi 5:16). Yet this "temple" was "not built of so many precious things" as Solomon's temple, *for they were not to be found upon the land*"! One may not refuse to ask what had become of the fine woods, the silver, and the gold, and the other precious ores of a few lines above! And this people of less than a hundred were manufacturing and working in iron and copper and brass, and steel and gold and silver in the New World? And they built a temple, like unto Solomon's temple "save it were not built of so many precious things"! What! one may ask, a people of less than a hundred in number — and many of these children — build a temple like unto Solomon's?

Let it be remembered that Nephi knew Solomon's temple. All his days he had lived in Jerusalem, and was familiar with the temple. He had often wandered about its courts, in his boyhood, played in its grounds, and with his sainted father worshipped within its walls. For more than three hundred years before Lehi left Jerusalem it had stood as the chief adornment of the holy city, and was world famed. All this that we may be reminded that Nephi must be regarded as knowing what he is talking about when he says that he built a temple and "did construct it after the manner of the temple of Solomon. . . . And the workmanship thereof was exceeding fine."

A description of Solomon's temple is found in I Kings, 6th chapter. Its form and its dimensions are there given. In shape its main hall was a rectangle, 60 cubits long, 20 wide and 30 high. As a cubit is about 18 inches, this gives us the dimensions in feet of 90 feet long, 30 feet wide and 45 feet high. On its east face it had a porch — forming an entrance — which extended across the whole front and added 10 cubits, or 15 feet, to the dimensions making the length of the building 105 feet. The height of the porch is given in II Chronicles (3:4) as 120 cubits, or 180 feet; but as this is regarded as out of proportion with other measurements, it is held to be a mistake. One of the Mss. of the Septuagint gives the height of the porch as 20 cubits, or 30 feet, and this is generally accepted. On three sides of the house were built a number of chambers — 7½, 9, and 10½ feet wide respectively, in three stories — Josephus says 30 — intended for the accommodation of the priests and for storing things required for the temple service. The beams that supported the ceilings of these three stories rested on ledges in the outer face of the temple wall formed by successive reductions of its thickness. Above the top most row of the chambers, the temple wall was pierced with windows of narrow lights of fixed lattice work. In the interior the main hall was divided into two chambers. The first, on the east, being called the Holy place—60 by 30 feet; the second, on the west, called the Most Holy place, or Holy of Holies, 30 by 30 feet, and 30 feet high, an exact cube.

Seven years was the time required to build Solomon's temple (I Kings 6:30)!

Two kingdoms were employed in the building it. The kingdom of Israel, and the kingdom of Tyre (see I Kings 5:12).

Solomon raised a levy out of Israel, of "thirty thousand men, and he sent them to Lebanon, ten thousand a month by courses, a month they were in Lebanon and two months at home. And Solomon had three score and ten thousand that bare burdens, and four score thousand hewers in the mountains; besides the chief of Solomon's officers which were over the work, three thousand and three hundred, which ruled over the people that wrought on the work" (I Kings 5:12-16).

Such the dimensions and general plan of Solomon's Temple. Such the time required to build it. Such the forces that worked upon it. And now, Nephi with his less than one hundred people, many of whom must have been children, built a temple "after the manner of Solomon's temple"—the manner of the construction was like unto the temple of Solomon; and the workmanship thereof was exceeding fine (!). Is it not pertinent to ask, is this statement from a great historical document, by one who knew Solomon's temple through all his boyhood and young manhood, or is it the reckless statement of an undeveloped mind that knew not what he was saying—which?

Of his part of Lehi's colony, Nephi is made king! And as elsewhere remarked, the title is fixed in a royal line of his descendants, to bear his name, Nephi II, Nephi III, and so following. "Thus they were called by the people, let them be of whatever name they would," says the Chronicle (see Jacob 1:9-11; cf. Mosiah 25:13). Just before his death, Nephi having grown old, "he anointed a man to be king and ruler over his people," "*according to the reign of the kings*"! To the credit of Nephi, be it said, he was desirous that his people should have no king, but in this he was overruled and became "king" of his little band of less than one hundred, and the succession of title was fixed as described above.

Again we may pause to note the parallelism between this procedure and that among the Jaredite colonists. They, too, though a small colony, must need have a "king." There is the same reluctance about establishing the "kingly" order of government. One of the sons of Moriancumr was first choice but he refused. The colony besought his father to constrain him, but his father "commanded them that they should constrain no man to be their king" (Ether 6:25). After many refused to be "king" one of the sons of Jared, Oriah by name, was found who accepted the honor, and the kingly form of government was established, followed by its train of evils.

One other thing in which this parallel between Nephites and Jaredites runs may be noted. That is in respect of what may rightly be called the tremendous credulity manifest in each. In the Nephite colony it was perhaps supremely expressed by Nephi when he said to his brethren, when reasoning with them upon his ability to build the ship he had been commanded of God to build. In assertion of what he could do—even greater things if God should command him—he said: "If God had commanded me to do all things, I could do them. If he should command me that I should say unto this water, be thou earth, it should be earth; and if I should say it, it would be done" (I Nephi 17:50). The colony was then at the head of the Arabian Sea or Gulf, which opens out and becomes one with the Indian Ocean, so that Nephi's suggestion is that if he said to the Ocean be thou dry land, it would be done. And, of course, granted the absolute sovereign power of God, and the contingent that he should command a man to say to the ocean, "be thou earth," it is not inconceivable that the miracle would be wrought; but so far within human experience that has not been done, and is not likely to be done, since it seems not to be the way of God's procedure. And that is not the point here to be either established or controverted—the possibility of the thing—but the Nephite belief in the possibility of its being done, and the Jaredite belief in the same absolute acceptance of God's sovereign power.

Among the Jaredites it finds its expression when Moriancumr took the sixteen small stones he had molten out of a rock, and asked God to touch them and so make them self-luminous—"I know, O Lord," said he, *that thou hast all power, and can do whatsoever thou wilt for the benefit of man;* therefore touch these stones, O Lord, with thy finger, and prepare them that they may shine forth in darkness; and they shall shine forth unto us in the vessels which we have prepared, that we may have light while we shall cross the sea" (Ether 3:4). And it was done, even as he had asked, and in the course of it Moriancumr saw first the "finger" of God and then his whole spirit personage. Subsequently this same prophet, Moriancumr—and it manifests the sovereign power of God, not only in theory, but in action—Moriancumr said unto a certain mountain, called "Zems" [Zerin], "*Remove and it was* removed" (Ether 12:30). This faith in the sovereign power of God results in the miracles of the Book of Mormon surpassing the miracles of the Bible.

Mormon in giving a summary of miracles wrought by the Saints of the New World said, "In his (the Christ's) name could they remove mountains, and in his name could they cause the earth to shake; and by the power of his words did they cause prisons to tremble to the earth, yea even the fiery furnace could not harm them, neither wild beasts nor poisonous serpents, because of the power of his (the Christ's) word."

The whole atmosphere of the book is miracle—miracle! Sometimes it takes on almost childish expression, illustrated by the following circumstance. The first Nephi in one of the many controversies had with his older brothers so reproved and rebuked them that he was so wrought upon that he had no strength left in his body; and now his story:

"And now it came to pass that when I had spoken these words they were angry with me, and were desirous to throw me into the depths of the sea; and as they came forth to lay their hands upon me I spake unto them, saying: In the name of the Almighty God, I command you that ye touch me not, for I am filled with the power of God, even unto the consuming of my flesh; and whoso shall lay his hands upon me shall wither even as a dried reed; and he shall be as naught before the power of God, for God shall smite him. And it came to pass that I, Nephi, said unto them that they should murmur no more against their father; neither should they withhold their labor from me, for God had commanded me that I should build a ship. . . . And it came to pass that I, Nephi, said many things unto my brethren, insomuch that they were confounded and could not contend against me; neither durst they lay their hands upon me nor touch me with their fingers, even for the space of many days. Now they durst not do this lest they should wither before me, so powerful was the Spirit of God; and thus it had wrought upon them. And it came to pass that the Lord said unto me; Stretch forth thine hand again unto thy brethren, and they shall not wither before me, so powerful was the Spirit of God; and thus it had wrought upon them. And it came to pass that the Lord said unto me: Stretch forth thine hand again unto thy brethren, and they shall not wither before thee, but I will shock them, saith the Lord, and this will I do, that they may know that I am the Lord their God. And it came to pass that I stretched forth my hand unto my brethren, and they did not wither before me; but the Lord did shake them, even according to the word which he had spoken. And now, they said: We know of a surety that the Lord is with thee, for we know that it is the power of the Lord that has shaken us. And they fell down before me, and were about to worship me, but I would not suffer them, saying: I am thy brother, yea, even thy younger brother: wherefore, worship the Lord thy God, and honor thy father and thy mother, that thy days may be long in the land which the Lord thy God shall give thee" (I Nephi 17:48-55).

III

PARALLELS FOUND IN NEPHITE TRAITS AND INCIDENTS IN DIFFERENT
NEPHITE PERIODS: ANTI-CHRISTS—SHEREM, NEHOR, KORIHOR

Having seen how strong parallelism obtains between Jaredite and Nephite
peoples in the matter of their migration, and their movements after
arriving in the promised land, it remains in somewhat the same manner
to show that a like sameness of repetition or parallelism obtains among
the Nephites at different periods showing the same limitations, and leading
to the same conclusions respecting the authorship of the Book of Mormon.

I begin with the appearance of Anti-Christs among the Nephites.
Of these there are about five, who appeared between 544 B.C. to 50 B.C.
The principal trait of all of them — as the term Anti-Christ would imply —
was a denial of the Christ, more especially of the fact of his coming.
This fact of the coming of the Christ in the flesh to redeem the world
was very plainly revealed to the Nephites, and their prophets dwelt upon
it with very great emphasis, and with startling clearness: whereas in the
Old Testament prophecies, as we know them, the matter of the coming
of the Christ and the purpose of his mission are somewhat veiled, and
without the aid of the interpretation afforded by the New Testament, it
would scarcely be discerned that the mission of the Christ was revealed
in the Old Testament. But among the Nephites, and also among the
Jaredite prophets, knowledge of the Christ and the fact of his coming
to bring to pass the redemption of man through atonement for sin is
the prevailing and protruding thought of all their visions and messages.
This is true in the case of Lehi, who led the little colony from Jerusalem,
I Nephi ch. 10, and more especially was it true of Nephi, his son, who
had a pre-vision of the birth, and life, and mission of the Christ and of
his apostles so vivid that it could almost be regarded as history rather
than prophecy (I Nephi chs. 11 and 12). Nephi sets forth the whole
Book of Mormon attitude upon the subject in the following passage:

"We labour diligently to write, to persuade our children, and also
our brethren, to believe in Christ, and to be reconciled to God; for we
know that it is by grace that we are saved, after all we can do. And
notwithstanding we believe in Christ, we keep the law of Moses, and
look forward with steadfastness unto Christ until the law shall be fulfilled;
for this end was the law given; wherefore the law hath become dead
unto us, and we are made alive in Christ, because of our faith; yet we
keep the law because of the commandments; and we talk of Christ, we
rejoice in Christ, we preach of Christ, we prophesy of Christ, and we

write according to our prophecies, that our children may know to what source they may look for a remission of their sins" (II Nephi 25:23-26).

It is the denial of this knowledge that the Anti-Christs of the Book of Mormon make as would be presumed from the descriptive term, "Anti-Christs."

The first of them was one Sherem, a "learned" man, who "had a perfect knowledge of the language of the people, wherefore he did use much flattery, had much power of speech according to the power of the devil." He arose in the life time of Jacob, brother of Nephi, therefore, he appears in a most ingratiating manner to Jacob. He had sought "much opportunity" to speak to Jacob (544-420 B.C.): "for I have heard," said he, "and I also know that thou goest about much, preaching that which ye call the gospel, or the doctrine of Christ. And ye have led away much of this people (it should be held in mind that the Nephite people were still few in number; by now, all told, not to exceed above two hundred) that they pervert the rightway of God, and keep not the law of Moses, which is the right way; and convert the law of Moses into the worship of a being which ye say shall come many hundred years hence. And now behold, I Sherem declare unto you that this is blasphemy; for no man knoweth of such things; for he cannot tell of things to come. And after this manner," adds Jacob, "did Sherem contend against me." "But behold, the Lord God poured in his Spirit into my soul, insomuch that I did confound him in all his words." The controversy then proceeds, Jacob speaking: "Deniest thou the Christ who should come? And he said: If there should be a Christ, I would not deny him; but I know that there is no Christ, neither has been, nor ever will be. And I said unto him; Believest thou the scriptures? And he said, Yea. And I said unto him. Then ye do not understand them; for they truly testify of Christ. Behold, I say unto you, that none of the prophets have written, nor prophesied, save they have spoken concerning this Christ. And this is not all: it has been made manifest unto me, for I have heard and seen; and it also has been made manifest unto me by the power of the Holy Ghost; wherefore, I know if there should be no atonement made, all mankind must be lost.

"And it came to pass that he said unto me, Shew me a sign by this power of the Holy Ghost, in the which ye know so much. And I said unto him, What am I that I should tempt God to shew unto thee a sign in the thing which thou knowest to be true? Yet thou wilt deny it, because thou art of the devil. Nevertheless, not my will be done; but if God shall smite thee, let that be a sign unto thee that he has power, both in heaven and in earth; and also that Christ shall come. And thy will, O Lord, be done, and not mine. And it came to pass that when I, Jacob, had spoken these words, the power of the Lord came upon him, insomuch, that he fell to the earth. And it came to pass that he was nourished for the space of many days. And it came to pass that he said unto the people, Gather together on the morrow, for I shall die; wherefore, I desire to speak unto the people before I shall die.

"And it came to pass that on the morrow the multitude were gathered together; and he spake plainly unto them and denied the things which he had taught them; and confessed the Christ, and the power of the Holy Ghost, and the ministering of angels. And he spake plainly unto them, that he had been deceived by the power of the devil. And he spake of hell, and of eternity, and of eternal punishment. And he said, I fear lest I have committed the unpardonable sin, for I have lied unto God; for I denied the Christ, and said that I believed the scriptures; and they truly testify of him. And because I have thus lied unto God, I greatly fear lest my case shall be awful; but I confess unto God. And it came to pass that when he had said these words, he could say no more, and he gave up the ghost. And when the multitude had witnessed that he spake these things as he was about to give up the ghost, they were astonished exceedingly; insomuch that the power of God came down upon them, and they were overcome, that they fell to the earth. Now, this thing was pleasing unto me, Jacob, for I had requested it of my Father who was in heaven: for he had heard my cry and answered my prayer. And it came to pass that peace and the love of God was restored again among the people; and they searched the scriptures, and hearkened no more to the words of this wicked man" (Jacob 7:1-23).

Thus the Nephite Christian triumphed over the stickler for the law of Moses, the Anti-Christ. I ask judgment upon this story as it stands. Is there not about it a certain "raw"ness? a certain amateurishness? In conception and handling the work of a boy—an undeveloped mind?

The next Anti-Christ was Nehor—some three hundred years after Sherem. He was a large man, and was noted for his much strength:

"And he had gone about among the people, preaching to them that which he termed to be the word of God, bearing down against the church; declaring unto the people that every priest, and teacher ought to become popular; and they ought not to labour with their hands, but that they ought to be supported by the people; and he also testified unto the people that all mankind should be saved at the last day, and that they need not fear nor tremble, but that they might lift up their heads and rejoice; for the Lord had created all men, and had also redeemed all men; and in the end, all men should have eternal life. And it came to pass that he did teach these things so much, that many did believe on his words, even so many that they began to support him and give him money; and he began to be lifted up in the pride of his heart and to wear very costly apparel; yea, and even began to establish a church after the manner of his preaching" (Alma 1:1-6).

Unhappily in a contention with an old Nephite hero — one Gideon — Nehor became enraged and killed him, for which crime he was tried and convicted and sentenced to execution: "And it came to pass that they took him; . . . and they carried him upon the top of the hill Manti, and there he was caused, or rather did acknowledge between the heavens and the earth, that what he had taught to the people was contrary to the word of God; and there he suffered an ignominious death" (Alma 1:2-15).

So passed away Nehor, the Anti-Christ. The story is somewhat different from that of Sherem in its viewpoint, but in the end confession of error by the Anti-Christ, an ignominious death, the triumph of the orthodox faith, the same amateurish spirit characterizing the narrative.

But while it was true that Nehor thus perished, his cult survived him; and a few years later, a Nephite prophet, Aaron by name, preaching to a faction among the Nephites called Amalekites, and at a place called Jerusalem, was opposed by one of Nehor's disciples, an Anti-Christ, in a small way. It was a controversy of the same color of the others thus far considered. "What is that which thou hast testified? Hast thou seen an angel? Why do not angels appear to us? . . . Thou sayest, except we repent we shall perish. . . . How knowest thou that we have cause to repent? . . . Behold, we have built sanctuaries and we do assemble ourselves together to worship God. We do believe that God will save all men."

And then the same old formula of the Nephite prophets:

"Now Aaron said unto him, Believest thou that the Son of God shall come to redeem mankind from their sins? And the man said unto him, We do not believe that thou knowest any such thing. We do not believe in these foolish traditions. We do not believe that thou knowest of things to come, neither do we believe that thy fathers, and also that our fathers did know concerning the things which they spake, of that which is to come. Now Aaron began to open the Scriptures unto them concerning the coming of Christ, and also concerning the resurrection of the dead, and that there could be no redemption for mankind, save it were through the death and sufferings of Christ, and the atonement of his blood. And it came to pass as he began to expound these things unto them, they were angry with him, and began to mock him; and they would not hear the words which he spake" (Alma 21).

And so Aaron withdrew from that city and went to another, a slight variation from the usual conclusions of these controversies, a variation, however, which only emphasizes the otherwise monotonous parallelism.

Twenty years later came Korihor: "and he was Anti-Christ, for he began to preach unto the people against the prophecies which had been spoken by the prophets concerning the coming of Christ." "And this

Anti-Christ . . . began to preach unto the people that there should be no Christ. And after this manner did he preach, saying:

"O ye that are bound down under a foolish and a vain hope, why do ye yoke yourselves with such foolish things? Why do ye look for a Christ? For no man can know of any thing which is to come. Behold, these things which ye call prophecies, which ye say are handed down by holy prophets, behold, they are foolish traditions of your fathers. How do ye know of their surety? Behold, ye cannot know of things which ye do not see; therefore ye cannot know that there shall be a Christ. Ye look forward and say that ye see a remission of your sins. But behold, it is the effect of a frenzied mind; and this derangement of your minds comes because of the traditions of your fathers, which lead you away into a belief of things which are not so. And many more such things did he say unto them, telling them that there could be no atonement made for the sins of men, but every man fared in this life according to the management of the creature; therefore every man prospered according to his genius, and that every man conquered according to his strength; and whatsoever a man did was no crime. And thus he did preach unto them, leading away the hearts of many, causing them to lift up their heads in their wickedness; yea, leading away many women, and also men, to commit whoredoms; telling them that when a man was dead, that was the end thereof."

So he proceeded through various parts of the land teaching these doctrines, until he was finally brought before the high priest of the land, Alma; and here the controversy was carried on in a manner strongly reminiscent of the controversy between Jacob and Sherem.

"And he (Korihor) did rise up in great swelling words before Alma, and did revile against the priests and teachers, accusing them of leading away the people after the silly traditions of their fathers, for the sake of glutting in the labors of the people."

This Alma denied: "And now if we do not receive anything for our labors in the church, what doth it profit us to labor in the church, save it were to declare the truth, that we may have rejoicings in the joy of our brethren? Then why sayest thou that we preach unto this people to get gain, when thou, of thyself, knowest that we receive no gain? And now, believest thou that we deceive this people, that causes such joy in their hearts? And Korihor answered him, Yea. And then Alma said unto him, Believest thou that there is a God? And he answered, Nay. Now Alma said unto him, Will ye deny again that there is a God, and also deny the Christ? For behold, I say unto you, I know there is a God, and also that Christ shall come. And now what evidence have ye that there is no God, or that Christ cometh not? I say unto you that ye have none, save it be your word only. But, behold, I have all things as a testimony that these things are true; and ye also have all things as a testimony unto you that they are true; and will ye deny them? Believest thou that these things are true? Behold, I know that thou believest, but thou art possessed with a lying spirit, and ye have put off the Spirit of God that it may have no place in you; but the devil has power over you, and he doth carry you about, working devices, that he may destroy the children of God. And now Korihor said unto Alma, If thou wilt shew me a sign, that I may be convinced that there is a God, yea, shew unto me that he hath power, and then will I be convinced of the truth of thy words.

"But Alma said unto him, Thou hast had signs enough; will ye tempt your God? Will ye say, Shew unto me a sign, when ye have the testimony of all these thy brethren, and also all the holy prophets? The scriptures are laid before thee, yea, and all things denote there is a God; yea, even the earth, and all things that are upon the face of it, yea, and its motion; yea, and also all the planets which move in their regular form, doth witness that there is a Supreme Creator; and yet do ye go about, leading away the hearts of this people, testifying unto them there is no God? And yet will ye deny against all these witnesses? And he said, Yea, I will deny, except ye shall shew me a sign. And now it came to pass that Alma said unto him, behold, I am grieved because of the hardness of your heart yea, that ye will still resist the Spirit of the truth, that thy soul may be destroyed. But behold, it is better that thy soul should be lost, than that thou shouldst be the means of bringing many souls down to destruction, by thy lying and by thy flattering words; therefore if thou shalt deny again, behold, God shall smite thee, that thou shalt become dumb, that thou shalt never open thy mouth any more, that thou shalt not deceive this people any more. Now Korihor said unto him, I do not deny the existence of a God, but I do not believe that there is a God; and I say also, that ye do not know that there is a God; and except ye shew me a sign, I will not believe. Now Alma said unto him, This will I give unto thee for a sign, that thou shalt be struck dumb, according to my words; and I say, that in the name of God, ye shall be struck dumb, that ye shall no more have utterance. Now when Alma had said these words, Korihor was struck dumb, that he could not have utterance, according to the words of Alma. And now when the Chief Judge saw this, he put forth his hand and wrote unto Korihor, saying: Art thou convinced of the power of God? In whom did ye desire that Alma should shew forth his sign? Behold, he has showed unto you a sign; and now will ye dispute more? And Korihor put forth his hand and wrote, saying: I know that I am dumb, for I cannot speak: and I know that nothing, save it were the power of God, could bring this upon me; yea, and I also knew that there was a God. But behold, the devil hath deceived me; for he appeared unto me in a form of an angel, and said unto me,

Go and reclaim this people, for they have all gone astray after an unknown God. And he said unto me, There is no God; yea, and he taught me that which I should say. And I have taught his words; and I taught them, because they were pleasing unto the carnal mind; and I taught them, even until I had much success, insomuch that I verily believed that they were true; and for this cause, I withstood the truth even until I have brought this great curse upon me. Now when he had said this, he besought that Alma should pray unto God, that the curse might be taken from him. But Alma said unto him, If this curse should be taken from thee, thou shouldst again lead away the hearts of this people; therefore, it shall be unto thee, even as the Lord will. And it came to pass that the curse was not taken off of Korihor; but he was cast out, and went about from house to house, begging for his food. Now the knowledge of what had happened unto Korihor was immediately published throughout all the land; yea, the proclamation was sent forth by the Chief Judge to all the people in the land, declaring unto those who had believed in the words of Korihor, that they must speedily repent, lest the same judgments would come unto them. And it came to pass that they were all convinced of the wickedness of Korihor; therefore they were all converted again unto the Lord; and this put an end to the iniquity after the manner of Korihor. And Korihor did go about from house to house, begging food for his support. And it came to pass that as he went forth among the people, yea, among a people who had separated themselves from the Nephites, and called themselves Zoramites, being led by a man whose name was Zoram; and as he went forth amongst them, behold, he was run upon and trodden down, even until he was dead; and thus we see the end of him who perverteth the ways of the Lord; and thus we see that the devil will not support his children at the last day, but doth speedily drag them down to hell" (Alma 30).

I shall not apologize for giving the story at so great length. It is instructive. The two Anti-Christs — Sherem and Korihor — the stories of their unbelief and the treatment of them, how alike they are! In both the denial of the Christ; the charge against the ministry, that they mislead the people; that they could not know of things yet future; the denial of the Christ, and of the scriptures; the same method of attack by the prophets — "believest thou the scriptures?" "deniest thou the Christ," "believest thou there is a God"? The same hesitancy on the part of the Anti-Christ in answering directly; the same demand for a sign. The same hesitancy on the part of the prophet to invoke the power of God in a sign. In both cases the sign given upon the person of the blasphemer; in one case stricken that he fell of a mortal sickness; in the other stricken with dumbness, shortly afterwards to be run over and trodden to death. In both cases a confession of being deceived by the devil and in both cases a vain repentance. When the people saw what befell Sherem, they were so overcome, "that they fell to the earth. . . . And it came to pass that peace and the love of God was restored again among the people." And when the people throughout the land learned what had happened to Korihor, "it came to pass that they were all convinced of the wickedness of Korihor; therefore they were all converted again unto the Lord."

But in addition to the striking parallelism in these incidents of Anti-Christs of the Book of Mormon, with the strong implication that they have their origin in one mind, I call attention again to the fact of "rawness" in dealing with this question of unbelief, the evidence of "amateurishness" increasingly evident in this story of Korihor. Does it not carry with it the proof that it is the work of a pious youth dealing with the very common place stock arguments clumsily put together for the belief in the existence of God, with an awkward turning from the request for a special miracle, in proof of God's existence, to the standing miracle of the creation and an orderly universe for that truth, rather than an adult appeal and argument on the great questions involved? And is not the vindication of God and his truth by a vindictive miracle on the person of the ranting blasphemer, rather the dream of a pious boy of what might very well have happened, rather than a matter of actual experience?

There were other Anti-Christs among the Nephites, but they were more military leaders than religious innovators, yet much of the same kidney in spirit with these dissenters here passed in review; but I shall hold that what is here presented illustrates sufficiently the matter taken in hand by referring to them, namely that they are all of one breed and brand; so nearly alike that one mind is the author of them, and that a young and undeveloped, but piously inclined mind. The evidence I sorrowfully submit, points to Joseph Smith as their creator. It is difficult to believe that they are the product of history, that they come upon the scene separated by long periods of time, and among a race which was the ancestral race of the red man of America.

IV

PARALLELS CONTINUED: WAR CHIEFTAINS; WAR METHODS AND
PRINCIPLES; MIRACLES AND ABSURDITIES; NEPHITE AND JAREDITE WAR
OF EXTINCTION; THE QUESTION OF HISTORY OR WONDER-TALE

The parallelism which I have noted first between Jaredite and Nephite experiences and traits, and now among Nephites at different periods in respect of the Anti-Christs who appear among them, holds also as to their military chieftains and their methods of warfare. I shall not follow this, however, in the same detail as in the case of their Anti-Christs, but it is just as true in the one case as the other.

In the method of carrying on war, and in the descriptions of battles, the same tendency to repetition, to recurrence to the marvelous is found. The cause of war seems to be always the same, or else without cause — they seem to be wars just stuck in at supposed needed intervals — especially during the earlier centuries of Nephite history — with monotonous regularity. The battles were bloody, heroic, and often attended with marvelous personal encounters between the leaders. The whole matter of war seems to be treated from the amateurish notion that the wicked are invariably punished, the righteous always victorious. The whole treatment of war and battles, some will say, bears evidence of having originated in one mind and that mind pious but immature.

As an illustration of the amazingly miraculous events connected with Nephite wars, reference is made to the performances of a corps of 2,000 — ultimately 2,060 — young men, "striplings," who fought through what could appropriately be called the Thirteen Years War, since it lasted that long — 73 B.C. to 60 B.C. These "striplings" fought in many battles, *yet none of them were killed.* They were the sons of a Lamanite colony brought from among that people by one of the many Nephite missionary expeditions among the Lamanites. This colony had contracted such a hatred for war that they entered into an oath-binding covenant that they would not resort to war under any circumstances, no, not even in self-defense; and many of them when put to the test, being assailed by their Lamanite kindred, suffered death without resistance. It was to preserve them from such assaults that they had been brought into Nephite lands. But when they saw their Nephite friends sorely beset by Lamanite armies, they were tempted to break their oath. This their religious leaders would not consent to. Then they bethought themselves of the sons born to them in Nephite lands who were not under this oath, and these were desirous of taking up arms in aid of their friends, the Nephites. This they did, under the leadership of one Helaman, more prophet than military leader, and they performed prodigies of valor and prowess in the war, but none of them could be killed in battle. For their mothers had taught them that by having faith God would protect them; "if they did not doubt, God would deliver them." "We do not doubt," they said in telling Helaman of their faith — "We do not doubt our mothers knew"! "Never were men known," says Helaman in relating the story of their valor, "to have fought with such miraculous strength; and with such mighty power did they fall upon the Lamanites that they did frighten them." Often they saved the day at critical periods of battle, and though many of them were wounded, yet none were slain, to the amazement of both armies. On one occasion two hundred of the 2,060 "fainted because of loss of blood." "Nevertheless according to the goodness of God . . . not one soul of them did perish." "Yea," and speaking of this same particular battle, *"neither was there one soul among them who had not received many wounds"*!

Beautiful story of faith! Beautiful story of mother-assurance! Is it history? Or is it a wonder-tale of a pious but immature mind?

In some cases blundering expressions bordering on comedy are found in recounting war events. This for instance. A Lamanite army is summoned to surrender, "and when they heard the words of Moroni, their chief captains, *all those who were not slain*(!) came forth and threw down their weapons of war at the feet of Moroni."

Again in describing a Nephite mobilization of the people preparatory to a war—about 16 A.D.—it is said that the chief judge "sent a proclamation among all the people that they should gather together their women and children, their flocks and their herds, and all their substance, *save it were their land unto* one place"(!) (III Nephi 3:13); and still again, in describing a mobilization of the Jaredites, preparatory to their battles which were to end in their extermination, it is recorded that "they did gather together all the people, upon the face of the land, who had not been slain"(!) (Ether 15:12).

On one occasion the Nephites captured a city by getting the Lamanite guards drunk. The Lamanites sought reprisals in kind, but without success. "Many times did they attempt to minister their wine to the Nephites, that they might destroy them with poison or with drunkenness," but the Nephites were "not to be taken in their snares." Imitators are seldom successful. The Nephites "would not partake of their wine, save they had first given to some of the Lamanite prisoners." "They were thus cautious that no poison should be administered among them." Then this solemn asseveration: *"For if their wine would poison a Lamanite, it would also poison a Nephite"*! "And thus they did try all their liquors" (Alma 55).

By a peaceful revolution in 91 B.C. the form of Nephite government was changed from monarchy to a republic, or "reign of judges," chosen by the "voice of the people"; and a number of their most sanguinary wars were occasioned by efforts of men "who would be kings" to overthrow the republic and reestablish monarchy in its stead. The great Thirteen Years War was occasioned by such a purpose. One Moroni, perhaps the most heroic of all the Book of Mormon heroes, a staunch republican, and one who patriotically held democracy to his heart, was the leader of the Nephite forces during this Thirteen Years War. At one time he found the civil forces within the capital city, Zarahemla, and other central positions of the land, were not responding to the needs of his own and other armies in the field for fresh levies of men and provisions; that there had come about a suspension of activities and co-ordination of the civil with the military authorities. As a result the armies in the field were unable to maintain themselves against the enemy. Cities they had taken from the Lamanites at great cost were retaken by the enemy; the tide of war was running against the Nephites, and it looked as if they must be overwhelmed. Under these circumstances Moroni "wrote epistles" to the chief judge at Zarahemla. The first earnestly protesting the apparent neglect of the civil authorities. This producing no results, the second "Epistle" was written in anger. In his wrath Moroni apparently forgot the existence of the "republic," and said: "We desire to know the cause of this exceeding great neglect; yea, we desire to know the cause of your thoughtless state. *Can you think to sit on your thrones in a state of thoughtless stupor*, while your enemies are spreading the work of death around you?" He seemed to like this form of appeal for later in the epistle he returns to it: "Behold, could ye suppose that *ye could sit upon your thrones*, and because of the goodness of God ye could do nothing and he would deliver you?" (Alma 60:7, 11).

Also there was a break in these epistles, in the usually accepted philosophy governing in Nephite warfare — viz., and roughly — be good and you will win wars. This new departure was evidently taught by the sanguinary character of this war with its successes and its losses surging first from one side to the other. "Do you suppose," wrote Moroni, "that because so many of your brethren have been killed, it is because of their wickedness? I say unto you, if ye have supposed this, ye have supposed in vain: for I say unto you, there are many who have fallen by the sword; and behold it is to your condemnation: for the Lord suffereth the righteous to be slain that his justice and judgment may come upon the wicked; therefore ye need not suppose that the righteous are lost because they are slain; but behold, they do enter into the rest of the Lord their God" (Alma 60:12, 13).

Also Moroni almost slipped in these epistles, in his inspirational or prophetic knowledge of conditions existing in the interior of the republic. He had assumed in his epistles to the chief executive judge, Pahoran, head of the civil administration—that the failure to support him and his armies was due to the indifference and wickedness of those in civil authority. Hence in his admonition to Pahoran to *"begin to be up and doing"* (Alma 60:24) and to "bestir" himself in the defense of his country, he said: *"Ye know that ye do transgress the laws of God, and ye do know that ye do trample them under your feet. Behold, the Lord saith unto me, if those whom ye have appointed your governors do not repent of their sins and iniquities, ye shall go up to battle against them."* Now the facts were that the chief judge and the legally constituted authorities at Zarahemla had had a rebellion on their hands; a civil war broke out and had overthrown the civil authority. Pahoran, the chief judge, who was just as patriotic as Moroni, had been driven from the capital city to Gideon. "King men were established in usurped power at the capital, and were negotiating an alliance with the King of the Lamanites."

Moroni on hearing this by return epistle from Pahoran marched an army to Zarahemla, put down the rebellion, and restored Pahoran; after which Nephite affairs ran smoothly. But what of Moroni's inspired conception of the cause of the interrupted co-ordination of the civil with the military powers, and his commandment from the Lord to go up to battle against "those whom ye have appointed your governors," if they "do not repent of their sins" etc. (For above cf. Alma 60; 61).

This Thirteen Years War was full of wordy heroics, ecstatic preachments, and miracles. As an example of this General Moroni, early in the war, dramatically raised what was really a standard of liberty, called by him, however, "The Title of Liberty." This he raised against the King men among the Nephites. Four thousand of these were hewn down by the sword, and their leaders cast into prison, and those that remained were compelled "to hoist the Title of Liberty upon their towers and in their cities. . . . And thus he (Moroni) put an end to the stubbornness and the pride of those people who professed the blood of nobility."

This "Title of Liberty" was born of the patriotic fervor of Moroni, angered upon hearing of the dissensions of the King men among the Nephites, even while he was preparing armies against the threatened invasion of the Nephite lands.

"It came to pass that he rent his coat; and he took a piece thereof, and wrote upon it.

"*'In memory of our God, our religion, and freedom, and our peace, our wives, and our children'; and he fastened it* upon the end of a pole thereof.

"And he fastened on his head-plate, and his breast-plate, and his shields, and girded on his armour about his loins; and he took the pole, which had on the end thereof his rent coat (and he called it the Title of Liberty), and he bowed himself to the earth, and he prayed mightily unto his God, for the blessings of liberty to rest upon his brethren so long as there should a band of Christians remain to possess the land; for thus were all the true believers of Christ, who belonged to the church of God, called by those who did not belong to the church; and those who did belong to the church were faithful; yea, all those who were true believers in Christ, took upon them gladly, the name of Christ or Christians, as they were called, because of their belief in Christ, who should come.

"And therefore, at this time, Moroni prayed that the cause of the Christians, and the freedom of the land might be favored. (This, it should be remembered, was in 73 or 70 B.C.) And it came to pass that when he had poured out his soul to God, he gave all the land which was south of the land Desolation: yea, and in fine, all the land, both on the north and on the south, a chosen land, and the land of liberty. And he said, surely God shall not suffer that we, who are despised because we take upon us the name of Christ, shall be trodden down and destroyed, until we bring it upon us by our own transgressions. And when Moroni had said these words, he went forth among the people, waving the rent of his garment in the air, that all might see the writing which he had wrote upon the rent, and crying with a loud voice, saying (The committee editing the current or 1921 edition of the Book of Mormon have taken large liberties with the text of the first edition, and also with many subsequent editions of the book—in this chapter, in order to get rid of the supposed absurdity of *"waving the rent of his coat,"* that the people might see what "he had wrote upon the rent." I doubt if the editors have much improved it; and in any event, in this writing we are entitled to use the text of the first edition. p. [351]):

"Behold, whosoever will maintain this title upon the land, let them come forth in the strength of the Lord, and enter into a covenant that they will maintain their rights, and their religion, that the Lord God may bless them. And it came to pass that when Moroni had proclaimed these words, behold, the people came running together with their armours girded about their loins, rending their garments in token, or as a covenant, that they would not forsake the Lord their God, or, in other words, if they should transgress the commandments of God, or fall into transgression, and be ashamed to take upon them the name of Christ, the Lord should rend them even as they had rent their garments" (Alma 46).

"Surely," someone will say, "this is dramatically heroic enough to satisfy the wildest desire of a pious boy of fervid imagination." Also written clumsily enough to justify the thought that it was written by one ignorant of English composition; and others will think the phrases of the passage too closely akin to New Testament phraseology about "Christ" and "Christians" to be used in far off America about 70 B.C.

In fine antithesis to the virtuous, patriotic and heroic leadership of the Nephites was the leadership of the Lamanites. The chief Lamanite commanders were the ideal villainous leaders of bad causes. Amalickiah, who started the revolt leading to this Thirteen Years War, was "a large and strong man"; also "a cunning man," and a man of many flattering words, by which he "seduced the people" from their allegiance to democratic principles and government — unscrupulous, treacherous. Of Ammoron, the brother of Amalickiah, and who succeeded that brother in Lamanite leadership of the war, we know nothing physically, but for the rest we know him haughty, courageous, an atheist, bitter in his hatred of the Nephites, whom he regarded as usurpers of power in the land. He was descendant of that Zoram, servant of Laban, keeper of the records of the house of Joseph, at Jerusalem, whom Nephi pursuaded to join Lehi's colony, but to whom Ammoran refers in a letter to Moroni, as "Zoram, whom your fathers pressed and brought out of Jerusalem." He closed his epistle, in bombastic phraseology which some would say was well suited to a school boy's "defi" of the times which witnessed the incubation of the Book of Mormon, and of the vicinage:

"Behold, I am a bold Nephite; . . . And I close my epistle to Moroni."

The allusions here to absurdities of expressions and incidents in the Book of Mormon are not made for the purpose of ridiculing the book, or casting undue aspersions upon it; but they are made to indicate what may be fairly regarded as just objects of criticism under the assumption that the Book of Mormon is of human origin, and that Joseph Smith is its author. For these absurdities in expression; these miraculous incidents in warfare; those almost mock — and certainly extravagant — heroics; these lapses of the main characters about conditions obtaining, are certainly just such absurdities and lapses as would be looked for if a person of such limitations as bounded Joseph Smith undertook to put forth a book dealing with the history and civilization of ancient peoples.

Only one more reference to Nephite wars will be necessary — and this the war that destroyed their civilization and annihilated them as a people. This war is mentioned here because it will bring us once more face to face with that strange parallelism we have found so many times in Book of Mormon events. This time it will have to do with so important a matter as a war of extinction of two peoples, the Nephites and the Jaredites, on the self same battle site, with the same "hill" marking the axis of military movements. By the Nephites this "hill" was called the "Hill Cumorah," by the Jaredites the "Hill Ramah"; it was that same "hill," in which the Nephite records were deposited by Mormon and Moroni, and from which Joseph Smith obtained the Book of Mormon, therefore the "Mormon Hill," of today — since the coming forth of the Book of Mormon — near Palmyra, New York. For identification of the "Hill Cumorah" with the "Hill Ramah" of the Jaredites, cf. Mormon 6:1-11; and Ether 15:11. Also in Oliver Cowdery's Letters on "Early Scenes and Incidents in Church History" there is an identification of Cumorah and Ramah.[17] It will be remembered that Cowdery was associated with Joseph Smith in bringing forth the Book of Mormon, and hence would be capable of interpreting the statements of the book. This word on identification of Cumorah with Ramah, because certain students of Book of Mormon geography want to be rid of the necessity of both Jaredites and Nephites being extended so far northward as Cumorah.

But now to deal the last war between the Nephites and Lamanites, about Cumorah-Ramah, and their parallelisms.

This last war here to be considered in many respects was similar to the Great Robber War of 16 A.D., and more especially in respect to the mobilization of the people. This mobilization in the Robber War is also reminiscent of and even more like the last Jaredite mobilization than the Nephite. The fact that there are three mobilizations, each resembling the other, emphasizes the parallelisms we are noting in Book of Mormon wars.

The Robber War came about as follows:

Of course the conversion of the people at the time the "sign" of Messiah's birth was given was nearly universal both among Nephites and Lamanites; but immediately "then began to be lyings sent forth among the people by Satan, to harden their hearts to the intent that they might not believe in those signs and wonders which they had seen; but notwithstanding these lyings and deceivings the more part of the people did believe" (III Nephi 1:22). Still insidious heresies respecting the relation of the law of Moses to the Christian faith, now that the sign of the Christ's coming had been given, brought division among believers; also there was wickedness in "the rising generation" that played havoc with the faith of the believing Lamanites who had been converted by the "sign." The secret cult, the "Gadianton robbers," brought into existence by one Gadianton about 50 B.C., now also arose to plague the people. This Gadianton was an "expert" in deviltry, and especially "expert in many words, and also in his craft to carry on the secret work of murder and robbery." He it was who founded the evil cult which ever after bore his name (Helaman 2). An uprising of this band brought on the Great Robber War.

It took on all the usual characteristics of a Book of Mormon war. Giddianhi was the leader of the Gadiantons; Gidgiddon was the chief commander of the Nephite armies. The Lamanite leader was the typical leader of bad causes. The Nephite commander—"This Gidgiddoni"—was a righteous man and a great prophet among the Nephites as was also the chief judge. There was the same exchange of war epistles, as in the case of Moroni and Ammoron, and later between Mormon and the Lamanite king—insolence on the part of the Lamanite chieftain, silence or defiance on the part of the Nephite commanders.

There was the same gathering together of the people—men, women and children—with movable goods and chattels—to *one place*, as later occurred at Cumorah. It was this proclamation ordering the mobilization that contained the unguarded invitation to sarcasm already noted in a former paragraph, commanding that the people, should gather together their women and children, the flocks and their herds and all their substance, "*save it were their land,* unto one place." And this they did, taking "their horses and their chariots and their cattle, and all their flocks and their herds and their grain and all their substance, and did march forth by thousands and tens of thousands until they had all gone forth to the place which had been appointed" (III Nephi 3; cf. Mormon 6; also cf. Ether 15:11-15). When all preparations were ended the war began. "And (speaking of the first engagement) great and terrible was the battle thereof, yea, and great and terrible was the slaughter thereof, insomuch that there never was known so great a slaughter among all the people of Lehi since he left Jerusalem."* This must have been said while the great battles of the Thirteen Years War was fresh in the mind of the Nephite Historian!

The Nephites were victorious. Giddianhi was slain, "and thus was the end of Giddianhi." It comes like a refrain of a familiar song, this accounting for the disastrous ending of Lamanite leaders. Giddianhi was succeeded by one Zemnariah—the succession is a close repetition of the succession of Lamanite leaders in the Thirteen Years War, in the case of Amalickiah and Ammoron; and as in that instance this second leader was over come and slain dramatically, hanged on a tree, in fact, the tree was felled, the people with a loud voice, saying—

"May the Lord preserve his people in righteousness and in holiness of heart, that they may cause to be felled to the earth all who shall seek to slay them because of power and secret combinations, even as this man hath been felled to the earth. And they did rejoice and cry again with one voice, saying, May the God of Abraham, and the God of Isaac, and the God of Jacob, protect this people in righteousness, so long as they shall call on the name of their God for protection" (III Nephi 4:29, 30).

And now to deal with the last war between the Nephites and the Lamanites.

---

* This appears to be a favorite expression with the author of the Book of Mormon. It is said of the great battle fought by Nephites and Lamanites in 77 B.C. when "tens of thousands of Lamanites were slain or scattered abroad" (Alma 28).

The Nephite Concentration, 400 A.D.

After a long war, in which many battles with varying success had been fought, Mormon, the chief general of the Nephite forces, wrote an epistle to the king of the Lamanites expressing the desire that he would grant that the Nephite people might gather "to the land of Cumorah, by a hill which is called (Cowdery's letters, the latest publication of them, will be found in *Improvement Era*, for 1898 Vol. II.[18] They were first published in the *Saints Messenger and Advocate*, Kirtland, Ohio, 1834, No. I dated September 7th.) Cumorah, and there we would give them battle." This request was allowed:

"And it came to pass that we did march forth to the land of Cumorah, and we did pitch our tents round about the hill Cumorah; and it was in a land of many waters, rivers, and fountains; and here we had hope to gain advantage over the Lamanites. And when three hundred and eighty and four years had passed away, we had gathered in all the remainder of our people unto the land Cumorah. And it came to pass that . . . we had gathered in all our people in one to the land of Cumorah."

The Jaredite Concentration, 600 B.C.

And now for the Jaredites concentration one thousand years before this Mormon Nephite period. The opposing commanders Coriantumr and Shiz:

After a protracted war, in which many battles had been fought with varying success, the armies of Coriantumr "came to the waters of Ripliancum, which by interpretation is large or to exceed all" — "the land of many waters" in Mormon's description — and both descriptions met by great and small lake conditions in the western New York State. Here a battle was fought and Coriantumr's armies were successful, and Shiz and his army fled southward.

But the army of Coriantumr "did pitch their tents by the hill Ramah, and it was the same hill," says Moroni, who relates the story, "where my father Mormon did hide up the records unto the Lord which were sacred." Then began the Jaredite concentration at that place.

"And it came to pass that they did gather together all the people, upon all the face of the land, who had not been slain . . . and the people who were for Coriantumr, were gathered together to the army of Coriantumr; and the people who were for Shiz, were gathered together to the army of Shiz; wherefore they were for the space of four years, gathering together the people, that they might get all who were upon the face of the land, and that they might receive all the strength which it was possible that they could receive."

Opening of the Nephite Series of Battles Leading to Extermination of the Nephites

"And it came to pass that my people, with their wives and their children, did now behold the armies of the Lamanites marching towards them; and with that awful fear of death which fills the breasts of all the wicked did they await to receive them. And it came to pass that they came to battle against us, and every soul was filled with terror, because of the greatness of their numbers."

Opening of the Jaredite Series of Battles Leading to Extermination of Jaredites

"And it came to pass that when they were all gathered together, every one to the army which he would, with their wives and their children; both men, women and children being armed with weapons of war, having shields, and breast-plates, and head-plates, and being clothed after the manner of war, they did march forth one against another, to battle; and they fought all that day, and conquered not."

Progress of the Nephite Battle, Lamantations for the Slain

"And it came to pass that they did fall upon my people with the sword, and with the bow, and with the arrow, and with the axe, and with all manner of weapons of war. And it came to pass that my men were hewn down, yea, even my ten thousand who were with me, and I fell wounded in the midst; and they passed by me that they did not put an end to my life. And when they had gone through and hewn down all my people save it were twenty and four of us (among whom was my son Moroni) and we having survived the dead of our people, did behold on the morrow, when the Lamanites had returned unto their camps, from the top of the hill Cumorah, the ten thousand of my people who were hewn down, being led in the front by me; and we also beheld the ten thousand of my people who were led by my son Moroni."

So Mormon continues to enumerate divisions of ten thousands, until an army of men of 240,000 are accounted for, and, of course the women and children belonging to these armies, "Yea, even all my people," said Mormon, "save it were those twenty and four who were with me, and also a few who had escaped into the south countries, and a few who had deserted over unto the Lamanites." These twenty-four, including General Mormon himself, were all afterwards slain, except Moroni; and the few who escaped to the south country were also "destroyed." So for the Nephites it was a war of utter extinction: All "had fallen," lamented Mormon as he viewed the slain from the summit of Cumorah; "and their flesh, and bones, and blood lay upon the face of the earth, being left by the hands of those who slew them, to moulder upon the land, and to crumble and to return to their mother earth. And my soul was rent with anguish, because of the slain of my people, and I cried, O ye fair ones, how could ye have departed from the ways of the Lord! . . . O ye fair sons and daughters, ye fathers and mothers ye husbands and wives, ye fair ones, how is it that ye could have fallen! But behold, ye are gone, and my sorrows cannot bring your return." And more to the same effect.

Progress of the Jaredite Battles; Lamentations for the Slain

"And it came to pass that when it was night they were weary, and retired to their camps; and after they had retired to their camps (this was the second day of the battle), they took up a howling and a lamentation for the loss of the slain of their people; and so great were their cries, their howlings and lamentations, that it did rend the air exceedingly. And it came to pass that on the morrow they did go again to battle, and great and terrible was that day; nevertheless they conquered not, and when the night came again, they did rend the air with their cries, and their howlings, and their mournings, for the loss of the slain of their people. . . . But behold, the Spirit of the Lord had ceased striving with them, and Satan had full power over the hearts of the people, for they were given up unto the hardness of their hearts, and the blindness of their minds that they might be destroyed; wherefore they went again to battle." So they continued fighting day after day until millions had wasted away to thirty two men on the one side, to 27 men on the other. These "were large and mighty men. And they slept and prepared for death on the morrow." They fought for three hours the next day, and then "fainted with the loss of blood." Coriantumr's men sought to escape by flight, but it was vain; all were slain until the two leaders alone remained; and one of these, Shiz, had fainted "with the loss of blood." "And it came to pass, when Coriantumr had leaned upon his sword, that he rested a little, he smote off the head of Shiz. *And it came to pass,* that after he had smitten off the head of Shiz, that Shiz raised upon his hand and fell; and after that he had struggled for breath, he died."

Coriantumr wandered about some time alone, and at last fell in with the colony of Mulek, which about this time arrived in America, with whom he died.

The Two Witnesses to these Annihilations — Moroni and Ether

Of these wars of extinction each had its witness. The Nephite witness was

Moroni: he participated actively in the last battle of his people, while the Jaredite witness did not. Still the important part assigned to Moroni was that of witnessing and recording these last scenes connected with his people. He wandered about alone, adding from time to time to the record he was making, until he came to his uncertain end — in what manner and where he died, we know not.

Ether: Ether did not participate as a warrior in the last battles of his people. He dwelt in the cavity of a rock by day, and went forth only by night to note the progress of Jaredite destruction. And after the duel between Coriantumr and Shiz, in which Shiz was slain and "Coriantumr fell to the earth and became as if he had no life"; then "the Lord spake unto Ether, and said unto him, Go forth. And he went forth, and beheld that the words of the Lord had all been fulfilled; and he finished his record."

The Last Words of the Witnesses

Moroni: "And now I bid unto all, farewell. I soon go to rest in the paradise of God, until my spirit and body shall again re-unite, and I am brought forth triumphant through the air, to meet you before the pleasing bar of the great Jehovah, the eternal Judge of both quick and dead. Amen."

Ether: "Now the last words which are written by Ether, are these whether the Lord will that I be translated, or that I suffer the will of the Lord in the flesh, it mattereth not, if it so be that I am saved in the kingdom of God. Amen."

In all this war of extinction, and destruction there is only one important variation, and that is that in the case of the Jaredites, the annihilation was complete for both sides down to the last man; in the case of the Nephites and Lamanites only the Nephites were wholly annihilated; the Lamanites, their opponents, survived but only in a state of anarchy leading ultimately to the barbarism and semi-barbarism in which they were found by the Europeans a thousand years afterward.

And now, I doubt not, at the conclusion of this review of the Nephite and Jaredite wars of extinction, some will be led to exclaim — and I will set it down for them — "Is all this sober history inspired written and true, representing things that actually happened? Or is it a wonder-tale of an immature mind, unconscious of what a test he is laying on human credulity when asking men to accept his narrative as solemn history?"

V

PARALLELISM IN THE BOOK OF MORMON! THE SIMILARITY OF
CONVERSIONS IN THE DIFFERENT PERIODS OF BOOK OF MORMON
HISTORY AND THE LIKENESS OF THESE TO THE CHRISTIAN CONVERSIONS
OF THE PERIOD AND VICINAGE WHEN AND WHERE THE BOOK OF
MORMON WAS "TRANSLATED" AND PUBLISHED

It should be remembered that Book of Mormon peoples were granted
an exceptionally clear understanding by revealed knowledge of the life,
mission and character of the Christ, and of the purpose of the Gospel.
Although required to live under the law of Moses until the coming of
Messiah in the flesh, yet they lived in anticipation of the coming of the
Christ, and believed in the necessity and effectiveness of the Saviour to
come, and of his Gospel. So that "conversions" among Book of Mormon
peoples relate to conversions to the Christ that was to come, and to the
Gospel as the plan for man's salvation—happily called, in some places
"the plan of happiness." The first Nephi, as early as the sixth century
B.C., taught that there was "none other name given under heaven save
it be this Jesus Christ . . . whereby man can be saved." Also he said:
"We labor diligently to write, to persuade our children, and also our
brethren, to believe in Christ, and to be reconciled to God"; also *we
know that it is by the grace of God that we are saved, after all that we
can do.* And notwithstanding we believe in Christ, we keep the law of
Moses, and look forward with steadfastness unto Christ, until the law
shall be fulfilled; for, for this end was the law given; wherefore the law
hath become dead unto us, and we are made alive in Christ, because of
our faith; yet we keep the law because of the commandments" (II Nephi
25). And this runs throughout the book; so that "conversion" in the
Book of Mormon has reference to conversion to the Christ and his
Gospel—to Christian conversion. And these conversions, I say in my
headlines to this division, and also religious experiences after conversion,
I would add, are alluded throughout various periods of the Book of
Mormon by the same emotional phenomena—faintings or swoonings,
"the falling power," unconsciousness, and usually attended by visions or
ecstasies of supposed highly spiritual experiences.

This sort of thing begins in the very first chapter of the Book of
Mormon, and with its first prophet Lehi. This man who had lived all
his days in Jerusalem, and who was a very pious man, heard certain
prophets prophesying unto the people of that city, saying that they must
repent or the city would be destroyed:

"Wherefore it came to pass that my father, Lehi, as he went forth,
prayed unto the Lord, yea, even with all his heart, in behalf of his people.

And it came to pass, as he prayed unto the Lord, there came a pillar of fire and dwelt upon a rock before him; and he saw and heard much; and because of the things which he saw and heard, he did quake and tremble exceedingly. And it came to pass that he returned to his own house at Jerusalem; and he cast himself upon his bed, being overcome with the Spirit and the things which he had seen.

"And being thus overcome with the Spirit, he was carried away in a vision, even that he saw the heavens open, and he thought he saw God sitting upon his throne, surrounded with numberless concourses of angels in the attitude of singing and praising their God. And it came to pass that he saw one descending out of the midst of heaven, and he beheld that his lustre was above that of the sun at noon day; and he also saw twelve others following him, and their brightness did exceed that of the stars in the firmament; and they came down and went forth upon the face of the earth; and the first came and stood before my father, and gave unto him a book, and bade him that he should read. And it came to pass that as he read, he was filled with the Spirit of the Lord, and he read, saying, Wo, wo unto Jerusalem! for I have seen thine abominations; yea, and many things did my father read concerning Jerusalem that it should be destroyed, and the inhabitants thereof, many should perish by the sword, and many should be carried away captive into Babylon. And it came to pass that when my father had read and saw many great and marvelous things, he did exclaim many things unto the Lord; such as great and marvelous are thy works, O Lord God Almighty! Thy throne is high in the heavens, and thy power, and goodness, and mercy are over all the inhabitants of the earth; and because thou art merciful, thou wilt not suffer those who come unto thee that they shall perish! And after this manner was the language of my father in the praising of his God; for his soul did rejoice, and his whole heart was filled, because of the things which he had seen; yea, which the Lord had shewn unto him."

I quote this at such length because it is so typical both of what we shall find in various parts of the Book of Mormon, and of the period in the early decades of the 19th century when the Book of Mormon was incubated.

The first Nephi also was given similar rapturous vision, for he desired to see the same things that his father had seen, and as he sat pondering these things in his heart he was "caught away in the spirit of the Lord, yea into an exceeding high mountain," he says, "which I had never before seen"; and there his father's visions were given unto him and even more extended ones, and more marvelous. He returned to the tent of his father and became the interpreter of these things to his brethren.

Also he was subject to the same ecstasy as was his father, both in seeing visions and in fervor of teaching: "I glory in plainness; I glory in truth; I glory in my Jesus, for he hath redeemed my soul from hell. I have charity for my people, and great faith in Christ, that I shall meet many souls spotless at his judgment seat" (II Nephi 33:6, 7).

And when this young prophet was resisted in his preachments to his older brethren he was so filled with this "power of God" that it was dangerous to oppose him. On one occasion when they were tempted in their anger to throw him into the depths of the sea, and came forth to lay their hands upon him, he said: "In the name of the Almighty God, I command you that ye touch me not, for I am filled with the power of God, even unto the consuming of my flesh; and whoso shall lay their hands upon me, shall wither even as a dried reed; and he shall be as naught before the power of God, for God shall smite him." After this outburst the elder brothers dare not touch him "so powerful was the spirit of God" upon Nephi, and "so had it wrought upon them," his brethren.

Then there was relenting, and the Lord told Nephi to stretch forth his hand to his brethren and touch them, and they should not wither, but the contact should "shock them. This that they may know that I am the Lord their God," said the Lord to Nephi, and this was done; "and the Lord did shake them." Then the elder brothers said to Nephi: "We know of a surety that the Lord is with thee, for we know that it is the power of the Lord that has shaken us. And they fell down before me, and were about to worship me, but I would not suffer them, saying I am thy brother, yea, even thy younger brother; wherefore, worship the Lord thy God, and honour thy father and thy mother, that thy days may be long in the land which the Lord thy God shall give thee" (I Nephi 17). The closing admonition was doubtless needful as those to whom it was addressed had been in frequent disobedience and rebellion against their father.

Another early Nephite character—544-421 B.C.—one Enos, son of Jacob, brother of the first Nephi, tells of his conversion:

"My father . . . he was a just man . . . and blessed by God for it (!) and I will tell you of the wrestle which I had before God, before I received a remission of my sins. Behold, I went to hunt beasts in the forest; and the words which I had often heard my father speak concerning eternal life, and the joy of the saints, sunk deep into my heart. And my soul hungered; and I kneeled down before my Maker, and I cried unto him in mighty prayer and supplication for mine own soul; and all the day long did I raise my voice high that it reached the heavens. And there came a voice unto me, saying, Enos, thy sins are forgiven thee, and thou shalt be blessed, and I, Enos, knew that God could not lie, wherefore, my guilt was swept away. And I said, Lord, how is it done? And he said unto me, Because of thy faith in Christ, whom thou hast never before heard nor seen. And many years pass away, before he shall manifest himself in the flesh; wherefore, go to, thy faith hath made thee whole" (Enos 1:2-8).

How like to a good Christian "'experience' this is," some will be led to exclaim, "of the period of 1820-1830"?

About 100 B.C. one Alma—he was the son of the high priest of the Church whose name also was Alma—was about to overthrow the Church by reason of his cunning and flattery, "for he was a man of many words . . . therefore he led many of the people to do after the manner of his iniquities." Joining with the four sons of the reigning king, they were playing, joining with the four sons of the reigning king in riotous living and idolatry, he was raising havoc with moral and spiritual affairs of the Nephites. In answer to the prayers of his father, the high priest of the Church, an angel of the Lord, appeared unto him and his four princely companions "and he spake as it were with a voice of thunder," which caused the earth to shake upon which they stood. "And so great was their astonishment, that they fell to the earth, and understood not the words which he spake unto them. Nevertheless he cried again, saying, Alma, arise and stand forth, for why persecuteth thou the church of God? For the Lord hath said, This is my church, and I will establish it; and nothing shall overthrow it, save it is the transgression of my people. . . . And now behold, can ye dispute the power of God? For behold, doth not my voice shake the earth? And can ye not also behold me before you? And I am sent from God. Now I say unto thee, Go, and remember the captivity of thy fathers in the land of Helam, and in the land of Nephi; and remember how great things he has done for them: for they were in bondage, and he has delivered them. And now I say unto thee, Alma, go thy way, and seek to destroy the church no more, that their prayers may be answered; and this even if thou wilt of thyself be cast off. And now it came to pass that these were the last words which the angel spake unto Alma, and he departed. And now Alma, and those that were with him, fell again to the earth, for great was their astonishment; for with their own eyes they had beheld an angel of the Lord; and his voice was as thunder, which shook the earth; and they knew that there was nothing save the power of God that could shake the earth and cause it to tremble, as though it would part asunder. And now the astonishment of Alma was so great, that he became dumb, that he could not open his mouth; yea, and he became weak, even that he could not move his hands; therefore he was taken by those that were with him, and carried helpless, even until he was laid before his father."

The father believing the visitation to be of God rejoiced in it, and with his fellow priests "prayed that the Lord their God would open the mouth of Alma, that he might speak; and also that his limbs might receive their strength, that the eyes of the people might be opened to see and know of the goodness and glory of God." And this was done, for—

"It came to pass after they had fasted and prayed for the space of two days and two nights, the limbs of Alma received their strength, and he stood up and began to speak unto them begging them to be of good cheer"; and straightway he entered upon such admonitions and doctrinal exegesis of the "new birth" and other doctrinal subjects of the gospel it causes one to be amazed: "For, said he, I have repented of my sins, and have been redeemed of the Lord; behold I am born of the Spirit. And the Lord said unto me, Marvel not that all mankind, yea, men and women, all nations, kindreds, tongues and peoples, must be born again; yea, born of God, changed from their carnal and fallen state, to a state of righteousness, being redeemed of God, becoming his sons and daughters; and thus they become new creatures; and unless they do this, they can in no wise inherit the kingdom of God. I say unto you, unless this be the case, they must be cast off; and this I know, because I was like to be cast off. Nevertheless, after wandering through much tribulation, repenting nigh unto death, the Lord in mercy hath seen fit to snatch me out of an everlasting burning, and I am born of God: My soul hath been redeemed from the gall of bitterness and bonds of iniquity. I was in the darkest abyss; but now I behold the marvelous light of God. My soul was racked with eternal torment; but I am snatched, and my soul is pained no more. I rejected my Redeemer, and denied that which had been spoken of by my fathers; but now that they may foresee that he will come, and that he remembereth every creature of his creating, he will make himself manifest unto all; yea, every knee shall bow, and every tongue confess before him. Yea, even at the last day, when all men shall stand to be judged of him, then shall they confess that he is God; then shall they confess, who live without God in the world, that the judgment of an everlasting punishment is just upon them; and they shall quake, and tremble, and shrink beneath the glance of his all-searching eye" (Mosiah 27).

After this experience he and his princely companions become faithful servants of the Church. "And how blessed are they! For they did publish peace: they did publish good tidings of good; and they did declare unto the people that the Lord reigneth."

All four of the sons of King Mosiah went among the Lamanites as missionaries, where they all had remarkable spiritual experiences, but especially the oldest one, Ammon. To achieve his purposes as a missionary, he became a servant to one of the petty kings of the Lamanites. There was such a marvelous display of miraculous power in his service that the king, his "master" suspected him of being the "Great Spirit" himself, come down among men.

He sent for him to come into his presence, and yet when he was come he durst not speak to him, and for the space of one hour (it seems they divided the day in hours!) the king answered him not. Then Ammon knew the king's thoughts and opened conversation with him. He started with the Book of Mormon initial question of so many discourses — "Believe thou that there is a God?" Then Ammon expounded all things from the creation up to the opening of this incident at the Lamanite king's court, stressing evidently the hand-dealings of the Lord with the Nephites. Then Lamoni — for such was the Lamanite king's name — believing all the words of Ammon began to cry unto the Lord saying: "O Lord, have mercy; according to thy abundant mercy which thou hast had upon the people of Nephi, have upon me, and my people. And now, when he had said this, he fell unto the earth, as if he were dead. And it came to pass that his servants took him and carried him in unto his wife, and laid him upon a bed; and he lay as if he were dead for the space of two days and two nights; and his wife, and his sons, and his daughters mourned over him, after the manner of the Lamanites, greatly lamenting his loss" (Alma 18:41-43).

So long had the king lain as if dead that his people began to prepare to bury him; but Ammon favored by the queen with an interview assured her the king was not dead, "but he sleepeth in God, and on the morrow he shall rise again."

And when the king rose on the morrow according to this word — "he stretched forth his hand" unto his wife who had faithfully watched by his side and began blessing God and saying: "As sure as thou livest, behold, I have seen my Redeemer; and he shall come forth, and be born of a woman, and he shall redeem all mankind who believe on his name. Now when he had said these words, his heart was swollen within him and he sunk again with joy; and the queen also sunk down, being overpowered by the Spirit. Now Ammon seeing the Spirit of the Lord poured out according to his prayers upon the Lamanites, his brethren, who had been the cause of so much mourning among the Nephites, or among all the people of God because of their iniquities and their traditions, he fell upon his knees, and began to pour out his soul in prayer and thanksgiving to God, for what he had done for his brethren; and he was also overpowered with joy; and thus they all three had sunk to the earth. Now, when the servants of the king had seen that they had fallen, they also began to cry unto God, for the fear of the Lord had come upon them also, for it was they who had stood before the king, and testified unto him concerning the great power of Ammon. And it came to pass that they did call on the name of the Lord, in their might, even until they had all fallen to the earth, save it were one of the Lamanitish women, whose name was Abish, she having been converted unto the Lord for many years, on account of a remarkable vision of her father; thus having been converted to the Lord, never had made it known; therefore when she saw that all the servants of Lamoni had fallen to the earth, and also her mistress, the queen, and the king, and Ammon lay prostrate upon the earth, she knew that it was the power of God; and supposing that this opportunity, by making known unto the people what had happened among them, that by beholding this scene, it would cause them to believe in the power of God, therefore she ran forth from house to house, making it known unto the people."

This spreading of the news abroad resulted in bringing a great throng together, but it was variously moved by what was seen, and not all of it to the liking of Abish; for one sought to kill Ammon with a sword. "And as he lifted the sword to smite him, behold, he fell dead." And when Abish saw the contentions which were among the multitude she was exceeding sorrowful even to tears: "And it came to pass that she went and took the queen by the hand, that perhaps she might raise her from the ground; and as soon as she touched her hand she arose and stood upon her feet, and cried with a loud voice, saying, O blessed Jesus, who has saved me from an awful hell! O blessed God, have mercy on this people. And when she had said this, she clasped her hands, being filled with joy, speaking many words which were not understood; and when she had done this, she took the king, Lamoni, by the hand, and behold he arose and stood upon his feet. And he immediately, seeing the contention among his people, went forth and began to rebuke them, and to teach them the words which he had heard from the mouth of Ammon; and as many as heard his words, believed, and were converted unto the Lord. But there were many among them who would not hear his words; therefore they went their way. And it came to pass that when Ammon arose, he also administered unto them, and also did all the servants of Lamoni; and they did all declare unto the people the self same thing: that their hearts had been changed; that they had no more desire to do evil" (Alma 19).

Aaron, another of the sons of Mosiah and brother of Ammon, had spiritual experiences nearly equal to those related above of Ammon. He came before the king of the land of Nephi, father of King Lamoni.

Aaron began his work with this king at the same initial point, characteristic of Book of Mormon preachments: "Believest thou that there is a God?" Then identification of God with the "Great Spirit" of the Lamanites' mind. Then the king is left to pray: "O God, Aaron hath told me that there is a God; and if there is a God, and if thou art God, wilt thou make thyself known unto me, and I will give away all my sins to know thee, and that I may be raised from the dead, and be saved at the last day. And now when the king had said these words, he was struck as if he were dead."

There was a near riot in this case when the queen heard of it and the multitude gathered to the presence of the unconscious king. Seeing this Aaron put forth his hand and raised the king from the earth, and said unto him, stand, and he stood upon his feet, receiving his strength. "Now this was done in the presence of the queen and many of the servants. And when they saw it, they greatly marvelled, and began to fear. And the king stood forth, and began to minister unto them. And he did minister unto them, insomuch that his whole household were converted unto the Lord" (Alma 22).

These Lamanite converts of Ammon and Aaron et al. were gathered to the Nephites and were the fathers and mothers of those 2,000 valiant young men who could not be killed in battle, mentioned in a former chapter of this writing.

These instances of conversion might be thought sufficient for illustration of the matter in hand—the comparison of these instances with that manner of hysterical conversion so common to the time and place of the coming forth of the Book of Mormon; but I desire that it shall be known that this trait of emotional conversion continues throughout the Book of Mormon.

At the time the sign of the birth of the Christ was given in the New World, namely, the continuance of light through the day and the night and the day—"which should be as one day, as if there were no night"—and the appearance of the promised "New Star"—all this predicted wonderful display of signs, as might be expected, when fulfilled, was attended with widespread, emotional phenomena among the Nephite people.

The record does not disappoint one. To heighten the dramatic interest in the event, the unbelievers in the prophecies which predicted these things had set a time limit in which they must come to pass, or belief in them be abandoned by the "Christians," or those who looked for their fulfillment. Happily, the sign was given within the time limit fixed and the believers saved from those who threatened them. The story of the event follows: "And it came to pass that the words which came unto Nephi were fulfilled, according as they had been spoken; for behold at the going down of the sun, there was no darkness; and the people began to be astonished, because there was no darkness when the night came. And there were many, who had not believed the words of the prophets, *fell to the earth and became as if* they were dead, for they knew that the great plan of destruction, which they had laid for those who believed in the word of the prophets, had been frustrated; for the signal which had been given was already at hand; and they began to know that the Son of God must shortly appear; yea, in fine, *all the people upon the face of the whole earth from the west to the east, both in the land north and in the land south,* were so exceedingly astonished *that they fell to the earth;* for they knew that the prophets had testified of these things for many years, and that the sign which had been given was already at hand; and they began to fear because of their iniquity and their unbelief."

The above represents a whole continent of people — millions of them at the same time — prostrate under the "falling power," and lying felled to the earth "as if they were dead"! A spectacle, to say the least of it, the like of which enters not into the experiences of men anywhere else in all the history of the world. "Did it occur here," the skeptic will ask; "or is it one more wonder-tale from an overwrought enthusiast's mind, lost to all sense of the proportion of things?" Nothing surpasses this in Book of Mormon wonder lore, except it might be the account which tells us how immediately following this manifestation of signs of the Christ's birth, there was such a recurrence of widespread wickedness that there was one of the most tremendous battles in all the war experience of the Nephites, and a near-overthrow of Nephite civilizations. This could well be called the Great Robber War; and it was brought on within eighteen years from the time the signs of the Christ's birth were given, and the whole people prostrate upon the earth at the feet of God!

After the dramatic ending of this war in favor of the believers in Christ, then came the characteristic Nephite, hysterical joy, taking on a religious fervor, so many examples of which we have aleady seen:

"And it came to pass that they did break forth, all as one, in singing, and praising their God for the great thing which he had done for them, in preserving them from falling into the hands of their enemies: Yea, they did cry, Hosanna to the Most High God; and they did cry, Blessed be the name of the Lord God Almighty, the Most High God. And their hearts were swollen with joy, unto the gushing out of many tears, because of the great goodness of God in delivering them out of the hands of their enemies; and they knew it was because of their repentance and their humility that they had been delivered from an everlasting destruction" (III Nephi 4:31-33).

There were given, according to the Book of Mormon, far greater signs to witness the death of the Christ, his lying in the tomb, than at the time of his birth; and in every way they exceeded those signs given in the Old World. At Jerusalem during the Messiah's crucifixion there was "darkness over all the land" from the sixth to the ninth hour; but in America there were three days of terrible complete and awful darkness; and there was one earthquake at Jerusalem, but evidently only of a few moments' duration; but in America the awful quaking of the earth and the storm and tempest which attended upon it and "deformed" the "face of the whole earth" continued "for about the space of three hours." It can well be supposed that the attendant mourning and "howling" of the people in the New World would be in something like a just ration to the larger destruction that attended upon these direful events in Messiah's life. And so indeed they did for—"There was great mourning, and howling, and weeping among all the people continually; yea, great were the groanings of the people, because of the darkness and the great destruction which had come upon them. And in one place they were heard to cry, saying, O that we had repented before this great and terrible day, and then would our brethren have been spared, and they would not have been burned in the great city Zarahemla. And in another place they were heard to cry and mourn, saying, O that we had repented before this great and terrible day, and had not killed and stoned the prophets, and cast them out; then would our mothers and our fair daughters, and our children have been spared, and not have been buried up in that great city Moronihah; and thus were the howlings of the people great and terrible" (III Nephi 8:23-24).

Then came a voice "heard among all the inhabitants of the earth, upon all the face of the land," meaning, doubtless, and only, all the inhabitants of the New World. And the voice cried:

"Wo, wo wo unto this people; wo unto the inhabitants of the whole earth, except they shall repent, for the devil laugheth, and his angels rejoice, because of the slain of the fair sons and daughters of my people; and it is because of their iniquity and abominations that they are fallen. Behold that great city Zarahemla have I burned with fire, and the inhabitants thereof. And behold, that great city Moroni have I caused to be sunk in the depths of the sea, and the inhabitants thereof to be drowned" (III Nephi 9:2-4).

And so throughout many paragraphs, cities are enumerated that have been variously destroyed, and their inhabitants denounced for their wickedness.

Of course with the appearing of the Christ to the Nephites there was further manifestation of the "falling power." For when Jesus appeared to a large number of Nephites in the land Bountiful, and announced himself as the predicted Messiah:

"The whole multitude fell to the earth; for they remembered that it had been prophesied among them that Christ should show himself unto them after his ascension into heaven." And after they had witnessed for themselves that this was he by thrusting their hands into his wounds, "they did cry out with one accord, saying: Hosanna! blessed be the name of the Most High God! And they did fall down at the feet of Jesus, and did worship him" (III Nephi 11:17).

So this sort of ecstatic utterance continues throughout the Nephite period; it is characteristic. It appears through the days of Mormon centuries after the appearing of the Christ. Mormon, in his own book, speaking upon the redemption, employs language closely akin to the phraseology of early nineteenth-century sectarian phraseology when dealing with the same theme. He represents the Christ as having brought to pass "the redemption of the world"—

"Whereby he that is found guiltless before him at the judgment day, hath it given unto him to dwell in the presence of God in his kingdom, to sing ceaseless praises with the choirs above unto the Father, and unto the Son, and unto the Holy Ghost, which is one God, in a state of happiness which hath no end" (Mormon 7:7).

The same style of supplication, self-abasement, and hysterical pleading is to be found in Moroni's translation of the Jaredite record, brought over into the English by Joseph Smith. The Brother of Jared is pleading with the Lord to provide means by which their dish-tight barges might be illuminated and thus avoid the horror of darkness in a journey of nearly a year in the sea:

"And it came to pass that the Brother of Jared cried unto the Lord, saying, O Lord I have performed the work which thou hast commanded me, and I have made the barges according as thou has directed me. And behold, O Lord, in them there is no light, whither shall we steer? And also we shall perish, for in them we cannot breathe, save it is the air which is in them; therefore we shall perish" (Ether 2:18, 19).

"O Lord, thou hast said that we must be encompassed about by the floods. Now behold, O Lord, and do not be angry with thy servant because of his weakness before thee; for we know that thou art holy, and dwellest in the heavens; and that we are unworthy before thee; because of the fall, our natures have become evil continually: nevertheless, O Lord, thou hast given us a commandment that we must call upon thee, that from thee we may receive according to our desires. Behold, O Lord, thou hast smitten us because of our iniquity, and hath driven us forth, and for this many years we have been in the wilderness; nevertheless, thou hast been merciful unto us. O Lord, look upon me in pity, and turn away thine anger from this thy people, and suffer not that they shall go forth across this raging deep in darkness, but behold these things which I have molten out of the rock" (Ether 3:2, 3).

The stones were touched in answer to the prayer, and then: "And it came to pass that the wind did never cease to blow towards the promised land, while they were upon the waters; and thus they were driven forth before the wind; and they did sing praises unto the Lord all the day long; and when the night came, they did not cease to praise the Lord" (Ether 6:8, 9).

So with the last of the Jaredite prophets as well as with the first. He lived in the days of the declination of the Jaredites—in the days of Coriantumr:

"And he began to prophesy unto the people and could not be restrained because of the spirit of the Lord which was upon him. For he did cry from the morning, even until the going down of the sun, exhorting the people to believe in God unto repentance, lest they should be destroyed, saying unto them, that by faith all things are fulfilled; wherefore, whoso believeth in God might with surety hope for a better world, yea, even a place at the right hand of God, which hope cometh of faith, maketh an anchor to the souls of men, which would make them sure and steadfast, always abounding in good works, being led to glorify God" (Ether 12:3, 4).

Thus throughout the Book of Mormon, from first to last, and among both its distinct peoples, both Jaredites and Nephites, and in widely separated periods of time and of place, are to be found these hysterical religious extravagancies of both speech and action. Traces of the same traits may be found in the experiences of Joseph Smith. His first vision, in which he claims to have communed in vision with both God the Father and God the Son, was preceded by a fearful struggle with the powers of darkness in which he felt that his own destruction was inevitable when, just as the evil power seemed about to prevail, he was released by entering upon his vision of God. He had become unconscious to things about him, however, for according to his own description of the circumstance he tells us that—

"*When I came to myself again I found myself lying on my back looking up into heaven.* When the light had departed (in which he had been enveloped during his vision) I had no strength; but soon recovering, in some degree, I went home" (*Hist. of the Church*, 1:6).

Also in his visions of and interview with Moroni which resulted in his obtaining the Book of Mormon, the same trait of the "falling power," so frequently exhibited in religious experiences recounted in the Book of Mormon, is to be found. Following the first visit of the angel Moroni to him, during the night of September 23rd, 1823, there came another visitation on the following day.[19] The previous night having been spent in receiving three visitations of the angel, it was but natural that the young prophet should feel unfit for labor in the fields on the next day. His father laboring beside him, observing his abstraction and weakness, directed him to go to the house. He started with the intention of doing so, but in attempting to cross the fence out of the field, behold, "My strength," he says, "entirely failed me, and I fell helpless on the ground, and for a time was quite unconscious of any thing. The first that I can recollect was a voice speaking unto me, calling me by name. I looked up, and beheld the same messenger (Moroni) standing over my head, surrounded by light as before" (*History of the Church*, 1:14, 15).

So also at the first conference of the then-forming Church held in June, 1830, there was further manifestation of this power. Newel Knight was again overcome, and I choose his experience rather than the others because of the close resemblance of his experience to that of other experiences outside the church of the Latter-day Saints to be noted later. "Much exhortation and instruction was given," says the prophet, writing of this conference, "and the Holy Ghost was poured out upon us in a miraculous manner — many of our number prophesied, whilst others had the heavens opened to their view, and were so overcome that we had to lay them on beds or other convenient places; among the rest was Brother Newel Knight, who had to be placed on a bed, being unable to help himself. By his own account of the transaction he could not understand why we should lay him on the bed, as he felt no sense of weakness. He felt his heart filled with love, with glory, and pleasure unspeakable, and could discern all that was going on in the room; when, all of a sudden, a vision of the future burst upon him. He saw there represented the great work which through my instrumentality was yet to be accomplished. He saw heaven opened, and beheld the Lord Jesus Christ, seated at the right hand of the Majesty on high, and had it made plain to his understanding that the time would come when he would be admitted into His presence to enjoy His society for ever and ever. When their bodily strength was restored to these brethren, they shouted hosannas to God and the Lamb, and rehearsed the glorious things which they had seen and felt, whilst they were yet in the spirit.

"Such scenes as these were calculated to inspire our hearts with joy unspeakable, and fill us with awe and reverence for that Almighty Being, by whose grace we had been called to be instrumental in bringing about, for the children of men, the enjoyment of such glorious blessings as were now at this time poured out upon us" (*Hist. of the Church*, 1:85).

Something of the same nature to this "falling" and "overwhelming power," resulting in unconsciousness and other forms of emotionalism, was experienced also by many early converts to Mormonism. The following circumstance is related by the Prophet himself. The Prophet had urged upon his young friend, Newel Knight, a very estimable man to pray, to pray for divine guidance respecting the new work then coming forth; but this on one pretext or another he declined to do. Finally, however, he attempted it in secret. He was unable to pray, however, and this led him to feel very uneasy in his mind, and he started for home. On reaching home his appearance was such as to alarm his wife. He requested her to bring the Prophet to him. "I went," says the Prophet, "and found him suffering very much in his mind, and his body acted upon in a very strange manner; his visage and limbs distorted and finally he was caught up off the floor of the apartment and tossed about most fearfully." His relatives and some of the neighbors, having heard of his condition, soon gathered at his house and witnessed his distress. The Prophet after some effort caught him by the hand, and immediately Newel spoke to him and asked him to cast out the evil spirit. "If you know that I can," said Joseph, "it shall be done." And then almost unconsciously the Prophet rebuked the evil spirit and commanded him in the name of Jesus Christ to depart from the afflicted man. Newel was instantly relieved: his countenance became natural, the distortions of his body ceased. He himself declared that he saw the evil spirit leave him and vanish from sight. His relief from this mental distress, however, was attended with great physical weakness. But after the storm came the calm. His friends laid him upon his bed, and then was witnessed a most remarkable scene. Newel himself afterwards narrated it as follows:

"I now began to feel a most pleasing sensation resting upon me, and immediately the visions of heaven were opened to my view. I felt myself attracted upward, and remained for some time enwrapt in contemplation, insomuch that I knew not what was going on in the room. By and by, I felt some weight pressing upon my shoulder and the side of my head, which served to recall me to a sense of my situation, and I found that the spirit of the Lord had actually caught me up off the floor, and that my shoulder and head were pressing against the beams."

This is usually called "the first miracle in the Church." It was witnessed by eight or ten adult persons, most of whom afterwards joined the Church. The Prophet himself ascribed the power by which the evil spirit was cast out, to God; saying: "It was not done by man, nor the power of man; but it was done by God, and by the power of godliness: therefore, let the honor and the praise, the dominion and the glory, be ascribed to the Father, Son and Holy Ghost, for ever and ever. Amen" (*History of the Mormon Church*, pp.188-89).[20]

Spiritual manifestations in various degrees continued in the Church, and at one time in Kirtland broke out in such unseemly fashion as to be rebuked severely by the Prophet. This, however, was not to such an extent as to "quench the spirit," and at the time the Temple at Kirtland was dedicated there were further "Manifestations of the Spirit." The following instances are given by the Prophet himself in his own journal history; speaking of the closing scenes of the first day's services in the Temple. "I . . . called upon the congregation to speak, and not to fear to prophesy good concerning the Saints, for if you prophesy the falling of these hills and the rising of the valleys, the downfall of the enemies of Zion and the rising of the kingdom of God, it shall come to pass.

Do not quench the Spirit, for the first one that open his mouth shall receive the spirit of prophecy.

"Brother George A. Smith arose and began to prophesy, when a noise was heard like the sound of rushing mighty wind, which filled the Temple, and all the congregation simultaneously arose, being moved upon by an invisible power; many began to speak in tongues and prophesy; others saw glorious visions; and I beheld the Temple was filled with angels, which fact I declared to the congregation. The people of the neighborhood came running together (hearing an unusual sound within, and seeing a bright light like a pillar of fire resting upon the Temple), and were astonished at what was taking place. This continued until the meeting closed at eleven p.m." (*History of the Church*, 2:428).

Such manifestations continued through the subsequent days of the dedication of the Temple, and afterwards, from time to time.

Morbid imagination, morbid expression of emotions, have, undoubtedly, an extended history; and in some cases Bible warrant can be cited in support of spiritual exaltation and rhapsodies which seem closely allied to these. But it will not be necessary to enter into a consideration of this history. It will be sufficient just to acknowledge, in passing, the long historical existence of these things, and then come to the period when such phenomena are likely to find their way to the knowledge of Joseph Smith and influence his conceptions of spiritual things — manifestations and experiences; and which, on the supposition that the Book of Mormon is of merely human origin, and Joseph Smith its author, would find their way into the web and woof of the Book of Mormon narrative of spiritual experiences.

In dealing with these emotional or supposed spiritual phenomena, for our purpose, it will not be necessary to go further back in time than 1735. It was about that time the revival methods and emotional extravagancies, begun in England under the preaching of Wesley and Whitefield, began to be developed in America, in various parts of New England, but chiefly under the preaching of Jonathan Edwards at Northampton, Mass. At this time the manifestations became so extravagant that they fell into disrepute and they subsided — which whole circumstance Mr. Edwards deplored. There was, however, a revival of the phenomena, in a more moderate form in 1740-42; and it is in this period that I note what occurred, relying chiefly upon the high authority of Mr. Edwards for an account of these things.

In the month of May 1741, a sermon was preached in a private house. Near the conclusion one or two persons were so greatly affected with a sense of greatness and glory of divine things, and the infinite importance of the things of eternity, that they were not able to conceal it — "The affection of their minds overcoming their strength, and having a visible effect upon their bodies."

"When the exercises were over, the young people that were present removed into the other room for religious conference; and particularly that they might have opportunity to inquire of those that were thus affected, what apprehensions they had, and what things they were that thus deeply impressed their minds; and there soon appeared a very great effect of their conversation; the affection was quickly propagated throughout the room; many of the young people and children, that were professors, appeared to be overcome with a sense of the greatness and glory of divine things, and with admiration, love, joy, and praise, and compassion to others, that looked upon themselves as in a state of nature; and many others at the same time were overcome with distress, about their sinful and miserable estate and condition; so that the whole room was full of nothing but outcries, faintings, and the like. Others soon heard of it in several parts of the town, and came to them; and what they saw and heard there, was greatly affecting to them, so that many of them were overpowered in like manner, and it continued thus for some hours" (Edwards's *Works*, p. c).[21]

These emotional "affections" extended to children, and it was generally among the young people that these phenomena were most pronounced. Reciting events following upon those noted above, Mr. Edwards says:

"A little after it, at the conclusion of the public exercises on the sabbath, I appointed the children that were under seventeen years of age, to go from the meeting-house to a neighbouring house, that I might there further enforce what they had heard in public, and might give in some counsels proper for their age. The children were there very generally and greatly affected with the warnings and counsels that were given them, and many exceedingly overcome; and the room was filled with cries; and when they were dismissed, they almost all of them went home crying aloud through the streets, to all parts of the town. The like appearances attended several such meetings of children, that were appointed. But their affections appeared by what followed, to be of a very different nature; in many, they appeared indeed but childish affections, and in a day or two would leave them as they were before. . . . About the middle of the summer, I called together the young people that were communicants, from sixteen to twenty-six years of age, to my house; which proved to be a most happy meeting; many seemed to be very greatly and most agreeably affected with those views, which excited humility, self-condemnation, self-abhorrence, love, and joy: many fainted under these affections. We had several meetings that summer, of young people, attended with like appearances. It was about that time, that there first began to be cryings out in the meeting-house; which several times occasioned many of the congregation to stay in the house after the public exercises were over, to confer with those who seemed to be overcome with religious convictions and affections, which was found to tend much to the propagation of their impressions, with lasting effect upon many; conference being, at these times, commonly joined with prayer and singing. . . . The months of August and September were the most remarkable of any this year, for appearances of the conviction and conversion of sinners, and great revivings, quickenings, and comforts of professors, and for extraordinary external effects of these things. It was a very frequent thing, to see a house full of outcries, faintings, convulsions, and such like, both with distress, and also with admiration and joy. It was not the manner here, to hold meetings all night, as in some places, nor was it common to continue them till very late in the night; but it was pretty often so, that there were some that were so affected, and their bodies so overcome, that they could not go home, but were obliged to stay all night where they were" (Id., p. c).

Edwards gives an account of a revival that took place in Northampton, Mass.—his place of residence—during his absence under a Mr. Buell, and the conditions he found on his return.

"When I came home, I found the town in very extraordinary circumstances, such as, in some respects, I never saw it in before. Mr. Buell continued here a fortnight or three weeks after I returned: There being still great appearances attending his labours; many in their religious affections being raised far beyond what they had ever been before: and there were some instances of persons lying in a sort of trance, remaining perhaps for a whole twenty-four hours motionless, and with their senses locked up; but in the mean time under strong imaginations, as though they went to heaven, and had there a vision of glorious and delightful objects. But when the people were raised to this height, Satan took the advantage, and his interposition, in many instances, soon became very apparent: and a great deal of caution and pains were found necessary, to keep the people, many of them from running wild" (Id., p. ci).

It was during the ministry of Mr. Buell that the experiences of Mrs. Edwards, wife of Jonathan Edwards, reached their climax. Those experiences began some time before Buell's arrival in Northampton, under the following circumstances, as related by Mrs. Edwards herself:

"To my mind there was the clearest evidence, that God was present in the congregation, on the work of redeeming love; and in the clear view of this, I was all at once filled with such intense admiration of the wonderful condescension and grace of God, in returning again to Northampton, as overwhelmed my soul and immediately took away my bodily strength. This was accompanied with an earnest longing, that those of us, who were the children of God, might now arise and strive. It appeared to me, that the angels in heaven sung praises, for such wonderful, free, and sovereign grace, and my heart was lifted up in adoration and praise. I continued to have clear views of the future world, of eternal happiness and misery, and my heart full of love to the souls of men. On seeing some, that I found were in a natural condition (unconverted), I felt a most tender compassion for them; but especially was I, while I remained in the meeting-house, from time to time overcome, and my strength taken away, by the sight of one and another, whom I regarded as the children of God, and who, I had heard, were lively and animated in religion. We remained in the meeting-house about three hours, after the public exercises were over. During most of the time, my bodily strength was overcome; and the joy and thankfulness, which were excited in my mind, as I contemplated the great goodness of God, led me to converse with those who were near me, in a very earnest manner" (Id., p. civ).

Thus Mr. Buell came. Mrs. Edwards rejoiced when she saw "the honor which God put upon him" in his ministry. "I found rest and rejoicing in it, and the sweet language of my soul continually was '*Amen, Lord Jesus! Amen Lord Jesus!*'

"When I came home, I found Mr. Buell, Mr. Christophers, Mr. Hopkins, Mrs. Eleanor Dwight, the wife of Mr. Joseph Allen, and Mr. Job Strong, at the house. Seeing and conversing with them on the Divine goodness renewed my former feelings, and filled me with an intense desire that we might all arise, and with an active, flowing, and fervent heart give glory to God. The intenseness of my feelings again took away my bodily strength" (Id., p. cvi).

A few days later:

"About 11 o'clock, as I accidentally went into the room where Mr. Buell was conversing with some of the people, I heard him say, 'O that we, who are the children of God, should be cold and lifeless in religion!' and I felt such a sense of the deep ingratitude manifested by the children of God, in such coldness and deadness, that my strength was immediately taken away, and I sunk down on the spot. Those who were near raised me, and placed me in a chair; and from the fulness of my heart, I expressed to them, in a very earnest manner, the deep sense I had of the wonderful grace of Christ towards me, of the assurance I had of his having saved me from hell, of my happiness running parallel with eternity, of the duty of giving up all to God, and of the peace and joy inspired by an entire dependence on his mercy and grace. Mr. Buell then read a melting hymn of Dr. Watts's, concerning the loveliness of Christ, the enjoyments and employments of heaven, and the Christian's earnest desire of heavenly things; and the truth and reality of the things mentioned in the hymn made so strong an impression on my mind, and my soul was drawn so powerfully towards Christ and heaven, that I leaped unconsciously from my chair. I seemed to be drawn upwards, soul and body, from the earth towards heaven; and it appeared to me that I must naturally and nec- essarily ascend thither. These feelings continued while the hymn was reading, and during the prayer of Mr. Christophers, which followed. After the prayer, Mr. Buell read two other hymns, on the glories of heaven, which moved me so exceedingly, and drew me so strongly heav- enward, that it seemed as it were to draw my body upwards, and I felt as if I must necessarily ascend thither. At length my strength failed me, and I sunk down; when they took me up and laid me on the bed, where I lay for a considerable time, faint with joy, while contemplating the glories of the heavenly world. After I had lain a while, I felt more perfectly subdued and weaned from the world, and more fully resigned to God, than I had ever been conscious of before. I felt an entire indifference to the opinions, and representations, and conduct of mankind respecting me; and a perfect willingness that God should employ some other in- strument than Mr. Edwards, in advancing the work of grace in North- ampton. I was entirely swallowed up in God, as my only portion, and his honour and glory was the object of my supreme desire and delight. At the same time, I felt a far greater love to the children of God than ever before. I seemed to love them as my own soul; and when I saw them, my heart went out towards them, with an inexpressible endeared- ness and sweetness. I beheld them by faith in their risen and glorified state, with spiritual bodies re-fashioned after the image of Christ's glorious body, and arrayed in the beauty of heaven. The time when they would be so appeared very near, by faith it seemed as if it were present. This was accompanied with a ravishing sense of unspeakable joys of the upper world. They appeared to my mind in all their reality and certainty, and as it were in actual and distinct vision; so plain and evident were they to the eye of my faith, I seemed to regard them as begun. These antic- ipations were renewed over and over, while I lay on the bed, from twelve o'clock till four, being too much exhausted by emotions of joy, to rise and sit up; and during most of the time, my feelings prompted me to converse very earnestly with one and another of the pious women, who were present, on those spiritual and heavenly objects, of which I had so deep an impression" (Id., pp. cvi-cvii).

There is much more to the same effect in the experience of Mrs. Edwards, as quoted in "Memoirs of Jonathan Edwards" (see *Works*, 1 ("Memoirs"): c-cvii). Repeatedly her "bodily strength was taken away," and there were repeated "faintings" and rhapsodies. At times her friends feared for her life. At which she would respond—"I should be willing to die in darkness and horror if it was most for the glory of God."

In the above extended quotation from the case of Mrs. Edwards will be found a close parallel to the experiences of Newel Knight as related by Joseph Smith and quoted in a previous page of this chapter.

Mr. Edwards gave his approval to this revival of religion, both of 1735-37, and 1740-42, though he deplored some of the extravagances into which it ran; and withstood Whitefield's extravagances ("Mem.," p. cxiii) on the occasion of one of the English revivalist's visits to New England. Yet he devotes a long defensive treatise of this movement under the title of "Religious affections" (*Works,* 1:234-343); and still another defense in what he calls "A Faithful Narrative of the Surprising work of God in the conversion of many hundred souls in Northampton" (*Works,* 1:344-64); and again in "Some thoughts Concerning the Present Revival of Religion in New England" (Id., pp. 365-430). His own viewpoint of the subject may be judged by the following passage:

"There are false affections, and there are true. A man's having much affection does not prove that he has any true religion: but if he has no affection, it proves that he has no true religion. The right way is not to reject all affections, nor to approve all: but to distinguish between them, approving some and rejecting others; separating between the wheat and the chaff, the gold and the dross, the precious and the vile" (*Works,* 1:244).

Answering some objections to violent manifestations of religious "affections," he says—and by what he says in defense of these manifestations one may see the nature of them:

"The most specious thing alleged against these extraordinary effects on the body is that the body is impaired, and that it is hard to think that God, in the merciful influences of his Spirit on men, would wound their bodies, and impair their health. But if it were in multiplied instances (which I do not suppose it is) that persons received a lasting wound to their health by extraordinary religious impressions made upon their minds, yet it is too much for us to determine that God shall never bring an outward calamity, in bestowing a vastly greater spiritual and eternal good."

As a further description of this work as it appeared in his time, in New England, Mr. Edwards says:

"Whatever imprudences there have been, and whatever sinful irregularities; whatever vehemence of the passions, and heats of the imagination, transports, and ecstasies: whatever error in judgment, and indiscreet zeal; and whatever outcries, faintings, and agitations of the body; yet, it is manifest and notorious, that there has been of late a very uncommon influence upon the minds of a very great part of the inhabitants of New England, attended with the best effects. There has been a great increase of seriousness, and sober consideration of eternal things; a disposition to hearken to what is said of such things, with attention and affection; a disposition to treat matters of religion with solemnity,

and as of great importance; to make these things the subject of conversation; to hear the word of God preached, and to take all opportunities in order to do it; to attend on the public worship of God, and all external duties of religion, in a more solemn and decent manner; so that there is a remarkable and general alteration in the face of New England in these respects. Multitudes in all parts of the land, of vain, thoughtless, regardless persons, are quite changed, and become serious and considerate. There is a vast increase of concern for the salvation of the precious soul, and of that inquiry, What shall I do to be saved? The hearts of multitudes had been greatly taken off from the things of the world, its profits, pleasures, and honours. Multitudes in all parts have had their consciences awakened, and have been made sensible of the pernicious nature and consequences of sin, and what a dreadful thing it is to be under guilt and the displeasure of God, and to live without peace and reconciliation with him. They have also been awakened to a sense of the shortness and uncertainty of life, and the reality of another world and future judgment, and of the necessity of an interest in Christ. They are more afraid of sin, more careful and inquisitive that they may know what is contrary to the mind and will of God, that they may avoid it, and what he requires of them, that they may do it, more careful to guard against temptations, more watchful over their own hearts, earnestly desirous of knowing and of being diligent in the use of the means that God has appointed in his word, in order to salvation. Many very stupid, senseless sinners, and persons of a vain mind, have been greatly awakened.
. . . Now, through the greatest part of New England, the holy Bible is in much greater esteem and use than before. The great things contained in it are much more regarded, as things of the greatest consequence, and are much more the subjects of meditation and conversation: and other books of piety that have long been of established reputation, as the most excellent, and most tending to promote true godliness, have been abundantly more in use. The Lord's day is more religiously and strictly observed. And much has been lately done at making up differences, confessing faults one to another, and making restitution: probably more within two years than was done in thirty years before. It has been undoubtedly so in many places. And surprising has been the power of this spirit, in many instances, to destroy old grudges, to make up long-continued breaches, and to bring those who seemed to be in a confirmed irreconcilable alienation, to embrace each other in a sincere and entire amity. Great numbers under this influence have been brought to a deep sense of their own sinfulness and vileness; the sinfulness of their lives, the heinousness of their disregard of the authority of the great God, and of their living in contempt of a Saviour. They have lamented their former negligence of their souls, and their neglecting and losing precious time.

The sins of their life have been extraordinarily set before them; and their enmity against that which is good, and proneness to performances, how unworthy of God's regard were their prayers, praises, and all that they did in religion. It has been a common thing, that persons have had such a sense of their own sinfulness, that they have thought themselves to be the worst of all, and that none ever was so vile as they. And many seem to have been greatly convinced that they were utterly unworthy of any mercy at the hands of God, however miserable they were and though they stood in extreme necessity of mercy; and that they deserved nothing but burnings. . . . And not only do these effects appear in new converts, but great numbers of those who were formerly esteemed the most sober and pious people have, under the influence of this work, been greatly quickened, and their hearts renewed with greater degrees of light, renewed repentance and humiliation, and more lively exercises of faith, love, and joy in the Lord. Many have been remarkably engaged to watch, and strive, and fight against sin; to cast out every idol, sell all for Christ, give up themselves entirely to God, and make a sacrifice of every worldly and carnal thing to the welfare and prosperity of their souls. And there has of late appeared in some places an unusual disposition to bind themselves to it in a solemn covenant with God. And now, instead of meetings at taverns and drinking-houses, and of young people in frolics and vain company, the country is full of men, women, and little children—to read and pray, and sing praises, and to converse of the things of God and another world. In very many places the main of the conversation in all companies turns on religion, and things of a spiritual nature. Instead of vain mirth among young people, there is now either mourning under a sense of the guilt of sin, or holy rejoicing in Christ Jesus: and, instead of their lewd songs, there are now to be heard from them songs of praise to God, and the Lamb that was slain to redeem them by his blood. And there has been this alteration abiding on multitudes all over the land, for a year and a half, without any appearance of a disposition to return to former vice and vanity" (Id., p. 374).*

This revival work even extended to the Indians of New England:

"And, under the influences of this work, there have been many of the remains of those wretched people and dregs of mankind, the poor Indians, that seemed to be next to a state of brutality, and with whom,

---

*This is strongly reminiscent of what the father of King Lamoni said to Aaron, the missionary, when brought to conviction of sin: "What shall I do that I may have this eternal life of which thou hast spoken? Yea, what shall I do, that I may be born of God, having this wicked spirit rooted out of my breast, and receive his Spirit, that I may be filled with joy, that I may not be cast off at the last day? Behold, said he, I will give all that I possess; yea, I will forsake my kingdom, that I may receive this great joy" (Alma 22:15).

till now, it seemed to be to little more purpose to use endeavours for their instruction and awakening, than with the beasts. Their minds have now been strangely opened to receive instruction, and been deeply affected with the concerns of their precious souls; they have reformed their lives, and forsaken their former stupid, barbarous, and brutish way of living; and particularly that sin to which they have been so exceedingly addicted, their drunkenness. Many of them to appearance brought truly and greatly to delight in the things of God, and to have their souls very much engaged and entertained with the great things of the gospel. And many of the poor negroes also have been in like manner wrought upon and changed. Very many little children have been remarkably enlightened, and their hearts wonderfully affected and enlarged, and their mouths opened, expressing themselves in a manner far beyond their years, and to the just astonishment of those who have heard them. Some of them for many months have been greatly and delightfully affected with the glory of divine things, and the excellency and love of the Redeemer, with their hearts greatly filled with love to and joy in him; and they have continued to be serious and pious in their behaviour" (Id., p. 375).

Here and there throughout the several treatises cited above, Mr. Edwards deals at length with the character and extent of these religious emotional phenomena, but what has now been set down will be enough to disclose their general character. After 1742, these manifestations of the spirit "began to wane, much to the regret of Mr. Edwards." "I am full of apprehension," he wrote to Rev. William M'Culloch, under date of September 23rd, 1747, "that God has no design of mercy to those that were left unconverted, of the generation that were on the stage, in the time of the late extraordinary religious commotion, and striving of God's Spirit; unless it be perhaps a small gleaning from among them. But it may be, when their little ones, the generation that was then in their childhood, are brought fully on the stage of action, God will abundantly pour out his Spirit, and revive and carry on his work, here and elsewhere in the Christian world."

"It was postponed," remarks the editor of the "Memoirs," in a footnote, "to the time of the Children of the generation here referred to."

"It is deserving perhaps of inquiry," says the "Memoirs," in an other place, and referring to the setback the great revival of 1740-42 received as a result of certain extravagant excesses of that period, "whatever the subsequent slumber of the American Church, *for nearly seventy years* may not be ascribed in an important degree, to the fatal reaction of these unhappy measures" (*Works*, 1:cxiii).

At any rate, after the subsidence of this religious emotionalism in

1742, it was about seventy years before there came a reappearance of it.

This brings us to the early decades of the 19th century. It was in 1800 that what was known as the "Kentucky revival" began, which is thus described by Prof. J. B. Turner, author of *Mormonism in All Ages:*[22]

"In the year 1800, the great revival in Kentucky, as it is called, commenced. The people were accustomed to assemble, sometimes to the number of ten or twelve thousand, and they often continued together, in devotional exercises, for several days and nights. Here the people were sometime seized with general tremor, the pulse grew weaker, their breathing difficult, and, at long intervals, their hands and feet became cold, and finally they fell, and both pulse and breath, and all symptoms of life forsook them for nearly an hour, during which time they suffered no pain, and were perfectly conscious of their condition, and knew what was passing around them.

"At one time, during service, several shrieks were uttered, and people fell in all directions. Not less than one thousand fell at one meeting. Their outward expressions of devotion consisted in alternate singing, crying, laughing, shouting, and every variety of violent motion, of which the muscular system is capable. These violent motions they soon became unable to resist. They were violently thrown upon the ground by the convulsions, where their 'motions resembled those of a fish upon land.' This disease lasted through several years, in some cases, and propagated itself by sympathetic imitation, from one to another, with astonishing rapidity, in crowds, and often in small assemblies" (*Mormonism in All Ages*, p. 272).

This was the beginning of the re-appearance of the emotional phenomena of the days of Mr. Edwards. Later, as this method of reaching men became popular, the crowds were even larger and the encampments extended through many weeks. "Such was the eagerness of the people to attend," says Henry Howe, author of *Historical Collections of the Great West*,[23] "that entire neighborhoods were forsaken, and the roads literally crowded by those pressing forward on their way to the grove." The great assemblies being too large for one person to address them, they would divide into several congregations and be addressed by as many different speakers. "The whole grove," writes Mr. Howe—the encampments were usually held in groves—"the whole grove at times became vocal with the praises of God, and at others pierced with the cries of distressed penitents" (*Historical Collections of the Great West*, p. 205). Strange nervous contortions often attended upon manifestations of this religious fervor. Men and women acted as if they were beside themselves. There would be "shoutings," "fallings," "jerkings," and all manner of emotional frenzy manifested. Sometimes large numbers in a congregation would be seized with a tremor. The pulse of one so attacked would grow weaker, his breathing become more difficult, and at intervals hands and feet would grow cold, and finally he would fall. "Both pulse and breath, and all symptoms of life," says Professor J. B. Turner of Illinois College, in describing the malady — I can think of it as nothing else — "forsook them for nearly an hour, during which time they suffered no pain, and were perfectly conscious of their condition, and knew what was passing around them."

It will not be necessary to further repeat the scenes, nor describe again the manner of these "religious" manifestations. It is clearly established now that these scenes of religious frenzy were common in the vicinage where Joseph Smith resided in his youth and early manhood. The writings of Jonathan Edwards were commonly accessible throughout New England in those days; and Joseph Smith himself came in contact with these emotional phenomena in his own experience after their rebirth in the early decades of the 19th century. The question is, did his knowledge of these things lead to their introduction into the Book of Mormon narrative? I think it cannot be questioned but where there is sufficient resemblance between the Book of Mormon instances of religious emotionalism and those cited in the foregoing quotations from the works of Edwards *et al.* to justify the thought that the latter might well have suggested and indeed become the source of the former.

VI

There can be no doubt but what the style of preaching, exhortation, warning, praying, admonition together with the things emphasized and the ends aimed at in such work of the Christian ministry as came to the attention of Joseph Smith were all largely and deeply influenced by those first and greatest evangelical popular prachers of Protestant Christianity, John Wesley, George Whitefield, Jonathan Edwards, and Dr. Thomas Loke *et al.* In saying this I am not unmindful of the fact that these great lights of the Protestant Churches wrought their work in the generation preceeding the one in which Joseph Smith lived, and that he never came in contact with them—Wesley, Whitefield, and Dr. Coke on their several visits to America, or with Dr. Edwards in New England. Still that revival of religion which marked the early decades of the 19th century, with which Joseph Smith was familiar, took on pretty much all of its coloring from the spirit and manner in which these above named evangelists conducted their work. The generation of men following them—the men with whom Joseph Smith came in contact, during his boyhood and early manhood, and though whom he heard of these "giants" of ultra-Protestantism of the former generation were but imitators of these in spirit, in matter, and in manner. The impression which these ultra-Protestant leaders of the preceding generation made upon their own generation and upon the one following was profound. This may be witnessed by the revival of religious emotionalism in the early decades of the 19th century. It was with these leaders of the previous generation that this sort of religious phenomena had its origin, among English Protestants—and when it had its re-birth in the generation following, it came back with what one may call increased fury, and a wider response on the part of the people than in the previous generation. It was a success that was achieved by adopting both matter—i.e., doctrine and manner, and method of those who began it, in the previous generation. This second heat of ultra-Protestantism was at its full height then in the boyhood and early manhood of Joseph Smith. It was the only kind of "religion" he came in contact with—this ultra-Protestantism of the aggressive sects—this frenzied sort. He did not come in contact with, nor hear much about the more conservative forms, of Protestantism. He knew but little of the Episcopal Church of England, or of the Roman Catholic Church, or of the Lutheran, or the Greek Church; and what little he knew or had heard of these large subdivisions of the Christian world would likely be, not only fragmentary, but distorted.

The upshot of all this would be that if the Book of Mormon is of merely human origin, and Joseph Smith is its author, then all these facts here considered would be reflected in the Book of Mormon. Are they? That is the test to which the Book is now to be submitted.

What may be regarded as the principal characteristic of ultra-Protestantism and its methods is a pride in excessive humility, a glorying in self-abasement, and self-accusation; all the more so, perhaps, because of a subconscious realization that there is in their scheme of divine ordering a free pardon for all their sin; hence the consequences of sin upon themselves will not be greater because the sins are many or of the baser sort; and it is evident upon this theory, carried to its logical conclusion, the greater and more numerous the sins the greater the power and the glory of the pardoning power—God. Then why not the penitent self-accuse, self-abase, and proclaim himself the vilest of men, since it will eventuate in the increased power and glory of God, as a mighty savior of sinful man?*

But in the first place let us note how the spirit of self-abasement and self-accusation has got itself expressed in the Book of Mormon.

The preaching of ultra-Protestant ministers had for its object the excitement of this consciousness of sin, the confession of it, and a firm reliance upon a free pardon of it through the free grace of the Lord Jesus Christ. Hence the preaching of these evangelists was an appeal to the emotions, rather than to the understanding—to the intellect. This kind of preaching brought on such ecstatic appeals as this from a frantic appeal to sinners, by White and Old:

"The Lord help you to think! O think how soon your sun will go down and even your bodies will feel damnation, not only in respect to pain, but loss. . . . Those who value themselves most on this beauty and dress, and do not love God on earth, will be most deformed in hell, and their bodies suffer proportionally there. There is no dressing in hell, nothing but fire and brimstone there, and the wrath of God always awaiting on thee, O sinner, who ever thou art, man or woman. . . . When you are damned, the days of your mourning will be but at the beginning; there is no end to your mourning in hell. There is but one song, if it may be called so, in hell, to wit . . . 'how am I tormented in this flame!' Consider this, ye that forget God; and O that God may bless you tonight with Godly sorrow. Believers, pray for them; Lord help you, sinners, to pray for your vile selves. Some may think, what do you cry for? (The preacher, as was his wont was crying copiously), why, I cry for you. . . . May the love of God make you cry! May you not go home tonight without an arrow steeped in the blood of Christ. It was wonderful what

_____
*The evil and extreme effects of the doctrine of justification by faith without works is, perhaps.[24]

a good woman awaking thought she saw written over her head, O earth, earth, hear the word of the Lord! May every faithful soul be made to hear it; to awake, arise from their sleep in sin. The sun is going down, and death may put an end to all tonight: the Lord help you to come though it is the eleventh hour; o that you would fly, fly this night to Christ, lest God destroy you forever. Jesus stands ready with open arms to receive you whom he has first pricked to the heart, and made you cry out, What shall I do to be saved! He will then make you believe in his name, that you may be saved: God grant this may be the case of all here tonight. Amen" (From a sermon of George Whitefield, from a collection of *Eighteen Sermons* by him published in 1808, reported by Joseph Gurney. Sermon VIII, pp. 160, 161.)[25]

On another occasion this:

"I was preaching in Scotland, and saw ten thousand affected in a moment, some with joy, others crying I cannot believe; others, God has given me faith, some fainting in their friends arms: seeing two stout creatures upon a tombstone, hardened indeed, I cried out, you rebels come down, and down they fell directly, and cried before they went away; What shall we do to be saved? . . . O may God bring down you rebels tonight; may this be the happy hour you may be cast down and disquieted within you. What can I say more? *I would speak till I burst, I would speak till I could say no more,* O poor souls, that hast been never yet cast down. I will tell you, if you die without being cast down, however you may die and have no pangs in your death, and your carnal relations may thank God that you died like lambs, but no sooner will your souls be out of your bodies, but God will cast you down to hell, you will be lifting up your eyes in yonder place of torment, you will be disquieted, but there will be nobody there to say, hope thou in God, for I shall yet praise him, &c. O my God, when I think of this, I could go to the very gates of hell to preach. I thought the other day, O if I had my health, I would stand on the top of every hackney coach, and preach Christ to those poor creatures. Unconverted old people, unconverted young people, will you have no compassion on your own souls; if you will damn yourselves, remember I am free from the blood of you all. O if it be thy blessed will, Lord most holy, O God most mighty, take the hearts of these sinners into thy hand. Methinks I see the heavens opened, the Judge sitting on his throne, the sea boiling like a pot, and the Lord Jesus coming to Judge the world, well, if you are damned, it shall not be for want of calling after. O come, come, God help you to come, whilst Jesus is standing ready to receive you. O fly to the Saviour this night for refuge; remember if you die in an unconverted state you must be damned forever" (Id., pp. 230, 231, 232).

The basis of appeal to the sinner was that he might become heir to the righteousness of Christ through imputation of that righteousness to him: the following excerpt from a sermon on "Repentance and Conversion" is an illustration of both the doctrine and the appeal made upon it:

"But some go further, they think they are converted because they are reformed: they say, a reformed rake makes a good husband, but I think a renewed rake will make a better. Reformation is not renovation: I may have the outside of the platter washed; I may be turned from profaneness to a regard for morality; and because I do not swear, nor go to the play as I used to do; have left off cards, and perhaps put on a plain dress; and so believe, or rather fancy, that I am converted; yet the old man remains unmortified, and the heart is unrenewed still. Comparing myself with what I once was, and looking on my companions with disdain, I may there stick faster in self, and get into a worse and more dangerous state than I was before. If any of you think me too severe, remember you are the person I mean; for you think me so only because I touch your case. . . . You have not heard me, I hope, speak a word against reformation; you have not heard me speak a word against being converted from the church of Rome; against being converted to the church of England; or against being good: no; all these are right in their place; but all these conversions you may have, and yet never be truly converted at all. What is conversion then? I will not keep you longer in suspense, my brethren: man must be a new creature, and converted from his own righteousness to the righteousness of the Lord Jesus Christ; conviction will always precede spiritual conversion: and therefore the Protestant divines make this distinction, you may be convinced and not converted, but you cannot be converted without being convinced; and if we are truly converted we shall not only be turned and converted from *sinful self,* but we shall be converted from righteous self . . . in vain we may talk of being converted till we are brought out of ourselves; to come as poor lost undone sinners, to the Lord Jesus Christ; *to be washed in his blood; to be clothed in his glorious imputed righteousness:* the consequence of this imputation, or application of a Mediator's righteousness to the soul, will be a conversion from sin to holiness. . . . They that are truly converted to Jesus, and are justified by faith in the Son of God, will take care to evidence their conversion, not only by having grace implanted in their hearts, but by that grace diffusing itself through every faculty of the soul, and making a universal change in the whole man. I am preaching from a title that saith, He that is in Christ is a new creature, old things, not will be, but are passed away, all things, not only will, but are become new. As a child when born has all the several parts of a man, it will have no more limbs than it has now, *if it lives to fourscore years and ten.* So when a person is converted to God, there are all the features of the new creature and growth, till he becomes a young man and a father in Christ; till he becomes ripe in grace, and God translates him to glory. Anything short of this is but the shadow instead of the substance; and however persons may charge us with being enthusiasts, yet we need not be moved either to anger or sorrow, since St. Paul says, I travel in birth till Christ be formed in your hearts" (Whitefield's *Sermons*, pp. 90, 91, 92, 93).

Then in closing, not the above sermon, but one in much the same strain, Whitefield made the following appeal:

"And if God hath not wrought this in any of you that are here, which perhaps may be the case, though I cannot think what should bring anybody here if they had not a desire of the salvation of their souls; if God hath not wrought it in you yet, O that this may be the time; O that God may give us some parting blessing; that some poor creatures that have nothing but the devil's work in them yet may now seek after the blessed work of the Holy Ghost. If we may ask what God has wrought, let me ask you what the devil hath wrought in you; O thou unconverted soul, sin has made thee a beast, made thy body, which ought to be the temple of the living God, a cage of every unclean bird; what hath Satan wrought in thee? but made thee a nest of vile stinking swine; and what will he give thee? *Hell, hell, hell.* The wages the devil gives no man can live by; the wages of sin is death: and here I come to bring you good news, glad tidings of great joy. O that God may now counter-work the devil, and take thee into his own workmanship, create thee anew in Christ Jesus, give thee to feel a little of his Spirit's work on thy heart, and make thee, of a child of the devil, a child of God! Say not, it cannot be; say not, it shall not be; say not, it is too late; say not, it is for others but not for me; my brethren, God help you to cry, and to try tonight, if thou canst turn the text into a prayer, Lord God, I have felt the devil work in me, now good God, let me know what it is for thee to work in me; make me a new creature, create a new spirit within me, that I may join with thy dear people in singing, what hath God wrought! What hath he wrought! How am I come to this place of torment! I sold my birthright for a mess of pottage! Heaven or hell is set before you tonight; Jesus grant that the terrors of the Lord may awaken you tonight, and that you may not rest till you have comfort and support from God" (Id., pp. 195, 196).

So also Wesley: whose manner and subject matter is thus given by Southey: "It was a peculiarity of Wesley, in his discourses, that in winding up his sermons — in pointing his exhortations and driving them home — he spoke as if he were addressing himself to an individual, so that every one to whom the condition which he described was applicable felt as if he were singled out; and the preacher's words were then like the eyes of a portrait which seem to look at every beholder. "Who," said the preacher, "who art thou, that now seest and feelest both thine inward and outward ungodliness? Thou art the man! I want thee for my Lord, *I challenge thee for* a child of God by faith. The Lord hath need of thee. Thou who feelest thou art just fit for hell are just fit to advance his glory—the glory of his free grace, justifying the ungodly and him that worketh not. O, come quickly! Believe in the Lord Jesus: and thou, even thou, art reconciled to God." And, again—"Thou ungodly one, who hearest or readest these words, thou vile, helpless, miserable sinner, I charge thee before God, the judge of all, go straight unto Him, with all thy ungodliness! Take heed thou destroy not thine own soul by pleading thy righteousness, more or less. Go as altogether ungodly, guilty, lost, destroyed, descrying, and dropping into hell; and thou shalt then find favor in His sight, and know that He justifieth the ungodly. As such thou shalt be brought unto the blood of sprinkling, as an undone, helpless, damned sinner. Thus look unto Jesus! There is the Lamb of God, who taketh away thy sins! Plead thou no works, no righteousness of thine own! No humility, no contrition, sincerity! In no wise! That were, in very deed, to deny the Lord that bought thee. No. Plead thou singly the blood of the covenant, the ransom paid for thy proud, stubborn, sinful soul" (*The Life of Wesley*, by Robert Southey, 1:336-37).[26]

The effect of such appeals is given in numerous instances in some work of which the following are but examples: "One day, after Wesley had expounded the fourth chapter of Acts," the persons present "called upon God to confirm his word." "Immediately," he adds, "one that stood by, to our no small surprise, cried out aloud, with the utmost vehemence, even as in the agonies of death; but we continued in prayer, till a new song was put in her mouth, a thanksgiving unto our God. Soon after two other persons (well known in this place as laboring to live in all good conscience toward all men) were seized with strong pain, and constrained to roar for the disquietness of their heart. But it was not long before they likewise burst forth into praise to God their Savior. The last who called upon God, as out of the belly of hell, was a stranger in Bristol; and in a short space he also was overwhelmed with joy and love, knowing that God had healed his backslidings. So many living witnesses hath God given, that his hand is still stretched out to heal, and that signs and wonders are even now wrought by his holy child Jesus." At another place, "a young man was suddenly seized with a violent trembling all over, and in a few minutes, the sorrows of his heart being enlarged, sunk down to the ground; but we ceased not calling upon God till he raised him up full of peace and joy in the Holy Ghost." Preaching at Newgate, Wesley was led, insensibly, he says, and without any previous design, to declare strongly and explicitly that God willeth all men to be saved, and to pray that, if this were not the truth of God, he would not suffer the blind to go out of the way; but if it were, that he would bear witness to his word. "Immediately one, and another, and another, sunk to the earth; they dropped on every side as thunderstruck." "In the evening I was again pressed in spirit to declare that Christ gave himself a ransom for all. And almost before we called upon him to set his seal, he answered. One was so wounded by the sword of the spirit, that you would have imagined she could not live a moment. But immediately his abundant kindness was showed, and she loudly sung of his righteousness" (Southey, 1:220-21).

Southey gives the following account of John Hayden of Bristol: "Wesley describes him as a man of regular life and conversation, who constantly attended the public prayers and sacraments, and was zealous for the church, and against dissenters of every denomination. What he saw satisfied him so little, that he went about to see his acquaintance, one after another, till one in the morning, laboring to convince them that it was all a delusion of the devil. This might induce a reasonable doubt of his sanity at the time; nor is the suspicion lessened by the circumstance, that when he had sat down to dinner the next day, he chose, before he began to eat, to finish a sermon which he had borrowed upon Salvation by Faith. In reading the last page he changed color, *fell off his chair*, beat himself against the ground and screamed so terribly that the neighbors were alarmed and ran into the house." Wesley was presently informed that the man was fallen raving mad. "I found him," he says, "on the floor, the room being full of people, whom his wife would have kept without, but he cried out aloud, 'No, let them all come, let all the world see the *just judgment of God!*' Two or three men were holding him as well as they could. He immediately fixed his eyes upon me, and stretching out his hand, cried, 'Aye, this is he who *I said* was a deceiver of the people! But God has overtaken me. I said it was all a delusion; but this is no delusion!' He then roared out, 'O thou devil, thou cursed devil, yea, thou legion of devils! thou canst not stay! Christ will cast thee out! I know his work is begun! Tear me to pieces if thou wilt; but thou canst not hurt me!' He then beat himself against the ground again, his breast heaving at the same time as in the pangs of death, and great drops of sweat trickling down his face. We all betook ourselves to prayer. His pangs ceased, and both his body and soul *were at* liberty." The next day Wesley found him with his voice gone, and his body weak as an infant's, "but his soul was in peace, full of love, and rejoicing in hope of the glory of God" (Southey, 1:222-23). This borders closely on the casting out of devils.

Southey also relates the following as to the effect of Dr. Coke's preaching in America. Dr. Coke, it be remembered, was Mr. Wesley's representative in America: "It appears that the spirit of riotous devotion, which afterward produced the fanatical extravagances of the camp-meetings, began to manifest itself in the early days of American Methodism, and that it was encouraged by the superiors, when it might have been repressed. At Annapolis," says Dr. Coke, "after my last prayer, the congregation began to pray and praise aloud in a most astonishing manner. At first I found some reluctance to enter into the business; but soon the tears began to flow, and I think I have seldom found a more comforting or strengthening time. This praying and praising aloud is a common thing throughout Virginia and Maryland. What shall we say? Souls are awakened and converted by multitudes; and the work is surely a genuine work, if there be a genuine work of God upon earth. Whether there be wildfire in it, or not, I do most ardently wish that there was such a work at this present time in England." At Baltimore, after the evening service was concluded, "the congregation began to pray and praise aloud, and continued so to do, till two o'clock in the morning. Out of a congregation of two thousand people, two or three hundred were *engaged at the same time in praising God, praying for the conviction* and conversion of sinners, or exhorting those around them with the utmost vehemence; and hundreds more were engaged in *wrestling* prayer, either for their own conversion, or sanctification. The first noise of the people soon brought a multitude to see what was going on. One of our elders was the means that night of the conversion of seven poor penitents within his little circle in less than fifteen minutes. Such was the zeal of many, that a tolerable company attended the preaching *at five the next morning,* notwithstanding the late hour at which they parted." The next evening the same uproar was renewed, and the maddened congregation *continued in their excesses as long and as loud as before.* The practice became common in Baltimore, though that city had been one of the "calmest and most critical" upon the continent. "Many of our elders," says Coke, "who were the softest, most connected and most sedate of our preachers, have entered with all their hearts into this work. And gracious and wonderful has been the change, our greatest enemies themselves being the judges, that has been wrought on multitudes, on whom the work began at those wonderful seasons" (Southey's *Life of Wesley,* 2:260-61).

NOTES

1. Elias Boudinot, *A Star in the West, or, a Humble Attempt to Discover the Long Lost Ten Tribes of Israel, Preparatory to their Return to their Beloved City, Jerusalem* (Trenton, N.J.: Published by D. Fenton, S. Hutchinson, and J. Dunham, George Sherman, Printer, 1816). In twelve chapters Boudinot defended the Indians against accusations they were cruel savages; pointed out that the

Jews were the chosen people of God; and decided, after reading the second apocryphal book of Esdras and examining Indian culture, that the Indians were descended from the Ten Lost Tribes of Israel.

2. Joseph Sabin, *A Dictionary of Books Relating to America,* 29 vols. (New York: Biographical Society of America, 1892-1928), 176-77.

3. Orson Pratt, an outstanding intellectual leader of the early Mormon Church, was born September 19, 1811, in Hartford, New York, became a member of the Church in 1830, and served as one of the Twelve Apostles from 1835 until his death on October 3, 1881. He spent most of his life as a missionary, was widely known for his ability as a mathematician and as a writer in defense of Mormonism, and served as historian for his Church during the last seven years of his life. In August 1870 he met Dr. John P. Newman in a famous debate on polygamy and became known nationwide as a stalwart defender of the practice. A polygamist himself, he was the father of forty-five children.

4. As Roberts said in his *Comprehensive History,* Joseph Smith experienced his first vision as a boy of fourteen in the spring of 1820, when he reported that God and Jesus Christ appeared to him and instructed him that he must not join any of the churches because "they were all wrong." Three years then intervened before he experienced a second heavenly visit. Joseph Smith recounted that on September 1, 1823, the Angel Moroni, a resurrected being from the Book of Mormon period, appeared and told him of the existence of some gold plates in a hill not too far distant that contained an abridged history of the ancestors of the American Indians and that with the records was a breast-plate holding two stones, the "Urim and Thummim," with which he would be expected to translate the records. Moroni returned two more times during the night to repeat the message of the Book of Mormon and to warn the young man he was to divulge this information only to certain designated people as "commanded." B. H. Roberts, *A Comprehensive History of the Church of Jesus Christ of Latter-day Saints,* 6 vols. (Salt Lake City: Deseret News Press, 1930), 1:52-55, 70-75. While Roberts merely recounted the story of the "first vision" as reported by Joseph Smith, Dean C. Jessee has clearly indicated that there are contradictory accounts of this asserted heavenly visitation. See his review of Milton V. Backman, Jr., *Joseph Smith's First Vision: The First Vision in Its Historical Context* (Salt Lake City: Bookcraft, 1971), in *Dialogue: A Journal of Mormon Thought,* 6 (Spring 1971):85-88.

5. Jonah 4:6-7: "And the Lord God prepared a gourd, and made it come up over Jonah, that it might be a shadow over his head, to deliver him from his grief. So Jonah was exceeding glad of the gourd. But God prepared a worm when the morning rose the next day, and it smote the gourd that it withered."

6. The first (1830) edition of the Book of Mormon was a single narrative. Orson Pratt, in 1879, added references and divided the book into chapters and verses. In 1920 the Book of Mormon was published with double-column pages, chapter headings, chronological data, revised footnote references, a pronouncing vocabulary, and an index.

7. Joseph Smith, *History of the Church of Jesus Christ of Latter-day Saints,*

with an introduction and notes by B. H. Roberts, 6 vols. (Salt Lake City: Deseret News Press, 1902).

8. William Wines Phelps was a well-educated convert to the Mormon Church in 1831. He never became an apostle and, in fact, was once excommunicated but within two years was back in the Church and remained faithful to his beliefs the rest of his life, his death occurring on March 7, 1872, in Salt Lake City. He was the subject of a revelation by Joseph Smith (Doctrine and Covenants, Section 55) and was prominent in producing many publications for his Church, including "The Evening and Morning Star." He served several terms in the Utah legislature, was involved in early educational activities in the Territory, and had been a strong supporter of Brigham Young in the fight with Sidney Rigdon over who should succeed Joseph Smith as leader of the Mormon Church.

9. Despite Robert's statement that a photograph was included with the manuscript, only this crude pencil drawing remains.

10. Lucy Smith, *History of the Prophet Joseph* (Salt Lake City: Improvement Era, 1902), 84.

11. Parley Parker Pratt, a brother of Orson Pratt and a member of the Council of Twelve Apostles from 1835 to 1857, was born in Burlington, New York, on April 12, 1807. He traveled to Utah in 1847 and served in the legislature of Utah Territory. He was assassinated on May 13, 1857, while traveling near Van Buren, Arkansas. He was the author of the famous pamphlet, *Voice of Warning,* and also a *History of the Missouri Persecutions.* Parley P. Pratt, Jr., ed., *The Autobiography of Parley Parker Pratt* (New York: Published for the Editor and Proprietor by Russell Brothers, 1874).

12. Oliver Cowdery, ed., "Letter of Joseph Smith, Jr., to Oliver Cowdery," *Latter Day Saints Messenger and Advocate,* 1 (Dec. 1834):40.

13. Edward W. Tullidge, *Tullidge's Histories, Containing the History of All the Northern, Eastern and Western Counties of Utah; Also the Counties of Southern Idaho, with a Biographical Appendix* (Salt Lake City: Press of the Juvenile Instructor, 1889), 271-72. Anson Call became a member of the Church on May 21, 1836. He arrived in Salt Lake Valley on September 9, 1848; served in the territorial legislature; became a probate judge; and helped plant colonies on the Colorado River and in Box Elder County, Utah.

14. Franklin D. Richards and James A. Little, *A Compendium of the Doctrines of the Gospel* (Salt Lake City: Geo. Q. Cannon & Sons, Printers, 1898).

15. Orson Pratt, "A Series of Pamphlets," in his *Works* (Liverpool: R. James, 1851).

16. *The Book of Mormon; an Account Written by the Hand of Mormon, upon Plates Taken from the Plates of Nephi.* By Joseph Smith, jun., author and proprietor (Palmyra, N.Y.: Printed by E. B. Grandin, for the author, 1830).

17. Oliver Cowdery, "Early Scenes and Incidents in the Church," *Improvement Era,* Letter VII, vol. 2, no. 9 (July 1899):652-58.

18. The eight letters by Oliver Cowdery in the *Improvement Era,* vol. 2 for 1898-99, may be found on the following pages: Letter I, Part I, no. 3 (Jan. 1899):186-93; Letter II, Part I, no. 4 (Feb. 1899):267-74; Letter III, Part I, no. 5 (Mar. 1899):347-50; Letter IV, Part I, no. 6 (Apr. 1899):419-24; Letter V, Part

II, no. 7 (May 1899): 529-33; Letter VI, Part II, no. 8 (June 1899):590-97; Letter VII, Part II, no. 9 (July 1899):652-58; Letter VIII, Part II, no. 10 (Aug. 1899):729-34.

19. Smith, *History of the Church,* 11, gives the date for the first visit of Moroni as being September 21, 1823.

20. Brigham H. Roberts, "History of the Mormon Church," *Americana,* 5 (Feb. 1910):188-89. The incident involving Newel Knight and the "first miracle" of the Church is also narrated in Smith, *History of the Church,* 82-84.

21. Jonathan Edwards, *The Works of President Edwards* (Orig. publ., London, 1817 in 10 vols.; reprint ed., New York: Burt Franklin, Research and Source Series No. 271, 1968). Volume 4, in three parts, is entitled *A Treatise Concerning Religious Affections,* in which Edwards attempted to establish criteria for determining "Distinguishing Signs of Truly Gracious and Holy Affections."

22. J. B. Turner, *Mormonism in All Ages, or the Rise, Progress, and Causes of Mormonism; with the Biography of Its Author and Founder, Joseph Smith, Junior* (New York: Platt & Peters, 1842). Turner, a professor at Illinois College, Jacksonville, thought that "it is time the absurdities of their scheme were exposed. . . . They are, in truth, the most dangerous and virulent enemies . . . that now exist in the Union."

23. Henry Howe, *Historical Collections of the Great West, Containing Narratives of the Most Important and Interesting Events in Western History,* 2 vols. in one book (Cincinnati: Published by Henry Howe, at E. Morgan & Co.'s, 1855).

24. Roberts did not complete this footnote.

25. George Whitefield, *Eighteen Sermons Preached by the late Rev. George Whitefield . . . ,* taken verbatim in shorthand, and faithfully transcribed by Joseph Gurney. Revised by Andrew Gifford (Springfield, Mass.: Thomas Dickman, 1808).

26. Robert Southey, *The Life of John Wesley,* abridged, and newly edited, with notes, etc., by Arthur Reynolds (London: Hutchinson, 1904). A later printing based on the 3rd edition of 1846 and edited by Maurice H. Fitzgerald in two volumes appeared in 1925 (London: Oxford University Press, 1925).

"A PARALLEL"

As B. H. Roberts explained to Richard R. Lyman in his letter of October 24, 1927, he was sending Lyman a "Parallel between some main outline facts pertaining to the Book of Mormon and matter that was published in Ethan Smith's *View of the Hebrews*," but which was "not one fourth part of what can be presented in this form." But it was this abbreviated version of his longer "A Book of Mormon Study" that became known to a small circle of interested Mormons during the late 1920s and the 1930s until his son, Ben E. Roberts, decided to distribute copies during a dinner address at the Timpanogos Club in 1946. Because it became so well known and the subject of analysis by both Mormon and non-Mormon scholars, it is being produced here as it appears in the typescript copy in the B. H. Roberts Papers in the Marriott Library.

Someone, perhaps Ben E. Roberts or B. H. Roberts's secretary, made some editorial changes from the author's original by correcting misspelled words, inserting punctuation, adding citations, and completing quotations that had only been quoted in part. The only substantive change perceived by the present editor occurs in item #13 where B. H. Roberts inserted a phrase in parentheses in a sentence quoted from II Nephi 10:8-18 of the Book of Mormon: "I will afflict thy seed (meaning the American Indians) by the hand of the Gentiles" In the mimeographed version distributed by Ben E. Roberts that entire sentence was omitted. With that exception, no substantive changes were made by the unknown editor, and Mervin B. Hogan made a "faithful copy" of the eighteen similarities in his article, "'A Parallel': A Matter of Chance versus Coincidence," as it appeared in the *Rocky Mountain Mason*, January 1956.

A PARALLEL

<table>
<tr><td>

BOOK OF MORMON
1830

</td><td>

VIEW OF THE HEBREWS
1823-5

</td></tr>
</table>

(1) *Place:* Sharon, Windsor Co., Vermont: And Palmyra, Ontario (now Wayne) County, New York.

(1) *Place:* Poultney, Rutland Co. Vermont (adjoining county on the west from Windsor County, Vermont, where Smith family lived).

(2) *Title:* "Book of Mormon," by the hand of Mormon," ascribing Origin of American Indians to certain Tribes of the Hebrews. Translated by Joseph Smith.

(2) *Title:* "View of the Hebrews" or "The Tribes of Israel in America" written by Ethan Smith, Minister.

(3) *Revealed Existence* of the Book of Mormon to Joseph Smith September 22, 1823.

Gold Plates of Book of Mormon given into custody of Joseph Smith for translation, September 22, 1827.

Book of Mormon published the latter part of March, 1830. "To the convincing of the Jew and the Gentile that Jesus is the Christ." (Preface Title page)

(3) *"View of the Hebrews" published (1st Ed.)* 1823.

Second Edition published 1825; considerably enlarged by quotations from Baron Humbolt's "New Spain" (Black's translation) American Edition, 1811 Copious quotations on ruined cities of America, Temples, and the story of Quetzalcoatl — Reminiscent of Moses *"as a type of the Christ."*

(4) *Origin of Am Indians*

It is often represented by Mormon speakers and writers, that the Book of Mormon was the first to represent the American Indians as descendants of the Hebrews: holding that the Book of Mormon is unique in this. The claim is sometimes still ignorantly made.

(4) *Origin of Am Indians*

In his index to the "View of the Hebrews" (p. 10) Mr. Ethan Smith informs us that from page 114 to page 225 (111 pages) will be devoted "to promiscuous testimonies," to the main fact for which his book stands, viz. *the Hebrew origin of the American Indians.* He

BOOK OF MORMON
1830

VIEW OF THE HEBREWS
1823-5

(4) *Origin of Am Indians* (continued):
brings together a very long list of writers and published books to show that this view very generally obtained throughout New England. One hundred and eleven pages devoted to evidence alone of the fact of such Hebrew origin gives space for much proof. Referring to Adair's testimonies on the subject, the "View of the Hebrews" *lists twenty-three arguments to prove such origin.* (pp. 147-8)

(5) *The Hidden Book Revealed:* On finding of the Book of Mormon Joseph Smith states that the Angel Moroni said that there was a book deposited written upon gold plates giving an account of the former Inhabitants of this continent and the source whence they sprang- - - -Convenient to the village of Manchester- - -stands a hill of considerable size- - -On the west side of the hill, not far from the top, under a stone of considerable size lay the plates, deposited in a stone box. This stone was thick and rounding in the middle on the upper side and thinner toward the edges, so that the middle part of it was visible above the ground, but the edge all around was covered with earth. Having removed the earth, I obtained a lever, which I got fixed under the edge of the stone, and with a little exertion

(5) *The Lost Book:* Dr. West of Stockbridge gave the following information: "An old Indian informed him that his fathers in this country had not long since had a book which they had for a long time preserved. But having lost the knowledge of reading it, they concluded it would be of no further use to them; and they buried it with an Indian chief." It was spoken of "as a matter of fact." (View of the Hebrews p. 223)

"Some readers have said: If the Indians are of the Tribes of Israel, some decisive evidence of that fact will ere long be exhibited. This may be the case. * * * * *Would evidence like the following be deemed as verging toward what would be satisfactory? *Suppose* a leading character in Israel—where ever they are—should be found to have in

BOOK OF MORMON 1830	VIEW OF THE HEBREWS 1823-5

(5) The Hidden Book Revealed (continued):

raised it up.*- - -The box in which they (the plates) lay, was formed by laying stones together in some kind of cement. In the bottom of the box were hid two stones crossways of the box, and on these stones lay the plates and the other things with them.- - -I looked in, and there indeed did I behold the plates. (P.G.P. 89, 93)

(5) The Lost Book (continued):

his possession some Biblical fragment of ancient Hebrew writing. This man dies and it is buried with him in such manner as to be long preserved. Some people afterwards removing that earth, discover this fragment, and ascertain that it is an article of ancient Israel. Would such an incident- - - -be esteemed of weight? Something like this may probably have occurred in favor of our Indians being of Israel." (p. 217)

Finding the Pittsfield Parchment: (Hebrew). Mr. Merrick gave the following account: That in 1815, he was leveling some ground under and near an old wood-shed standing on a place of his, situated on Indian Hill (a place in Pittsfield so called, and lying, as the writer

---

*Has your attention ever been called to at least one striking passage in the Solomon Spaulding Book as published by our Church, which suggests something of a parallel. The description given above of this stone box as found by our Prophet, it is given by Spaulding in connection with his finding the manuscript of his book and is as follows:

"As I was walking and forming various conjectures respecting the character, situation, and numbers of those people who far exceeded the present race of Indians in works of art and ingenuity, I happened to tread on a flat stone. This was at a small distance from the fort: and it lay on the top of a small mound of earth exactly horizontal, the face of it had a singular appearance. I discovered a number of characters which appeared to me to be letters—but so much effaced by the ravages of time, that I could not read the inscription. *With the assistance of a lever I raised the stone,* but you may easily conjecture my astonishment when I discovered that its *ends and sides rested on stones and that it was designed as a cover* to an artificial cave. I found on examining that its sides were lined with- - -build in a conical form with- - -down- -and that it was about eight feet deep.

This opening led to the cave. "within the cavity I found an earthen box with a cover which shut it perfectly tight—*the box was two feet in* length, one & half in breadth and one and three inches in diameter.- - - -When I had removed the cover I found that it contained twenty-eight sheets of parchment and that when- - -appeared to be manuscripts written in an elegant hand with Roman letters and in the Latin language. (Mss. Found p 1-2)

BOOK OF MORMON 1830	VIEW OF THE HEBREWS 1823-5

(5) *The Lost Book* (continued): was afterwards informed, at some distance from the middle of the town where Mr. Merrick is now living)- - -he plowed and conveyed away old chips and earth. After the work was done he discovered near where the earth had been dug the deepest a kind of black strap about six inches in length- - -He found it was formed of pieces of thick raw hide- - -and in the fold it contained four folded leaves of old parchment. These leaves were of a dark yellow (suggesting gold color?) and contained some kind of writing. (they turned out to be Bible quotations) They were written in Hebrew with a pen, in plain and intelligible writing.

(Query: Could all this have supplied structural work for the Book of Mormon)

(6) *Inspired Seers and Prophets:* Ammon to King Limhi of the Jaredite records: "I can assuredly tell thee O King, of a man that can translate the records; for he hath that wherein he can look, and translate all records;- - -and it is a gift from God. And the things are called Interpreters, and no man can look in them except he be commanded.- - -And whosoever is commanded to look in them, the same is called SEER."

"And the King said that a Seer is greater than a Prophet. And Am-

(6) *Inspired Prophets — Spirit Gifts.* "The Indian tradition says, that their fathers were possessed of an extraordinary divine spirit, by which they foretold things future, and controlled the common course of nature: *and this they transmitted to their offspring provided they obeyed the sacred laws annexed* to it."

"Ishtoallo (Mr. Adair says of those Indians) is the name of their priestly order: And their pontifical office descends by inheritance to the Eldest."

BOOK OF MORMON 1830	VIEW OF THE HEBREWS 1823-5

(6) *Inspired Seers and Prophets* (continued):

mon said that a Seer is a Revelator and a Prophet also; and a gift which is greater can no man have except he possess this the Power of God which no man can,- - -But a Seer can know of things which have past and also of things that which are to come, and by them shall all things be revealed." (Mosiah Ch. 9)

"And now Urim and Thummim he [Mosiah] translated them [the records of the Jaredites] by the means of the two stones which were fastened into the two rims of a bow. *Now these things were prepared from the beginning, and handed down from generation to generation,* for the purpose of interpreting languages- - -And whosoever has these things is called SEER after the manner of Old Times (Mosiah ch. 28)

(7) *Urim & Thummim & Breast Plate:* "I looked in and there indeed did I behold the plates, the Urim and Thummim, and the Breast Plate as stated by the messenger (i.e. Moroni) P. of G.P. 53.

"With the records was found a curious instrument, which the ancients called "Urim & Thummim, which consisted of *two transparent stones set in the brim of a bow fastened to a breast plate.*

Through the medium of the Urim and Thummin I translated the record by the gift and power

(7) *Urim & Thummim & Breast Plate:* "The Indian Archimagus (the High Priest) officiates in making the supposed holy fire for the yearly atonement for sin, the Sagan (Waiter upon the High Priest) clothes him with a white Ephod, which is a waist-coast without sleeves. In resemblance of the Urim and Thummim, the American Archimagus wears *a breast plate made of a white conch shell, with two holes bored in the middle of it, through which he puts the ends of an otter skin strap, and fastens a*

BOOK OF MORMON
1830

VIEW OF THE HEBREWS
1823-5

(7) *Urim & Thummim & Breast Plate* (continued):
of God." (Wentworth Letter, History of the Church, Vol. 4, p. 537)

(7) *Urim & Thummim & Breast Plate* (continued):
buckhorn white button to the outside of each, *as if in imitation of the precious stones of the Urim* (View of the Hebrews p. 150).

The dress of the High Priest of the Osage Indians: "His cap was very high.- - -His robe was a buffalo skin decorated with various colored feathers.- - -And he wore on his breast suspended from his neck a dressed beaver skin stretched on sticks, on which were painted various hieroglyphic figures in different colors. The Indians speak of similar characters being among other tribes. Here as in Mr. Adair's account is their High Priest and breast plate." (View of the Hebrews p.166)- - -"The official dress of their High Priest, and his resemblance of the breast plate and other things," The "View of the Hebrews" urges as evidence of Hebrews origin. (p. 167)

7 Urim & Thummim & Breast Plate

See the Phelps "Peep Stone" Deseret Museum

[Roberts neglected to provide the illustration for the original manuscript.]

Also see Frontis Piece — Engraving — in Priest's American Antiquities.

Describing a buried chieftain in one of the Ohio Mounds:
"On the breast lay a piece of copper; also a curious stone five inches in length, two in breadth, with two perforations through it. Containing a string of sinews of some animal. On this string were many beads of ivory, or bone. The whole appeared to have been designed to wear upon the neck as a kind of breastplate. (View of the Hebrews p. 195)

BOOK OF MORMON 1830	VIEW OF THE HEBREWS 1823-5
(8) *Characters in Which Book of Mormon was Engraved on Gold Plates:* "These records were engraven on plates which had the appearance of Gold- - -they were filled with engravings, in Egyptian characters, and bound together in a volume as the leaves of a book, with three rings running through the whole.- - -The characters on the unsealed part were small and beautifully engraved. The whole book exhibited many marks of antiquity in its construction and much skill in the art of engraving." (Jos.Smith Wentworth Letter, Church History Vol. 4 p. 537) The first Nephi speaking of the record he was making of events of his times says: "Yea, I make a record in the learning of the Jews and the language of the Egyptians. And I know that the record which I make is true; And I make it with mine own hand; and I make it according to my knowledge." (6th Cent. B.C. I Nephi, ch. 1) This strange manner of making record continued through the whole Nephite period: for Mormon in the 4th Century A.D. says: And now behold we have written this record [meaning the whole abridgment of the Book of Mormon] according to our knowledge in the *characters, which are called among* us the reformed Egyptian, being handed down and altered by	(8) *Evidence of Mexican Indians anciently in contact with "Egyptian Hieroglyphics:" (View of the Hebrews* on Authority of Humbolt) "On the northwest coast between Nootka and Cook river- - -the natives display a decided taste *for hieroglyphical paintings- - -A* harp (says Humbolt) represented in the *hieroglyphical paintings* of the northwest coast of America, is an object at least as remarkable, as the famous harp on the tombs of the kings of Thebes." Humbolt is cited as giving it as his opinion "that these more improved tribes in New Mexico came from the north west coast and left some of their half civilized brethren there. *Among the hieroglyphical paintings of the latter, it seems, the harp was found. Was not this a noted Is-raelitish musical instrument?* How should the American Indians be led to paint the Jewish harp? The Jews in Babylon "hung their harps upon willows." And it is as natural an event that their brethren, in the wilds of America should place them in their silent *hieroglyphical paintings.* Whence could have been derived the knowledge of the *accurate hieroglyphical paintings,* which this most learned author (meaning Humbolt) exhibits as found among some of the Indians *unless they had learned them from people to whom the knowledge of hiero-glyphics had been transmitted from*

BOOK OF MORMON
1830

VIEW OF THE HEBREWS
1823-5

(8) *Characters in Which Book of Mormon was Engraved on Gold Plates* (continued):
us according to our manner of speech.

(8) *Evidence of Mexican Indians anciently in contact with "Egyptian Hieroglyphics"* (continued):
Egypt, its original source." (View of the Hebrews pp 184-5)

Was this sufficient to suggest the strange manner of writing the Book of Mormon in the *"learning of the Jews, and the language of the Egyptian? But in an altered Egyptian.* See Mormon cited above, left.

(9) *Accounting for two classes of people in America, one barbarous the other civilized:*
The descendants of Lehi, sometime after his death were divided by the withdrawal of the younger son I Nephi, and those he persuaded to follow him, from the elder sons of Lehi, Laman and Lemuel and their sympathizers, and this was the beginning of the establishment of civilized and barbarous peoples in America. Nephi describes both.

Of those who went with him he said:

"We did observe to keep the judgments and the statutes and the commandments of the Lord in all things according to the law of Moses. And the Lord was with us; and we did prosper exceedingly; and we did sow seed and we did reap again in abundance and we began to raise flocks and herds and animals of every kind- - -And I did teach my people to build buildings

(9) *Accounting for an Overthrown Civilization in America as witnessed by the Ruined Monuments of it; and the existence of barbarous peoples occupying America at the advent of Europeans:*
Mr. Ethan Smith found opposition to his views growing out of the supposition that if the American Indians were descendants of the lost tribes of Israel, then they would have been a civilized rather than a barbarous people when discovered. Of this he says:

"Some have felt a difficulty arising against the Indians being the ten tribes from their ignorance of the *mechanic arts of writing and of navigation.* Ancient Israel knew something of these, and some imagin, that these arts being once known could never be lost. But no objection is hence furnished against our scheme. The knowledge of mechanic arts possessed in early times has been lost by many nations.- - -And Israel, in an outcast

BOOK OF MORMON 1830	VIEW OF THE HEBREWS 1823-5

(9) *Barbarous & Civilized People* (continued):

and to work in all manner of wood, and of iron, and of copper, and of brass, and of steel, and of gold, and of silver, and of precious ores *which were in great abundance."*

"And I Nephi did build a temple and I did construct it after the manner of the temple of Solomon safe it were not build of so many precious things; *for they were not to be found upon the land.* Wherefore, it could not be build like unto Solomon's temple, but the manner of the construction was like unto the Temple of Solomon and the workmanship thereof was *exceeding* fine. And it came to pass that I Nephi did cause my people to be industrious and to labor with their hands" (and Nephi became their king) (II Nephi 5:6-18)

In relation to the other part of the Colony from whom Nephi and his following had withdrawn, called henceforth Lamanites, this is recorded of the same period. He [God] had caused the cursing to come upon them. Yea, even a sore cursing because of their iniquity, for behold they had hardened their hearts against Him, that they had become like unto a flint; wherefore as they were white and exceeding fair and delightsome, that they might not be enticing unto my people, the Lord did cause a skin of blackness to come upon them and thus said the Lord God: I shall cause that they shall be loathsome

(9) *Barbarous & Civilized People* (continued):

state, might as well have lost it. It seems a *fact* that Israel *have* lost it, let them be who or where they may, otherwise they must have been known in the civilized world.

But the people who migrated to this western world did possess some knowledge of the mechanic arts (as much doubtless, as was possessed by Israel when they disappeared in the East) appears from incontestable facts which are furnished in Baron Humbolt's "New Spain" and the "American Archeology" such as the finding of brick, earthenware, sculptures, some implements of iron, as well as other metals and other tokens of considerable improvements which furnishes an argument in favor of the Indians having descended from the ten tribes.- - -

"The probability then is this; that the ten tribes arriving in this continent with some knowledge of the arts of civilized life, finding themselves in the vast wilderness filled with the best of game inviting them to the chase, *most of them fell into a wandering idle hunting life.* Different clans parted from each other, lost each other, and formed the separate tribes. *Most of them formed a habit of this idle form of living and were pleased with it.*

More sensible parts of this people associated together to improve their knowledge of the arts and *probably continued thus for ages.*

BOOK OF MORMON 1830	VIEW OF THE HEBREWS 1823-5

(9) *Barbarous & Civilized People* (continued):

to thy people safe they shall repent of their iniquity- - -And because of their cursing which was upon them they did become an idle people full of mischief and subtility *and did seek in the wilderness for beasts of prey.*" II Nephi 5:20-24.

This occurred thirty years after the Colony of Lehi left Jerusalem.

The Nephites are again described two hundred years later as follows:

"We, [Nephites] multiplied exceedingly and spread upon the face of the land and became exceeding rich in gold and in silver and in precious things and in the workmanship of wood, in buildings, and in machinery and also in iron, and copper, and brass, and steel, making all manner of tools of every kind to till the ground and weapons of war—yea, the sharp-pointed arrow and the quiver and dart and the javolin and all preparations for war."

Of the Lamanites of this period this same writer (Jarom) says that the Lamanites were "scattered upon much of the face of the land." "And they were exceeding more numerous than were they of the Nephites and they loved murder and did drink the blood of beasts. And it came to pass that they came many times against us, the Nephites, to battle. But our kings and our leaders were mighty men in the

(9) *Barbarous & Civilized People* (continued):

From these the noted relics of civilization discovered in the west and south were furnished. But the savage tribes prevailed; *and in process of time their savage jealousies and rage annihilated their more civilized brethren.* And thus as a wholly vindictive providence would have it, and according to ancient denunciations all were left in an 'outcast' state. This accounts for their loss of their knowledge of letters, of the art of navigation and of the use of iron, and such a loss can no more operate against their being the ten tribes, then against their being of any other origin.

It is highly probable that the more civilized part of the tribes of Israel after they settled in America *became wholly separated from the hunting and savage tribes of their brethren;* that the latter lost the knowledge of their having descended from the same family with themselves; *that the more civilized part continued for many centuries, that tremendeous wars were frequent* between them and their savage brethren until *the former became extinct.* (!)

This hypothesis accounts for the ancient works, forts, mounds, and vast enclosures as well as tokens of a good degree of civil government which are manifestly very ancient and for centuries before Columbus discovered America.

BOOK OF MORMON
1830

VIEW OF THE HEBREWS
1823-5

(9) *Barbarous & Civilized People* (continued):
faith of the Lord.- - -wherefore we withstood the Lamanites and swept them away of our land and began to fortify our cities or whatsoever place of our inheritance. (Jarom 1:5-8)

Three hundred years later, the following is the description of this savage division of the people in America: They are spoken of as a wild and a hardened and a jealous people: A people who delighted in murdering the Nephites [the civilized branch of America's population] and robbing and plundering them; and their hearts were set upon riches or upon gold and silver or precious stones; yet they sought to obtain these things by murdering and plundering that they might not labor for them with their own hands, and thus they were a very indolent people, many of whom did worship idols and the curse of God had fallen upon them because of the traditions of their fathers." (Alma 17:14-15)

This parallel between these two peoples continues until finally about 400 A.D. the Lamanites entirely destroyed the Nephites at Cumorah, where dreadful battles were fought, where no quarter was asked or given between the parties.

Description of the final battles are given where armies perished in groups of tens of thousands. (Mormon, Chapter 6)—Mormon was the leader of the Nephite division.

(9) *Barbarous & Civilized People* (continued):
These partially civilized people became extinct and what account can be given of this, but that the savages extirpated them after long and dismal wars? And nothing appears more probable than that they were the better part of the Israelites who came to this continent who for a long time retained their knowledge of the mechanic and civil arts, while the greater part of their brethren became savage and wild."

Then he adds this in conclusion of the theme:

"But however vindictive the savages must have been;—however cruel and horrid in extirpating their own civilized brethren, yet it is a fact that there are many excellent traits in their original character. (View of the Hebrews pp 171-173)

Let it be remembered that the work from which the above is quoted existed from three to five years before the publication of the Book of Mormon, and the two editions of the work flooded the New England states and New York.

BOOK OF MORMON 1830	VIEW OF THE HEBREWS 1823-5

(9) *Barbarous & Civilized People* (continued):

The complete destruction of the Nephites is witnessed by Moroni, son of above Mormon.

A few Nephites had escaped from Cumorah and of these Moroni said:

"Now it came to pass that after the great tremendeous battles of Cumorah behold the Nephites who had escaped into the country southward were hunted by the Lamanites *until they were all destroyed.*" (Moroni 8:2) He alone was left of his people.

It will be remembered that the same thing happend in the destruction of the Jaredite nation which preceded the Nephite and Lamanite occupation of the land, annihilation to the very last man.

(10) *Jerusalem:*

The destruction of Jerusalem pending and actual features largely and early in the Book of Mormon. Although Lehi and his colony left Jerusalem some years before its destruction, yet by vision to this Prophet its destruction was made known.

"Behold," said he, "I have seen a vision in which I know that Jerusalem is destroyed, and had we remained in Jerusalem, we should have perished. (II Nephi 1:4)

The same is repeated in II Nephi 6:8. It is a subject frequently referred to from pp 1-50

(9) *Barbarous & Civilized People* (continued):

Overthrown Civilization of America

(10) *Jerusalem:*

In the "View of the Hebrews" the whole of chapter I, pages 13-46 *is devoted to the destruction of Jerusalem,* the historical account of it.

Would this treatise of the destruction of Jerusalem suggest the theme to the Book of Mormon author is the legitimate queery. Since the "View of the Hebrews" was published eight to five years before the Book of Mormon.

BOOK OF MORMON
1830

VIEW OF THE HEBREWS
1823-5

(11) *Israel:*

The Book of Mormon has many references to both the scattering and the gathering of Israel *in the last days.* These references occurr more abundantly in the forepart of the Book of Mormon, especially in First Nephi, chapter 19, 20, 21, and Second Nephi, chapter 25.

(11) *Israel:*

The "View of the Hebrews" has many references to both the scattering and gathering of Israel *"in the last days."* The second chapter of the "View of the Hebrews" is entitled *"The certain Restoration of Judah and Israel,"* and in this section is quoted nearly all the references to Isaiah that are referred to but quoted more full in the Book of Mormon.

(12) *Isaiah:*

Lehi's Colony brought with them from Jerusalem the Old Testament, (the whole Bible) down to the days of Jeremiah — about 600 BC; yet about the only books extensively quoted before the coming of Christ to America is Isaiah! Jacob, brother of First Nephi, quotes nearly all of 49, 50, and 51st chapters; and Nephi quotes about thirteen full chapters from Isaiah (see "Synopsis of chapters" in current editions of B. of M. p 524)

The Hebrew records possessed by the Nephites on brass plates are spoken of as containing more matter more than the Old Testament had among the Gentiles (I Nephi 13-20-23) Then why are quotations and references to this great and rich Hebrew literature confined practically to Isaiah alone? (see opposite column)

(12) *Isaiah:*

Ethan Smith's "View" quotes copiously and chiefly from Isaiah in relation to the scattering and gathering of Israel. In this second chapter on "the Certain Restoration of Israel" he quotes from six different chapters in Isaiah. In his fourth chapter and in the few pages he devotes to a "Conclusion" he returns to the subject of the "restoration of Israel," and here he quotes from *twenty chapters* of Isaiah! He quotes Isaiah 18th chapter complete, but verse by verse with comment, and makes of it an "Address" of Isaiah to the U.S. *to save Israel.*

Query: Did the Author of the Book of Mormon follow too closely the course of Ethan Smith in this use of Isaiah would be a legitimate query. The "View of the Hebrews" was published eight to five years before the Book of Mormon.

BOOK OF MORMON 1830	VIEW OF THE HEBREWS 1823-5

(13) *A great Gentile Nation to be raised up in America, the promised land to save Israel in America, in the last days.*

"Following is the vision of Nephi on the founding of a great Gentile nation in the land of Promise, America: "Thou beholdest that the Gentiles who have gone forth out of captivity and have been lifted up by the power of God above all other nations, upon the face of the land which is choice above all other lands (America) which is the land that the Lord God hath covenanted with thy Father (Lehi) that is said he should have for the land of his inheritance; - - -thou seest that the Lord God will not suffer that the Gentiles will utterly destroy the mixture of thy seed which are among thy brethren, neither will he suffer that the Gentiles shall destroy the seed of thy brethren. - - -I will be merciful unto the Gentiles under the visiting of the remnant of the house of Israel in great judgment. I will be merciful unto the Gentiles in that day insomuch that I will bring forth unto them in mine own power much of my Gospel, which shall be plain and precious saith the Lamb." I Nephi 13:30-34—I Nephi 21st chapter, the Prophet Nephi quotes the whole of Isaiah which relates largely to the building up and establishment of Israel in the last days. *And then in chapter 22, Nephi is questioned by his brethren as to whether the prophecies of the 49th chapter of* Isaiah

(13) *The American Gentile Nation (U.S.) appealed to in the "View of the Hebrews" to become the savior of Israel in America.*

Ethan Smith's chapter four in the "View of the Hebrews" is devoted to an appeal to the Christian Nation of the United States *to become the instrument for teaching the Gospel to the American Indians and restore them to the favor and blessing of God.*

The title of the fourth chapter is "An address of the Prophet Isaiah Relative to the Restoration of His People." The chapter is really an exposition of Isaiah 18, which he interprets to be an appeal of the ancient Prophet to this great nation of the West—"away over the mouths of the Nile. It will be remembered that Isaiah 18, opens with the exclamation "Woe to the land shadowing with wings" it would seem to be denunciation. This Ethan Smith changes to "Ho, lands shadowing with wings," saying that the best expositors agree on his interpretation and that the salutation is a friendly calling of attention instead of a denunciation, and what follows in the chapter is an invitation to the land shadowing with wings to participate in the bringing unto the Lord of Hosts as a present a "people scattered and peeled." The whole chapter must needs be read, we can only give a few excerpts "The duty of sending to them (the American Indians) the Gospel and of being at any expense to teach

BOOK OF MORMON
1830

VIEW OF THE HEBREWS
1823-5

(13) *A Great Gentile Nation* (continued):
which he has read are to be taken literally or are they spiritual or is a spiritual interpretation to be had of them. Nephi replies that they are both temporal and spiritual but in the main argues for a literal interpretation. In closing of which he refers to the mighty nation among the Gentiles whom God will raise up to bless Israel. He says 'and it [The Prophecy of Isaiah] meaneth that the time cometh that after all the House of Israel have been scattered and confounded that the Lord God will raise up a mighty nation among the Gentiles yea even upon the face of this land and by them shall our seed be scattered and after our seed is scattered the Lord God will proceed to do a marvelous work among the Gentiles which shall be of great worth unto our seed; wherefore it is likened unto their being nursed by the Gentiles and their being carried upon their arms and upon their shoulders, and it shall also be of worth unto the Gentiles and not only unto the Gentiles, but unto all the House of Israel. (I Nephi 22:7-9)

Another Book of Mormon Prophet, Jacob, brother of Nephi, speaking of the gathering of Israel and their restoration to their lands, is represented as saying: "It shall come to pass that they shall be gathered in from their long dispersion from the isles of the sea and from the four parts of the earth

(13) *A Great Gentile Nation* (continued):
them Christianity and the blessings of civilized life is great and urgent on every principle of humanity and general benevolence and this duty peculiarly attaches to the people who are now in possession of the former inheritance of those natives; and from too many of whom that people have received insufferable injuries. - - -An address is found in the 18th chapter of the Prophet Isaiah, which is apprehended to be of deep interest to America. The writer- - -found it to be an address to some Christian people of the last days, just at the time of the final restoration of God's ancient people; An address to such a people beheld in vision away over the mouths of the Nile or in some region of the West; a call and solemn divine charge to them to awake and aid that final restoration."

The call then must be to a people of the last days; a nation now on earth; and a nation to be peculiarly instrumental in the restoration of the Hebrews in the last days, for this is the very object of the address; to go and collect the ancient people of God; because in 'that time shall the present be brought unto the Lord of Hosts of a people scattered and peeled (the very people of the ancient covenant in manifest description repeatedly given) to the place of the name of the Lord of Hosts, the Mt. Zion.'

BOOK OF MORMON 1830	VIEW OF THE HEBREWS 1823-5

(13) *A Great Gentile Nation* (continued):

and the nations of the Gentiles shall be great in the eyes of me, saith God in carrying them forth to the lands of their inheritance, yea, the kings of the Gentiles shall be nursing fathers unto them and their queens shall become nursing mothers, wherefore the promises of the Lord are great unto the gentiles, for he hath spoken it and who can dispute. But behold this land, said God, shall be the land of thine inheritance and the gentiles shall be blessed upon the land- - -I will afflict thy seed (meaning the American Indians) by the hand of the Gentiles, nevertheless I will soften the hearts of the Gentiles, that they shall be like unto a father to them; wherefore the Gentiles shall be blessed *and numbered among the House of Israel.*" II Nephi 10:8-18

From all which it would appear that the great American nation, the Gentile nation is to take an important part in the gathering and establishment of Israel in their promised land, America.

(13) *A Great Gentile Nation* (continued):

Dealing with the prophecies of Isaiah 49 and other chapters of Isaiah and Jeremiah, *Ethan Smith argues as Nephi did on the 48th and 49th chapter of Isaiah, viz., that the prophecies are to be literally fulfilled and not treated as mystical passages and that the restoration spoken of "is to be in* the latter days." As to the land addressed—this land shadowing with wings, he holds to be America, the continent of those two great wings shall be found at last most interesting in relation to your Hebrew brethren (addressing the people of those continents) and those two great wings shall prove but an emblem of a great nation then on that continent (i.e. in the last days); Far sequestered from the seat of anti-Christ and of tyrany and blood; and whose asylum is equal rights, liberty and religion shall be well represented by such a national coat of arms—the protecting wings of a great eagle; which nation in yonder setting of the sun (when in the last days judgments shall be thundering through the nations of the eastern continents) shall be found a realm of peaceful protection to all who fly from the abodes of despotism to its peaceful retreat, even as an eagle protects her nest from all harm, yea, a land, that when all other lands shall be found to have trampled on the Jews, shall be found to have protecting wings for

BOOK OF MORMON 1830	VIEW OF THE HEBREWS 1823-5
(13) *A Great Gentile Nation* (continued):	(13) *A Great Gentile Nation* (continued):

them. Free from such cruelty and ready to aid them. - - -

Ye friends of God in the land addressed (the land shadowing with wings—America) can you read this prophetic declaration of the ancient Prophet Isaiah without having your hearts burning within you? Surely you can not, if you can view it as an address of the Most High to you. God here exalts you in the last days, the age of terror and blood, as high as the standard to be raised for the collection of the seed of Abraham on the mountains! - - -If these views be correct, Christians in our land may well

A Great Gentile Nation to be raised up in America, the promised land to save Israel in America, in the last days.

praise God that it is their happy lot to live in this land shadowing with wings; this protecting realm, an asylum of liberty and religion; a land so distanct from the seat of anti-Christ and of the judgments to be thundered down upon all the corrupt establishments in the last days; and their devout gratitude to heaven ought to rise for the blessing of having their existence so near the period alluded to in this sublime prediction when this land of liberty is beginning to feel her distinction, immunities compared with the establishments of tyrany and corruption in the old continent. - - -

"Ho, thou nation of the last days shadowing with the wings of liberty and peace; pity, instruct, and save my ancient people and breth-

BOOK OF MORMON 1830	VIEW OF THE HEBREWS 1823-5

(13) *A Great Gentile Nation* (continued):

(See Preface on Title page of the Book of Mormon:)

"which is to show unto the remnant of the House of Israel what great things the Lord hath done for their fathers; and that they may know the covenants of the Lord, that they are not cast off forever. *And also* (the Book of Mormon was written and preserved) *to the convincing of the Jew and Gentile that Jesus is the Christ, the Eternal God.*

This the mission of the United States according to the Book of

---

(13) *A Great Gentile Nation* (continued):
ren; especially that outcast branch of them, who were the natives of this soil."

Much more to the same effect—but this in conclusion)—and still addressing the Gentile Nation.

"Tell them [the Indians] what their ancient fathers, the prophets, were inspired to predict in their behalf; and the charge here given for their restoration; assure them this talk of a prophet is for them, and they must listen to it, and obey it. *That the great spirit above the clouds now calls them by you to come and receive his grace by Christ* and the true staff, in Jacob, the Shilo who has come, and to whom the people must be gathered. Inform them that by embracing this true seed of Abraham, *you and multitudes of other gentiles, have become the children of that ancient patriarch. And now that they must come back as your brother in the Lord.* Unfold to them their superlative line of the entail of the covenant; that as touching this election they are beloved for the fathers' sakes; that they were for their sins excluded for this long period, until the fullness of the Gentiles be come in, and so all Israel shall be saved.

"Go thou nation (U.S.) highly distinguished in the last days, save the remnant of my people, bring me a present of them to the place of the Lord of Host, the Mt. Zion."

BOOK OF MORMON 1830	VIEW OF THE HEBREWS 1823-5
(13) *A Great Gentile Nation* (continued): *Mormon;* (but the "View of the Hebrews" preceded the Book of Mormon by five years)!	**(13)** *A Great Gentile Nation* (continued): *This is the Mission of the United States according to the "View of the Hebrews"**
(14) *Love of Riches Among Nephites — Pride:* Jacob, son of Lehi on the Nephites says: "And they began to search much gold and silver, and began to be lifted up somewhat in pride." (Jacob 1:15, 16) And again to the Nephites: "Many of you have begun to search for gold- - -that you have obtained many riches: and because some of you have obtained more abundantly then that of your brethren ye are lifted up in pride of your hearts. - - -Do ye suppose that God justifieth you in this thing? Nay!- - -The one being is as precious in his sight as the other." (Jacob 2:12, 13, 21)	**(14)** *Love of Riches — Pride:* "A Chief of the Delaware Indians - - -said he knew it to be wrong if a poor man came to his door naked to turn him away empty.- - -He believed God loved the poorest of men better than he did proud, rich men." ("View" p 104)
(15) *Polygamy:* "The people of Nephi began to grow hard in their hearts, *and indulged themselves somewhat in*	**(15)** *Polygamy:* "Longtime ago" the Delaware Chief said, "It was a good custom among his people to take but one

*See *Star of the West* (by Boudinot) p. 297.

MOSES DU PRATZ
Author of
History of Louisiana, written about 1730.
Star of the West, P 133.

Natchez named for tribe of Indians of that name. Boudinot makes much of "O-E-A" or Yo-he-vah (as does Ethan Smith) see Star of the West, P 178 et sq.

"Much is to be done who when the signal is set up among the nations; and these children of God's watch, free providence, shall be manifestly discovered, i.e. lost tribes *they are to be* converted to the faith of Christ, & instructed in their religious prerogatives, and prepared and assisted to return to their own land & their ancient city, *even the city of Zion,* which shall become a praise to all the earth. . . . Who knows but God has raised up these U.S. in these last days for the very purpose of accomplishing his will in bringing his beloved people to their own land."

Star of the West, P 297.

BOOK OF MORMON 1830	VIEW OF THE HEBREWS 1823-5

(15) *Polygamy:* (continued) *wicked practices, such as like unto David of old desiring many wives and concubines:* - - -

Jacob to the Nephites: This people begin to wax in iniquity; they understand not the scriptures, for they seek to excuse themselves in committing whoredoms, because of the things which are written concerning David and Solomon.- - -David and Solomon had many wives and concubines, which thing was abominable before me saith the Lord.- - -.Wherefore my brethren, hearken to the word of the Lord; for there shall not any man among you have save it be one wife and concubines he shall have none. For I the Lord delight in the chastity of women" (Jacob, 2:27, 28)

(15) *Polygamy:* (continued) wife, and that for life. But now they [the Indians] had become so foolish, and so wicked that they would take a number of wives at a time and turn them away at pleasure." (View of the Hebrews p 104)

(16) *Lamanite Virtues:*

Jacob contrasts the Nephites with the Lamanites to the Nephites' disadvantage in respect of chastity and single marriages; and says of the Lamanites: *"Behold their husbands love their wives, and the wives love their husbands; and their husbands and their wives love their children."* (Jacob 3:7)

(16) *Indian Virtues:*

"They are just, honest, liberal, hospitable to strangers, considerate, loving, and *affectionate to their wives* and relations, *fond of their children,* frugal, and persevering; charitable- - -living in love, peace, and friendship." (View of the Hebrews p. 175)

Query: "Were the passages in this colum[n] sufficient to suggest what appears in the left hand column?

(17) *Civilization in America:*

Broadly the Book of Mormon represents the Nephites and Jaredites as being civilized people, with National Governments, Kingdoms, Republics, with trade, and

(17) *Civilization in America:*

In the "View of the Hebrews" quite an elaborate account is given of the civilization that must have existed in Mexico and Central America in ancient times. This is

BOOK OF MORMON
1830

VIEW OF THE HEBREWS
1823-5

(17) *Civilization in America:* (continued)
commerce, navigation, education, written culture, Religion; settled orders of living, cities, connected with highways, military establishments, etc., etc..

This idea of all this, however, is better obtained from general and incidental statements in the Book of Mormon rather than from any formal and elaborate and definite description of what their civilization consisted.

The first allusion to the civilized status occurs at about thirty years after Lehi's Colony left Jerusalem. The first Nephi says: "I did teach my people to build buildings and to work in all manner of wood, and of iron, and of copper, and of brass, and of steel, and of gold, and of silver, and of precious ores, which were of great abundance- - -and it came to pass that I Nephi, did cause my people to be industrious and to labor with their hands, and it came to pass that they would that I should be their King." And he reluctantly accepted this office.

Similar descriptions are several times given in the B. of M.

(18) *The Messiah on the Western Continent:*
It may be said that the chief event, the greatest and most important of all events in the Book of Mormon, is the appearance of

(17) *Civilization in America:* (continued)
summarized largely from Baron Humbolt's "New Spain" published first in Germany, 1808-9 and translated into English by John Black in 1811, and quoted copiously by Ethan Smith in his second edition of the "View of the Hebrews" 1825.

In these excerpts from Humbolt are descriptions of pyramids Temples, ruined cities, high-ways with some speculations as to their resemblances to the Egyptian pyramids. Ethan Smith quotes extensively from the Archaeologia Americana published at Worcester, Mass. 1820.

On these authorities Ethan Smith says:

"The people, however, who traversed Mexico, left behind them traces of cultivation and civilization- - -The Taultees introduced the cultivation of Maize and Cotton; they built cities made roads and constructed those great pyramids, which are yet admired, and the faces are very accurately laid out." (p. 189)

Some twenty pages are devoted to describing civilization traits as seen in Temples, pyramids and ruined cities.

(18) *Quetzalcotle* (So often called in literature *"The Mexican Messiah"*):
The legends of Quetzalcotle are stated in the "View of the Hebrews" at some length, I greatly abbreviate. "The pyramids of

BOOK OF MORMON 1830	VIEW OF THE HEBREWS 1823-5

(18) *The Messiah on the Western Continent* (continued):

the Christ — the Hebrew Messiah — in the western world. He was anticipated in prophecy, and spoken of in expectation of His coming, and the purpose of that coming. Finally, in third Nephi, a magnificent description of His appearing to the Nephites is given, an account of His ministry among the Nephites. His stay was comparatively brief, and when he departed in light and glory, He promised at some future time to return. (See III Nephi ch. 11 et sq.

(18) *Quetzalcotle* (So often called in literature *"The Mexican Messiah"*) (continued):
Cholula was an altar dedicated to Quetzalcotle or the serpent of green feathers; as his name is said to imply. This is the most mysterious being of the whole Mexican mythology. He is said to be a white and bearded man. He was High Priest of Tula, legislator, chief of a religious sect, who inflicted on themselves the most cruel penance — "he appeased by his pennance divine wrath, (In other words atonement). — The reign of Quetzalcotle was a golden age of the people of Anahuac, he dwelt twenty years among them, ordered fasts and regulated the Taltic year. "He preached peace to men"- - - He disappeared after he had declared to the Cholulans that he would return and govern them again and renew their happiness."

Ethan Smith speaks of him as "appeasing divine wrath," "may have a striking allusion to the system of the Mosaic sacrifices including also the mediation of Moses, *as a type of Christ, and God's turning away his fierce wrath from Israel at his intercession as was repeatedly the case.* ("View of the Hebrews" pp. 206—)

The legitimate query: did this character spoken of in the "View of the Hebrews," published five years before the Book of Mormon, furnish the suggestion of the *Christ* on the *Western Continent?*

Bibliography

As already indicated, the Brigham H. Roberts Papers at the Marriott Library of the University of Utah form the basis for this book. The items listed under Roberts in the Bibliography have been selected from among his numerous writings as the important documents relating to his specific interest in the Book of Mormon and for his concerns as a historian. The manuscript of his "Life Story" was especially helpful in setting events in chronological order and in explaining the background for significant events in his career, and the two letters cited from the Scott Kenney Papers provided insight into Roberts's feelings about the intellectual climate of Mormon Utah. This essay examines the books and documents used or cited by Roberts except for the last few pages, which are concerned with Mormon and non-Mormon writings involved in recent interest in Ethan Smith's *View of the Hebrews*.

Before describing the published works related to B. H. Roberts's analyses of the origin of the Book of Mormon, it should be noted that, although he makes no reference to them, he had access to a series of pamphlets that could have been of much help in his investigations of the archeological evidence concerned with the Mormon scripture. Louis E. Hills, a scholar in the Reorganized Church of Jesus Christ of Latter-Day Saints, published a series of eight articles and pamphlets during the years 1917 to 1924 that examined very carefully such subjects as Book of Mormon geography, the historical data from the ancient records and ruins of Mexico and Central America, the latest discoveries in the area by archeologists, and even an examination of the "Popol vuh and the traditional history of the ancient Americans." Basing most of his argument to prove the authenticity of the Book of Mormon on the evidence presented in *Native Races*, written by that "great historian," Hubert H. Bancroft, Hills also cited many of the antiquarian and modern works that B. H. Roberts used in his studies, suggesting the possibility that Roberts may have been guided in his choice of monographs and documents by reference to Hills's writings. Hills attempted to use the Book of Mormon record itself to try to establish the location of ancient cities in Central America and Mexico rather than using the ruins to prove the

Mormon scripture. It is interesting that Hills sought to use scientific and antiquarian documents to prove the Book of Mormon while Roberts quoted some of the same volumes to raise questions about the book's divine origin.

Of the two chief biographies of Roberts, Robert H. Malan's *B. H. Roberts: A Biography* is a brief report arranged topically but, as Davis Bitton has indicated, lacks "real penetration" and offers only the "thin gruel served up in most life stories of church leaders." The more recent and more comprehensive biography by Truman G. Madsen, *Defender of the Faith,* is particularly good in the description of Roberts's early life in which the author's graceful prose introduces a quite sympathetic picture of the Mormon leader. But both biographies betray their subject by failing to treat at all Roberts's controversial parallel study of the Book of Mormon with Ethan Smith's *View of the Hebrews.* The exclusion, for whatever reason, would have been abhorred by the four-square Roberts, who had written in the preface to his *A Comprehensive History of the Church* that events "considered detrimental to the reputation of either the leaders of the church or of its membership" should not be left out but should be included, "allowing the line of condemnation or of justification to fall where it may." Madsen did discuss the problem of the similarities in an earlier article in the summer 1979 issue of *BYU Studies,* in which he advanced the explanation that Roberts was playing "Devil's Advocate" and that to "resurrect" the study of *View of the Hebrews* was "not a service to scholarship."

In his most recent article, "B. H. Roberts after Fifty Years: Still Witnessing for the Book of Mormon," *Ensign* (December 1983): 11-19, Madsen repeated the assertion of his 1979 article, "B. H. Roberts and the Book of Mormon," *BYU Studies,* 19 (Summer 1979): 427-45, that Roberts continued to maintain his belief in the Book of Mormon during the eleven years after his 1922 study of the book until his death in 1933. After a short review of Roberts's life Madsen describes the three studies included in the present volume and notes that Roberts explained in a March 14, 1932, letter to Elizabeth Skolfield, his former secretary in the Eastern States Mission, that he had been unable to present the manuscript studies to the First Presidency and Twelve Apostles since returning from the mission field because they were "not in a studious mood." Madsen assures his readers on the basis of the later letters that Roberts did not mean what he said in the Book of Mormon studies, and offers his own explanation of the problems discussed by Roberts: "Ethan Smith published a book on revelation in 1833, endorsed by several ministers in New York and Massachusetts. He also published *View of the Hebrews,* revised and enlarged, in 1835. Both books were published long after the Book of Mormon began circulation. If critics can claim that Joseph Smith was aware of Ethan Smith's novel, it surely can also be claimed that Ethan Smith was aware of Joseph Smith's." Ethan Smith's *View of the Hebrews* was, of course, not a "novel" in any sense of the word, but was a serious analysis of current archeological discoveries and the known cultural studies of Indian tribes in order to prove the theory that the American Indians were of Israelitish descent. Also, as Madsen had pointed out earlier in his article, *View of the Hebrews,* appeared in a first edition in 1823, several years before the Book of Mormon was published in 1830.

In identifying the participants in the drama staged by Roberts when he presented his Book of Mormon "Study" to the General Authorities of his Church, The *Deseret News* and *Salt Lake Tribune* were helpful in giving the details of the lives and careers of these men. Andrew Jenson's *Latter-day Saint Biographical Encyclopedia* and Edward W. Tullidge's *Histories* are always useful for additional biographical information, and *Boyd's Directory of the District of Columbia* offered the best clues to the identity of the Mr. Couch who originally sparked the Roberts's investigation.

Of the few references to early anti-Mormon literature, the most significant, as far as Roberts was concerned, were probably Alexander Campbell's *Delusions — An Analysis of the Book of Mormon* and J. B. Turner's *Mormonism in All Ages,* in which both writers attacked the claims made for the Book of Mormon. Mormon writers of the early period whose works were cited included Oliver Cowdery's "letters," found in the *Latter Day Saints' Messenger and Advocate,* and his series of eight letters of "Early Scenes and Incidents in the Church," printed in the *Improvement Era* issues of 1899. Orson Pratt's *Works* and Parley P. Pratt's *Autobiography* were both mentioned. Lucy Smith's *History of the Prophet* came in for some discussion, and, of course, both the first edition of the Book of Mormon (1830) and the Doctrine and Covenants with Joseph Smith, Jr., as author, were cited. The Journal History of the Latter-day Saints Church, a combination of daily narrative and newspaper scraps, is invaluable for any investigation of Mormon history. Among the references to Mormon leaders, Roberts, in a handwritten note, cited a unique sermon delivered by Brigham Young just a few months before his death in 1877 in which Young described, in fanciful detail, the wagon-loads of gold plates which Joseph Smith had been shown in a cave in the Hill Cumorah.

In researching these and other Mormon records cited by Roberts, the editor was able to find most of the documents and books in the Special Collections division of the Marriott Library. For the few that were not available at the Marriott Library, the staff members at the L.D.S. Archives were most gracious and helpful in granting use of some materials,

but the editor was denied access to the Roberts collection of correspondence and papers; to Roberts's theological work, "The Truth, the
Way, the Life"; and to minutes and correspondence of the First Council
of Seventy. These apparently have been open to students for some time,
but their use was not allowed in this instance.

In his investigation, Roberts turned to commonly used Bible references and commentaries, of which there were sometimes so many
editions that it was not always possible to locate the exact one. Among
those he used were: Samuel W. Barnum, ed., *A Dictionary of the Bible,*
and William Smith, *A Dictionary of the Bible;* Robert Jamieson et al., *A
Commentary . . . on the Old and New Testaments;* Samuel M. Jackson,
ed., *The Schaff-Herzog Encyclopedia of Religious Knowledge;* and Philip
Schaff, ed., *Wilmore's new analytical reference Bible.* For an examination
of some of the apocryphal books, Jacob M. Myers's *I and II Esdras*
proved to be helpful.

The reference works and early Mormon sources mentioned above,
although used by Roberts in his investigations of the Book of Mormon
story, were really secondary to his main interest, the archeological and
antiquities evidence of native American civilizations and its relationship
to the Mormon scripture. In describing the materials he researched, it
will be convenient to divide them chronologically into the rather antiquarian writings of the 1600s to the early 1800s, then the more objective
examinations of the late nineteenth century, and finally the first scientific
and scholarly studies from 1900 to 1920, when Roberts was conducting
his explorations of Book of Mormon origins.

In 1632 Gabriel Sagard, a lay brother in the Catholic Church, published his *Le grand voyage des pays des Hurons,* which examined, in
highly descriptive prose, most phases of Huron life, with special emphasis
on the tribe's language. Such general works were used by Roberts to
compare the customs, myths, and other cultural attributes of American
Indians with those described as being part of the lifestyle of the Book
of Mormon Nephite and Lamanite peoples.

But more to the point of the Mormon record was the stream of
early investigators who were convinced that the American Indians were
the descendants of the Ten Lost Tribes of Israel and those students who
were just as sure that the theory was quite preposterous. Among the first
was Thomas Thorowgood, who argued in 1650 that the *Jewes in America,
or Probabilities That the Americans are of that Race.* He was answered
by Hamon l'Estrange with *Americans no Jewes, or Improbabilities that
the Americans are of that race.* Gregorio Garcia continued the theme of
Israelitish origin in his 1729 *Origen de los Indios de el Nuevo mundo*
but was outdone by James Adair, possibly because the latter's book
appeared in English. Adair's *History of the American Indians* was pub-

lished in London in 1775 and was the result of about forty years of residence as a trader among the Indians in the American southern colonies. His book strongly supported the Lost Tribes theory and became the basis for many other treatises on the subject.

Alexander von Humboldt's famous *Political Essay on the Kingdom of New Spain* (1814) did not get involved in the discussion of Hebrew origins but became a standard text for many religious and historical scholars who had an interest in the antiquities of Mexico. Its precise statistics and rather scientific appraisal of the industry and culture of the people caused it to be quoted widely. At about the same time as its appearance, Peter S. Duponceau translated *A Grammar of the Language of the . . . Delaware Indians* from the German edition of the work by the Reverend David Zeisberger and presented it to the American Philosophical Society. Zeisberger contended that the languages of the native Americans lacked the diversity of those found in the Eastern Hemisphere and really had no resemblance to the Eastern tongues.

Then, during the early 1800s, there seemed to be a revival of interest in the possibility of an Israelitish relationship with the American Indians. Elias Boudinot's *A Star in the West* (1816) proposed that the second apocryphal book of Esdras helped prove that the Ten Tribes had wandered a long way to an uninhabited country and had then "passed a great water" to arrive in the Americas. In 1825 Josiah Priest continued the theme in his *The Wonders of Nature and Providence* with "Proofs that the Indians of North America are lineally descended from the ancient Hebrews. Extracted from the Reverend E. Smith's *View of the Hebrews*, with some additional remarks." The above two works were next in importance to Ethan Smith's book in the arguments advanced by Roberts in his study of the Book of Mormon. Priest's later book, *American Antiquities and Discoveries in the West*, expanded the theory of Hebrew descent, but it was published in 1834, four years after the appearance of the Book of Mormon. The third author of this period to achieve prominence with an obsession to prove the Israelitish origin of the American Indians was Lord Viscount Kingsborough, who spent a lifetime gathering the material for this elaborate argument in the nine-volume work, *Antiquities of Mexico*. One critic has described Kingsborough's work as "a storehouse of analogies in support of the Hebrew theory" (Allen Thorndike Rice in introduction to Désiré Charnay, *The Ancient Cities of the New World*). But the most extreme of those who supported the Lost Tribes theory was Charles Etienne Brasseur de Bourbourg, whose *Histoire des nations civilisées du Mexique et de l'Amerique-Centrale* (1857) advanced the Hebrew connection plus such droll theories as that of finding that the Maya had used the electric telegraph 100,000 years ago.

To round out this first category of part-fact, part-fiction speculations by very early investigators of American Indian civilizations, Henry R. Schoolcraft produced his *Historical and Statistical Information Respecting the History, Conditions and Prospects of the Indian Tribes of the United States* (1851) in six volumes. The work contains valuable information on the origins, traditions, mental types, antiquities, physical geography, tribal organizations, history and government, and the intellectual capacities of about seventy tribes east of the Rocky Mountains. But at the same time, Schoolcraft included two articles by the Reverend Thomas Hurlburt and the Reverend William Hamilton, who both found a resemblance between the Indian and Hebrew languages. The final book of this series, Henry Howe's *Historical Collections of the Great West*, was a miscellaneous assortment of sketches of frontier life with an interesting section on the excesses of emotion produced in frontier camp meetings, a phenomenon that interested Roberts.

After examining the antiquarian and early attempts at describing the possible origins and the cultures of the native American races, Roberts found a more rewarding field in late nineteenth-century investigations by the better-trained scholars of the time, although an occasional Bourbourg appeared here also. For example, there was Augustus Le Plongeon, whose *Sacred Mysteries among the Mayas and the Quiches* insisted that the Maya hieratic alphabet was similar to the Egyptian alphabet and whose *Queen Moo and the Egyptian Sphinx* went so far as to claim that a group of Mayan people had crossed the Atlantic to settle on the river Nile under the rule of the Egyptian Queen Moo. Another book entitled *Life in Ancient Egypt*, by Adolf Ermon, described, among other things, the delight which Egyptian rulers took in warfare. Roberts also consulted John G. Wilkinson's *The Manners and Customs of the Ancient Egyptians*, looking for any evidence of a relationship with American civilizations, and he even read Edward Gibbon's *The History of the Decline and Fall of the Roman Empire*, searching for clues. He did find in *The Cities and Cemeteries of Ertruria*, by George Dennis, reference to short curved swords, which might have been similar to the "scimeters" mentioned in the Book of Mormon.

A more productive series of books dealt with discoveries about ancient American peoples, and Roberts paid some attention to E. A. Allen's *The prehistoric world: or, Vanished Races* (1885); Albon Jasper Conant's *Footprints of vanished races in the Mississippi Valley—being an account of some of the monuments and relics of pre-historic races* (1879); and, more frequently, to Jean Francois Nadillac's *Pre-historic America* (1885). He quoted extensively from John D. Baldwin, "a kind of handbook," on *Ancient America, in Notes on American Archaeology*, and the book is filled with Roberts's handwritten marginal notes on such subjects as "Sailing vessels used by Native Am." and "May not Maya come from Moron." Similarly, Roberts relied heavily on Hubert Howe Bancroft's *The Native Races,* in five volumes, which became a standard text for its time on the subjects listed in the volume titles: *Wild Tribes, Civilized Nations, Myths and Languages, Antiquities,* and *Primitive History.*

With specific reference to the ancient civilizations found in Mexico and Peru, Roberts first turned to William H. Prescott and his classic histories of the conquest of the two areas as well as to such lesser-known authorities as Johann Jakob Tschudi, *Travels in Peru,* and with co-author Ribero y Ustáriz, *Peruvian Antiquities,* and John L. Stephens, *Incidents of Travel in Central America, Chiapas, and Yucatan.* He also found some interest in the French writer, Désiré Charnay, whose *The Ancient Cities of the New World: Being Voyages and Explorations in Mexico and Central America from 1857-1882* concluded that the civilizations of these areas were comparatively modern and of Toltec origin, and an article by Charnay, "The Ruins of Central America," in the October 1880 issue of the *North American Review* that discussed, among other things, the fact that copper took the place of iron and steel among the ancient Mexicans.

Specific studies of the former Indian inhabitants of what is now the United States led to a reading of J. D. Whitney's article on skeletal remains found in the "Auriferous Gravels of the Sierra Nevada of California" but, more important, to an examination of two other standard works of the time. John T. Short, *The North Americans of Antiquity,* studied the mound builders and cliff dwellers of the western United States to try to determine what relationships existed between them and the more advanced civilizations of Mexico and Central America. Almost as a footnote, Short dismissed the Book of Mormon story as a "pretentious fraud." The second book was John Wesley Powell's famous *Seventh Annual Report of the Bureau of Ethnology* (1891), one of whose various authors questioned some of the exaggerations of Henry Schoolcraft and another discussed the "Classification of the North American Languages," a subject of much concern to Roberts.

In his investigations of the origin of Native American languages and their possible relationship with European or Middle Eastern tongues, Roberts turned to the works of two German philologists: Heymann Steinthal's *Die Classification der Sprachen* (1850) and his "On the origin of language," in the *North American Review* of April 1872; and F. Max Müller's nine *Lectures on the Science of Language* (1866) and his *Chips from a German workshop* (1887), a five-volume work on the science of language, which incidentally referred to the Iroquois language. An American scientist, William Dwight Whitney, in *Language and the Study of Language; Twelve Lectures on the Principles of Linguistic Science* (1888), ridiculed the attempts to identify the Ten Lost Tribes with the American

Indians and declared that the languages of North and South America were "all descended from a single parent language." When Roberts began investigating treatises of the first twenty years of the twentieth century, he also had access to Franz Boas's *Handbook of American Languages* (1911); Sylvanus G. Morley's *An Introduction to the Study of the Maya Hieroglyphs* (1915); and even H. G. Wells's *The Outline of History*, 1 (1920), which held that the American Indian languages "are separable from any Old World group."

Scientific writers of the early 1900s could still speculate, as did G. Elliott Smith in his article, "The Origin of the Pre-Columbian Civilization of America," published in *Science* magazine of August 11, 1916, that the culture of Egypt reached the Pacific Coast sometime between 4000 and 900 B.C. and "leavened" the aboriginal peoples already in America, but most accepted the conclusion of such distinguished anthropologists as Ales Hrdlicka, who, in *Skeletal Remains Suggesting or Attributed to Early Man in North America,* concluded that "America was peopled by immigration from the Old World" but not before the Pleistocene age. A good general discussion of knowledge about pre-Columbian civilizations could be found in Peter De Roo's *History of America before Columbus* (1900).

Roberts made early attempts to satisfy his doubts on specific Book of Mormon problems that modern scientific discoveries were beginning to emphasize, such as references to the horse and to silk, in the Nephite record. In an article by Woods Hutchinson in the *Saturday Evening Post* of December 24, 1921, on "Insect-Borne Diseases," the author quoted Dr. Henry Fairfield Osborn, who speculated that a plague of tsetse flies might have wiped out the early horse population of the Americas. An L. E. Wyman pamphlet, *Notes on the Pleistocene Fossils Obtained from Rancho La Brea Asphalt Pits* (1915), seemed only to cast doubts for Roberts on the possibility of horses existing in the Western Hemisphere at the time of the Nephites. The possibility that silk was known by Book of Mormon peoples Roberts attempted to establish by reference to such accounts as Li Ung Bing's *Outline of Chinese History* (1914), which explained that the weaving of silk was known in China as early as 2640 B.C., and to M. D. C. Weaver's article, "The Master Weavers of the Desert Empire," in *Harper's Magazine* of July 1916, which pointed out that cotton had been woven in such a fine fabric that it could easily be mistaken for silk.

To marshal significant evidence pro and con on questions raised by the Book of Mormon story, Roberts came to rely upon several works of the early 1900s that he quoted often and extensively. William M. Beauchamp's *A History of the New York Iroquois* (1905) and an earlier one, *The Iroquois Trail, or Foot-prints of the Six Nations* (1892), he used occasionally but seems to have become enamored with John Fiske's *The Discovery of America,* 1 (1902), and his *Excursions of an Evolutionist* (1894), the first of which he must have worn out if his lengthy quotations from the book are any guide. Fiske's first volume in his twelve-volume history of America dealt with almost every conceivable aspect of the ancient civilizations of the Western Hemisphere and with pre-Columbian voyages. Of almost equal importance to Roberts was his copy of Daniel G. Brinton's *The American Race* (1891), which is heavily noted by Roberts in the margins. Brinton declared that his book was the first "attempt at a systematic classification of the whole American race on the basis of language." Some of Roberts's marginal notations included "No domestic animals," "Diversity of Tongues," and "The Mayas: & Their Architecture, Sculpture—achieved without metal tools—or Bronze chisels."

Another favorite treatise of the early 1900s was Frederick S. Dellenbaugh's *The North Americans of Yesterday* (1906), which Roberts also marked with typical notes in the margin: "Race Unity," "*Conclusion:* No evidence of out-side derivation of Am. Race," "Use this if you argue for restricted area for N. & Lamanites," and "As for the Lost-Tribes-of-Israel theory, on which Kingsborough was wrecked, *no archaeologist of today would be willing* to give it a second thought." And again, Roberts found ideas with which he was comfortable in William F. Holmes's *Handbook of Aboriginal American Antiquities* (1919), which discussed the scope of archeological science, race origins, migrations, cultural evaluations, chronology, substances employed in the arts, and the manipulation of stones.

Finally, in this series of early twentieth-century scientific studies of American cultures, Roberts quoted profusely from two works on the American Indians: Clark Wissler's *The American Indian* (1917), a general summary of anthropological research in the New World, and Frederick Webb Hodge's, *Handbook of American Indians North of Mexico* (1907), a descriptive list of the Indian tribes and settlements north of Mexico. Wissler maintained that America was peopled by a Mongoloid race during the Stone Age whose long history finally led to many varieties of culture. Hodge's book described the history, archeology, manners, arts, customs, and institutions of the native Americans.

In the final section of his "A Book of Mormon Study," it seems apparent that in calling attention to certain emotional religious excesses in the environment of Joseph Smith, Roberts is suggesting a possible connection with the Book of Mormon. He did so by quoting at length from the works of three famous evangelists and by referring to a fourth: Robert Southey's, *The Life of Wesley* (1846), George Whitefield's *Works— Eighteen Sermons* (1808), Jonathan Edwards's *The Works of President Edwards* (1817), and Charles Grandison Finney's *Lectures on Revivals of*

Religion (1868). All described the efficacy of "forest-preaching" and the positive results coming from a hell-fire and brimstone type of sermon. Edwards wanted to show "the distinguishing marks of a work of the Spirit of God," or in other words what was "the nature of true religion."

Because Roberts became the lightning rod for heated questions directed to Church officials concerning the Book of Mormon and other theological conundrums, he received and answered scores of letters from puzzled Mormons and inquiring Gentiles alike during his lifetime. Of two typical letters, one was from a Spencer, Iowa, lawyer (November 7, 1903), asking for an explanation of how the Book of Mormon was translated, and a second was from G. A. Marr, a troubled Latter-day Saint, who also inquired about the method of translation employed by Joseph Smith and posed other troubling questions. And Roberts could step in without invitation to lambaste fellow Mormons who he thought were adopting irrelevant or even contemptuous approaches to the solution of complex issues in Mormonism. They ranged from the mild speculation of D. M. McAllister's conviction in his article, "Important Appeal to Native Hawaiians and Other Polynesians," that the Hawaiian race came originally from America, to Franklin D. Richards's and James A. Little's assumptions about the exact route taken by Lehi, as outlined in their *A Compendium of the Doctrines of the Gospel.* Roberts seemed particularly grieved by J. M. Sjodahl's "Book of Mormon Facts" in the *Juvenile Instructor* of June 1922, which asserted that Ouija boards led to the "spiritist" magic prophesied by the Book of Mormon.

The personal journals of three prominent L.D.S. officials were quite helpful in providing information about what transpired during the meetings of the winter of 1922 in which B. H. Roberts presented his "Book of Mormon Difficulties" to Church authorities. The James E. Talmage Journals at Brigham Young University were especially useful. The others were the Diaries of George Franklin Richards in the L.D.S. Archives and the Anthony W. Ivins Papers held by the Utah State Historical Society. The Wesley P. Lloyd Personal Journal gave particular insight for the reactions of both Church leaders and Roberts to the presentation of his "Book of Mormon Difficulties." And for the five-year period of his tour of duty as president of the Eastern States Mission, the Papers of Brigham Henry Roberts (1857-1933) at the University of Utah furnished important information about Roberts's research activities in the sources concerned with the origins of the Mormon Church. The Roscoe A. Grover interview of 1979 gave insight into the personality and character of Roberts, while the Massachusetts Conference of Eastern States Mission, President's Records, in the L.D.S. Archives also contributed to an understanding of his career as a mission executive.

Finally, this essay on sources would not be complete without a statement about the recent articles and books on the subject of the possibility that Ethan Smith's *View of the Hebrews* might have served as a basic plan for the Book of Mormon. The *Wayne Sentinel*, published in Palmyra, was invaluable in giving a picture of the town in the 1820s and for the specific information about the availability of books and the fact that Ethan Smith probably visited Palmyra. Perhaps the first Mormon interest in Ethan Smith's book was that of George Reynolds, a member of the First Council of Seventy and the author of three works concerned with the Book of Mormon, who, in the *Juvenile Instructor* of October 1, 1902, penned a short article on *View of the Hebrews* in which he was delighted to report that it advanced "strong evidences in favor of the genuineness of the Book of Mormon." Apparently, very little attention came from this introduction, and when Roberts published his *New Witnesses for God* in 1909 he listed the book, along with three others, as possible supporting evidence to substantiate the authenticity of the Book of Mormon. He later explained in his "A Book of Mormon Study" that at that time he was unaware of the Ethan Smith book "except by report of it, and as being in my hands but a few minutes." But by the time he wrote his letter to Apostle Richard R. Lyman on October 24, 1927, he had obtained his personal copy and had constructed his brief "A Parallel" and his much longer "A Book of Mormon Study," both analyses of similarities between the two works.

With Roberts's submission of "A Parallel" to Richard R. Lyman, copies of that document were circulated among interested Mormons. As indicated, Ariel L. Crowley asked for and received assurances from Ben E. Roberts in 1939 that the study did not reflect on the integrity of Joseph Smith or his story of the writing of the Book of Mormon. Crowley later published his *About the Book of Mormon* (1961), including the reassuring letter from Ben E. Roberts, and discounted the rumors about B. H. Roberts's study of *View of the Hebrews* as casting doubts, in any way, on the divine origin of the Nephite record.

While I. Woodbridge Riley in his *The Founder of Mormonism* (1903) mentioned Ethan Smith's book, Fawn M. Brodie may have been the first serious scholar to use Roberts's list of parallels as a platform on which to raise doubts about the authenticity of the book when she postulated in her biography of Joseph Smith, *No Man Knows My History* (1945), that *View of the Hebrews* gave Smith "the idea of writing an Indian history in the first place." Talk about the existence of the Roberts manuscript came to an end on October 10, 1946, when Ben E. Roberts handed out copies of his father's "A Parallel" after speaking to the Timpanogos Club in Salt Lake City. Since then, that eighteen-page analysis, in digested form, of Roberts's more comprehensive work on the

Book of Mormon has been public property, and scholars on both sides of the issue have given it careful attention.

Hugh Nibley, in perhaps the most sophisticated analysis, argued in his *No, Ma'am, That's Not History,* "The fact that two theories or books present parallelism, no matter how striking, may imply a common source, but it certainly does not prove that the one is derived from the other." Nibley continued this theme in two articles entitled "The Comparative Method," published in two issues of the *Improvement Era,* October and November 1959—"In every case where the Book of Mormon *might* have borrowed from him [Ethan Smith], it might much more easily have borrowed from the Bible or prevailing popular beliefs." Francis W. Kirkham in his *A New Witness for Christ in America* (1951) similarly declared that the Book of Mormon "differs so widely in content and purpose that the knowledge of . . . [*View of the Hebrews*] could have had little, if any influence on the material published in the Book of Mormon."

A more cautious approach to the controversy was taken by L.D.S. historian Marvin S. Hill in his "Survey: The Historiography of Mormonism," in *Church History* (December 1959), in which he said that the "most plausible exposition" of Ethan Smith's hypothesis was made by Fawn Brodie in her Joseph Smith biography. HIll made no other judgment except to conclude generally that "Mormonism has been plagued by too much emotion, too much description and too little interpretation."

Defending the Book of Mormon against the Ethan Smith theory was not left to Utah Mormons alone, because three members of the Reorganized Church of Jesus Christ of Latter-Day Saints entered the fray. Charles A. Davies's article, "View of the Hebrews and the Book of Mormon," in the *Saints' Herald* (August 1, 1962), held that B. H. Roberts's "parallels" study was "an interesting piece of research" but still "no evidence has been produced that the two men [Ethan and Joseph Smith] ever met or that Joseph Smith had access to the other's works." F. Edward Butterworth and Roy E. Weldon, in their *Criticisms of the Book of Mormon Answered* (1973), listed seventeen reasons why Joseph Smith was not influenced by Ethan Smith's *View of the Hebrews,* concluding that the only similarity between it and the Mormon scripture was the claim that the American Indians were descended from the Hebrew people.

A few critics have used the Ethan Smith book and Roberts's study of parallels to attempt to prove the spuriousness of the Book of Mormon. Hal Hougey's "A *Parallel*"—*The Basis of the Book of Mormon* (1963) made the point that Joseph Smith's scribe, Oliver Cowdery, lived in Poultney, Vermont, until 1825, the same town where Ethan Smith resided when he published his book. Hougey reproduced Roberts's eighteen-point "Parallel" and added his own notes to prove how counterfeit he thought the Mormon scripture was. Larry W. Jonas, in *Mormon Claims Examined* (1961), contended that Ethan Smith's book furnished the plot for the Book of Mormon and gave examples of pages from the Smith book to demonstrate its connection with the Nephite record. A third skeptic, Robert N. Hullinger, published in the *Lutheran Quarterly* (August 1970) "The Lost Tribes of Israel and the Book of Mormon," in which he listed some of the Roberts's "Parallels"; he charged that Nibley had "failed to destroy the argument" of the Ethan Smith work and that Joseph Smith had depended on the *View of the Hebrews* for his basic theme. A final but more circumspect scholar, Wesley M. Jones, concluded in his *A Critical Study of Book of Mormon Sources* (1964) that "evidences supporting Ethan Smith's theory also support the Book of Mormon."

A number of Mormon scholars who wrote in the 1960s and early 1970s rushed to defend the Book of Mormon from the "parallels": Spencer J. Palmer and William L. Knecht, "View of the Hebrews: Substitute for Inspiration?" in *BYU Studies* (Winter 1964); Sidney B. Sperry, *Problems of the Book of Mormon* (1964); William L. Riley, "A Comparison of Passages from Isaiah and Other Old Testament Prophets in Ethan Smith's *View of the Hebrews* and the Book of Mormon" (M.A. thesis, Brigham Young University, 1971); and Bruce D. Blumell, "I Have a Question," a response to the theories that the Book of Mormon was based on the Spaulding manuscript or on Ethan Smith's *View of the Hebrews,* in *Ensign* (September 1976).

Quite recently two questioning students of the Book of Mormon, also knowledgeable about the Roberts "Parallels," have published articles in the May-June 1981 *Sunstone* magazine. Madison U. Sowell, in his "Defending the Keystone: The Comparative Method Reexamined," studied rather carefully the history, pro and con, of the Ethan Smith book and finally advised his readers to "a prayerful examination" of the Book of Mormon, while at the same time encouraging the use of the comparative method employed by Roberts. George D. Smith, Jr., was more pointed as he wrote "Defending the Keystone: Book of Mormon Difficulties," describing Roberts's 141-page study in answer to the five questions propounded by Mr. Couch of Washington, D.C., and proposing that there were still many questions to be examined about the origin of the Book of Mormon.

Adair, James. *The History of the American Indians.* London: E. and C. Dilly, 1775.

Allen, E. A. *The prehistoric world: or, Vanished races.* Cincinnati: Central Publishing House, 1885.

Ashment, Edward H. "The Book of Mormon—A Literal Translation." *Sunstone,* 5 (Mar.-Apr. 1980):10-14.

Baldwin, John D. *Ancient America, in Notes on American Archaeology*. New York: Harper & Brothers, 1878.

Bancroft, Hubert Howe. *The Native Races*. 5 vols. San Francisco: A. L. Bancroft & Co., Publishers, 1883.

Barnum, Samuel W., ed. *A Dictionary of the Bible*. New York: D. Appleton and Co., 1880.

Bartholomew, Daphne. Librarian of Poultney (Vt.) Public Library. Letter to Editors, Aug. 20, 1982.

Beauchamp, William Martin. *A History of the New York Iroquois, now commonly called the Six Nations*. Albany, N.Y.: New York State Education Department, 1905.

———. *Iroquois Folk Lore Gathered from the Six Nations of New York*. Selected and arranged by the Rev. Wm. M. Beauchamp . . . for the Onondaga Historical Association. Syracuse: N.Y.: Dehler Press, 1922.

———. *The Iroquois trail, or Foot-prints of the Six nations, in customs, traditions, and history*. Fayetteville, N.Y.: Printed by H. C. Beauchamp, 1892.

Bing, Li Ung. *Outlines of Chinese History*, ed. Joseph Whiteside. Shanghai: Commercial Press, 1914.

Bitton, Davis. "Mormon Lives," a review of *B. H. Roberts: A Biography*, by Robert H. Malan. *Dialogue: A Journal of Mormon Thought*, 2 (Winter 1967):120-23.

Blair, Emma Helen, ed. *The Indian Tribes of the Upper Mississippi Valley and Region of the Great Lakes as Described by Nicolas Perrot, French Commandant in the Northwest*. 2 vols. Cleveland: Arthur H. Clark Co., 1911.

Blumell, Bruce D. "I Have a Question." *Ensign*, 6 (Sept. 1976):84-87.

Boas, Franz. *Handbook of American Languages*. Smithsonian Institution, Bureau of American Ethnology, Bulletin 40, Part I. Washington, D.C.: Government Printing Office, 1911.

———. *The History of the American Race*. New York: Annals, New York Academy of Sciences, vol. 21, 1912.

Boudinot, Elias. *A Star in the West, or, a Humble Attempt to Discover the Long Lost Ten Tribes of Israel, Preparatory to their Return to their Beloved City, Jerusalem*. Trenton, N.J.: Published by D. Fenton, S. Hutchinson, and J. Dunham, George Sherman, Printer, 1816.

Bourbourg, Charles Etienne Brasseur de. *Histoire des nations civilesées du Mexique et de l'Amérique-Centrale*. 4 vols. Paris: Arthur Bertrand, 1857.

Brinton, Daniel G. *The American Race: A Linguistic and Ethnographic Description of the Native Tribes of North and South America*. Philadelphia: D. McKay, 1901.

Boyd's Directory of the District of Columbia. Washington, D.C.: R. L. Polk & Co., 1921.

Brodie, Fawn M. *No Man Knows My History*. 2d ed. New York: Alfred A. Knopf, 1979.

Butterworth, F. Edward, and Roy E. Weldon. *Criticisms of the Book of Mormon Answered*. Independence, Mo.: Herald House, 1973.

Call, Lamoni. *2000 Changes in the Book of Mormon.* Bountiful, Utah: Lamoni Call, 1898.

Campbell, Alexander. *The Millennial Harbinger.* Vol. 2. Bethany, Va.: Printed and Published by the Editor, 1831.

Chamberlain, H. "Letter to B. H. Roberts, from Spencer, Iowa, November 13, 1903." *Improvement Era,* 7 (Jan. 1904):193-96.

Charnay, Désiré. *The Ancient Cities of the New World: Being Voyages and Explorations in Mexico and Central America from 1857-1882,* trans. J. Gonino and Helen S. Conant. New York: Harper & Brothers, 1887.

———. "The Ruins of Central America." *North American Review,* 287 (Oct. 1880):301-21.

Cheesman, Paul R. *The Keystone of Mormonism.* Salt Lake City: Deseret Book Co., 1973.

Clark, J. Reuben. Papers. Harold B. Lee Library, Brigham Young University, Provo, Utah.

Conant, Albon Jasper. *Foot-prints of vanished races in the Mississippi valley— being an account of some of the monuments and relics of pre-historic races scattered over its surface, with suggestions as to their origin and uses.* St. Louis: C. R. Barnes, 1879.

Condon, George E. *Stars in the Water: The Story of the Erie Canal.* New York: Doubleday, 1974.

Cowdery, Oliver. "Early Scenes and Incidents in the Church." *Improvement Era.* Letter VII, 2 (July 1899):652-58.

———. "Letter of Joseph Smith, Jr. to Oliver Cowdery." *Latter Day Saints Messenger and Advocate,* 1 (Dec. 1834):40.

———. "Letters." *Improvement Era.* Letter I, Part I, 3 (Jan. 1899):186-93; Letter II, Part I, 4 (Feb. 1899):267-74; Letter III, Part I, 5 (Mar. 1899):347-50; Letter IV, Part I, 6 (Apr. 1899):419-24; Letter V, Part II, 7 (May 1899):529-33; Letter VI, Part II, 8 (June 1899):590-97; Letter VII, Part II, 9 (July 1899): 652-58; Letter VIII, Part II, 10 (Aug. 1899):729-34.

Crawford, M. D. C. "The Master Weavers of the Desert Empire." *Harper's Magazine* (July 1916):287-96.

Crowley, Ariel L. *About the Book of Mormon.* Salt Lake City: Deseret News Press, 1961.

Davies, Charles A. "'View of the Hebrews' and the Book of Mormon." *Saints' Herald,* 109 (Aug. 1, 1962):9-11.

Dellenbaugh, Frederick S. *The North Americans of Yesterday: A Comparative Study of North American Indian Life, Customs, and Products, on the Theory of the Ethnic Unity of the Race.* New York: G. P. Putnam's Sons, 1906.

Dennis, George. *The Cities and Cemeteries of Etruria.* 2d ed. 2 vols. London: John Murray, 1883.

DeRoo, Peter. *History of America before Columbus, according to Documents and Approved Authors.* Philadelphia: J. B. Lippincott, 1900.

Deseret News, 24 Feb. 1881, 29 May, 11 June 1904; 12 Sept. 1919; 9 Apr. 1928;

8 Apr. 1929; 26 Oct. 1932; 23 Sept. 1934; 8 Dec. 1938; 4 June 1953; 29 Dec. 1979.

The Doctrine and Covenants of the Church of Jesus Christ of Latter-day Saints; Containing the Revelations Given to Joseph Smith. Salt Lake City: Church of Jesus Christ of Latter-day Saints, 1921.

Edwards, Jonathan. *The Works of President Edwards.* 10 vols. Originally published, London, 1817. Reprinted: New York: Burt Franklin, Research and Source Series No. 271, 1868.

The Encyclopedia Americana. New York: Encyclopedia Americana Corporation, 1918-20.

The Encyclopaedia Britannica. New Werner ed., 9th ed. Akron, Ohio: Encyclopaedia Britannica, 1904.

Erman, Adolf. *Life in Ancient Egypt,* trans. Helen Mary Tirard. New York: Macmillan, 1894.

Finney, Charles Grandison. *Lectures on Revivals of Religion.* Oberlin, Ohio: E. J. Goodrich, 1868.

Fiske, John. *The Discovery of America.* 3 vols. Cambridge, Mass.: Printed at the Riverside Press, 1902.

————. *Excursions of an Evolutionist.* 16th ed. Boston: Houghton, Mifflin, 1894.

Foster, Lawrence. *Religion and Sexuality.* New York: Oxford University Press, 1981.

Fry, Evan A. *The Restoration Faith.* Indpendence, Mo.: Herald Publishing House, 1962.

Garcia, Gregorio. *Origen de los Indios de el Nuevo mundo, e Indias Occidentales, averigvado con discurso de opiniones por el padre presentado Fr. Gregorio Garcia.* Madrid: En la imprenta de F. Martinez Abad, 1729.

Griffith, Michael T. "Readers' Forum." *Sunstone,* 6 (July-Aug. 1981):2-4.

Gibbon, Edward. *The History of the Decline and Fall of the Roman Empire,* 8 vols. London: Murray's British Classics, 1887.

Gilbert, Grove Karl. *Sixth Annual Report of the Committee of the New York State Reservation.* Albany, 1890.

Grover, Roscoe A. Interview by Gordon Irving, Salt Lake City, Feb.-Mar. 1979. Oral History Program. L.D.S. Archives, Salt Lake City.

Hill, Marvin S. "Survey: The Historiography of Mormonism." *Church History,* 28 (Dec. 1959):418-26.

Hills, Louis Edward. *Friendly Discussion of the Book of Mormon Geography by L. E. Hills and F. F. Wipper at the Stone Church, Independence, Mo., May 20 to May 30, 1924.* Independence, Mo.: Zion's Religious Literary Society, 1924.

————. *Geography of Mexico and Central America from 2234 B.C. to 421 A.D.* Independence, Mo., 1917.

————. *Historical Data from Ancient Records and Ruins of Mexico and Central America.* Independence, Mo., 1919.

————. *New Light on American Archaeology.* Independence, Mo.: Lambert Moon Printers and Stationers, 1924.

———. *A Short Work on the Geography of Mexico and Central America, from 2234 B.C. to 421 A.D.* Independence, Mo., 1917.

———. *A Short Work on the Popol and the Traditional History of the Ancient Americas.* Kansas City, Mo.: Franklin Hudson Publ., 1918.

———. *A Study of the Geography of the Book of Mormon.* N.p., n.d.

———. *Traditional History of Ancient Americans in Mexico and Central America.* Independence, Mo., 1918.

Hodge, Frederick Webb, ed. *Handbook of American Indians North of Mexico.* Smithsonian Institution, Bureau of American Ethnology, Bulletin 30, in two parts. Washington, D.C.: Government Printing Office, 1907.

Hogan, Mervin B. "'A Parallel': A Matter of Chance versus Coincidence." *Rocky Mountain Mason,* 4 (Jan. 1956):17-31.

Holmes, William H. *Handbook of Aboriginal American Antiquities.* Smithsonian Institution, Bureau of American Ethnology, Bulletin 60. Washington, D.C.: Government Printing Office, 1919.

Hougey, Hal. *"A Parallel" — The Basis of the Book of Mormon.* Concord, Calif.: Pacific Publishing, 1963.

Howe, Henry. *Historical Collection of the Great West, Containing Narratives of the Most Important and Interesting Events in Western History.* 2 vols. in one book. Cincinnati: Published by Henry Howe, at E. Morgan & Co.'s, 1855.

Hrdlicka, Ales. *Skeletal Remains Suggesting or Attributed to Early Man in North America.* Smithsonian Institution, Bureau of American Ethnology, Bulletin 33. Washington, D.C.: Government Printing Office, 1907.

Hullinger, Robert N. "The Lost Tribes of Israel and the Book of Mormon." *Lutheran Quarterly,* 22 (Aug. 1970):319-29.

Humboldt, Alexander von. *Political Essay on the Kingdom of New Spain.* 2d ed., 4 vols. Trans. J. Black. London: Longman, Hurst, Rees, Orme, and Brown, and H. Colburn, 1814.

Hunter, Milton R., and Thomas L. Ferguson. *Ancient America and the Book of Mormon.* Oakland, Calif.: Kolob Book, 1950.

Hutchinson, Woods. *Common Diseases.* Boston: Houghton Mifflin, 1913.

———. "Insect-Borne Diseases." *Saturday Evening Post,* 194 (Dec. 24, 1921):14-15, 61-62.

———. *Preventable Diseases.* Boston: Houghton Mifflin, 1909.

Ivins, Anthony Woodward. Collection. Utah State Historical Society, Salt Lake City.

Jackson, Samuel M., ed. *The Schaff-Herzog Encyclopedia of Religious Knowledge.* New York: Funk and Wagnalls, 1908.

Jacobsen, Virginia Budd. "James Edward Talmage: A Portrait of the Second President of the University of Utah." *Utah Alumnus* (Dec. 1936): 9,16.

Jamieson, Robert, A. R. Fausset, and David Brown. *A Commentary: critical, practical and explanatory, on the Old and New Testaments.* 4 vols. New York: F. H. Revell, 189[?].

Jenson, Andrew. *Latter-day Saint Biographical Encyclopedia.* Salt Lake City: Andrew Jenson History Co., 1920.

Jessee, Dean C. "The Reliability of Joseph Smith's History." *Journal of Mormon History,* 3 (1976):23-46.

Jonas, Larry W. *Mormon Claims Examined.* Grand Rapids, Mich.: Baker Book House, 1961.

Jones, Wesley M. *A Critical Study of Book of Mormon Sources.* Detroit: Harlo Press, 1964.

Journal History. L.D.S. Church Archives, Salt Lake City.

Keller, Jeffrey. "Discussion Continued: The Sequel to the Roberts/Smith/Talmage Affair." *Dialogue,* 15 (Spring 1982): 79-98.

Kenney, Scott G. Papers. Special Collections, Marriott Library, University of Utah, Salt Lake City.

Kingsborough, Edward King. *Antiquities of Mexico.* 9 vols. London: R. Havell, etc., 1831-48.

Kirkham, Francis W. *A New Witness for Christ in America.* Salt Lake City: Utah Printing, 1959.

Larsen, Wayne A., Alvin C. Rencher, and Tim Layton. "Who Wrote the Book of Mormon?: An Analysis of Word Prints." *BYU Studies,* 20 (Spring 1980): 225-51.

Le Plongeon, Augustus. *Queen Moo and the Egyptian Sphinx.* New York: Published by the Author, 1896.

_____. *Sacred Mysteries among the Mayas and the Quiches.* New York: Robert Macoy, 1886.

L'Estrange, Hamon. *Americans no Jewes, or Improbabilities that the Americans are of that race.* London: Printed by W. W. for Henry Seile, 1652.

Lloyd, Wesley P. Personal Journal. In private possession.

McAllister, Duncan M. "Important Appeal to Native Hawaiians and Other Polynesians." *Improvement Era,* 24 (June 1921):703-12.

Madsen, Truman G. "B. H. Roberts after Fifty Years: Still Witnessing for the Book of Mormon." *Ensign* (Dec. 1983):11-19.

_____. "B. H. Roberts and the Book of Mormon." *Brigham Young University Studies,* 19 (Summer 1979):427-45.

_____. *Defender of the Faith.* Salt Lake City: Bookcraft, 1980.

_____. "The Meaning of Christ—The Truth, the Way, the Life: An Analysis of B. H. Roberts' Unpublished Masterwork." *Brigham Young University Studies,* 15 (Spring 1975):259-92.

Malan, Robert H. *B. H. Roberts: A Biography.* Salt Lake City: Deseret Book Co., 1966.

Marr, G. A. Letter to B. H. Roberts, March 19, 1925. L.D.S. Church Archives, Salt Lake City.

Massachusetts Conference of Eastern States Mission, President's Records. L.D.S. Church Archives, Salt Lake City.

Morley, Sylvanus Griswold. *An Introduction to the Study of the Maya Hieroglyphs.* Smithsonian Institution, Bureau of American Ethnology, Bulletin 57. Washington, D.C.: Government Printing Office, 1915.

Müller, F. Max. *Chips from a German Workshop.* 5 vols. New York: Charles Scribner's Sons, 1887.

————. *Lectures on the Science of Language.* Delivered at the Royal Institution of Great Britain in 1861 and 1863. 2 vols. New York: C. Scribner, 1886.

Myers, Jacob M. *I and II Esdras.* Garden City, N.Y.: Doubleday, 1974.

Nadaillac, Jean François Albert du Pouget. *Pre-historic America,* trans. N. d'Auvere [pseud.] and ed. W. H. Dall. New York: G. P. Putnam's Sons, Knickerbocker Press, 1893.

Nibley, Hugh. *An Approach to the Book of Mormon.* 2d ed. Salt Lake City: Deseret Book Company, 1964.

————. "Mixed Voices." *Improvement Era,* 62 (1959): Kangaroo Court," 145-48, 184-87, 224-26, 300-301; "Just Another Book?" 345-47, 388-91, 412-13, 501-3, 530-31, 565-66; "The Grab Bag," 530-33, 546-48; "What Frontier, What Camp Meeting?" 590-92, 610-15; "The Comparative Method," 744-47, 759, 848, 854-56.

————. *No Ma'am That's Not History.* Salt Lake City: Bookcraft, 1946.

————, and others. *F. M. Brodie's Reliability as a Witness to the Character and Accomplishments of Joseph Smith.* Four reviews of *No Man Knows My History.* N.p., n.d.

Osborn, Henry Fairfield. *Men of the Old Stone Age.* 2d ed. New York: Charles Scribner's Sons, 1916.

————. *The Origin and Evolution of Life.* New York: Charles Scribner's Sons, 1918.

Palmer, David A. "A Survey of Pre-1830 Historical Sources Relating to the Book of Mormon." *Brigham Young University Studies,* 17 (Autumn 1976):101-7.

Palmer, Spencer J., and William L. Knecht. "View of the Hebrews: Substitute for Inspiration?" *Brigham Young University Studies,* 5 (Winter 1964):105-13.

Powell, John Wesley. *Seventh Annual Report of the Bureau of Ethnology to the Secretary of the Smithsonian Institution, 1885-'86.* Washington, D.C.: Government Printing Office, 1891.

Pratt, Orson. "A Series of Pamphlets." *Works.* Liverpool: R. James, 1851.

Pratt, Parley P., Jr., ed. *The Autobiography of Parley Parker Pratt.* New York: Published for the Editor and Proprietor by Russell Brothers, 1874.

Prescott, William H. *History of the Conquest of Mexico.* 3 vols. Philadelphia: David McKay, 1891.

————. *History of the Conquest of Peru,* ed. John Foster Kirk. 2 vols. Philadelphia: J. B. Lippincott, 1890.

Priest, Josiah. *American Antiquities and Discoveries in the West.* Albany, N.Y.: Printed by Hoffman & White, 1834.

————. *The Wonders of Nature and Providence, Displayed.* 1st ed. Rochester, N.Y.: 1824; 2d ed. Albany: Published by Josiah Priest, E. and E. Hosford, Printers, 1825; 3rd ed. Albany: E. and E. Hosford, 1826.

Reynolds, George. "View of the Hebrews." *Juvenile Instructor,* 37 (Oct. 1, 1902):595-97.

Richards, George Franklin. Diaries. L.D.S. Church Archives, Salt Lake City.

Richards, Franklin D., and James A. Little. *A Compendium of the Doctrines of the Gospel*. Salt Lake City: Geo. Q. Cannon & Sons, 1898.

Riley, I. Woodbridge. *The Founder of Mormonism*. New York: Dodd, Mead, 1903.

Riley, William L. "A Comparison of Passages from Isaiah and Other Old Testament Prophets in Ethan Smith's *View of the Hebrews* and the Book of Mormon." M.A. thesis, Brigham Young University, 1971.

Roberts, B. H. *A Comprehensive History of the Church of Jesus Christ of Latter-day Saints, Century I*. Volumes 1-6. Salt Lake City: Deseret News Press, 1930.

_____. "An Objection to the Book of Mormon Answered." *Improvement Era* 12 (July 1909):681-89.

_____. "Attack on Book of Mormon." 1903. L.D.S. Archives, Salt Lake City.

_____. "B. H. Roberts on the Intellectual and Spiritual Quest." *Dialogue: A Journal of Mormon Thought* 13 (Summer 1980):123-28.

_____. "Christ in the Book of Mormon." *Improvement Era* 27 (Jan. 1924):188-92.

_____. "Christ's Personal Appearance in the Western Hemisphere." *Improvement Era* 20 (Apr. 1917):477-99.

_____. Collection. Special Collections, Marriott Library, University of Utah, Salt Lake City.

_____. Conference Reports. L.D.S. Archives, Salt Lake City.

_____. *Corianton, a Nephite Story*. Salt Lake City: N.p., 1889.

_____. *Defense of the Faith and the Saints*, Vols. I and II. Salt Lake City: The Deseret News, 1907, 1912.

_____. *Discourses of B. H. Roberts*. Salt Lake City: Deseret Book Company, 1948.

_____. *The Gospel: an Exposition of Its First Principles*. Salt Lake City: Contributor Company, 1888.

_____. "Higher Criticism and the Book of Mormon." *Improvement Era* 14 (June 1911):665-77; 14 (July 1911):774-86.

_____, ed. *History of the Church of Jesus Christ of Latter-day Saints. Period I: History of Joseph Smith, The Prophet by Himself*. Volumes I-VI. Salt Lake City: Deseret News, 1902-12.

_____, ed. *History of the Church of Jesus Christ of Latter-day Saints. Period II: From the Manuscript History of Brigham Young and Other Original Documents*. Volume VII. Salt Lake City: Deseret News, 1932.

_____. "Joseph Smith: An Appreciation." *Improvement Era* 36 (Dec. 1932):81.

_____. Life Story of B. H. Roberts. Special Collections, Marriott Library, University of Utah, Salt Lake City.

_____. *The Life of John Taylor, Third President of the Church of Jesus Christ of Latter-day Saints*. Salt Lake City: George Q. Cannon & Sons, 1892.

_____. Memorial Library. L.D.S. Church Archives, Salt Lake City.

_____. *The Missouri Persecutions*. Salt Lake City: George Q. Cannon & Sons, 1900.

_____. *The Mormon Battalion; Its History and Achievements.* Salt Lake City: Deseret News, 1919.

_____. *New Witnesses for God,* Volumes II and III. Salt Lake City: The Deseret News, 1909.

_____. "Originality of the Book of Mormon." *Improvement Era* 8 (Oct. 1905):881-902.

_____. "The Origin of the Book of Mormon." *American Historical Magazine* 3 (Sept. 1908):441-68; 3 (Nov. 1908):551-80; 4 (Jan. 1909):22-44; 4 (Mar. 1909):168-96.

_____. *Outlines of Ecclesiastical History: A Textbook.* Salt Lake City: George Q. Cannon & Sons, 1893.

_____. "A Plea in Bar of Final Conclusions." *Improvement Era* 4 (Feb. 1913):309-25.

_____. *Rasha—The Jew; A Message to All Jews.* Salt Lake City: Deseret News Press, 1932.

_____. "Review of the New Manual." *Improvement Era* 8 (Aug. 1905):783-89.

_____. *The Rise and Fall of Nauvoo.* Salt Lake City: The Deseret News, 1900.

_____, ed. *The Seventy's Course in Theology.* Salt Lake City: Deseret News, 1907, 1908, 1910, 1911, 1912.

_____. "Translation of the Book of Mormon." *Improvement Era* 9 (Apr. 1906):425-36; 9 (May 1906):546-53.

_____. "What College Did to My Religion." *Improvement Era* 36 (Mar. 1932):259-62.

Sabin, Joseph. *A Dictionary of Books Relating to America.* New York: Biographical Society of America, 1892-1928.

Sagard-Théodat, Gabriel. *Le grand voyage des pays des Hurons, situé en l'Amerique vers la mer douce, és derniers confins de la Nouvelle France, diete Canada.* Paris: Chez Denys Moreau, 1632.

_____. *The Long Journey to the Country of the Hurons,* ed. George M. Wrong and trans. H. H. Langton. Toronto: Champlain Society, 1939.

Schaff, Philip, ed. *Wilmore's New Analytical Reference Bible.* New York: Funk and Wagnalls, 1918.

Schoolcraft, Henry R. *Historical and Statistical Information Respecting the History, Conditions and Prospects of the Indian Tribes of the United States.* 6 vols. Philadelphia: Lippincott, Grambo, 1851.

Sherlock, Richard. "'We Can See No Advantage to a Continuation of the Discussion': The Roberts-Smith-Talmage Affair." *Dialogue,* 13, 3 (Fall 1980):63-78.

Short, John T. *The North Americans of Antiquity: Their Origin, Migrations, and Type of Civilization Considered.* 3rd ed. New York: Harper & Brothers, 1882.

Sjodahl, J. M. "Book of Mormon Facts." *Juvenile Instructor,* 6 (June 1922):305-9.

Smith, Ethan. *View of the Hebrews.* Poultney, Vt.: Smith & Shute, 1823; 2d ed., 1825.

Smith, George D., Jr. "Defending the Keystone: Book of Mormon Difficulties." *Sunstone*, 6 (May-June 1981):45-50.

Smith, G. Elliott. "The Origin of the Pre-Columbian Civilization of America." *Science*, 44 (1916).

Smith, Joseph, Jr. *The Book of Mormon*. Palmyra, N.Y.: Printed by E. B. Grandin, for the Author, 1830.

Smith, Joseph Fielding. *Essentials in Church History*. Salt Lake City: Deseret News Press, 1922.

Smith, Lucy. *History of the Prophet Joseph*. Salt Lake City: Improvement Era, 1902.

Smith, Scott S. "Readers' Forum." *Sunstone*, 6 (July-Aug. 1981):2.

Smith, William. *A Dictionary of the Bible: Comprising Its Antiquities, Biography, Geography, and Natural History, . . . also Archaeology and Literature*. Boston: Thomas Y. Crowell, n.d.

Southey, Robert. *The Life of John Wesley*, abridged and ed. Arthur Reynolds. London: Hutchinson & Co., 1904.

Sowell, Madison U. "Defending the Keystone: The Comparative Method Reexamined." *Sunstone*, 6 (May-June 1981):44, 50-54.

Sperry, Sidney B. *The Problems of the Book of Mormon*. Salt Lake City: Bookcraft, 1964.

Steinthal, Heymann. *Die Classification der spracken*. Berlin: Ferd. Dümmler's Buchhandlung, 1850.

————. "On the Origin of Language." *North American Review*, 225 (Apr. 1872):272-308.

Stephens, John L. *Incidents of Travel in Central America, Chiapas, and Yucatan*. 2 vols. New York: Harper & Brothers, 1871.

Talmage, James E. Journals, Jan. 1922-July 1933. Harold B. Lee Library, Brigham Young University, Provo, Utah.

Taylor, Samuel W. *Nightfall at Nauvoo*. New York: Macmillan, 1971.

Thomas, Mark. "Scholarship and the Future of the Book of Mormon." *Sunstone*, 5 (May-June 1980):24-29.

Thompson, Zadock. *History of Vermont*. Burlington, Vt.: Chauncey Goodrich, 1842.

Thorowgood, Thomas. *Jewes in America, or, Probabilities that the Americans are of that Race*. London: Printed by W. H. for Tho. Slater, 1650.

Tschudi, Johann Jakob von. *Travels in Peru*. New York: A. S. Barnes, 1854.

————, and Eduardo de Ribero Ustariz. *Peruvian Antiquities*, trans. Francis L. Hawks. New York: A. S. Barnes, 1854.

Tullidge, Edward W. *Tullidge's Histories, Containing the History of All the Northern, Eastern and Western Counties of Utah; Also the Counties of Southern Idaho, with a Biographical Appendix*. Salt Lake City: Press of the Juvenile Instructor, 1889.

Turner, J. B. *Mormonism in All Ages, or the Rise, Progress, and Causes of Mormonism; with the Biography of its Author and Founder, Joseph Smith, Junior*. New York: Platt & Peters, 1842.

Walters, Wesley P. "The Use of the Old Testament in the Book of Mormon." M.A. thesis, Covenant Theological Seminary, 1981.

Wayne Sentinel (Palmyra, N.Y.), 1 Oct. 1823–13 June 1828.

Wells, H. G. *The Outline of History.* New York: Macmillan, 1920.

Wells, Junius F. "The Mormon Battalion." *Utah Genealogical and Historical Magazine* (July 1927):98-99.

Whitefield, George. *Eighteen Sermons Preached by the late Rev. George Whitefield. . .* Springfield, Mass.: Thomas Dickman, 1808.

Whitney, J. D. *Auriferous gravels of the Sierra Nevada of California,* vol. 6, no. 1. Cambridge, Mass.: Memorial Museum of Comparative Zoology at Harvard, 1880.

Whitney, William Dwight. *Language and the Study of Language: Twelve Lectures on the Principles of Linguistic Science.* New York: Charles Scribner's Sons, 1888.

Wilkinson, John Gardner. *The Manners and Customs of the Ancient Egyptians.* 5 vols. London: John Murray, 1847.

Wilson, Samuel Cole, ed. *Adair's History of the American Indians.* New York: Argonaut Press, 1966.

Wilson, James Grant, and John Fiske, eds. *Appleton's Cyclopaedia of American Biography.* New York: D. Appleton and Co., 1888.

Wissler, Clark. *The American Indian.* New York: Douglas C. McMurtrie, 1917.

Wyman, L. E. *Notes on the Pleistocene Fossils Obtained from Rancho La Brea Asphalt Pits.* Los Angeles: Los Angeles County Museum of Natural History, 1915.

Young, Brigham. "Discourse by President Brigham Young." Delivered at a special conference held at Farmington, Utah, June 17, 1877, and reported by D. W. Evans, George F. Gibbs, and others. *Journal of Discourses.* Liverpool: Printed and Published by William Budge, 1878.

Zeisberger, David. *A Grammar of the Language of the Lenni Lenape, or Delaware Indians,* vol. III. Trans. by Peter S. Duponceau. Presented to the American Philosophical Society at Philadelphia on December 2, 1816. Philadelphia: Printed by James Kay, Jun. & Co., 1830.

Afterword

When B. H. Roberts completed "A Book of Mormon Study" in early 1922, he could not have foreseen the interest that would be aroused by publication of this document he so carefully retained among his personal papers. Since the release in 1985 of *B. H. Roberts: Studies of the Book of Mormon* by the University of Illinois Press, the book went through three printings in hardcover before this current soft cover edition. In response to the growing interest in Roberts, Signature Books published in 1990 *The Autobiography of B. H. Roberts*. As the leading intellectual in the history of the Church of Jesus Christ of Latter-day Saints, Roberts seems to be attracting as much attention today as he did when he served as a member of the Church's First Council of Seventy from 1888 until his death on September 27, 1933.

The Roberts collection of papers held by the Marriott Library at the University of Utah also received an important addition since publication of *Studies of the Book of Mormon*. Mr. Thom D. Roberts, a great-grandson and Salt Lake City attorney, presented to the library B. H. Roberts's personal working copy of the 1825 edition of Ethan Smith's *View of the Hebrews*. The book has numerous marginal notes by Roberts, made as he constructed his comparison of this work with the Book of Mormon. The Roberts collection at the Marriott Library is much richer as a result of this gracious gift by Thom D. Roberts.

Since publication of *Studies of the Book of Mormon*, a number of readers has expressed interest in the March 14, 1932, letter of B. H. Roberts to his former Eastern States Mission secretary, Elizabeth Skolfield, as mentioned in the preface of this book. The letter is reported to be in possession of John Noble Henchley, but a relevant excerpt was quoted in an article entitled "B. H. Roberts After Fifty Years: Still Witnessing for the Book of Mormon," by Truman G. Madsen (*Ensign* 13 [December 1983]: 13). Ms. Skolfield had asked her former mission president about speculations concerning native American origins which had appeared prior to the publication of the Book of Mormon. Roberts answered as follows:

I am forwarding you with this mail an introductory chapter to a work of mine which is in typewritten form under the title "Book of Mormon Study." It makes 435 pages of typewritten matter. It is from research work I did before going to take charge of the Eastern States Mission [in May 1922]. I had written it for presentation to the Twelve and the Presidency, not for publication, but I suspended the submission of it until I returned home, but I have not yet succeeded in making the presentation of it, although a letter of submission was made previous to leaving the E.S.M. [in 1927]. I have made one feeble effort to get it before them since returning home, but they are not in a studious mood.

This new edition of Roberts's *Studies*, the result of continuing interest in his work, has permitted the editor to correct a few typographical errors which seem to creep into all books despite what care is taken.

Brigham D. Madsen
July 1992

Index

Adair, James: *The History of the American Indians,* 15, 68, 78, 156; available to Joseph Smith, 152; evidence of Israelite origins, 156-57; Indian religion, 207-8; racial color, 219

Alsup, Mr., Campbellite minister: debate with Roberts, 2, 3

Americana: articles by Schroeder and Roberts, 9, 18

Animals, 17, 22, 96-107, 114, 115, 198, 252, 257-58. *See also* Cattle; Dogs; Horses; Llamas

Anti-Christs: parallels among, 264, 267, 270-71; Sherem, 265-66; Nehor, 266-67; disciple of Nehor, 267; Korihor, 267-70

Archeology: Roberts's study of, 3; of Book of Mormon cataclysm, 7; lack of Book of Mormon artifacts, 14, 17, 130-31; fallacies exposed by, 77, 131-32; questions raised by, 140-41, 142-43

Aztecs: primitive culture of, 111, 198; textiles of, 114; history of, 128-29

Babel, tower of: in Book of Mormon, 1, 2; Indian tradition of, 15; chronology of, 66

Baldwin, John D.: *Ancient America,* 71; on iron, 109; Roberts's marginal notes in, 144n7

Bancroft, H. H.: linguistic similarities, 37, 89; Hebrew origin of Indians, 37; *The Native Races,* 37-38n3; Old World influences slight, 74-75, 88-89; Eastern influences slight, 89; iron unknown, 109; refuted, 130

Bolitho, Adolphus: Book of Mormon critique, 3-4

Book of Mormon: historical claims, xv-xvii, 12; Joseph Smith's account of, xv,

1; higher criticism, xxiv, 9, 11; Bible companion, 2, 13; miscellaneous anachronisms alleged, 2, 3, 4, 7; translation of, 7-9; literary style, 7-11, 23, 273, 276; grammatical errors, 8, 10, 16; contradictions in, 11, 259-60; purposes of, 13, 28, 323, 340; witnesses of, 13; Oliver Cowdery's account of obtaining, 47n3; migrations of, 162-68, 251-52, 258; summary of, 168-69; lack of historical perspective, 251; inconsistency of population and achievements, 259-60; miraculous battles, 272; changes in text, 276. *See also* Gold plates

"Book of Mormon Difficulties: A Study," xvii

Book of Mormon parallels
—biblical: 2, 7-11, 16-17, 237-40
—eighteenth-century America: Jonathan Edwards's revival, 298-303, 305-7; Edwards on the affections, 303-5; revival among the Indians, 305-6; revivalism of George Whitefield, 310-13; revivalism of John Wesley, 313-16
—internal: Nephites and Jaredites, 253-55, 259, 261, 262, religious extravagance, 295; anti-Christs, 264-71; warfare, 272, 277-83
—nineteenth-century America: conversion experiences, 284, 285, 287, 295; early Mormon experiences, 295-98; revivals, 307-8; self-abasement, 310
—Spaulding manuscript: discovery of box, 325n
—*View of the Hebrews:* Vermont origins, 27-28, 68n9, 155, 323; Indian origins, 170, 323-24; destruction of Jerusalem, 170, 172, 334; restoration of

Judah and Israel, 171, 172, 335; Isaiah cited, 171, 172-73, 174-75, 335; mission of America to Indians and Jews, 176-78, 336-41; literal interpretation of prophecy, 178-79; migrations, 183-86, 218-19; empty continent, 183, 205; names, 187; division of people, 188-90, 192, 332-34; loss of mechanic arts, 191-92, 196, 330; savages as scourge, 191, 192, 333; loss of navigation, 195-96, 197, 332; iron and steel, 197-99, 331-32; weapons rusted, 199, 200, 201; breastplates, 199-200; populations, 200, 332; ruined cities, 200-201; racial unity, 203, 205; language changes, 205-6; Urim and Thummim, 207-9, 327-28; idolatry and human sacrifice, 211; regard for the poor, 211-12; marriage, 213-14, 341-42; lost or hidden book, 215-17, 324-26; hieroglyphs, 217-18, 329-43; racial color, 219-20, 331; Egyptian influence, 220; fortifications, 221-23; towers, 221, 222, 223-24; government, 224-26; hunter's feast and foundation of Zion, 226-27; Jesus Christ (Quetzalcoatl) in New World, 228-36, 343-44; summary of, 240-42; seers and prophets, 326-27; love of riches, 341; high civilization, 342-43

"Book of Mormon Study": contrasted with *New Witnesses for God,* xvii; "devil's advocate" theory of, xviii, 346; importance of, xviii-xix; higher criticism in, xxiv; methodology of, xxiv, 186, 308, 309-10; structure of, 29; thesis of, 30

Boudinot, Elias: *A Star in the West,* 25, 157, 316-17*n1,* 349

Bourbourg, Charles E'tienne Brasseur de: critique of, 49, 51*n7*; similarities between Egypt and Mexico, 51*n7; Jews in America,* 90

Brinton, Daniel G.: Indian cultural unity, 41, 124; *The American Race,* Roberts's notations in, 44*n5;* rejection of Hebrew origins, 70; rejection of Polynesian migration, 71; Mayan-English similarities, 72; language stocks, 76-77; language changes slow, 86; absence of Old World influence, 87; domestic animals, 102-3; Stone Age Indians, 110,

198; Indian origins, 122-25
Brodie, Fawn M., 28-29

Call, Anson: Joseph Smith's Rocky Mountain declaration to, 246-47
Campbell, Alexander: critique of the Book of Mormon, 3
Cattle: in Book of Mormon, 96-98; unknown in pre-Columbian America, 98, 99, 100, 102; buffalo, 107
Chamberlin, Ralph V., 21; correspondence, 40-43
Chamberlin, William H., xxvi
Charnay, Desire: critique of Plongeon, 49; Central America studies, 51*n6;* toy chariots, 100-101; criticism of Bourbourg, 51*n7*
Cimeter. *See* Scimeter
Clark, J. Reuben: and Roberts, 19
Coke, Dr., 315-16
Compass: in Book of Mormon, 2; unknown in pre-Columbian America, 110, 125
Copper: in Book of Mormon, 107, 108, 112; biblical, 108; in New World, 111
Couch, Mr.: Book of Mormon questions, 20-21, 24, 36, 52, 63, 76, 95-96; identification, 37*n3*
Council of Twelve Apostles (LDS Church): meetings with Roberts, 21-22, 23, 47-48, 50, 57, 58-59, 62; correspondence, 46-47, 57-58
Council of Seventy (LDS Church): meetings with Roberts, 21-22, 23, 47-48, 50, 62; correspondence, 46-47
Cowdery, Oliver: relationship to Ethan Smith, 27; account of obtaining the gold plates, 47*n3;* identification of Cumorah as Ramah, 277-78
Cumorah: repository, 17-18; room in, 47*n3;* identified as Ramah, 277-78; final battle of, 280, 281-82, 283

De Bourbourg. *See* Bourbourg, Charles E'tienne Brasseur de
Dellenbaugh, Frederick S.: *North Americans of Yesterday,* languages, 72, 80-87; Indians indigenous, 73; refutation of Fiske, 84-86; dating American origins, 137-40; Roberts's marginal notes in, 145*n9*
Dogs: pre-Columbian, 98-99, 101, 102

Duponceau, Peter S.: unity of American languages, 41, 44*n*2, 349

Edwards, Jonathan: on revivals, 298-306
Egypt: writing compared with Book of Mormon, 16-17; culture of in America, 70; reformed writing used by Nephites, 83-84
Ericksen, E. E.: theory of Mormon history, xiii, xix; philosopher, xxvi
Esdras II: in *View of the Hebrews*, 183-84
Eskimo: language in America and Asia, 73, 90; relation to American Indians, 79, 80; ice age, 139, 140
Ether: speculation on "Ethan" connection, 187; witness of final battle, 283

First Council of Seventy. *See* Council of Seventy
First Presidency (LDS Church): supervision of Roberts, 6, 24; approval of Roberts's Isaiah solution, 9; meetings and correspondence with Roberts, 21-22, 23, 46-47, 57-59, 62
Fiske, John: languages change rapidly, 52-53, 82-83, 84; *Excursion of an Evolutionist*, 53; *The Discovery of America*, Indian origins, 78-80; on the Book of Mormon, 78; refutation by Dellenbaugh, 86-87; American-Asian intercourse denied, 87-88; domestic animals, 101-2; iron, 110-11, 198; misinformed, 130

Garcia, Gregario: *Origin of the Indians of the New World*, 68
"Gentiles": production of Book of Mormon, 177; restoration of Israel, 178-82; threat of judgment against, 181-82; converted, 181-82
Geography, Book of Mormon: identification problems, 13, 16; south of Mexico, 13, 14; Central America, 14, 66, 117, 138, 139-40; New England inconsistent with, 23; North America, 54, 65, 117; Roberts on, 92-93; hemispheric, 203-4, 252-53; Pratt's speculations on, 204-5
Gold plates: Book of Mormon written on, 1; others, 15, 26; weight, 17-18; Roberts's alternative to, 23; Oliver

Cowdery's account of, 47*n*3
Grant, Heber J., 21-22, 23, 46-50, 57-58, 62
Grover, Roscoe A.: recollection of Roberts, 25-26

Hamilton, Rev. William: remarks on the Iowa language, 69
Hayden, John: healing of, 315
Higher criticism: Book of Mormon, xxiv, 11. *See also* Isaiah
Hills, Louis E.: RLDS pamphlets, 345-46
Hodge, Frederick Webb: *Handbook of American Indians*, archeology, 140-41
Hogan, Mervin B., 27, 321. *See also* "A Parallel"
Holmes, William H.: textiles, 55, 114; *Handbook of Aboriginal American Antiquities*, 56*n*6; rejection of Old World influence, 77-78, 100; domestic animals, 99-100; misinterpretations of American antiquity, 129-36; Asian origins, 133-34; language stocks, 134; dating of cultural development, 134-37
Horses: in Book of Mormon, 17, 21, 22, 36, 42, 96-98; unknown in pre-Columbian America, 17, 21, 99, 101, 146*n*15; remains found, 38, 42, 104-5; prehistoric, 101, 104-7; after the flood, 103-4; intrusion into narrative, 198
Howe, Henry: *Historical Collections of the Great West*, 307-8
Humboldt, Alexander: books available to Joseph Smith, 15, 152; on American languages, 41; *Political Essay on the Kingdom of New Spain*, 44*n*3, 60, 349; citation by Ethan Smith, 158; hieroglyphs, 217-18; theocratic government, 224; gospel found in Mexico, 228
Hurlburt, Rev. Thomas: *Memoir on the Inflections of the Chippewa Tongue*, 69; cited as Schoolcraft, 69*n*11

Indians (American): traditions authenticate Book of Mormon, 7, 15, 16, 37; similarities with other cultures, 72, 125-26; cultural similarities of, 72-73, 125-26, 203-5; Old World influence denied, 73-75; Stone Age characteristics of, 110, 125, 140-41, 198; dating cultural development of, 135-38, 141;

religious traditions of, 207-8, 210-11. *See also* Languages, American Indian; Origins of American Indians

Iron: in Book of Mormon, 17, 22, 107-8, 122; ancient, 38, 42, 108, 110-11; Peruvian, 109-10; unknown in pre-Columbian America, 109; Roberts's conclusions, 112, 114, 115, 197-99

Isaiah: "problem" of, 8, 9; in Book of Mormon, 95-96; in *View of the Hebrews*, 174-78. *See also* Book of Mormon parallels

Ivins, Anthony W.: Roberts disappointed with, 23, 48

Jaredites: migration from the tower of Babel, 1, 118-19, 184-85, 253-54; in South and Central America, 14; barges, 17, 255-57, 294; Roberts's problem with, 23; literature of, 64, 66, 118-19, 164; language of, 75, 118; isolation of, 93, 117; metals of, 107-8; silk of, 113; in Central and North America, 117, 252-53; advanced civilization of, 117-19; history of, 162-64; population of, 164; kings of, 261; credulity of, 262. *See also* Book of Mormon parallels

Jarvis, Dr.: Israelite origins, 158

Jesus Christ: Book of Mormon appearances of, 2, 7, 15, 169, 231-32, 233, 343-44; gospel of in Book of Mormon, 2, 8, 16, 267, 284; Book of Mormon prophecies regarding, 8, 168, 236, 264-65; as Quetzalcoatl, 158, 228-40; signs regarding, 168, 236-38, 291-93; serpent connections, 229; as high priest, 230; as religious leader, 230-31; crucifixion of, 231; cup of, 231; travels of, 231-32; end of sacrifices, 232-33; golden age of, 233-34; disappearance and promise to return, 234-35

Jews: Book of Mormon written to, 13, 340; records of, 63, 65

Kingsborough, Lord Viscount: Indians and Ten Lost Tribes, 37-38, 40n5, 68, 78; theory rejected, 71; *Antiquities of Mexico*, 349

Kirtland temple: spiritual manifestations, 297-98

Knight, Newell, 296-97

La Brea, Rancho: asphalt pits, 104-5

Lamanites: ancestors of American Indians, 36, 63; reading ability, 64-65; history of, 166-67; black skin, 191, 192, 331; as scourge, 191, 192; ferocity of, 192, 332; villainous leaders of, 277

Languages, American Indian: diversity of, 21, 36, 53, 63, 72-73, 76-77, 80-81, 88, 90; lack of Hebrew characteristics, 21, 90n; lack of Egyptian characteristics, 21; unity of, 41, 72-73, 88, 203; Nephite influences, 65-67, 75; absence of Old World influence, 72-75, 82, 87-88; stocks and dialects, 81; absence of Eastern influence, 89-90; linked to Hebrew, 90, 203, 205-6; linked to other languages, 90; Roberts's conclusions, 91-94

Larned, Sylvester: translation of Pittsfield Hebrew manuscript fragment, 158

Le Piongeon. *See* Plongeon, Augustus Le

Liahona, 253, 255

Linguistics: rate of change, 41-42, 52, 53, 82-83, 134; Mayan, 72, 81, 86; language stocks, 75-77, 80-81; persistence of language, 84-87

Llamas, 98, 99, 101, 102

Lloyd, Wesley P.: conversation with Roberts, 22-24

Lost Atlantis theory, 70

Lost Tribes. *See* Ten Lost Tribes

Lyman, Richard R.: Book of Mormon questions, 21; objections of to Roberts's investigation, 23, 57, 59; correspondence, 26, 37-43, 58-59

"M." *See* "The Unknown"

Madsen, Truman G., xviii, xxxin12, 346-47

Mallory, Garrick: critique of Schoolcraft, 69

Mayan civilization: language, 49, 86; tools, 111; textiles, 113, 114; origins, 127, 128; collapse of, 128

Merrick, Joseph: Pittsfield Hebrew manuscript fragment, 158-59

Middleton, George W.: correspondence, 37-39

Migration theories: Book of Mormon, 1-2; multiple sources, 53, 70-71, 142; across Bering Strait, 68, 80, 127, 134, 183; from Africa, 70; from Polynesia,

70, 71, 126-27; from Asia, 70-71, 78, 126, 127, 133-34; from Old World, 79-80; Roberts's questions about, 92-94; from Egypt, 141-42. *See also* Ten Lost Tribes

Mormon: Book of Mormon chronicler, 2; abridgment by, 64; last battle of, 281-82

Mormonism: history, theory of, xiii, xix; B. H. Roberts period, xiii, xix-xx, xxvii; Joseph Smith period (Ohio, Missouri, Illinois), xiii-xiv, xix, 4-6; beliefs of, xiv-xv, xix, xxvii; historical claims of, xv-xvi; after Roberts, xx, xxiv-xxv

Moroni: visitations to Joseph Smith, 1, 295-96; Book of Mormon writings, 64, 66, 83, 164, 206; epistles of, 274-75; title of Liberty, 275-76; witness of final battle, 283

Mound builders: fallacies about, 77, 132; civilization of, 189-90

Mulek, 75, 121

Mulekites: language changes, 52, 82, 193; history of, 65-66, 119, 167-68; city of, 84; lack of records, 193

Names, Book of Mormon: original, 11; evident in Indian languages, 17; scimeter, 21, 36; Roberts's speculations, 144*n*7; Ether, 187

Nadaillac, Marquise de Jean Francois Albert du Pouget: *Pre-Historic America*, diversity of American languages, 52, 82; speed of change in aboriginal languages, 52, 82; rejection of Ten Lost Tribes theory, 71-72; citation of Squire, 90; on domestic animals, 100-101

Navigation, 125, 195-96, 197

Nephites: chronicle of, 2; in South and Central America, 13, 204, 252-53; Hebrew language, 21, 65, 84, 206-7; literature of, 50, 51*n*8, 63-65, 190; reformed Egyptian writing of, 83-84, 206-7; civilization of, 84, 119-22, 192-93; metals of, 108; history of, 164-66; stiff-necked, 193; travels of, 251-53. *See also* Book of Mormon parallels

New Witnesses for God: contrasted with "A Book of Mormon Study," xvii; research for, 3; translation theory of, 8; evaluation of, 11; purpose of, 12, 13;

methodology of, 13-14; summary, 13-18; Roberts's regrets about, 48, 109, 151-52

Origins of American Indians: in Book of Mormon, 2, 15, 116-17, 162-67; Hebrew (Israelite), 10, 28, 36, 37, 38, 67-70, 152-54, 157, 202; refutation of Israelite (Hebrew) theory, 70-71; Roberts's conclusion, 81-94; "empty continent" theory, 117, 119, 142, 164, 183-84, 252; Asian, 127. *See also* Ten Lost Tribes theory

Osborn, Henry Fairfield: tsetse fly, 106

Padden, William M., 7

Palmyra, New York: Erie Canal, 28; bookstores, 28

"A Parallel," 60*n*4; manuscript, 26-27; editorial changes in, 321; circulation of, 355

Peru: iron, 109-10; archaic culture, 111; textiles, 114

Pittsfield Hebrew manuscript fragment, 158-60

Plongeon, Augustus Le: *Sacred Mysteries among the Mayas and Quiches*, critique of, 48-50, 50-51*n*3

Powell, John Wesley: language stocks map, 80-81, 85-86; persistence of language, 86-87; common origin of American languages denied, 88

Pratt, Orson: Roberts compared to, xxv-xxvi; Jaredite population estimate, 164; Book of Mormon geography, 204-5

Pratt, Parley P.: characterization of Joseph Smith, 244-45

Prescott, William H.: *History of the Conquest of Mexico*, 55, 56*n*7; on silk and textiles, 114

Priest, Josiah: *American Antiquities*, 25, 152, 207, 209, 349; *Wonders of Nature and Providence*, 25, 28, 59, 60*n*3, 152, 153, 349; Israelite immigration, 90-91, 152-53; horses, 103-4; Roberts on, 109; influence on Joseph Smith, possible, 244

Priesthood: in Book of Mormon, 2; inspiration through channels of, 46; denied to blacks, 56-57; extended to blacks, 57*n*3

Quetzalcoatl. *See* Jesus Christ

Rigdon, Sidney, 7, 10, 16
Riley, Woodbridge: study of Joseph
    Smith, 16; *The Founder of Mormon-*
    ism, 28, 355
Riter, William E.: Book of Mormon
    questions, 20-21, 22, 23; correspon-
    dence, 35-36, 45-46, 51-57
Roberts, Ben, 27, 321
Roberts, Brigham Henry: intellectual
    leader, xiii, xv, xvi-xvii, xviii-xxi, xxiv-
    xxx passim; defense of the Book of
    Mormon, xvi-xviii, xxiv, 1, 2-4, 6-18,
    29, 30; conclusions about the Book of
    Mormon, xvii-xviii, 29-30, 251; auto-
    biography, xx; biographical summary,
    xx, xxix-xxx, 2-3; style of, xx-xxi,
    xxvi, 3, 10, 30; *The Mormon Doctrine*
    of Deity, xxi-xxii; historical perspec-
    tive, xxii-xxiii, xxv, 4, 5, 6, 13, 18-20,
    24; *A Comprehensive History,* xxii,
    xxiii, 18; *Outlines of Ecclesiastical*
    History, xxiii, 4; *History of the*
    Church, Period I, xxiii, 6; reading of,
    xxiv, 20, 25; "Higher Criticism and the
    Book of Mormon," xxiv; biblical liter-
    alism, xxv, xxviii; missionary work,
    xxv, xxix, xxx, 2-4, 24, 25-26, 29,
    60n1; theological perspective, xxv,
    xxvi-xvii, 13; on Darwin, xxvii-xxviii;
    "Man's Relationship to Deity," xxvii;
    pre-Adamite theory, xxviii; study of ar-
    cheology, 3; Horatio pseudonym, 4;
    Corianton: A Nephite Story, 4; *Mis-*
    souri Persecutions, 4-5; *The Rise and*
    Fall of Nauvoo, 5; John Taylor biog-
    raphy, 5-6; Book of Mormon transla-
    tion theory, 7-8; Book of Mormon,
    personal copy markings, 10-11; "Life
    Story," 18-19; *History of the Mormon*
    Church, 18, 20; *The Mormon Battal-*
    ion, 20; library of, 20; General Au-
    thorities, meetings with, 20-22, 23, 47-
    48, 50, 57, 58-59; revised interpreta-
    tion of the Book of Mormon re-
    ported, 23-24, 30; disputes with Gen-
    eral Authorities, 25-26; "What College
    Did to My Religion," 29; correspon-
    dence, 45-46, 47-60; pamphlets avail-
    able to, 345-46. *See also* "Book of
    Mormon Difficulties: A Study"; "A

Book of Mormon Study"; *New Wit-*
    nesses for God; "A Parallel"

Schoolcraft, Henry R.: Shemitic origin,
    68; criticism of, 69; *Reports to the Bu-*
    reau of Indian Affairs, 91, 157; *His-*
    torical and Statistical Information,
    349-50
Schroeder, Theodore, 9, 10, 18
Scimeter: in Book of Mormon, 21, 36,
    38, 112; pre-Christian, 43; name, 54
Seer stones, 208-9
Short, John T.: critique of Le Plongeon,
    48-49
Shoshone: stock, 85; extent of language,
    85-86
Silk: in Book of Mormon, 22, 36, 38-39,
    113; in China, 38, 39, 40n7, 54, 113;
    in Bible, 38-39, 54, 113; in Europe,
    39; from spiders, 43; lost art, 54; per-
    ishable nature of, 55; silk-like textiles,
    55, 113-14; unknown in pre-Colum-
    bian America, 113, 114
Smith, Ethan, 27, 155, 158, 159. *See also*
    View of the Hebrews
Smith, G. Elliot: Egyptian influence in
    New World, 141-42
Smith, George Albert, 23
Smith, Joseph: founding prophet, xiv, xv,
    4; visions of, 295-96, 298, 317n4; ac-
    count of the Book of Mormon, xv, 1-
    2, 17-18; doctrines of, xxvii; journal
    of, 6; death of, 6; translation of Book
    of Mormon, 7-8, 10; literary ability of,
    10, 16; books available to, 15, 27, 28,
    59, 151-53, 243 (*see also View of the*
    Hebrews); imaginative powers of, 23,
    243-50; Roberts's view of, 29-30; early
    life, 68n; "common knowledge" avail-
    able to, 153-56; recitations to family,
    243-44; ability to entertain, 244-45;
    adolescent follies of, 245; letters of,
    247-50; first miracle of, 296-97; reviv-
    alism, 309; visitations of Moroni,
    317n4
Smith, Lucy: *History of the Prophet Jo-*
    seph Smith, 243-44
Smith, William: *Dictionary of the Bible,*
    on steel, copper, and brass, 108-9
Spaulding theory: of origin of Book of
    Mormon, 2, 8, 9-10, 16, 31n27, 325
Steel: in Book of Mormon, 17, 21, 22,

36, 107-8, 122; terminology, 38; biblical (Jewish), 42, 108-9; Roberts's commentary on, 114, 115, 197-98

Steinthal, Heymann: unity of American languages, 41; linguistic work, 44*n*4

Talmage, James E.: influence on Roberts, xxvi; on religion and evolution, xxviii; Book of Mormon problems, 20-21, 22, 45, 46; account of General Authorities meeting, 21-22, 23; correspondence, 35-36

Temples, Book of Mormon: wooden, 14; compared to Solomon's, 17, 259-61, 331

Ten Lost Tribes (Hebrew, Israelite) theory: espoused, 10, 14, 37-38, 67-70, 90-91, 116 (*see also* View of the Hebrews); in Second Esdras, 67; rejected, 70-72, 77-78; Manasses Ben Israel, *The Hope of Israel,* 157

Textiles: ancient South American, 55, 113, 114; in Book of Mormon, 197

Thorowgood, Rev. Thomas, 90

Transportation, Book of Mormon: wheeled vehicles, 22, 99, 100, 115; chariots, 97, dogs, 98; llama, 99; sailing, 125

Turner, J. B.: *Mormonism in All Ages,* 307; religious malady, 308

Ultra-Protestantism, 309-16

"The Unknown" ("M"): attacks on the Book of Mormon, 7-8

Urim and Thummim: translation aid, 1, 7; Roberts's reported alternative to,

23; used to translate in Book of Mormon, 66, 118, 327-28; in Book of Mormon, 84, 253-54, 327; in *View of the Hebrews,* 207-8; Joseph Smith's description of, 208

View of the Hebrews: use by Roberts, xvii, 25, 26, 30, 62, 355; available to Joseph Smith, 15, 26, 28, 59, 152, 153, 155, 160, 170, 240; publication of, 68, 155; sources, 155-61; loss of mechanic arts, 188-89; as "ground plan" for Book of Mormon, 160-61, 235, 240; Israelite origins of American Indians, 160, 202; Great Spirit worship, 210-11; relationship to Book of Mormon, 235-36. *See also* Book of Mormon parallels

Weapons, Book of Mormon, 21, 36, 120, 166, 201. *See also* Scimeter

Wesley, John: address to sinners, 313-14; response of followers, 314 15; casting out devils, 315

Whitefield, George: appeal to sinners, 310-13

Widtsoe, John A., 22, 58, 58*n*3

Wissler, Clark: *The American Indian,* 55, 56*n*5, 73; textiles, 55; credentials, 73; languages, 73-76, 87; domestic animals, 98, 99; Stone Age culture, 111; Indian similarities with Asians and Polynesians, 125-29

Young, Brigham: administrator and colonizer, xiv-xv

STERLING M. MCMURRIN is E. E. Ericksen Distinguished
Professor at the University of Utah, Salt Lake City. He
received B.A. and M.A. degrees from the University of
Utah and a Ph.D. in philosophy from the University of
Southern California. Prior to joining the faculty of the
University of Utah in 1948, he taught philosophy at the
University of Southern California. His publications in-
clude A History of Philosophy (co-author), Contemporary
Philosophy (co-editor), The Theological Foundations of
the Mormon Religion, The Philosophical Foundations of
Mormon Theology, and Religion, Reason, and Truth. He
has authored numerous scholarly articles on philosophy,
religion, and education.

BRIGHAM D. MADSEN is professor emeritus of history at
the University of Utah, Salt Lake City. He received a B.A.
degree from the University of Utah and M.A. and Ph.D.
degrees in history from the University of California,
Berkeley. Prior to joining the faculty of the University of
Utah in 1965, he taught at Brigham Young University and
Utah State University. His publications include North to
Montana! (with Betty M. Madsen), The Lemhi: Sacaja-
wea's People, The Northern Shoshoni, Corinne: The Gentile Capital of Utah, and Gold Rush Sojourners in Great
Salt Lake City, 1849-50.